Spanish Marxism versus Soviet Communism

Spanish Marxism versus Soviet Communism

A History of the P.O.U.M.

Víctor Alba
and
Stephen Schwartz

Transaction Books
New Brunswick (USA) and Oxford (UK)

Copyright © 1988 by Transaction, Inc.
New Brunswick, New Jersey 08903

Library of Congress Catalog Number: 87-19199
ISBN: 0-88738-198-7
Printed in the United States of America

Library of Congress Cataloging-in-Publication Data

Alba, Victor.
  Spanish Marxism versus Soviet Communism.

  Includes bibliographies and index.
  1. Partido Obrero de Unificación Marxista—History
2. Communism—Spain—History.   3. Communist International
—History.   I. Schwartz, Stephen, 1948-
II. Title.
JN8395.A42   1987   324.246′02   87-19199
ISBN 0-88738-198-7

To the memory of

ANDREU NIN
1892-1937

and
JOAQUÍM MAURÍN
1896–1973

"Io desig ço que em pora ser gran cost,
i aquest esper de molts mals m'aconhorta"

"I desire what can only cost me greatly,
and this hope comforts me against many evils"
Ausias March

Contents

Preface

While there had always been some Marxists in Spain, there exists historically only one party that not only analyzed the reality of the country in the light of Marxism, but which tried to apply Marxism to the formulation of its political line. This was the Partido Obrero de Unificación Marxista, the Workers' Party of Marxist Unification, better known from its initials as the P.O.U.M. Another of its aspects makes this party special: it has been the only dissident, anti-Stalinist Communist movement, so far, not to remain a tiny grouping of intellectuals and students; The P.O.U.M. came to be a party of the worker masses and was, in reality, originally more powerful than the official Communist party from which the founders of the P.O.U.M. derived.

The history of how this party was organized—beginning within the ranks of the anarchosyndicalist National Labor Confederation (CNT), then passing through the Third (Communist) International, and finishing with an attempt at its physical elimination from the scene by representatives of the same Third International—is an especially instructive episode in the history of the labor movement, in Spain and worldwide.

The P.O.U.M. arrived early at an understanding of the true character of Stalinism—and this cost the lives of many of its militants, as well as obscuring its interpretation of Spanish social reality, which continues to be the most adequate, even with the coming of later changes.

The history of the P.O.U.M., then, proves that it is possible to cease being a "groupuscule" and swim against the political stream without for that reason losing influence, although probably not without running risks. It is, then, a living lesson for an epoch in which it seems everyone fears distancing themselves from commonly used cliches.

As indicated by its dual signature, this work is much more than a simple translation. Mr. Schwartz began by translating the Spanish manuscript of the French edition of Alba's work, HISTOIRE DU P.O.U.M., published in Paris. Mr. Schwartz cross-checked his translation work with the Spanish and Catalan original editions, the first under the title EL MARXISMO EN ESPANA (1919-1939): HISTORIA DEL B.O.C. Y DEL P.O.U.M., published in Mexico in 1973, in two volumes, the second as EL MARXISME A

CATALUNYA (1919-1939), published in four volumes in Barcelona in 1974 and 1975.

Mr. Schwartz, in addition, edited and amplified the work, using materials published in several languages since Professor Alba's works had their first editions, and, in particular, clarifying biographical information on some foreign participants in the Spanish Civil War. Mr. Schwartz is the sole author of chapter 7, on foreigners and the P.O.U.M.

Mr. Schwartz wishes to express his special thanks to the following: for special encouragement in pursuing this work: Wayne M. Collins Jr., Sandra Benedet, William Herrick, Manuel Fernández Grandizo (G. Munis), François Tara, Mary Low Machado, Ella Wolfe, Jean van Heijenoort, Morris Weisz, Carlos Béa Blanes, and Rebecca Long. Mr. Schwartz further enjoyed the active help of a number of historians in the field of Spanish civil war studies: Burnett Bolloten and his research assistant George Esenwein, Pierre Broué, and Rainer Tosstorff; the latter is author of a major academic study, "Die P.O.U.M. Wahrend des Spanischen Burgerkriegs," presented as a doctoral thesis at the University of Bochum, in 1986. Finally, to Horace and Eileen Schwartz, and to Barbara Szerlip for typing and indexing services, and to Phyllis Petel for proofreading.

Mr. Schwartz was supported in this project by the Institute for Contemporary Studies, San Francisco. Acknowledgements are also due the library and research staffs of the Houghton Library, Harvard University, and the Hoover Institution, Stanford University.

A Note on Catalan Orthography

Given that the events described in this book are focused almost entirely on the Catalan speaking areas of the Iberian peninsula, I have retained herein the Catalan spellings for those place-names, personal names, and some political titles that have their origins in the Catalan language. Thus, Lleida (Catalan) = Lérida (Castilian), Girona = Gerona, Castelló = Castellón, Alacant = Alicante, Saragossa = Zaragoza. "Plaça" and "carrer" are Catalan for "plaza" and "street."

In order to maintain a standard, a difficult matter when dealing with a genuinely bilingual situation such as has occurred in Catalunya, I have pluralized words ending in "ista" in accord with Catalan style. Thus, "*bloquista*" (sing.), *"bloquistes"* (pl.) The final "*e*" is pronounced like an unaccented "*a*"—more like the English than the Castilian pronunciation of "*istas*.") Other such plurals are "*cenetistes,*" "*sindicalistes,*" "*catalanistes,*" "*poumistes,*" and "*ugetistes.*"

Finally, a number of Catalan masculine given names are normally written in a form that can be confusing to English readers. For example, the well-known P.O.U.M. leader Gorkín's first name is Julián in Castilian, Julià (with the *j* equivalent to English *zh*) in Catalan. In the case of Gorkín I have retained the Castilian form since Gorkín has published so much in so many languages using the Castilian version of his first name. All of this is mentioned to underscore that the militia leader Marcià Mena (Marciano in Castilian) was, unlike another militia leader, Mika Etchebehere, male. So were Julià Maurín and Marià (Mariano) Vázquez.

Stephen Schwartz

BLOC OBRER I CAMPEROL/ THE WORKERS' AND PEASANTS' BLOC

1

From "Lucha Obrera" to "La Batalla"

The peripheral zones of the Iberian peninsula, Catalunya, and the Basque Country (Euzkadi), developed, were industrialized, and saw the emergence of the working class more quickly than the Castilian center did. Even under the despotic rule of Spain's political "ilustrados," the periphery exercised pressure in the direction of modernization: during the nineteenth century, it fought unsuccessfully to complete a bourgeois democratic revolution. Feudal forces—the "latifundista" aristocracy—dominated Spain, while the army transformed itself, after the Carlist wars, from a liberal to a conservative force.

The bourgeoisie—especially the Catalans—fought for political and social changes: ethnic autonomy, a republic, a reform in landholding. But when the working class, just then organizing itself, exercised pressure in its turn, the bourgeoisie renounced its demands for the moment, in exchange for the feudal state's protection against the workers and the middle class, which often sympathized with the workers.

Spanish society remained profoundly split, for more than a century, between two camps—monarchical and traditionalist versus democratic and free-thinking. This conflict extended from the largest cities to the smallest villages. It was a matter, in effect, of two cultures, if not two civilizations: one led by the priest and the landowner, the other usually, by the town doctor and pharmacist.

A tradition of political organization by the masses came forward during the struggle against Napoleon Bonaparte, and was accentuated under the mid-nineteenth century restorationist monarchy of Queen Isabella II. This allowed the working class, although small in numbers, to organize rapidly.

In 1840, workers' "resistance societies" had appeared, and in 1855, the first general strike in the history of the country took place in Barcelona. In 1868, the Spanish "regional" of the International Working Men's Association (First International) was organized, but quickly split into two tendencies: the antiauthoritarians, or Bakuninists, and the Marxists. In 1878, the

3

Spanish Workers' Socialist Party (Partido Socialista Obrero Español—P.S.O.E.) was set up, and in 1888, it established, at a congress in Barcelona, its own central trade union organization, the General Workers' Union (Unión General de Trabajadores—U.G.T.).

The anarchists, for their part, after numerous attempts at organization on a national scale, founded the Federation of Workers of the Spanish Region (Federación de Trabajadores de la Región Española—F.T.R.E.), and then, in 1910, the National Labor Confederation (Confederación Nacional del Trabajo—C.N.T.) became, in effect, the capital of the Spanish labor movement. Although the Socialists were stronger in Madrid and the North, the anarchists lead in Catalunya, the Llevant (Castelló, Valencia and Alacant), and among the *peones* of Andalucia.

The labor movement developed—through legal actions, anarchist terrorism, rationalist schools and workers' "ateneos," strikes and their constant repression—in a society unable to solve the problems that continued to divide it: the power of the big landowners, Church domination over culture and education, a centralist authority that throttled the minority nations within the Spanish state (Basques, Catalans, Galicians), and a tradition of military coups of which the last successful expressions came on September 23, 1923, led by Primo de Rivera, and on July 17, 1936, when the Spanish Civil War of 1936-39 began.

The Socialists, among whom there were only a few genuine Marxists (Julián Besteiro, Antonio García Quejido), saw a panacea in the concept of the republic; the anarchist answer was a society of federated communes. But both these objectives seemed too vague and far off to affect immediate problems. With the end of the First World War, it was felt that the workers' movement needed a fresh start.

For many, social conditions in Spain were similar to those in Czarist Russia. For that reason, the Russian revolution awoke great sympathy among Spanish socialists and anarchists. Among those early observers who had succeeded in getting Leon Trotsky out of prison when he passed through Spain in 1916, hardly any knowledge existed of what Lenin and the Bolsheviks signified. The Spanish socialists had participated very little in the life of the Socialist (Second) International and did not intervene in the great debates between Eduard Bernstein and Karl Kautsky, Rosa Luxemburg, and Lenin. They were as provincial as the country in which they acted. On the other hand, the new idea of the soviets and their original spontaneity, attracted many anarchists after 1917.

This sympathy was manifested in the second C.N.T. congress, held in the Teatro de la Comedia in Madrid in December 1919, with the participants representing some 600,000 workers (the U.G.T. at that time had only 150,000 members). The delegates affirmed that the C.N.T. fought for a "libertarian communist" regime; as the anarchist writer Manuel Buenacasa commented, "they came under the influence of the Russian revolution because they saw in it the revolution they had dreamed of. . . . Who in Spain, among the anarchists, hesitated [then] to call himself a Bolshevik?"[1]

One of those who felt no sympathy for the Bolsheviks was the Asturian anarchist Eleuterio Quintanilla. But neither he nor those who thought like him succeeded in preventing the 1919 congress from deciding that the C.N.T. should provisionally join the Communist (Third) International or Comintern, and send a delegation to Moscow. Of the delegates, only the well-known Barcelona union leader Ángel Pestaña made it to the Soviet Union. He was elected a member of the executive bureau at the second congress of the Third International. He was opposed to the calculated formation of Communist parties, for which he received a harsh reply from Trotsky. Refusing to concede, Pestaña voted against the twenty-one conditions of admission to the International proposed by the Bolsheviks, but at the same time signed the manifesto convoking the constituent congress of the new Red International of Labor Unions, known from its Russian abbreviation as the Profintern. Returning to Spain, he was arrested in Italy, and his report, later extended in his book *Setenta Días en Rúsia* (*Seventy Days in Russia*), was delayed in reaching the C.N.T. National Committee.

The Socialist Party also awaited a report. In effect, its youth organization, with 2,000 members, had already decided to split away and form a Communist Party. This decision by the Socialist Youth was adopted after a congress of the P.S.O.E. in December 1919 expressed its sympathy for the Russian revolution but voted not to join the Third International (by a tally of 12,497 in favor to 14,010 against). Nor did the U.G.T. support the Bolsheviks; (its vote, more strikingly, was 17,916 for and 110,902 against!)

But in June 1920, in a new Socialist Party congress, the partisans of the Third International won the contest, (with 8,268 in favor and 5,016 opposed). A delegation made up of Fernando de los Ríos and Daniel Anguiano went to Moscow. De Los Ríos was the person to whom Lenin formulated his famous question: "Freedom, for what?"

Having received the delegation's report, yet another Socialist congress decided not to affiliate with the Third International, but rather, to the Reconstruction International, which was maintained, in the early 1920s, apart from both the Second and Third, under the leadership of the Austrian Social Democratic Party. The final vote of the Spanish socialists was 8,808 to 6,025, against Moscow. Many of those in the pro-Soviet minority left the Socialist party and went on to form the Workers' Communist Party (Partido Comunista Obrero—P.C.O.). This new organization and the existing Communist Party created by the Socialist Youth, decided to fuse, following Moscow's advice to the two delegations at the third Comintern congress, or a single Communist Party (P.C.E.). The fusion was carried out under the supervision of the Italian socialist deputy Antonio Graziadei. The new party's organ was the Madrid weekly "La Antorcha (*The Torch*), and its general secretary was Rafael Milla, who was succeeded, following Milla's arrest, by Manuel Núñez Arenas. In the elections of 1923, the Communist Party gained, in Madrid, 2,476 votes, compared with 21,417 for the Socialists.

Maurín

Among those who felt the attraction of the Russian experience was a young schoolteacher from Lleida (Lérida) in Western Catalunya, Joaquím Maurín. Maurín, born in 1896 in Bozna Huesca (Aragon) had been editor of the Catalan-language Republican organ "El Ideal." Politically, he had, in this period, encountered in the Socialists "continuity and sense of responsibility" and in the anarchosyndicalists "a combative revolutionary spirit."

The second appeared to him to be "more realistic, more audacious, younger." Later, he would say that syndicalism as derived from Georges Sorel, "grounded in what is solid in Marxism, pragmatic and creative, favorably answered my questions."[2]

Maurín had become a friend of the famous Barcelona union leader Salvador Seguí—known as the "Noi del Sucre" or Sugar Boy—and other trade union and political figures, during a campaign "El Ideal" waged in favor of an amnesty for prisoners held following a failed revolutionary attempt in spring 1917. On ending his military service, Maurín returned to Lleida and was named secretary of the Provincial Committee of the C.N.T., editor of its widely respected organ, "Lucha Social," and director of the Workers Center school.

The year 1920 saw aggravation of a worldwide economic crisis that followed the end of the First World War. But the Catalan C.N.T. was strong, thanks, above all, to an organizational program, proposed by Seguí, based on the principle of the industrial or "single" union ("sindicato unico"). In anticipation of an employer offensive against the union movement, a pact was signed in August 1920 between the C.N.T. and U.G.T., on the initiative of the *cenetistes*. But this pact could not prevent the Catalan bourgeoisie from obtaining a commitment from the Madrid regime for a repressive policy. The police, headed by General Miguel Arlegui, and the civil authorities, under General Severiano Martínez Anido, collaborated in setting up, on the basis of a virtually nonexistent Catholic union apparatus, "free unions" ("sindicatos libres"), which served as a cover for groups of gunmen which today would be called "deathsquads," hired by the Barcelona em-

ployers and protected by the police. The Republican deputy Francesc
Layret, a lawyer for the C.N.T., was assassinated. Eveli Boal, secretary of
the National Committee of the C.N.T., was assassinated. The entire C.N.T.
Regional Committee for Catalunya was arrested, and another was set up in
its place, with Maurín representing Lleida. The link between the Regional
and National bodies was a thirty-year-old metalworker, Raimon Archs,
who organized, with an anarchist "specific (action) group" ("grupo es-
pecífico"), an attack on the head of the Madrid government, prime minister Eduardo Dato. Dato and Archs were killed; but the new head of the
government, José Sánchez Guerra, sent police from Madrid to protect the
lives of syndicalists in Barcelona, (including the recent pilgrim to Moscow,
Pestaña) who had been wounded in gunman attacks and were being threatened again by gunmen waiting at the hospital doors. Sánchez Guerra also
replaced Arlegui and Martínez Anido with civilians, and terrorism by both
the antisyndicalists and syndicalists abated somewhat.

Nin

To substitute for the murdered Eveli Boal as secretary of the C.N.T.
National Committee, the organization designated Andreu Nin, a schoolteacher born in 1892 in El Vendrell, Tarragona. Nin had been a journalist
for the Catalan periodicals "El Poble Catala" and "La Publicitat," had
taught in various workers' schools in Barcelona, had lived for a time in
Egypt, and had been first a supporter of the cause of left Republicanism in
its Catalan form, then of the Socialists. He had joined the C.N.T. Union of
Liberal Professions and become its president. Maurín and Nin were
friends, in spite of a profound difference in temperament between them.
Maurín was quiet, dry, patient, incisive. Nin was an extrovert, with tremendous vitality, a fine orator without flourishes. They had in common their
conception of politics as the education of the populace, their sympathy for
the Bolshevik revolution, and an impassioned interest in the Marxism they
had just begun to study.

In the 1919 C.N.T. congress, Nin had come out with those favoring
affiliation with the Third International. And when the National Committee met under his secretaryship, it was agreed the organization would send
to Moscow, for the founding congress of the Profintern, a delegation composed of Maurín, for Catalunya, Jesús Ibáñez, for Asturias, Hilari Arlandis, for Valencia, and Nin for the National Committee (along with the
French anarchist Gaston Leval, as representative for the anarchist groups).

Nin and Maurín left Spain together, with little money and no passports.
French syndicalists took care of them and conveyed them to the German
border, and German supporters took them to Berlin. There, Ibáñez was

arrested under suspicion of complicity in the killing of Dato. The Spanish government had offered a reward of one million pesetas in the case, and police forces throughout the world systematically harassed poor Spaniards in the hope of finding someone whose arrest could gain them this then-enormous sum. With Russian passports, prepared by the Soviet embassy, the *cenetista* delegates, once Ibáñez was freed, embarked in Stettin (now Szczeczin, Poland) and disembarked in Reval (now Tallinn) in then-independent Estonia, completing the journey by train to Petrograd (Leningrad) and Moscow.

The C.N.T. representatives and other syndicalists from various countries found themselves in a difficult situation at the Profintern meeting, because only two and a half months before, in March 1921, Trotsky had brutally suppressed the protests of the Kronstadt sailors, and many Russian anarchists were behind bars. The Spaniards interceded uselessly with Feliks Dzerzhinski, head of the secret police (the Cheka), then with Lenin, finally obtaining the release from prison and deportation from Russia of various anarchists. On the other hand, they had no success with their efforts to convince Trotsky to support with arms an immediate insurrection in Spain. Trotsky told them that since the arms were in the hands of the Spanish army, they had to "work on them" to bring the soldiers over to the people; this was not the last time Trotsky would, apparently, base his analysis of Spanish reality on his experiences in Russia.

At the third Comintern congress, beginning June 22, 1921, Lenin made a great impression on the Spaniards. Maurín would write of the experience half a century later, "Personally simple and modest, he gave the impression of being aware of his limitations. He was part theorist, part economist, part writer, part orator. . . . But as a political strategist he reached the proportions of genius."[3] Maurín's impression came from his hearing Lenin's speech in defense of the New Economic Policy (N.E.P.).

In July, at the Moscow House of Trade Unions, a former club of the nobility, the founding congress of the Profintern took place. Nin spoke in the plenary sessions in the name of the Spanish delegation, while the others worked in the commissions. All of them met at night in the Hotel Lux, with Victor Serge, a former anarchist converted to Bolshevism, who had participated in the C.N.T. and been imprisoned in Spain, and with the French revolutionary syndicalist leader Alfred Rosmer, a participant in the Zimmerwald antiwar conference in 1915. At the end of August, the delegation returned to Spain, leaving Nin in Moscow. The Spanish police considered him among those responsible for the Dato affair, since he had been secretary of the C.N.T. National Committee when it took place—demonstrating how little the police understood the functioning of the C.N.T.—and his comrades felt it would expose him to useless persecution if he were to return to Spain. In Moscow, Nin married a Russian woman, had two children, and worked in the Profintern secretariat, alongside Lozovsky (S.A. Dridzo), the Bolshevik "expert" on Western trade-unionism. In 1923, Nin became a member of the Russian Communist Party.

While serving as a Profintern functionary, Nin wrote reports and pamphlets, including a short survey of fascism that appeared in English as well as the other languages of the Moscow propaganda network, and which draws interestingly on the experience of the C.N.T. in the "social war" against the Barcelona gunmen.[4] He also traveled widely, and often clandestinely, in Germany, France (where he was arrested), and Italy (where he was when Lenin died in January 1924).

Meanwhile, in Barcelona, Maurín had been arrested on February 22, 1922. Maurín's imprisonment permitted the purely anarchist elements, unsympathetic to the Soviet project, to recover their preponderance in the C.N.T. National Committee, and a little afterward a plenum of regional C.N.T. organizations agreed to withdraw the provisional affiliation of the confederal movement with the Profintern and to send, by contrast, a delegation to a congress called in Berlin to "refound" the International Workers' Association, tracing its origins to the First International, as an organism for coordination between anarchist and anarchosyndicalist movements worldwide. The Spanish anarchists found it obvious—and in this they were right—that the Profintern was merely an appendix of the Comintern.

The C.N.T.'s decision put Maurín and his friends in a difficult situation, because they did not want to leave the organization, and at the same time, they did not agree that the movement should be exclusively anarchist in its orientation, since they sought an open entry for all tendencies. Soon, Nin found himself in Moscow, but representing nobody in Spain.

The Revolutionary Syndicalist Committees

Maurín and his associates felt that a decision such as that involving withdrawal from the pro-Soviet internationals could only be taken by a full C.N.T. congress, since the original decision had been adopted in a congress. Above all, they remained uneasy about the domination the strictly anarchist tendencies were gaining in the C.N.T. To try to counteract this influence, they created, at a conference in Bilbao at the end of 1922, the Revolutionary Syndicalist Committees (Comités Sindicalistas Revolucionarios—C.S.R.), which were meant to act within the ranks of the C.N.T. and not to divide it. The committees were intended to coordinate the actions of their sympathizers, supporting them in union assemblies, so they could gain new leadership positions and in this way, little by little, come to lead the C.N.T. Nin became the representative of the C.S.R. to the Profintern. With Maurín on the scene were Hilari Arlandis, Pere Bonet, Víctor Colomer, and David Rey (Daniel Rebull).

Following the custom in the Spanish labor movement, the first thing the C.S.R. did was to found a weekly, "La Batalla" ("The Battle"), edited by Maurín and published in Barcelona. The early series of "La Batalla" is an exceptionally interesting publication for present-day historians of the revolutionary Left, in that it is one of the first to present a discourse mingling the Bolshevik vanguard party theory and the liberation ethos of the historically established radical union movement, in the context of a small political grouping. This makes the early "La Batalla" strikingly resemble the special, "marginal" Left discourse that would come to influence the culture of the West during the 1960s.

The first issue of "La Batalla," in 3,000 copies, came out in December 1922. Its publisher, Josep María Foix, was murdered in April 1923, by the gunmen of the "sindicatos libres," during the still-raging "social war." "La Batalla" and the C.S.R. found a broad response in the *cenetista* rank and file. Three important Barcelona unions—transport, metal-working, and textile—were led by C.S.R. elements.

Meanwhile, the Communist Party (P.C.E.) had begun organizing itself. Its regional federations only had immediate influence in the Basque region, where it found support among the miners' unions, and in Catalunya, through the C.S.R., although the latter did not consider itself to be under Communist Party control.

In March 1922, the first P.C.E. congress had taken place, with the participation of a delegate from the Comintern, the Swiss Protestant minister Jules Humbert-Droz, who continued to represent the International in Spain until 1932. The congress, in accord with the united front slogan put forward by the Comintern, addressed an appeal to the C.N.T. and U.G.T., calling for an alliance with the Communists, but without response. At that moment, the Spanish party counted on no more than 500 members, and the C.S.R. had a few more.[5]

A second P.C.E. congress, held in March 1923, condemned terrorism as a weapon in the labor struggle, considering it favorable in the long run to the reactionary forces. During this period, an Italian, Secundino Tranquilli, functioned in Madrid, helping establish a branch of the International Red Aid, a Moscow-directed relief organization for left-wing prisoners in the capitalist countries. It would enjoy considerable success as a front organization for the Comintern, particularly in Spain but also in the United States where it was known as the International Labor Defense. Tranquilli was jailed, and from his cell he sent some articles to "La

Batalla," signed "Ignazio Silone," the name he would make famous as a novelist.

At this time, Lozovsky had invited Salvador Seguí, the "Noi del Sucre" who had become the leading figure in the C.N.T., to come to Moscow, and Nin added some personal lines to the invitation letter. But Seguí was killed by the "sindicatos libres" a few days after receiving the letter and before he could reply to it.

A little later that year, General Miguel Primo de Rivera, under pressure from the king and from elements of the Catalan bourgeoisie, carried out a coup. The P.C.E. contacted the Federation of Anarchist Groups (Federación de Grupos Anarquistas—F.G.A.) and the C.N.T., and the three organizations proposed a general strike to the P.S.O.E. and U.G.T. The Socialists did not reply. The military directorate now ruling the country lost no time in forcing the C.N.T. underground. The P.C.E. was partially tolerated, although its press was frequently suspended; however, for the C.S.R. the coming of the dictatorship signified the end of its activity, which was based, above all, on union meetings, which could not be held in clandestine conditions. "La Batalla" continued publishing, with large blank spaces imposed by the government's censorship, until its final suspension by state order, in summer 1924.

The C.S.R. had, just then, named a delegation to a congress of the Profintern. Maurín, at its head, recalled later that "the general impression [of life in Moscow] produced a greatly disagreeable reaction among the Spanish delegates. None of the four workers who made up the group felt any further attraction to communism."[6]

The Catalan-Balearic Federation of the P.C.E.

The impossibility of the C.S.R.'s continuing to function induced many of its militants to join the P.C.E.'s Catalan-Balearic Federation, which then had only thirty members.

Meanwhile, the P.C.E. was undergoing a crisis. Various of its formerly Socialist founding members had returned to the P.S.O.E. (Virginia González and her son, Ramón Lamoneda, as well as others). The general secretary of the executive committee of the party, Oscar Pérez Solís, a former army captain, was arrested and, while in jail, was visited by one Father Gafo, a Dominican priest who specialized in conversions of revolutionaries and who captured Pérez Solís for the church. (Following the 1936-39 civil war, in which he served on the Franco side, Pérez Solís would be rewarded with a bureaucratic post in the Spanish government oil company, C.A.M.P.S.A.) The other leaders of the party had gone to Paris, although the organization had not been legally banned. Across from its headquarters, in the calle Medrazo in Madrid, two royal police officers in helmet and saber were stationed, and its weekly periodicals were banned from time to time, but the Primo government did not consider it sufficiently important to actively persecute it. Similar tolerance was encountered by the Socialist Party and by a small Catalan organization that had been founded a week before the 1923 coup, the Socialist Union of Catalunya (Unió Socialista de Catalunya—U.S.C.), which brought together some professors and white-collar workers, led by Manuel Serra i Manet and Rafael Campalans, who were dissatisfied with the policies of the Republicans and uninterested in a Socialist Party dominated by Madrid's centralist outlook.

The "La Batalla" group was critical of the organizational passivity of the P.C.E. The party leadership believed that, being weak, they had to adapt to the situation, while Maurín felt they should lead the struggle against the dictatorship, although this would require them to concentrate their efforts underground.

In November 1924, a P.C.E. central committee plenum met in Madrid. The leadership was criticized, the executive committee resigned and a new one was elected, with Maurín representing Catalunya, González Canet the Levante, and Martín Sastre the North (the Basque Country and Asturias). The first decision was to launch a highly aggressive periodical, "Vanguardia."

The dictatorship reacted strongly, and in January 1925 the arrests began: Sastre and González Canet in Madrid, Maurín and others in Barcelona. The arrest of Maurín nearly cost him his life. On January 12, as he was leaving the Ateneu Barcelonés, he saw a group of men he presumed were policemen, tried to escape, and was shot in the leg. He was taken to the hospital and then to the fortress on Montjuic, from which he again tried to escape, hurting himself further in the attempt.

In November 1927, a diplomatic conference was called in Paris by the Spanish and French governments to discuss problems in Morocco. Maurín's comrades in Paris mobilized some well-known figures, who launched a campaign for his release. The Spanish government, afraid demonstrations would obstruct the conference, decided to free Maurín and his imprisoned companions. The government even overlooked a sentence of four years' imprisonment levied against him by a judge in Bilbao.

Maurín was now known to the police and could not participate in the underground movement. The party ordered him to Paris in October 1928. A little after he arrived there he married Jeanne Lifshitz, the sister of Boris Souvarine, whom he had met in Moscow four years before. They had a son, Mário.

In Paris, the situation of the party was much more unsettled. The echoes of the power struggle between Stalin and Trotsky had divided the communist parties throughout the world, while the leaderships, disciplined by the "Bolshevization" campaign undertaken in previous years by Grigory Zinovyev as head of the Comintern leaned toward Stalin. Maurín took no side, but nonetheless he refused to condemn Trotsky.

Andreu Nin, in Moscow, found himself at the center of the factional storm within the Bolshevik regime. As a member of the Russian Party, Nin had been elected to the Moscow City Soviet. In 1925, during a clandestine trip to Paris, in which he participated in meetings of the P.C.E. leadership, to which he had been named, he was arrested while leaving a trade union meeting and imprisoned for a month for passport fraud. He returned to Moscow as a Soviet subject, although he had never renounced his Spanish nationality.

Already, at the beginning of 1925, Nin had indicated his interest in the struggle within the Communist leadership, although his first instinct was toward support for the faction of Nikolai Bukharin. In May 1925, the following "Declaration of Comrade Nin" appeared in the weekly Comintern organ, "International Press Correspondence," under the rubric "For Leninism":

> In order to put an end, once and for all, to certain misunderstandings which exist with regard to my political attitude as to the inner discussions of the Russian Communist Party and the Communist International, I emphatically declare:
>
> 1. That during the Russian discussion from 1923 (through) 1924 I was against the opposition and for the line of the Central Committee.
>
> 2. That I am not in agreement with the explanation of the events of October 1917 and the role of the Party given by Trotsky.
>
> 3. That I am, on principle, not in agreement with the attitude of the Rosmer-Monatte group, which is endeavouring to revive an outlived revolutionary syndicalism and decidedly opposes the Communist International.
>
> 4. That I consider the political orientation of the Communist Party of France to be correct.
>
> 5. That I am decidedly on the side of the Executive Committee of the Communist International in the struggle against all right deviations.
>
> 6. That only the severest application of the Leninist principles and tactics can lead the world proletariat to victory in the struggle against the bourgeoisie.
>
> Andres Nin
>
> Moscow, April 1925.

Nin maintained his position within the Profintern and, in 1926, even temporarily substituted for Lozovsky as the top leader of the trade-union international. But by 1926, his position had evolved closer to that of Trotsky. That year, allied opposition groups led by Trotsky and Zinovyev formed an international commission, that included Victor Serge, Nin, a Bulgarian, Stepanov (Stoyan Minev), and another Russian member, Kharitonov. Nin was expelled from the Russian party early in 1928, but spoke at the fourth Profintern congress as late as March 1928. He was progressively removed from all political work and put under a form of house arrest until his return to Spain in 1930.[7]

In Paris, Julián Gómez, known as Gorkín, and other Spanish Communists were on the scene, as well as some of the Spanish anarchist leaders and a group around Colonel Francesc Macià, the leader of the Catalan independence movement, who had gone to Moscow in 1925 on a fruitless search for aid from the Comintern. Macià's request for support to a Catalanist insurrection was turned down by Zinovyev and Nikolai Bukharin. Nin had been Macià's host and interpreter during the latter's visit to the Soviet capital. At that time, Paris was also the residence of various elements from the Iberian Anarchist Federation (Federación Anarquista Ibérica—F.A.I.), set up at a secret meeting in Valencia in 1927.

The triumph of Stalin in the Comintern could not be doubted. The ideological colonialism implicit in the domination of the Comintern by the Russian Communist Party continued to make itself evident. At the sixth Comintern congress, in 1928, a new line of ferocious attack on the mainstream Social Democratic parties and labor movements, as "social fascists," was approved, along with reaffirmation of the "united front from below" tactic and the overall strategy of "class against class," slogans that opened the road in Germany to the victory of Hitler in 1933. Maurín and his comrades began to feel uncomfortable in the ranks of the Spanish Communist Party.

The P.C.E. then had no more than 500 members. Moscow had named as leaders José Bullejos and Gabriel León Trilla, soon adding Julián Adame to the team. Their major success was the recruitment of a group of workers in the port of Sevilla headed by José Díaz.[8]

Bullejos was called to Moscow to discuss the situation in the party. Maurín had already been asked for a report on the same matter. A commission made up of the French Communists Jacques Doriot and André Marty, the Italians Antonio Gramsci[9] and Verti, the Argentine Vittorio Codovilla, the Mexican Manuel Almanza, the Swiss Humbert-Droz, as well as Lozovsky and Nin, held discussions with Bullejos, Jesús Ibáñez, and Gorkín. The commission decided to recommend that Bullejos reorganize the Spanish party on the basis of the line adopted by the sixth Comintern congress.[10]

In 1929, the third P.C.E. congress was scheduled to be held. After overcoming various obstacles, including arrest of the delegates at the border and the illness of a party leader, the congress was held in Paris in August. Maurín and Pere Bonet represented the Catalan-Balearic Federation, but the Bullejos-Trilla-Adame *troika*, supported by the Comintern delegate, the Italian Ruggiero Grieco, decided that, since Maurín and Bonet were residing in France, they should be considered members of the French and not the Spanish party. Thus, opposition to the leadership was suppressed. The Catalan Communists, the largest section of the party, remained unrepresented and could not defend their political theses, which, according to Maurín, "will remain in the history of our movement as a magnificent intuition of how the revolutionary movement must develop in Spain." The theses stated that the revolution would be democratic, and they finished by proposing as a slogan for the period of dictatorship, a Democratic Federal Republic.

Maurín further noted, "the Theses of the Catalan Communist Federation were rejected by the Comintern as rightist. And, at the same time, the Comintern translated into Spanish the theses, exported [from Moscow], in favor of the 'democratic dictatorship of the workers and peasants.'

"The Comintern continued in an erroneous direction in Spain. It did not understand that the country was on the eve of a democratic revolution, and that the slogan that had been put forward would result in a complete divorce between the political aspirations of the worker masses and the Communist Party. Calling for one dictatorship to be replaced by another amounted to political suicide."[11]

It was obvious that the "Muscovite" Party leadership did not view the Catalan group favorably. While some of the members of the latter were in jail, in 1925, "a serious difference emerged between us and the group of functionaries," Maurín wrote, "when they, taking advantage of our imprisonment, had attacked our leadership in the party.

We held the opinion that it was necessary to continue with the political line we had already initiated, that is, to carry out further actions against the dictatorship, while at the same time concentrating the major activity of the party in Catalunya.

Bullejos and Trilla, who had first been Trotskyists, and who then became fulminating anti-Trotskyists when Trotsky was defeated, introduced into the Spanish Communist Party all the vices of bureaucratic degeneration. Lacking in the most basic political intelligence necessary to lead a party, once they felt they had the support of the Comintern they hardened in their positions and threw themselves into the magnificent task of 'structuring' the party. They expelled excellent comrades who, even if their positions were wrong, were nonetheless extremely valuable elements. The regional federations were mercilessly ground down. Leading committees were replaced wholesale, on the caprices of little dictators carried away with themselves. In a word, the party was 'bolshevized.'

Along with the dictatorship of the bureaucratic apparatus came the incorrect tactics of the Comintern, which never understood the essence of politics in Spain. In 1927, as a palpable demonstration of its absolute lack of comprehension, it wanted to impose on the Spanish C.P. a participation in Primo de Rivera's consultative assembly. This would have meant, literally, the death of Spanish communism for a very long time. The Comintern adopted a well-known resolution, in January 1927, obliging the Spanish party to take part in Primo's assembly. 'The tactic of boycotting the Assembly,' the resolution declared, 'would only be justified in a case where the political situation in Spain was that of immediate revolution, in a situation where the masses were stimulated to mobilize spontaneously against the (Primo) Directory in an active manner. But in the present situation, the calling of the Assembly and its eventual work must be considered as a point of departure for the work of agitation and organization.'

. . . In Catalunya, the former group around 'La Batalla,' which had undergone hard repression, seeing no possibility of any kind, given such an erroneous tactic, of seriously building up the Communist movement that they had begun against such odds, partially fell apart.

Many comrades thought along the following lines: 'Our position was strong and we made great progress so long as we remained on the margin of the Comintern's activity, tracing out our own path. But the moment we accepted the discipline and politics of the Comintern, we saw ourselves converted into foreigners in our own workers' movement, and we immediately found ourselves divorced from reality.' Those who thought that way were correct. It was obvious.

Others among us believed that it was necessary to hold out to the last moment to avoid a split in the Communist movement. We decided to remain inside the party and the International with hope, even, it is true, very weak, for a correction of its errors by the Comintern . . .

The Comintern had experienced defeat in Germany in 1923, in Estonia in 1924, in Bulgaria in 1925, in China in 1927. In 1922, it had not been able to stop Mussolini's fascists from taking power in Italy. Its policies had made possible the victory of Hindenburg, as president of Germany, in 1926. For the 'putschist' line of Zinovyev the Comintern substituted the right-wing policy of Bukharin and Stalin, which culminated in an alliance with Chiang Kaishek (Jiang Jieshi), at a moment when Chiang was preparing the brutal extermination of the heroic Chinese Communists.[12]

It is interesting to compare this political explanation of the crisis in the communist organization with the one given many years later by the P.C.E. itself:

"Trotsky, expelled from the Soviet Union in 1928 for his counter-revolutionary work, which aimed at the reestablishment of capitalism, then transferred the struggle to the international plane, attempting to create a common platform for all renegades and to force a split in the Communist International. In Spain the Trotskyists opened fire against the policy of the party on all the fundamental problems of the revolution, attempting to take over the leadership of the party in order to realize their counter-revolutionary aims.

"The Trotskyist maneuvers to divide the Communist Party of Spain failed. The party maintained itself, united and faithful to the Communist International.

"Nevertheless, in Catalunya, Maurín was able through evil works to carry away a part of the Catalan-Balearic Communist Federation. This shoddy affair had sad consequences for the development of the party in Catalunya, although in the face of this temporary reverse, a nucleus of firm militants reorganized the party's ranks."[13]

Still, in 1930, in a conference in Bilbao, the P.C.E. leadership attempted to claim that the Catalan-Balearic Federation remained with the party. But the federation considered itself excluded, and the *troika* considered some isolated individuals, who supported the line of the executive committee, to be their representatives. In reality, the federation no longer had anything to do with the party; it was an independent group, with something less than 200 members. But it was not the only communist group in Catalunya.

The Catalan Communist Party [Partit Comunista Català]

Many communists had stayed outside the P.C.E. organization. There was a communist tendency based simply on sympathy for the U.S.S.R., and on independent readings of Marx, Lenin, and other theoreticians. These were people, mostly young, who had seen the successive defeats of the republicans who did not proclaim the Republic, socialists who did not change society, *catalanistes* who did not achieve autonomy, and anarchists who did not establish libertarian communism. They believed that in Russia all of this had been accomplished, since what they knew of Russia consisted only of its brighter aspect and not its dark side.

Because of its dogmatism, the P.C.E. did not know how to capitalize on this diffuse sympathy. On the contrary, it rejected it. To say, as the Comintern commanded after 1928, that the socialists and anarchists were, in effect, allies of fascism, would attract nobody capable of thinking independently. To say that only the workers could destroy the Primo dictatorship when it was opposed by students, professionals, the middle class, and a section of the bourgeoisie, as well as the most conscious sectors of the working class, was to renounce any role in events.

In Catalunya various groupings also considered themselves Communists, particularly among students and in the ranks of Estat Català, the nationalist movement led by Macià. In Madrid, a group of Trotskyist intellectuals had appeared, and when Nin returned from the U.S.S.R. in 1930, a small anti-Stalinist nucleus was formed in Barcelona. Nin survived after 1928 on the income from his work as a translator (including a brilliant and today-classic series of great Russian novels in Catalan versions, the best known being Dostoyevsky's *Crime and Punishment*), but had finally gotten the Soviets to expel him along with his Russian wife, Olga Tayeyeva, and their two daughters.

The largest independent communist group, even larger than the Catalan-Balearic Federation, was the Catalan Communist Party [Partit Comunista Català], which included some former militants of the federation (for example, Víctor Colomer) who had left when they became convinced the P.C.E. could not be reformed from within. Joan Farré, from Lleida, and Jordi Arquer, from Barcelona, were among its leaders. The Partit Comunista Catala had been organized clandestinely in the Lleida railroad yards on November 2, 1928. It acted illegally and independently from Moscow and succeeded in launching a periodical, "Treball" ("Labor"). In 1930, it had 250 members.

In February 1930, the dictatorship fell. The government of general Dámaso Berenguer proclaimed an amnesty (including terrorists who had organized attacks on the king) and the exiles returned, Maurín among them. "La Batalla" reappeared legally, transformed into a weekly workers' newspaper of the highest quality, with four broadsheet pages dense with international information, theoretical discussion, and a great combativeness. The Spanish Revolution had begun.

Notes

1. Manuel Buenacasa, *El movimiento obrero espanol*, Barcelona, 1928, pp. 109-110.
2. Joaquím Maurín, "Hombres e Historia," series of articles in "España Libre" (New York), beginning February 19, 1960.
3. Joaquím Maurín, *Revolucion y contrarrevolucion en espana*, Paris, 1966, Appendix, p. 258.
4. Andreu Nin, *The Struggle of The Trade Unions Against Fascism.* Chicago, 1923.
5. Jules Humbert-Droz refers often to his stay in Spain in the text of his memoirs,

Dix Années au Service de L'Internationale Communiste, published in Neuchatel in 1971, long after he broke with Moscow. It reveals the fragmentary knowledge the Comintern delegates had of the countries in which they operated, which Humbert-Droz admits—he only found about a general strike by reading the newspapers.

6. Maurín, *Revolucion y contrarrevolucion*, p. 226.
7. Nin's declaration appeared in the English edition of "International Press Correspondence" for May 14, 1925. On point 2, it may be adduced that "the explanation ... of Trotsky" is a reference to the latter's pamphlet-length work, *The Lessons of October*, 1923. On the international opposition commission, see Victor Serge, *Memoirs of a Revolutionary*, Oxford, 1963. On Stepanov, see Branko Lazitch, *Biographical Dictionary of The Comintern*, Stanford, 1987. On Nin's expulsion from the Russian party, see Pierre Broué, "Cartes et Lettres d'Andres Nin a Trotsky (1928)," in "Cahiers Léon Trotsky" (Grenoble), June 1982; for Nin's speech at the 1928 Profintern congress see *Protokoll Uber Den 4 Kongress Der Roten Gewerkschafts-Internationale*, Moscow/Berlin, 1928, pp. 179-183. Andreu Nin's correspondence from Moscow with Maurín in Paris has recently been published; see Pelai Pagès, ed., "Correspondencia Nin-Maurín," "L'Avenç" (Barcelona) May-June and July-August 1982; also, "Lettre d'URSS d'Andreu Nin a Maurín," "Cahiers Léon Trotsky," December 1985.
8. Trilla stayed in the P.C.E. after Bullejos was removed from responsibility and expelled from the party. During the Second World War, he returned to Spain clandestinely, to reorganize the party. The leadership then in control, Dolores Ibárruri ("La Pasionaria") and Santiago Carrillo, feared him as a rival and in 1946 sent into Spain one Cristino García, who killed Trilla in the outskirts of Madrid, on their orders. García was arrested by the Spanish police, who knew nothing about the Trilla affair, but wanted García for his activities during the civil war. García was tried and executed. France reacted by closing its border with Spain, since García had been head of a French resistance group during the Second World War.
9. Jose Bullejos, *Europa entre dos guerras*, Mexico, 1945, reports the presence of Gramsci, although the latter was imprisoned in Italy beginning in November 1926. Bullejos wrote from memory, in exile in Mexico, without documents or archives. It is possible that the Italian mentioned was Palmiro Togliatti, then known as Ercoli.
10. Bullejos, op. cit., p. 100.
11. Joaquím Maurín, *El Bloque Obrero y Campesino*, Barcelona, 1932, pp. 18-19.
12. Maurín, *El Bloque ...*, op. cit., pp. 13-17.
13. *Historia del Partido Comunista de España*, edited by a commission of the Central Committee headed by Dolores Ibárruri, Paris, 1965, p. 82.

2

From the Workers' and Peasants' Bloc to the Workers' Alliance

The danger, in the eyes of Maurin and his friends, was that the proclamation of the Republic, which they believed was near, would excite unjustifiable illusions among the worker masses. The Socialists had no program for social measures, but only for political changes. The anarchists supported Republican politicians without obligating them, in exchange, to adopt a definitive position on social problems. The Republic appeared, to the majority, as a panacea. Maurin believed it was necessary to push for the Republic's proclamation, and, at the same time, to try to vaccinate the workers against Republican illusions, so they would not lessen pressure for their own demands.

The "La Batalla" group went, in other words, against the stream. It held out the hope that, directing itself above all to the C.N.T. rank and file, it would succeed in changing the direction of the current. The masses, in the final accounting, did not lack intuition. They impelled the Republicans and Catalan Left to sign a pact with the labor movement in San Sebastian in August 1930 and then to join in a revolutionary committee. The insurrections of some military men (Ramón Franco, aviator brother of the future dictator, along with the dictator's post-1936 collaborator, Gonzálo Queipo de Llano, rose in Cuatro Vientos, followed by the similar action of Fermín Galán and José García Hernández in Jaca) responded more to the pressure of the masses than to the decisions of the revolutionary committee. This situation, in which the masses dominated the political leadership rather than vice-versa, was to be repeated in 1931, in 1934, in 1937, and is not inconceivable in Spain today. It was necessary, then, to trust in the strength of the masses for the formation of a party capable of carrying out a bourgeois-democratic revolution.

But, for the moment, the "La Batalla" group limited itself to propaganda for its point of view through the weekly newspaper as well as through a monthly magazine, "La Nueva Era," founded in Paris in 1930 and shifted to Barcelona with the fall of the dictatorship. Another weekly, "L'Hora," in Catalan, echoed the same point of view. It was published by elements from the Partit Comunista Català (P.C.C.) and from Estat Català, including Jordi Arquer, Josep Rovira, and Daniel Domingo Montserrat.

Fusion

In June 1930, Maurín, Arquer, and other elements from the P.C.C. met in the Model Prison in Barcelona. Already, a year before, Arquer had visited Maurín in Paris but had failed to work out with him a clear position on the problem of the Iberian minority nationalities. His return to Barcelona brought about an evolution in Maurín's conceptions, and now, in jail, the two groups arrived at a coincidence of opinions. It was felt that between the two groups a single party could be formed.

At a beach near Barcelona, delegates of the Catalan-Balearic Federation met secretly. The majority was favorable to a fusion with the P.C.C. Among those who were opposed, some remained in the federation while others left to join the official, Muscovite P.C.E. In October 1930, the P.C.C. also held a secret congress. The majority, again, favored fusion with the federation. Those who did not left the organization's ranks; they were almost all journalists and other middle-class professionals. One of them held in his name the copyright to the title of the P.C.C. periodical, "Treball," so that this could not become the Catalan organ of the new party; taken up by the Stalinists, it became unfortunately notorious with the coming of the civil war in 1936.

Nin's Return

In September 1930, Nin returned to Barcelona, as previously noted. Maurín hoped he would enter the new party. But Nin, with all the friendship that linked him to Maurín and the sympathy he felt for the new party, was too closely tied to Trotsky. The latter demanded that his Spanish followers preserve their identity and continue working within the official P.C.E., under the banner of the "Communist Opposition."

On October 23, 1930, Nin wrote Trotsky his impressions following his return to Spain. Excerpts from their correspondence, as translated and circulated by Trotsky's "secretariat," included Nin's observations:

> Now we have: 1) the official [Communist] party, which has no effective force and no authority among the masses; 2) the Communist federations of Catalonia and Valencia, which have been excluded from the party and which, in

reality, together with the most influential groups of [Asturias] and a few other places, constitute in fact an independent party; 3) the Catalan Communist Party, which has a good elite leadership, counts on a certain influence among the dock workers of Barcelona and dominates the workers' movement in Lérida; and 4) the Left Opposition (Trotskyist). The latter has no force in Catalonia.

A week later (November 12), Nin wrote to Trotsky regarding Maurín, who, "notwithstanding his hesitations, is very intelligent, and above all, a very honest comrade." "La Batalla" seemed to him to be "confusionist" and he hoped Maurín would soon become a Trotskyist. "That would be an acquisition of great value, for . . . he is very well thought of and honest. We could spoil everything if we were to attack him in a manner that is too unjustified."

At the end of December 1930, Nin also found himself in the Model Prison, arrested after the general strike in Barcelona, called to support the military uprising of Galán and García Hernández in Jaca, and he wrote, from his cell, an article for "L'Hora," in which he defended the same point of view as Maurín on the necessity of the proletariat completing the bourgeois-democratic revolution.

Nin found himself, then, between a rock and a hard place: he wanted to enter the party that was being set up, and he knew that within it he would find a good place, but at the same time, out of loyalty to Trotsky, he felt this entry should be undertaken to conquer the new party and convert it into a Trotskyist organization. When, in February 1931, new elections were announced, Nin told the old Bolshevik exile that the federation would present his candidacy and proposed, as well, that two Trotskyists in Madrid enter the federation.

Following news of the coming elections, "L'Hora" suggested that a slate of political prisoners be assembled. But no legislative elections took place, only municipal voting, and the proposal for a joint candidacy was dropped.[1]

Events ran ahead of the fusion negotiations between the federation and the P.C.C. The insurrection at Jaca and the general strike in Barcelona prevented the holding of the fusion congress in December 1930, as planned. But militants of both groups, in jail and in the street, already acted together as members of the same party.

Precisely because events were moving quickly, it is necessary to draw a distinction between the positions of the groups. The federation published, in "La Batalla," an open letter to the Comintern executive committee, in which it put forward its criticisms of the official party line: the Muscovite leadership had done absolutely nothing to create in Catalunya, the Basque country, Galicia, and Andalucía, national independence movements intimately linked to the revolutionary working class. The letter pointed out what the party's policy should be in this area: "We demand a state for every nation."

It proposed, as well, the formation of revolutionary councils (juntas), since it seemed absurd to demand, as the official party did, "all power to the soviets," when in Spain soviets had never existed and few people knew what they were. The council was the spontaneous Spanish form of organization for a "counter-power" aiming to transform itself into a ruling power. Finally, the letter promised "to struggle with all our forces" for the completion of the democratic revolution.

General Dámaso Berenguer was soon replaced as head of government by Admiral Juan Bautista Aznar. Municipal elections were called. In March 1931, the members of the revolutionary committee set up following the pact of San Sebastian were condemned to six months in prison. The federation-P.C.C. fusion could no longer be delayed. A series of theses had been developed by teams from both groups for discussion in the cells of each organization.

In March 1931, at the same time as the government announced the holding of municipal elections for the following month, the fusion congress was held, in a bar in Terrassa, the center of the Catalan textile industry. A score of delegates participated. At any middle-class wedding more guests could be found.

The Workers' and Peasants' Bloc

The problems that were taken up by the members of the new party, to be known as the Workers' and Peasants' Bloc (Bloc Obrer i Camperol—B.O.C.), were largely new to the Spanish workers' movement, not in themselves, but in the manner in which they were treated. The *bloquistes,* as they would come to be known, had to invent new solutions and new answers. They were little interested in the efforts of others, whose positions they rejected, in the same direction—those of the antipolitical anarchists, those of Communist ideological colonialists, and those implied by the Republican evasions of the Socialists.

The vision of Spanish reality held by the *bloquistes* was summarized in the political theses approved by the Terrassa congress. Spain needed a bourgeois-democratic revolution, which must be carried out by the working class, since the bourgeoisie had demonstrated and would continue to demonstrate its incapacity to achieve it. Thus, the road was open to socialist revolution, a revolution to be undertaken with complete international independence, without submitting to any political line not determined by the Iberian workers themselves.

The international line of the new party was: to affiliate with none of the existing internationals and to defend the Bolshevik Revolution without abandoning the right and the duty to criticize what were considered to be the errors of the Muscovite leaders.

Given the diversity of the ideological origin of the *bloquistes,* there was much preoccupation with the position the B.O.C. would adopt on the national question. The theses of the congress presented it as a question that could not be discussed in isolation, but which must be related to the more general problem of the right of nationalities to self-determination, the rights of the various Iberian peoples, and other aspects of the democratic revolution. According to the theses:

> The Communists of Catalunya, who do not forget the double slavery suffered as workers submitted to the domination of the bourgeoisie and as Catalans ruled by a foreign power, demand the right of Catalunya, the right of all the Iberian nationalities, to free determination of their own fate, including separation.

> We do not mean to say here that we would separate ourselves from the other peoples of Iberia. We want only to say that, as Communists who are defenders of the free will of peoples, we cannot stand in opposition to the other nationalities that make up Spain demanding their freedom and organizing themselves separately.

> Naturally, we do not confuse this right with the needs of any bourgeoisie, which might wish to proclaim autonomy in order to satisfy its necessities as a class.

> But, as partisans of a state for each nation, the Communists of Catalunya call for the organization of all the Iberian nations into a federation of states on the basis of mutual recognition of complete internal freedom.

> Our demand is, with reference to the national question: Union of Iberian Republics.

> With regard to Morocco we demand its complete independence. Let the Moroccans organize their society as they see fit. We have no right to intervene in their decisions.

Holding positions that are considered correct is no guarantee that with them one can have any influence on reality. For that it is necessary for such positions to be supported by an organization with an audience among the masses. What must an organization be to gain this support? A mere Communist party, although internationally independent, would not suffice, the *bloquistes* believed. The Marxist education of the Iberian workers was either very superficial or nonexistent. The new party would have to be democratic and subject to control by its members' will. But this, in a non-Marxist environment like that of Catalunya, meant running the risk that the B.O.C. would quickly cease to be Marxist. To avoid that, it was proposed that the organization exist on two levels. On one, the militant Marxists would be grouped in the Communist Federation, while the other would be made up of sympathizers, who through the experience of struggle, would become members of the federation. The second level bore the title of the B.O.C. (In practice the name of the Bloc was used to designate the whole party, while that of the federation was common only inside the organization and, even there, was increasingly less used. It was a matter of not wishing to seem too sectarian.)

Against the Stream

The congress elected a central committee, which in turn named an executive committee, composed of Joaquím Maurín, general secretary, David Rey (Daniel Rebull), and Pere Bonet from the Catalan-Balearic Federation, with Jordi Arquer, Miquel Ferrer, and Víctor Colomer, from the P.C.C.

Soon after its formation, the new party counted 700 members. All were militants and all were known in their workplaces, unions, *ateneus,* towns, or neighborhoods. All had participated in the struggle against the dictatorship. At that time, the "official" Communist organization counted no more than fifty militants in Catalunya.[2]

Faced with the call for municipal elections, the Catalan Republican Left (Esquerra Republicana de Catalunya—E.R.C.), a party organized in great haste by Macià, with a membership of Catalan nationalists as well as Republicans, proposed that the Bloc enter an electoral coalition that it had established with the Unió Socialista de Catalunya. The Bloc declined, because it did not want to waste the possibilities the elections offered to become better known on its own.

Humbert-Droz, the Comintern delegate, affirmed in a report to Moscow:

> The Bloc is mounting in Catalunya a campaign of great violence against the party, and has consolidated its ranks, notwithstanding the claims of our comrades. The elements that two months ago we thought we had taken back are now functioning as candidates in Maurín's Bloc, in a way that makes me lose confidence in the statements of our comrades who every day talk more and more about the rapid disintegration of Maurín's party. The result of the elections will give a much more exact picture of this. I am not optimistic and hope that I am wrong.[3]

The Bloc presented candidates in the dozen or so towns—most of them in Lleida province—where the organization had local sections. The municipal program of the Bloc could be resumed in a single phrase: not a *centim* for the rich districts, everything for the poorer neighborhoods. It demanded, among other things, payments to unemployed workers, municipal buildings for the use of worker and union organizations, taxes on convents and churches, municipalization of public services, and (a very ingenuous proposal, not atypical for its time) importation of Soviet wheat to lower the price of bread. It also demanded the revision of the status of municipal councillors who were named by the regime from above and not elected.

In the elections, the highest total received by the Bloc was in Barcelona, where it received 2,176 votes against 43,000 for Macià Esquerra and 28,000 for the conservative Lliga Catalana. The results of the municipal elections were a surprise even for the victors. Not only in Catalunya, where the Esquerra swept the field, but in Spain at large, Republicans obtained a majority in every city.

What was to be done with this victory?

On the morning of April 14, 1931, "L'Hora" put out a special issue: "It is necessary to take advantage of the republican will of the people and proclaim the Republic." The Republic was indeed proclaimed that day, and the same journal called, in a special one-page extra, for action to prevent the king from fleeing and for the organization of citizens' guards. The provisional government sent three ministers to Barcelona to negotiate with Macià and to transform the "Catalan Republic" that he and his forces had proclaimed following the electoral sweep by the Esquerra, into an autonomous Generality (*Generalitat*), reviving the centuries-old form of local administration.

The Bloc foresaw many illusions on the part of the workers. To prevent the Republicans from taking advantage of these illusions to swindle the workers out of their possible gains, the executive committee of the Bloc proposed to the C.N.T. that revolutionary workers' councils be established. The C.N.T. did not reply, because its leaders wanted to help the Republicans gain time. At that moment, the C.N.T. was led by a group of union activists—Angel Pestaña, Joan Peiró—who had collaborated with the Republicans against the dictatorship and who then gave votes to Maciá. The B.O.C. wanted, by contrast, to exercise pressure so the change in regime would not remain merely political.

Thus, on April 17, in a manifesto, the B.O.C. demanded anew the formation of revolutionary councils, arming of the people, the land to those who tilled it, separation of church and state, recognition of the right of nationalities to self-determination and, if they wish, separation, aid for the unemployed, the setting up of revolutionary tribunals, and the establishment of a Union of Iberian Republics.

Such slogans were appropriate for a democratic revolution. But the Socialists and anarchosyndicalists exercised no pressure on the new government, and the Bloc was not strong enough to make its pressure felt. The same April 17, Maurín, in an article in "L'Hora," affirmed that it had been an error to let the king leave Spain, because "the monarch will be the center of attraction of the forces that are seeking revenge and this will make a civil war inevitable."

In the issue of "La Nueva Era" for April, the editorial pointed out that "the revolution has not ended, as the sectors that now hold power pretend, but rather, on the contrary, is in its full ascending phase."

The main forces of the revolution were the workers, the peasants, the Catalan nationalist movement, and an important part of the youth. For these forces to act together, it was indispensable that there be "an exact comprehension of the revolutionary phenomenon, above all in the leading sectors of the popular classes . . . A little revolution is necessary every day. Let the working classes play an increasingly active role in political events." It was necessary for the peasants to "anticipate (or act in advance of) the property laws that will be legislated by the future Constituent Cortes." Only when "a return to the past is no longer possible can we go forward toward the establishment of a socialist republic."

But in May, agitation had already begun to decline. No organization, apart from the Bloc, seemed to have doubts about the Republic. The provisional government wanted a constitution to precede the development of institutional changes and left all legislation of importance to the Constituent *Cortes*. The Bloc, on the other hand, called for the Republic to be constructed first in the streets and afterwards to be legalized through the *Cortes*.

This attitude attracted a considerable number of workers. In two months, the membership of the Bloc doubled. On the national scale, 1,400 militants did not count for much compared with the hundreds of thousands in the anarchist and Socialist union federations, as well as the tens of thousands in the Socialist party organization, although the virtual absence of the Socialists, both union and party, from Catalunya compensated in small measure. "La Batalla," which in April had reached a circulation of 30,000, stabilized its press run at 7,000 copies.

Organization

It was necessary to outweigh the numerical disadvantage the Bloc faced with the enthusiasm and organizational capacities of the members. The model adopted was based on the organic structure typical of Leninist parties: cells of five members at the base; local committees elected by the cells; city or province committees elected by the local committees; a congress made up of delegates drawn from the base, which would elect a central committee, from which the members of the executive committee would be named.

Further, trade union cells and union factional groups ("minorities") existed within the ranks of the C.N.T. and the "autonomous" or unaffiliated (mainly white-collar) unions to which the *bloquistes* belonged.

What distinguished the Bloc from the "official" Communist parties was that the democratic aspects of the system of organization really functioned and were not limited to an existence on paper. The Bloc maintained itself without outside subsidies, through the dues collected from the militants, and in the cells, the congress theses, the resolutions of the central committee—which met frequently—and the decisions of the executive committee were genuinely discussed. The congresses consisted of delegates elected by the rank and file.

Finance was a simple, but not an easy, problem. The militants paid dues monthly, and the rate of dues was the highest of all the Spanish workers' organizations. A percentage of the dues fund remained in the hands of the local committee for its expenses, and the rest went to the executive committee. There was only one paid position, at a salary half that of an average worker, that of general secretary. Money was always scarce. Many things had to be done by the militants themselves for free: posting notices and posters, which were often hand-written, cleaning the offices, etc. At a time when 200 pesetas per month was an average wage, the militants spent about twelve pesetas each, or 6% of their income, on the needs of the Bloc.

Naturally, the organizational system also included preparations for underground functioning, with alternate or parallel committees, etc. On the two occasions when the underground network was tested, in 1934 and after 1937, it worked well.

The Bloc was a party of workers. Not only in name, but in its actual composition. Few intellectuals, none of them famous at the time, joined, some professionals (lawyers, and a relatively large number of doctors), and a few other middle-class elements (above all, students). About 90% of the members were wage workers (with a high percentage, although not the majority, in the white-collar class), and, in the villages, peasants. The party's name reflected its reality: a worker and peasant party, to a much greater degree than the official Communist parties, and, also, with a higher proportion of workers than were present in any of the other dissident Communist or socialist groupings in the world (composed of intellectuals and white collar workers, but with few industrial workers.) There were relatively few women (most of them wives or daughters of members), but more than in the other workers' organizations in Spain, except, probably, the anarchists. A high percentage of the membership was aged under thirty years old.

The Bloc offered no hopes for the impatiently ambitious. It held positions that were anything but simple: it was Communist, but outside the Communist International; revolutionary and worker-based, but defending at that moment the necessity of a bourgeois democratic revolution in favor of the Republic, while working to avoid illusions among the people about it; Marxist, and, therefore, an adversary of anarchism, but working within the ranks of the C.N.T. internationalist, but defending the right of nationalities to self-determination. It demanded discipline in a country where it was "every man for himself"; and individual initiative and activism in a country where heretofore political parties had concentrated on the personalities of leaders ("personalismo").

With their demand to go further, to do more, the *bloquistes* yet again swam against the stream. When everybody was convinced freedom was secure, the *bloquistes* organized as if they might have to go underground the next day. People who felt an interest in these characteristics were different from those the C.N.T. or the Esquerra attracted: more demanding, more skeptical, and at the same time more enthusiastic, inclined to think for themselves, without adopting cliches; more disposed to discipline, and, at the same time, more intransigent with respect to their rights as organizational militants.

For the *bloquistes*, the revolution was more than an uprising, it was a way of life. Having no defined form, it was, rather, something one contributed to each day, and in that way its form emerged from what one was involved in. Notwithstanding the illusions of the Republic's first months, the *bloquistes* felt that the man in the street wanted more of what the Republic gave, and their mission was, then, to explain what this "more" consisted of and how to attain it.

This situation was made possible because of the conjunction of a series of special circumstances. There were few *bloquistes,* and this permitted them to know and understand one another. But there were not so few that there developed among them the spirit of the sect or the little chapel. And there were enough of them for there to be leaders and members, although not enough for differences to emerge between the two strata. Dialogue—if often carried out with raised voices and even shouts—was indispensable to all of them. The *bloquista* searched for opportunities to discuss. At work, at home, everywhere. He would go among groups of soccer fans, stamp collectors, or sellers of old books, transforming each discussion into a political encounter.

Bloc propaganda, which, to the extent possible, brought Marxism to the masses, was very special. Perhaps the fact of Maurín, Colomer and others having been school-teachers had something to do with it. The Bloc developed in a human environment that had never known anything serious about Marxism, and its propaganda had to take advantage of every political event to derive lessons from facts without using the typical Marxist phraseology, because that alone would have been enough to close everybody's ears. The history of the workers' movement, explained with a critical sense, was an excellent aid in this task, as was the analysis of the Spanish economy.

In this effort, different organizations created by the Bloc also helped. Its Red Aid (Socors Roig), for example, maintained through public donations, took care of political prisoners and other victims of repression. The electoral secretariat of each local committee trained militants in the monotonous work of vote supervision. The women's section worked not with the women comrades, who functioned through the cells, alongside the male militants, but as a medium for contact with the mass of women outside the organization, to politicize them, discussing with them the problems of the working woman as well as the working-class housewife. There was even a Proletarian Theatre, which organized some presentations by the surrealist painter Salvador Dalí during a brief period when that individual flirted with the Bloc in 1932. At one such event, the French surrealist writer René Crevel spoke on the theme of "The Mind Against Reason," the title of one of his books.

There was also, as is logical, a defense section, based on shock units known as the "B.O.C. Action Groups" or "*Gabocs*" ("Grups d'Acció del B.O.C."). The entire Bloc participated in the propaganda section, charged with the duty of coordinating the activity of a score of party orators, organizing meetings, planning posters, etc., and that gave special attention to conferences—here again, the pedagogical tendency previously noted. Finally, there was the B.O.C. Youth, to which the militants belonged in the period before their military service, at twenty-one. The Youth was set up at the end of 1931 and were always an important force within the party, as much for their numbers as for their activity. As can be imagined, the Youth made up a good part of the "Gaboc" shock units. Penetration of the student milieu was slow and not very extensive. The Youth were organized with the same structure as the federation: cells, committees, and congresses.

Trade Union Work

The worker masses were to be found in the ranks of the trade unions. It was, then, necessary to work within them. And the Catalan workers belonged to the C.N.T. As Maurín pointed out, "Lacking a genuine revolutionary party, the masses oriented themselves toward the C.N.T. . . . Anarchosyndicalism revived in an unexpected manner . . . In 1931, the C.N.T.-F.A.I. occupied, in their own way, a historical place comparable to that of the Bolshevik party in Russia in 1917."[4]

Within the C.N.T., three tendencies competed. The "sindicalista" or "business union" grouping, with Ángel Pestaña as its best known leader, controlled the organization at the moment of the Republic's proclamation, and had collaborated with the Republicans in the struggle against the monarchy. This tendency was displaced in the leadership during 1931-32 by the anarchist trend headed by the F.A.I. The members of the latter understood how to take advantage of a policy carried out by the Socialists in the Ministry of Labor under the new Republican regime, which consisted of forcing the workers to accept mixed boards ("jurados mixtos") for the resolution of labor disputes.

Naturally, the anarchosyndicalists were extreme partisans of direct action and enemies of any state intervention in labor questions; since the *sindicalistes* had collaborated with the Republicans and the Socialists the pure anarchists of the F.A.I. could accuse the *sindicalistes* of having abandoned their principles and, thus, could take their place in the C.N.T. leadership. The Socialists did not achieve their long-standing wish to destroy the C.N.T. and establish the domination of the U.G.T. in the former union's strongholds, but the Socialists did succeed in pushing the C.N.T. into the political margin and an anti-Republic position that culminated in a series of abortive insurrections aimed at the setting up of libertarian communism (four in 1932-33).

In opposition to these two tendencies in the C.N.T. was the *bloquista* minority that called itself the Revolutionary Union Opposition (Oposició Sindicalista Revolucionaria—O.S.R.) and that very slowly gained space for itself. It called for a C.N.T. in which all the tendencies could coexist and that would participate in future revolutionary actions alongside the rest of the workers' movement and not only in its own interest. Some Barcelona unions (printing workers, sales employees) were directed by *bloquistes,* who participated in union assemblies and tried to discuss the predominant positions and, when possible, to gain leadership posts. In general, they failed in the city of Barcelona but were able to win in many unions in the provinces of Girona and Tarragona and almost all of those in Lleida. It was not easy to make oneself heard in Barcelona union meetings, because the sindicalista and anarchist tendencies united against the *bloquistes* and tried to stop them from speaking. At times they came to blows.

Once the F.A.I. had achieved absolute predominance over the *sindicalistes*, the latter issued a notable manifesto, signed by thirty veteran leaders (which resulted in their being known as the "thirtyists" or *"tren-tistes"*), and split their unions away from the C.N.T., particularly in the provinces of Barcelona and Valencia. But the F.A.I. continued to dominate the key point: the city of Barcelona. The F.A.I. attempted, in a national plenum, at the beginning of 1932, to bar from union office anyone who had been an election candidate for a political party. This was aimed at the Bloc. Those unions that refused to remove leaders who had stood as candidates were expelled from the C.N.T.; some in Barcelona and the whole provincial organizations in Girona, Tarragona, and Lleida. These formed a group, coordinated by the trade union secretariat of the Bloc, under the direction of Pere Bonet, and titled themselves "C.N.T. Expelled Unions" ("Sindicats Expulsats de la C.N.T."), in the same way as those led by the *"trentistes"* referred to themselves as "C.N.T. Opposition Unions" ("Sindicats d'Oposició de la C.N.T.").

The Catalan union movement, then, found itself divided into three sectors: the anarchists, strong in Barcelona city and some places around that province; the *"trentistes,"* strong in the smaller industrial towns of Barcelona province (Sabadell, Terrassa, etc.), and the *bloquistes*, strong in the remaining three Catalan provinces. In the rest of Spain, the union movement was divided, also, into three sections: the anarchosyndicalist C.N.T., the Socialist U.G.T., roughly evenly matched at the beginning of the thirties, and the official Communist party's Unitary General Confederation of Labor (Confederación General de Trabajo Unitário—C.G.T.U.), without any strength save in some places in the North and in the port of Sevilla. The official Communists had tried to launch a "Reconstructed C.N.T." under their own control, but without going beyond their typically artificial propaganda efforts. Following the "third period" line dictated by the Comintern after 1928, the official party, rather than working within the ranks of the existing unions, sought to establish its own "dual" apparatus or, failing that, to simply destroy the established unions.

The trade union question brought forward the problem of anarchism. So long as this trend predominated in the Catalan labor movement, the perspectives of the Bloc would be limited. The defeat of anarchism as a doctrine would have to come, not through the maneuvers of the Socialists, which the Bloc opposed, nor through persuasion aimed at the anarchist leadership, but by making the worker mass think increasingly in a Marxist way.

For that reason, the Bloc criticized the policies followed by the Catalan anarchists, and anarchism as a doctrine, while defending the anarchists from, and protesting against, their persecution by the state. Thus, although the Bloc's criticism was among the harshest directed at the C.N.T., the anarchists had a certain respect for the Bloc.

This criticism affirmed that "Spanish anarchism has been indirectly an ally of the bourgeoisie, which has used it as a wedge into the labor movement," and therefore that anarchism "served as a springboard for bourgeois radicalism." The anarchists, "when they have had to intervene in politics, have done it through second parties; supporting candidates from the bourgeoisie. In reaction to this there is anarchosyndicalism and the C.N.T. But the C.N.T. lacked a revolutionary doctrine and did not know how to take advantage of circumstances in 1919 and 1920. The masses went further than the leaders. The C.N.T. then became "entangled in stupid terrorism," and did not understand how to fight against the dictatorship. In 1930, anarchism was reborn, "on the coat-tails of the bourgeoisie," and in 1931, in place of presenting their own candidate, they voted for the Republicans.

"As at the beginning of the century, the working masses entered a zone of petty-bourgeois influence. Anarchism made it more difficult for the workers to create their own class policy and opened the gates to the petty-bourgeois parties."[5]

Nothing seemed capable of weakening the anarchist influence in the C.N.T. The Republic undertook to provide the C.N.T. with a revolutionary image that its own leaders could not give it. With its dilatory behavior, the Republican leaders provoked impatience and disillusion in the worker masses. The Bloc, naturally, benefited from this, but not as much as the C.N.T.

At the beginning of June 1931, Maurín was invited to speak at the Ateneo of Madrid, an important forum for the progressive movement. There he tried to cleanse Communism of the disdain brought on by the policies of the official party—which continued to call for all power to the soviets—and affirmed that Spain at that moment needed a "Jacobin" republic. He said on that occasion, "We believe Spain has begun its revolution, and that every effective revolution has two stages: the democratic revolution and the socialist revolution. Without the first, the second is impossible. But our revolution must be Spanish in character. All great revolutions have been national phenomena, although basically, aside from their form, they have had universal effects. Formalist orthodoxy has always failed, in revolutions. For this reason, the Communist International suffered defeat in Germany [in 1923], in China, and in Bulgaria. The desire to reproduce in these countries the Russian formula was the cause of the defeat."

Andreu Nin, who spoke in the Ateneo the next day, was aware that the Maurín speech had caused a great impression in a public accustomed to usual vague remarks about day-to-day events and dedicated the entirety of his talk to combatting, from the Trotskyist point of view, the ideas put forward by Maurín. Maurín had friends in Madrid, founders of the official party who had since broken away and formed a Communist Group (Agrupación Comunista). Luis Portela, who published the weekly "La Antorcha" ("The Torch") was the best known among them. Without, at first, entering the Bloc, they collaborated with it.

For the moment, the main problem was that of propaganda. And problematical it was, particularly in the face of anarchist opposition to Marxist "authoritarianism." As described by the writer Francisco Madrid, "When Maurín stated in a meeting 'We must send to prison . . .' he was interrupted with shouts of 'Enough of prisons!' and when he tried to explain that it was necessary to execute speculators and hangmen, they shouted at him 'Dictator! Death to Russia!'"[6]

The Constituent Cortes

While in the Constituent Cortes, the projects for a constitution and then for the statute of Catalan autonomy and of the bases for agrarian reform were debated, the Bloc set up meetings almost every Sunday, in every location where there was a section, to develop a position on each of the questions considered important. The Bloc had no deputies, but it did not wish to be absent in the parliamentary debates, which were discussed by the public. In "La Nueva Era," number 7, for June-August 1931, an editorial summarized the themes of the campaign:

> The Republic has been a new attempt at government brought forward by the Spanish bourgeoisie to avoid its final collapse and the ensuing victory of the working class.
>
> The crisis of the semifeudal regime in Spain began to assume grave proportions in 1917-1919, when the working class, separating itself from petty bourgeois Republicanism, began to manifest a political personality of its own. The feudal-bourgeois balance had been able to maintain itself until then thanks to the alienation of the workers, as an independent class, from any political or social activity of importance.
>
> The bourgeoisie, feeling itself under attack by its historical adversary, broke, from this moment, with the appearance of constitutional legality and had recourse to the dictatorial regime.
>
> In the process of capitalist collapse, there have been three characteristic stages: a) 1917-1919. A period of coalition between the (conservative) Agrarian and industrial parties that, nevertheless, failed to provide a solution to the general crisis; b) 1923-1931. The stage of military dictatorship. Capitalism attempts to save itself by appealing to a regime of force bordering on fascism; c) The Republic. April 14 saw the fall of the monarchy, beginning the phase of definitive disintegration of the semifeudal regime. The bourgeoisie, finding itself in a situation from which it could not extricate itself, throws the mon-

archy overboard . . . An important change in the relationship of forces has, nevertheless, taken place.

The provisional government of the Republic is a compact bloc made up of the big rural landlord interests, represented by (Niceto) Alcalá Zamora; the financial oligarchies—(Miguel) Maura, (Alejandro) Lerroux, and (Indalecio) Prieto; the Catalan bourgeoisie—(Lluis) Nicolau d'Olwer; the petty bourgeoisie—(Claudio) Albornoz and (Marcelino) Domingo; the state bureaucracy—(Miguel) Azaña; and social democracy—(Francisco) Largo Caballero.

. . . The provisional government has been able during the first weeks to contain the revolutionary impulse by making promises and by leaving everything up to the Cortes.

. . . In Spain, we are now living through an extraordinarily disturbing moment. The working class and the bourgeoisie, facing each other, are each watching the other closely. The reaction is doing everything possible to make the proletariat begin the fight before it is sufficiently prepared.

. . . Until now, the unleashing of the reaction has been impeded, in great part, thanks to the revolutionary fact that has created a dual power: a provisional government in Madrid and the Generalitat government in Catalunya. The Generalitat, although it is a petty bourgeois government, has seen itself obliged, at various times, under the pressure of the workers, to serve as a breakwater against the reactionary trends.

The statute of the Generalitat, even if it does not incarnate the right of Catalunya to dispose of its own fate, is a wedge introduced into the structure of the old monarchical state. The general movement for autonomy that has surged forward throughout Spain as a reflection of events in Catalunya and as a centrifugal force against the state contributes to the disarticulation of the latter, indirectly aiding, in this way, the triumph of the working class.

The Spanish economic crisis is due in great part to the general capitalist crisis. And while the world crisis deepens daily, the economic collapse of Spain has no possibility of solution within the capitalist regime.

The economic crisis has acquired enormous proportions in Spain. Industry is paralyzed. The banks have collapsed and credit is tight. Foreign trade is diminishing. The purchasing power of the internal market is diminishing. The peseta currently stands at no more than 47% of its nominal value. A bad harvest has further increased the desperate character of the economic situation.

The solution to this antagonism between the productive forces and production relations can come through nothing other than a brusque rupture and the total triumph of the working class with a movement toward the restructuring of the economy along socialist lines.

In the beginning stage of our revolution, it is obvious that there is a great gap between the proletariat and the peasant masses. The peasants in the majority are still living through the period of democratic illusions.

A proletarian revolution that is not supported by the peasants, who in Spain make up the majority of the population, is condemned to defeat.

The proletarian movement and that of the peasants must come together so that the revolution will be impelled forward by both motive forces.

The mass of the working class continues to be almost totally influenced by social democracy and anarchosyndicalism. The first, converted into the fifth wheel of the bourgeoisie, wishes to use its power, not to bring to a head a socialist revolution, but to carry out a transitional policy like that of (Ramsay) Macdonald in England. Anarchosyndicalism rejects all political power.

For this reason, we see in Spain today a great economic offensive by the workers, but, in contrast, there is a great backwardness in its political evolution, in the direction of a march with rapid step toward the conquest of power.

When the working class reaches the point of giving its great strike movement a political content, the hour of its victory will be close.

The future of the revolution depends on the capacity of the working masses to react and adapt to the political rhythm of events. If this change takes place with greater slowness than that of the bourgeoisie in assuring its domination, the revolution will be smashed.

A socialist republic against a bourgeois republic! Here we have the stone on which must be built the castle of defense and attack.

On June 20, "L'Hora" published an interview with Maurín, on his return from Madrid. In it he explained that the Comintern had underhandedly carried out some efforts, rejected by Maurín and the executive committee of the Bloc, to bring them back into the official party.

"We want democracy and not bureaucracy," said Maurín. "We are opposed to the setting up of a Communist-controlled union federation. The official party demands a soviet republic. That is infantile communism. We must pass through the democratic experience and the masses must become disillusioned with the republic. We must create revolutionary councils to take advantage of this inevitable disillusionment. The syndicalists of the C.N.T. have been displaced (in leadership positions) by the F.A.I. because they had converted the C.N.T. into an appendix of the Republicans. The C.N.T. now is an organization directed not by revolutionaries, but by dogmatists."

On July 30, 1931, "La Batalla" affirmed: "The Republic is now exhausted. Three months of governing have sufficed to prove it completely. All power must go to the workers' organizations."

The Spanish monarchy, said the *bloquistes,* had served as an arbiter between the workers and the industrialists in the manner of an Asiatic despot, to borrow Marx's famous comparison. It was necessary not only to prevent the Republic from exercising the same role, but to assure that it take the side of the people, and this would only come about if the workers controlled the Republic, that is, came to power.

On August 1, "L'Hora" recommended a vote in favor of the draft statute on autonomy that was being submitted to a referendum in Catalunya, notwithstanding its finding the draft to be "reduced, limited," in that it ceded too much power to the central state and did not take into account the financing of economic development in Catalunya. Notwithstanding that, "to vote against the draft would be to give aid to centralism." But, the newspaper added, "if the Cortes mutilates the draft statute, it will be necessary to be ready to proclaim, anew, a Catalan Republic," as Maciá and the Esquerra had (briefly) done in Barcelona in April.

In October 1931, the first Spanish government of the Left took power, following the resignation of the right-wing Republican members of the provisional government (Alcalá Zamora, Maura) in protest against the articles in the new constitution governing religious matters. The new president was Manuel Azaña, a writer by profession.

Maurín stated in an interview with the Madrid anarchosyndicalist daily "La Tierra" that the crisis would better have been resolved by giving the executive not to a Republican, Azaña, but to the Socialists, which notwithstanding all their defects, were a workers' party.

On November 6, marking the anniversary of the Russian Revolution, "L'Hora" declared: "One thing is admiration and another is servility. Russia is the homeland of the Russians and nothing more."

Meanwhile, the Bloc had to occupy itself with electoral tactics in the face of no little police harassment. On August 2, a demonstration left three *bloquistes* wounded. On August 9, the Barcelona police, for the second time, entered the central office of the Bloc during a meeting of the central committee. On September 12, police fired on a fleeing crowd in front of police headquarters. On September 31, "L'Hora" was confiscated for a day for an article demanding the land for those who worked it.

None of this seriously threatened the Bloc or prevented the bloquistes from working very actively in a new electoral campaign. In the June 1931 Cortes ballotting, two of the successful (non-Bloc) candidates had been elected for districts in Lleida and Barcelona, and upon their renunciation of their Barcelona seats, by-elections were held. The Bloc nominated Maurín for both Barcelona seats, with the reasonable belief that he could win one of them. But the C.N.T. propagandized indirectly for a member of the Radical party (who did not win), and the first seat was taken by the Right, which gained 30,000 votes against 8,326 for Maurin (and 1,260 for the candidate of the official Communist party.) For the second seat, Maurin obtained 13,708, but with the help of the right, the seat was won by the conservative nationalist group Acció Catalana, with 42,000. The Bloc remained, then, without parliamentary representation. With a total of 17,536 votes throughout Catalunya in the June voting, the Bloc would have been entitled to one seat, had proportional representation been in effect. (The official C.P. gained 2,320 votes in the entirety of Catalunya in June.)

At the end of 1931, there were almost 4,000 *bloquistes*. A year before, there had been only 700. Neither electoral failures nor police action, then, could hold back the advance of the Workers' and Peasants' Bloc. This progress reflected the disenchantment of the people with the Republic, a disenchantment that the Bloc had predicted would occur and that it had hoped to avoid, by freeing the people of illusions. In its issue for September-October 1931, "La Nueva Era" explained the causes of this deception:

> The 1931 Republic is following in the footsteps of that of 1873. The democratic revolution is being drowned in blood.
>
> The democratic Revolution has four fundamental objectives that are to be realized: 1) The total destruction of the monarchy. 2) The general redivision of the land. 3) Separation of the church from the state. 4) The right of the nationalities to self-determination.
>
> What has been accomplished? What has been realized?
>
> The monarchy remains in place. The absence of the king does not mean the bases of the monarchy have been destroyed. The king represented nothing more than the point of an immense pyramid. The monarchy based itself, as well, on the church, the aristocracy, the big landlords, the banks, the financial oligarchies, the army, the guardia civil, the police, the bureaucracy, and historical routine. . . . What of all this has been destroyed? Nothing. There has been no change. The monarchy continues to maintain its tentacles deep in Spain's heart. The Republic supports itself on monarchical bases; it uses, in reality, the old monarchical organization to sustain itself.
>
> The bourgeoisie is incapable of destroying an archaic monarchy.
>
> The victory of the Republic gave considerable support to the agrarian insurrection, and to agitation among the peasants.
>
> What has the bourgeois republic done for the peasants?
>
> It has announced a program of agrarian reform. Reform is the antithesis of revolution. It is not reform, but revolution, that is presently necessary. Reform seeks to oppose Revolution.
>
> At the beginning of this century, Spain should have had an agrarian Revolution, such as France underwent at the end of the eighteenth century, like that carried out in Russia, which would have shaken the country in all directions, getting rid of the whole structure, leaving not one stone standing. Enough of court actions, enough of giant estates, enough of the sharecropping, enough of the *rabassa morta* [a form of land tenure in Catalunya under which peasants were granted sharecropping rights so long as the land was kept culti-

vated]! All these feudal survivals must be brutally extirpated by the plow of the agrarian revolution. The land to those who work it! That is to say, nationalization of the land and the free right of usufruct to those who work on it. The agrarian revolution will transform in a short time the entire soil of the peninsula! Unemployment will cease to be a problem. Chronic hunger will become a memory. The internal market will expand to fabulous lengths, and industry will escape its traditional weakness . . .

The bourgeoisie will, if it can, smash the peasant revolution.

The duty of a Republican government is to immediately break relations with the Vatican and to impose a brusque separation of church and state. To this prophylactic measure must be added the expropriation of all assets held by the church and the dissolution of the religious orders.

What has the government done in this regard?

It has tolerated the Church's plotting, with impunity, against the new regime. The religious orders have continued their role in education. The Jesuits have been allowed to export a good part of their capital.

Even more. The government has kept in constant contact with the Papal nuncio, seeking an agreement, which in its general lines seems already to have been sketched out. True, it brings about a separation of church and state, but . . . through a "process of adaptation," over ten years, the state will continue to support the church financially . . .

On the religious question, the bourgeoisie has equally tried to bring the revolution to defeat.

Catalunya, in proclaiming the Catalan Republic, sounded the call to arms that precipitated the fall of the monarchy. Catalunya conquered the right to govern itself freely. Nevertheless, the pan-Spanish bourgeoisie, over three days, swindled Catalunya out of its status as a Republic. The promise of the statute was what was given in return.

The autonomy movement continues to take on broad proportions throughout Spain. The revolution has permitted the historic divorce between nationality and the state to manifest itself. At bottom there is a deep rebellion against the oppressive, unitary state. Nevertheless, the bourgeoisie, and with it its fifth wheel, social democracy, are opposed, not only to recognition of the national right to separation, but even to a federal restructuring . . .

The Spanish bourgeoisie has lost any revolutionary character. Better said: It is a wall that raises itself to contain the revolutionary wave.

What is to be done, then?

When the bourgeoisie has given the full measure of which it is willing, then we must bring the working class to a point of conviction that it must take power, to complete the democratic revolution, and to go on, further, to the socialist revolution.

The Trotskyists and the B.O.C.

There were those who saw in this way of viewing things something petty bourgeois and nationalist; for example, the Trotskyists.

We have already explained how, on his return from Russia, Andreu Nin collaborated on "L'Hora" and sympathized with the B.O.C. The same day as the municipal elections that brought the Republic, Nin wrote to Trotsky, "We must enter the federation, carry on systematic work in it, and create our faction in it." This was the position of Trotskyists throughout the world: to form factions in the Communist parties, so as to effect their regeneration; in Catalunya, where the official party was nonexistent, this tactic would have had to be applied to the federation, had it not been, in fact, capably managing its own "regeneration." While such a tactic made sense with relation to the parties that remained under the Comintern's direction, the B.O.C. had already broken the connection. Trotsky himself failed to call for a full break with the Comintern until the disaster of the German Communist Party's complicity in the Hitler takeover, in 1933. The B.O.C. and Maurín were thus, arguably, years ahead of Trotsky.

At the same time, Nin had awakened something in the lethargic milieu of the small Trotskyist groupings, setting up the Spanish Communist Opposition (Oposición Comunista Española—O.C.E.), Spanish section of the international Trotskyist movement, and a monthly magazine, "Comunismo."[7] In its third issue, Nin wrote in criticism of the Bloc and Maurín and affirmed that the Bloc's electoral campaign had "very little that was Communist" in it.

Nin accepted, without much enthusiasm, what Trotsky wrote to him on June 29th: "We must submit Maurin to pitiless and incessant criticism; events will completely confirm our criticism." But what events reflected was the constant growth of the Bloc and the stagnation of the O.C.E.

Nin's position, obviously, was a disagreeable one for the *bloquistes*. On April 30, "L'Hora" described Trotskyism as an "illness of snobs" and on May 7 published an article by Jordi Arquer, "Against Communist Intestinal Struggles." When Nin, in May 1931, finally decided to apply for entry into the Bloc, the executive committee answered that his membership was, for the moment, inappropriate.

"Your evasive reply shows," Nin wrote in return, "that my sincere desires to contribute to the indispensable unification of Communist forces have not encountered among you the echo they deserve."

The executive committee rejected not Nin, but Trotskyism, and in doing so knew it was protecting the Bloc from the factional work that, as we have seen, the Trotskyists were prepared to carry out within its ranks.

On September 1, 1931, Trotsky, from exile on the isle of Prinkipo in Turkish waters, ordered the O.C.E. to break with the federation, and at the end of the month added "to enter the federation . . . would not only weaken but even disgrace the Left Opposition . . ." But facts proved the Bloc to have been right.

In March 1932, Nin was elected general secretary of the O.C.E., which changed its name to the Spanish Communist Left (Izquierda Comunista Española—I.C.E.). Relations between Trotsky and Nin grew cooler and were aggravated by differences over personalities within the "International Secretariat" of the Trotskyist movement. In August 1933, Trotsky, in a letter to all the sections of the Opposition, criticized the Spanish section and spoke of "the falseness and danger of the politics of Comrade Nin."

In September 1934, "Comunismo," in an editorial, informed its readers that the I.C.E. had broken with the international Trotskyist organization, because it had refused to accept the new tactic, put forward by Trotsky, of entering the Socialist parties (known as the "French turn," because it was inspired by the situation in France at that moment.) But although Nin and the I.C.E., in 1934, were to favor just such a unification with the Bloc, resulting in the organization of the P.O.U.M., and, indeed, called for "Marxist unity" to extend to the Socialists, with whom the I.C.E. and Bloc united in the Workers' Alliances, they resisted carrying out a "turn" in an artificial way. Had Nin been accepted into the Bloc in 1931, he would have had to defend the successive changes of line of the Trotskyists within the ranks of the Bloc, producing divisions and, necessarily, eventual expulsions.[8]

Nin had published, on returning to Spain, an answer to a book by the Catalan right-wing leader Francesc Cambó in which the latter gave advice to Primo de Rivera and analyzed Italian fascism. Nin's book, *Dictatorships in our Time—Els Dictadures dels Nostres Dies*, sold very well. He was also working on his translations of Russian novels into Catalan, essentially to earn his living, but in the process adding significantly to his reputation as a Catalan writer. Catalan intellectuals admired the translator and working-class leaders respected him as a militant. The Bloc certainly would have been pleased to include Nin in its ranks. They hoped his new Catalan experiences would eliminate the varnish which a nine-year stay in the U.S.S.R. had placed on his reactions.

The Official Communists and the B.O.C.

If the criticism of the Bloc by the Trotskyists was an echo of Trotsky's thought, that put forward by the official Communist P.C.E. was a bad translation of the Muscovite writings of the higher Comintern functionaries.

The official P.C.E. remained without a Catalan-Balearic section after the split with the federation. In 1931, a dozen members of the federation, who had dropped out of the organization, formed, in name only, an official Communist Party in Catalunya.

The International remained interested in attracting the federation back into its ranks. It carried out, unsuccessfully, some private efforts. For example, Humbert-Droz, the Comintern delegate, reported that "in Barcelona I have renewed my contact with the dissident party of Maurín, where there were some comrades in my confidence. But my efforts . . . did not succeed in becoming a reality."[9]

The Political Bureau of the official P.C.E. then met and decided to make a public offer: the dissidents could return to the party as if nothing had happened. Bullejos, who doubtless saw Maurín as a competitor for party leadership, was opposed to this offer being made. Humbert-Droz then decided to invite Maurín and other *bloquistes* to Moscow, where they could discuss all the matters in question with Bullejos, whom they would likewise order to go there. Maurín rejected the invitation.

It was a question not of who should lead the party, but of principles. Hilari Arlandis and some others, who now regretted having followed the federation, insisted on accepting the official P.C.E. offer, and some *bloquista* leaders did the same. But Maurín still refused to go, although he did not oppose sending a delegation. In view of this, the Comintern delegate withdrew the proposal, not only to Maurín, but to all of them. The *bloquistes* understood in the end that Moscow wanted Maurín to go to the Russian capital to prevent him returning to Spain; there was no longer room for doubt. But the official party still thought it possible to break Maurín away from the Bloc. The weekly "Mundo Obrero," the official party organ, toward the end of June 1931, published an appeal to the Bloc militants, inviting them to enter the party:

> The central committee of the Communist Party (Spanish Section of the Communist International) directs a warm appeal to you, in the hope that you will reenter its ranks, and declares that it is disposed to admit you as a group, on the basis of your acceptance without reservations of the program and the political line of the Communist International and its Spanish Section.[10]

The invitation received no response from the Bloc, but it provided a pretext for some federation elements that had unwillingly followed Maurín to return to an easier life (intellectually speaking) within the official party. These elements tried to divide the Bloc and were expelled by the central committee. The best known were Antoni Sesé and Hilari Arlandis.

Finally, in July 1931, the Comintern confirmed the decision of the official P.C.E. to expel the Catalan-Balearic Federation. In the resolution issued from Moscow, the Bloc was accused of "liberalism, Menshevism, petty bourgeois nationalism, and reflecting Trotsky's ideas," as well as of denying the leading role of the proletariat. It is curious to note that some of the same accusations were launched against the Bloc by the Trotskyists.

It was evident that Moscow—whose official party had fewer members in the whole of Spain than the Bloc had in Catalunya alone—had to create an organization that could confront the *bloquistes*. At that time, there had returned from Russia to Spain one Ramon Casanellas, who had taken refuge in Russia in 1921, after having participated in the assassination of Dato. He was accompanied by a Comintern representative, the Hungarian Erno Gerö, who after that period frequently acted in Catalyunya under the pseudonym of "Pedro." (After an extensive career during the 1936-39 civil war as a Comintern agent in Spain, Gerö would, decades later, become famous as an architect of repression in Hungary, before and during the insurrectionary events in Budapest in 1956.) Casanellas became the electoral candidate for the official party in Barcelona. He was neither a good orator nor did he enjoy much prestige with the masses. Moscow thought, without doubt, that his having been one of the authors of the attack on Dato would give him influence among the anarchists, but they considered him a renegade who had gone over to the Marxist enemy. In his brief period of activity (he died in 1933 in a traffic accident), he faithfully followed the commands of Gerö.

In March 1932, the fifth congress of the official party met in Sevilla, and, among other things, it decided to create a separate Communist Party in Catalunya, which would be apparently autonomous and which would affiliate directly with the Comintern. Although this maneuver was aimed at the *catalanistes,* the latter became aware that in it the Catalan Communists had not created their own party, but an organism established by the Spanish party following instructions by the Comintern.

In May, the official Partit Communista de Catalunya began functioning, with Casanellas as general secretary and with the weekly "Catalunya Roja" as its press organ. The Spanish party as well as the Catalan organization began a permanent campaign of anti-Bloc activity. A pamphlet, *Los Renegados del Comunismo—El Bloque Obrero y Campesino de Maurín*, summarized the arguments of the official Communists against the Bloc:

> The agents of the bourgeoisie hide not only behind the words 'socialism' and 'anarchism' but also 'communism.' The 'Workers' and Peasants' Bloc' of Maurín and the 'Communist Left' of the Trotskyists represent two organizations that carry out the orders of the bourgeoisie to weaken and break down the ranks of the Communist Party. The destruction of the traitor and renegade leaders of these organizations, the conquest for a truly Leninist communism of the revolutionary workers tricked by them, is an extremely important task of the Communist Party, as is the destruction of the social-fascist and anarchosyndicalist leaderships.[11]

To say the Azaña government was petty bourgeois, as Maurín did, was the same, according to this text, as supporting or propagating "the illusion that this government is not counterrevolutionary." To separate from the Comintern was the same as breaking with communism altogether. The slogan of the Bloc in favor of a seizure of power by factory committees appeared wrong to the official party because power could only be taken by the soviets.

The bilevel system of organization of the Bloc was an example of "liquidationism," and, in opposing the official party, the B.O.C. carried out "an indubitable order of the bourgeoisie." Maurín was "an agent of the bourgeoisie seeking the decomposition of the ranks of the communists and who uses a communist mask as a necessary tool in his treasonous work." The text further made a distinction between members of Nin's Trotskyist group, who were condemned as agents of centralist Spanish capitalism, and the *bloquistes,* who were scored as pawns of the Catalan bourgeoisie.

While a similarly deranged tone pervades the publications of Comintern organizations throughout the world during the "third period" after 1928, in the case of the Bloc, the resentment of the official apparatus was heightened by *bloquista* criticism of the Comintern's bureaucratic functioning. Maurín, for example, had written:

> Something that has contributed much to the strengthening of the B.O.C., although at certain moments it has constituted a source of great difficulty, is its poverty. It has no other resources than those it obtains through dues.
>
> The economic aid that the official communist parties receive from the Comintern is extremely pernicious. A permanent bureaucracy is created, which ends up acting in systematic agreement with whoever gives orders. Thus the affairs and activities of the parties depend on the percentage of aid they receive. The personality of the parties disappears, and they end up turned into cogs in a big bureaucratic machine . . .
>
> Experience has shown in an undeniable way that the regime of bureaucratic dictatorship that dominates the official communist parties is tremendously bad and dangerous for the vitality of the communist movement.[12]

Ateneus, Peasants, The Unemployed

The year 1932 brought the Bloc not only these and other criticisms, but also struggles, successes, and obstacles.

It began with the anarchist rising in the Catalan mining valley of Alt-Llobregat, January 21, which was put down by police action. But something interesting had happened: for the first time, anarchist committees, in the mining towns of Figols and Sallent, seized political power, taking over municipal halls and giving orders for the organization of life in these communities during the forty-eight hours in which they controlled them.

"La Batalla" on January 29 underscored the point: "We are in the presence of a historical fact of the greatest significance, which indicates, for the
march of our revolution, a most important turn. Anarchism has ceased to
exist. The workers and, among them, naturally, the anarchists, have accepted the Marxist thesis of the seizure of power." The facts, much later,
would demonstrate that this optimism was not justified.

Still, the events in Alt-Llobregat brought to the Bloc a number of C.N.T.
militants who participated in the struggle and learned the lessons thereof,
after their deportation to Bata, in then-Spanish Equatorial Guinea, by the
Azaña government. But these memberships did not mean the turn of a
significant current of C.N.T. members toward the Bloc. The reasons were
more psychological than political. A militant is, at once, a person who
thinks in specific ideological terms and a man who lives in a given environment, that of his organization. In the Bloc, anarchists felt outside their
natural home: among other obstacles, it was difficult to pass from the
vocabulary of the anarchists to that of the Marxists.

Other means for growth existed. One consisted in the "*ateneus*," a system of important labor educational institutions in Catalunya and in Spain
as a whole. The Ateneu Enciclopèdic Popular, which enjoyed a long and
honored tradition, and which exists at the time of this writing in Barcelona,
was conquered by the *bloquistes*. The *bloquistes* joined it en masse and
obtained a majority in its assembly, electing its governing council. Beginning with that moment, the "Enciclopèdic" doubled its activity, adopting
important initiatives in the field of education for working class children
(for example, leading a campaign for better schools), and organizing short
political courses led by well-known figures in the workers' movement.

The Bloc also conquered other *ateneus* in the working-class neighborhoods and in various provincial cities; where they did not already exist,
the Bloc established them. In the *ateneus* the cream of the proletariat was
to be found and the Bloc attracted the best elements from this selection by
giving them a role in the leadership of the *ateneus*. *Bloquista* orators knew
they had access to a prestigious forum from which to put forward their
viewpoint, but they made no attempt to monopolize it.

Another area in which the Bloc advanced was that of the unions. A
Catalan regional C.N.T. plenum, held in Sabadell in April 1932, had expelled the local federations of Lleida and Girona, led by *bloquistes,* and in
May the Regional Committee expelled the Tarragona local federation for
the same reason. It was a kind of revenge by the anarchists for *bloquista*
criticism of the insurrectional adventure in Alt-Llobregat.

Alongside these organizations of industrial workers, the *bloquistes* set up
peasant organizations. In Catalunya, this stratum was unorganized, except
for the "rabassaires"—vineyard cultivators bound by the "*rabassa morta*"

contract, whose union had come under the control of the Esquerra, although the *bloquistes* slowly penetrated it. In 1932, they founded, in Lleida, the Unió Agraria (Agrarian Union) and, in Girona, Acció Social Agraria (Agrarian Social Action). In 1934, the Lleida Unió had almost as many members as the Unió de Rabassaires (18,000), and in Girona membership reached about 12,000.

In the union field, the Bloc took a further significant initiative. The country was undergoing a strong economic crisis, an echo of the worldwide depression, but aggravated by the flight of capital and economic sabotage by the industrialists and big landowners who opposed the Republic. There were 400,000 unemployed, most of them in the countryside, and 34,000 in Barcelona province.[13]

For a workers' party, it was a duty, as well as an opportunity, to organize the unemployed. The Bloc threw itself into this task. Josep Coll, an unemployed stonemason, was the brain of the campaign. The effort found echoes and led to the formation of a Workers Front Against Unemployment, led by *bloquistes*. The Bloc convened a conference on unemployment, which met on February 22, 1933, with delegates from the Bloc, the Unió Socialista (U.S.C.), various autonomous unions, and the *bloquista*-led federations expelled from the C.N.T. Neither the official P.C.E., nor the C.N.T., nor the "*trentistes*" participated.

This conference approved a list of demands: a six-hour work day, unemployment insurance, a rise in relief payments (thirty-five pesetas per week for each worker, with fifty for those who were married), and a tax reform to finance these measures. The Bloc, in calling the conference, had stated:

> It is necessary for the working class to make its immediate aspirations concrete through its slogans. But in making these aspirations concrete we do not allow ourselves the illusion that the problem of unemployment can be resolved under the capitalist regime . . . The workers who have jobs must put themselves at the side of the jobless. They must struggle for the triumph of the unemployed workers' demands out of class solidarity and because tomorrow these slogans will be directly meaningful to them.

In April, the Workers' Front Against Unemployment communicated with the deputies in the Catalan Parliament. The Socialists, at the same time, introduced a bill therein, calling for a six-hour workday. The Parliament rejected the bill and in exchange set up an Institute Against Unemployment, with an annual budget of 65.7 million pesetas. The latter measure, introduced by the Esquerra, was broader than that proposed by its allies among the Catalan Socialists. But without the campaign and conference organized by the Bloc, none of this would have been successful.

But small successes of this kind did not make the *bloquistes* lose their heads. The situation of the country was disturbing. On August 10, 1932, General José Sanjurjo led a rising against the Republic from Sevilla. A general strike frustrated this attempt. The Bloc, which had denounced the coup preparations for several months, demanded Sanjurjo's execution (he was tried, condemned to death, and pardoned on petition of the Socialists).

The same day as the rising, "Mundo Obrero," the official Communist newspaper, published, in a full-page headline, "The Azaña government is the center of the fascist counterrevolution." For this and other evidence of lack of political sense, Moscow finally removed the *troika* of Bullejos, Trilla, and Adame, and substituted for it a new team headed by José Díaz, who continued as party chief until his suicide in Soviet Georgia, after the Spanish Civil War. But nothing changed in the official party, because the problems were caused not by the overthrown *troika,* but by the party's submission to Moscow. The new leadership continued with the tactic of attacking the Socialists as "social-fascists," which in Germany was being used to prepare the way for Hitler's takeover.

Criticizing the Socialists and anarchists, as the Bloc did, did not mean they were to be considered the "last step before fascism" as the official P.C.E., under orders from Moscow, insisted. It was for these reasons that the official P.C.E. in Catalunya remained skeletal. In the elections for deputies to the Catalan Parliament in November 1932, the Bloc gained 12,000 votes, with 3,565 in Barcelona, and the official party received 1,216. The conservative Lliga took 37,000 votes and the Esquerra 65,000 in Barcelona.

The Second Bloc Congress and the National Question

The difference between the political positions of the Bloc and those of any other workers' organization may be seen clearly in the proceedings of the second congress of the Catalan-Balearic Communist Federation (that is to say, the organization of Bloc militants).

The congress was held in April 1932, in a new headquarters location, in the carrer del Palau no. 6. Two months before, "La Batalla" published the theses that were discussed at the congress, so that they could be debated in the cells. The congress approved a name change for the federation, which would now be titled the Iberian Communist Federation (Federación Comunista Iberica—F.C.I.), in order to bring in small groups of sympathizers in Asturias, Madrid, and Valencia. Some delegates were opposed, because they considered it premature for the federation to extend itself outside Catalunya.

Perhaps the most interesting document was the thesis on the national question, mostly written by Jordi Arquer. It is worth partially reproducing because it analyzes the position of other working class forces regarding this problem and because it shows there was a full coincidence of views between the *bloquistes* who had come out of the Catalan Communist movement and those coming from the C.N.T. or from the official Communist party. New elements had, in reality, undergone a submergence and blending with these founding groups. Thus, the Bloc declared:

1. The fall of the monarchy and the implantation of the Republic, since this political change was not accompanied by the incorporation into the new political state of the program of democratic revolution, does not represent a particularly ordered advance, not only in the sphere of relations between the conflicting social classes, but also in that of the relations between the national collectivities that live, for better or for worse, within the context of the Spanish state.

2. Under the monarchy, the pan-Spanish imperialist state, formed historically by diverse nationalities, upon which the feudalism of Castilla exercised its hegemony, linked closely with the monarchy and exercising its domination through the big capitalist institutions superposed upon a semifeudal and petty bourgeois economy, had not succeeded in forging a single national spirit. The assimilationist spirit of Castilian imperialism did not succeed in winning out over the personality of the nations on the periphery: Catalunya, Galicia, the Basque country.

The state was formed before the nation. The Castilian state had succeeded little by little in exercising its hegemony over the other Iberian nationalities, destroying the state bodies created by these nationalities [e.g., the Catalan Generalitat]. The historic formation of the Spanish state was accomplished without the support of the bourgeoisie, but retained its feudal characteristics, and was, for that reason, hostile to industrial capitalism. Within the Spanish state, supremacy has been exercised not by the nations that were the most progressive and enjoyed the highest level of industrial development—Catalunya, the Basque country—but the most backward: the centers ruled by agrarian feudalism—Castilla, Andalucia, Extremadura, etc. This fact partially explains the historical contradiction because of which capitalism has not evolved and has lacked initiative, since it must live under the control and rule of a state of the feudal type which is opposed to industrial capitalism, existing always under the shadow of the tariff, a concession made to it by agrarian latifundism as a payment for political submission. . .

8. The workers' movement in Catalunya, over which anarchism has for some decades exercised its hegemony, is disinterested in political problems, and, lamentably confusing the anecdotal aspect of *Catalanisme*—the fact of its control by the bourgeoisie—with the essential reality of a collectivity that has begun demanding its right to an independent personality, has produced the paradox that an essentially liberating movement is not of interest for the worker masses and that the winning of its demands find no place in class programs.

This attitude of incomprehension on the part of the anarchosyndicalists has not changed in the most minimal degree until now. In the name of the "revolutionary unity (?) of the proletariat," the leading elements of the 'C.N.T.' have arrived at the suicidal, centralist, and reactionary affirmation that 'they would rise up in arms against any attempt at separation,' thus offering support to feudal centralism and putting themselves in a situation eminently contrary to libertarian principles.

9. The position on the problem of the Iberian nationalities taken by those of the 'Spanish Workers Socialist Party' shares neither more nor less the position adopted by its colleagues, the Socialist parties that operate in the orbit of the Second International. With the sole difference that, while the Socialist parties in the rest of Europe have made some theoretical declarations, exclusively on paper, proclaiming the right to freedom of 'advanced' nations—thereby sustaining in a direct manner the rights of the imperialist powers over the colonial peoples—while at the same time doing nothing to practically aid the 'advanced' peoples to obtain their independence, the 'Spanish Workers Socialist Party' has not even made these theoretical declarations. Worse yet: as good supporters of pan-Spanish imperialism, they have pronounced themselves in a brutally imperialist way against the demands of the peoples of Spain.

10. The 'Communist Party of Spain' has never held a correct position on the national question. In these, as in so many other aspects, its mental myopia in the face of reality has been the main cause of its inability to influence in even the most minimal way the movement for emancipation of the Iberian nationalities. Officially obligated by the Communist International, they have in a cold and mechanical manner added to their programs and their slogans the right of Catalunya, the Basque country, and Galicia to their freedom and their independence. For this reason, this acceptance of the principle of the right of peoples to self-determination has remained no more than a simple verbal formality so as not to put the party in conflict with the declarations and resolutions of the Comintern regarding the role the communist parties must play in the national liberation movements . . .

12. The approval of the Catalan autonomy statute can in no way serve as a solution for the Catalan question. The statute was elaborated behind the backs of the people and gained approval through 'blackmail.' The worker and peasant mass did not feel it was represented. The statute is a shameful example of yielding in the face of the imperialist state.

13. The 'Catalan-Balearic Communist Federation' as the leading nucleus of the 'Workers' and Peasants' Bloc' mass organization declares: that with the national question being one of the basic points in the program of the democratic revolution that has not been achieved as the bourgeoisie wished, merely by substituting, for the monarchical regime, a Republican one, it will struggle for the right of the peoples to determine their own destiny, arriving if necessary at a point of separation, if such is their will . . .

17. The problem of breaking down the remains of Spanish feudalism, linked today because of the bourgeoisie with the present restructuring of the Spanish economy, must be the task of the working class. In this struggle, an extremely important role belongs to the struggle for the freedom of Catalunya, the Basque country, Galicia, and Morocco. The 'Catalan-Balearic Communist

Federation,' conscious of its historic duty as the leading nucleus of the working masses, in accepting the responsibility for the leadership of this struggle to the death against the feudal remnants and against the impotent bourgeoisie that sustains them with its weaknesses, declares itself in a clear manner that will leave no room for doubts or errors: we accept and we support separatism as a factor in the decomposition of the Spanish state, although as communists we are not separatists in the bourgeois nationalist sense.

But notwithstanding the struggle we maintain against the Spanish imperialist state for the freedom of the oppressed nations, not only will this not be the motive for provoking a rupture between the proletarians of the peoples of Spain, but in the interests of this same struggle against a common enemy, the proletarians of Catalunya, Morocco, the Basque country, and Galicia will maintain themselves united with the proletariat of the other lands of the Spanish state. If we accept separatism 'as communists' it is only to promote the disarticulation of the Spanish state. More than once, had we gained this victory and were the proletariat the master of state power, effectively guaranteeing the absolute freedom of all the Iberian peoples, there would have been no interest in pushing for a suicidal separation. We are not interested in the balkanization of the Iberian peninsula. On the contrary, we make our own the formula of Lenin: 'Separation in the interest of union.' That is: first separate, then unite. Only the proletariat in power can achieve what the bourgeoisie has been incapable of producing: that the Iberian nationalities voluntarily federate and form a political unity that in fact has never existed within the Spanish state. The working class is called, then, to complete the unity of Iberia, reincorporating Portugal in the general revolutionary rhythm of the federal proletarian state and ransoming Gibraltar from the vassalage of British imperialism to which it is submitted . . .

19. To win this goal, the Catalan-Balearic Communist Federation will struggle tirelessly to avoid the working class integrating itself into the specifically 'nationalist' organizations that hope to solve the social question after having obtained the freedom of Catalunya, forgetting lamentably that the problem of Catalunya's freedom can only find a solution when the working masses have carried out a social revolution that will make them masters of state power. We will combat, therefore, this type of nationalist revolutionary extremism, which remains a bourgeois tendency, a leftist opportunism, inside the movement for liberation of the Iberian nationalities.[14]

An international thesis was also discussed. The Bloc was the only party in the country that had shown an interest in world problems and the only one that actively condemned Spanish policy in occupied Morocco and agitated for the independence of the "protectorate." This was natural, because the reasons that led to the foundation of the Bloc had an international character. In 1932, the events in Germany seemed, to the *bloquistes,* destined to have great influence in Spain. The international thesis pointed out the responsibility of German social democracy in the rise of Hitler through its policy of "lesser evil," and of the communists through their policy of attacking "social fascism." Thanks to the split between Spanish Socialists and anarchists, fascism might soon rise in Spain as well.

The political thesis had as its title "The Spanish Revolution and the Tasks of the Proletariat." In it was put forward the many-times previously cited interpretation of the Spanish revolution as a democratic bourgeois revolution that the working class must complete, given the incapacity of the bourgeoisie to carry it out. It added that "Communism, even having long accepted the fundamental principles of Marxism and Leninism, nevertheless could not conquer the leadership of the working class without being the direct product of Iberian historical reality, and not a standardized model subject to bureaucratic orders completely foreign to our revolution. The Spanish revolution must be made by the Spanish workers themselves. Revolutionary colonialism is disastrous for the march of the revolution."

In relation with this, the congress also approved theses on communist unification, in which one read: "Communism, aiming at an authentic democracy cleansed of all class vestiges, must conserve and foster as a precious asset the elements of democracy historically acquired in the class struggle and should only refuse the benefits of democracy to those that consciously or not wish to deprive the proletariat of them."

The congress finally elected a new central committee, and, from that, a new executive committee: Maurín, Arquer, Rovira, Bonet, Colomer, David Rey, Ferrer.

In the closing act of the congress, Maurín summarized the situation as follows:

> There exist objective conditions favorable for the complete triumph of the revolution: incapacity and chaos at the top, unease at the bottom, provoked by the tremendous economic crisis the country is suffering. What is lacking, nevertheless, is real understanding on the part of the proletariat that only if it takes power will the democratic revolution fully triumph; that a strong Communist Party . . . must exist, and that it must create an alliance between the proletarians and the peasantry.

The Communist Federation and the Workers and Peasants Bloc, based in Catalunya, understood that it was indispensable to extend their organization throughout Spain for any final victory.

The Spanish Revolution

In this period, two books written by *bloquistes* came out, along with a series of booklets. The first was *From Jaca to Sallent—De Jaca a Sallent*, by Jaume Miravitlles, in Catalan[15]. At Jaca in December 1930, the two army captains, Galan and García Hernández, had risen against the monarchy, and were then shot: Sallent was the city where the F.A.I. took over power locally in January 1932. The book compared the two ways of putting forward the problem of the revolution: the Marxist and the anarchist.

It began by noting that Spain had had neither a Cromwell nor a Luther, nor an industrial revolution, nor bourgeois parliamentarism or nation-building. The results of these failures included a scarcity of industry, a scarcity of population, a scarcity of parliamentarism.

In Spain, a country without a revolution, there were two revolutionary theories: that of the nonexistent revolution as practiced by anarchosyndicalism and that of the incorrect revolution through the military coup. For the Spanish, revolution meant conspiracy. But conspiracies always fail. Miravitlles noted that for the anarchists, as for the bosses, there were two kinds of worker: the good and the bad. The good worker for one was the bad for the other, and vice versa. The anarchosyndicalists confused politics with elections. For this reason they had never had a political position on wages, on the redistribution of wealth, etc.

Reformism, Miravitlles went on to say, was doomed to defeat in Spain because the ruling system was unreformable. And the anarchists, even when they wanted to make revolution, thought in terms of reforms.

The January 1932, insurrection put in evidence that "the basic cell of the Spanish revolution will not be the soviet, but the trade union and the municipality. The impatience of the F.A.I. is the fermentation agent of the proletarian movement; produced by a fact of temperament, of a biological order, it can lead us to catastrophe. One cannot play with insurrection . . . The defeat of an insurrection opens the door to fascism."

A more general analysis, not limited to the anarchists, is to be found in the other book, written by Maurín beginning in autumn 1931, and published in summer 1932, by Editorial Cenit: *The Spanish Revolution: From Absolute Monarchy to Socialist Revolution—La Revolucion Espanola: De La Monarquia Absoluta a La Revolucion Socialista.* It provided an interpretation of the events taking place in the country after the fall of the dictatorship, and of the significance of the Republic. It caused a lesser impression than Maurín's earlier work, and its theses were greeted with silence in the press.

Following his custom of putting every problem in historical terms, he began by pointing out that Spain was the first European country to achieve national unity, not through the work of the bourgeoisie, but of the absolute monarchy, mortgaged by the church through the struggle of the *Reconquista,* against the Arabs. Feudalism struggled against the bourgeoisie through theology (the counterreformation and the Jesuits), through expulsion (of the Jews and Moors and their descendants), through emigration (America, the escape valve for the energies that, remaining in the peninsula, would have become revolutionary), and by extermination (the war against the brotherhoods known as "*germanías*" and the local communes). The marriage of national unity and absolutism had failed to produce a bourgeois revolution.

Since then, the bourgeoisie, allied with other forces, tried to reform the country, but always, fearful of its own allies, finished by putting itself at the side of the feudal forces. Little by little, the feudal monarchy, to survive, came to support the bourgeoisie, making concessions to it, persecuting the workers' movement, and trying to force artificial industrialization. But it would never dare the revolution in the countryside that was indispensable for industry to expand. The masses were disturbed, and to prevent the masses from overthrowing the king, the king was overthrown by members of the gentry converted to Republicanism.

What was the Republic? Maurín answered with a quotation from Marx, written for the *New York Tribune* in 1854.

> One of the characteristics of the [Spanish] revolution consists in the fact that the people, precisely at the moment in which it was ready for a great leap forward and the beginning of a new era, fell under the power of past illusions and all the forces and all the influences conquered at the cost of such sacrifices, passed into the hands of men that appeared as representatives of the popular movements of the previous epoch.

Maurín added, "In 1931, Marx would have begun his article in the same way. The leadership of Spanish political life passed, at the triumph of the Republic, to the most typical representatives of the old regime. . . . The two most important offices [in the provisional Republican government], the presidency and the chief ministry (*de Gobernación*), were occupied by two monarchists . . ."

The latter had supported the Catalan autonomy with the hope of forging an alliance between the big landlords in Andalucía and the Catalan petty bourgeoisie. But this did not work:

> The bourgeoisie, once again, has demonstrated its intelligence by tying the Socialists to the cart of power. And, in friendship, they offered them the three thorniest ministries: those of the interior, labor, and justice.

> The main problems of the Spanish revolution were to be dealt with, precisely, by the ministries occupied by the Socialists. The economic crisis, the workers' movement, the property laws, and the relationship between the state and the church, were left to the Socialist ministers.

While the constitution was under discussion, in the street important things took place:

At the same time as the Cortes debated the religious problem, the peasants of Andalucía seized the estates and divided up the land. Agrarian revolts broke out everywhere. The agrarian revolution suddenly took on an unanticipated thrust.

The bourgeoisie needed to maneuver rapidly, to strangle the peasant revolution. Alcalá Zamora and Maura were two obstacles. . . . Alcalá Zamora and Maura had to be sacrificed to proceed rapidly, through a tactical coup, to a republican dictatorship. With both of them, ipso facto out of the picture, the Republican government of Azaña assumed a draconian legal position, muzzling the workers' movement and trying to hold the revolution in check [through application of the so-called Law for the Defense of the Republic].

But the Cortes did not pay attention to what was happening in the street:

The healthy solution would be not a Constituent Cortes, which had to look for intermediate solutions, but a convention that incarnated the revolutionary impetus of the working masses. The Constituent Cortes, nevertheless, had triumphed over the concept of a revolutionary convention.

Finally, the Cortes approved a constitution:

The constitution elaborated by the Cortes is a bridge between revolution and counterrevolution, between the democratic Republic and a fascist Republic. It is neither the Magna Carta of a nation, nor the law code of a triumphant revolution . . .

A constitution, by its own definition, cannot be a standard to which the future should be subjected, but must be the consecration of a fully realized fact. The constitution is born of the revolution and does not precede it. It must be an index, not a preface.

When the book was published, the Cortes was discussing the autonomy statute for Catalunya:

The approval by the Cortes of the statute for Catalunya will not solve the national question. The problem is much deeper. The statute will be no more than an autonomous constitutional charter that confers on Catalunya a measure of power—but not power itself—in secondary administrative matters. Catalunya will not recover its national personality. It will remain subject to the will of the pan-Spanish bourgeoisie.

The Cortes also debated a basic project for agrarian reform. Maurín disagreed regarding how the problem should be developed:

The solution of the problem of the peasantry in Spain is not a simple redivision of the land—a division the bourgeoisie of the Republic will not carry out—but in the general industrialization of the country. The agrarian revolution and the industrial revolution are the two sides of the same coin. One cannot exist without the other. We would enter, then, into a full social revolution. The bourgeois state is incapable of industrializing, because this would suppose a break with the capitalist world. Spain, under the bourgeoisie, will not escape its status as a colony. The bourgeoisie, whether monarchist or Republican, lacks the boldness to confront the consequences of trying to establish a new nation.

Spain can only be saved if the state, during the period of transition to socialism, transforms itself into a large enterprise that, nationalizing the land, the banks, the mines, transportation, communications, acting boldly according to a plan previously developed in a scientific way, is prepared to change Spain from head to foot.

Naturally, this undertaking must belong to the working class.

These and other problems, as the Bloc incessantly insisted, could only be resolved by the working class. But the working class does not exist in isolation; rather, it is a product of the same society it must transform:

The Catalan proletariat, to which history has given the grave responsibility of being the agent of greatest importance in the social transformation of Spain, has not been able to completely form its proletarian consciousness because of the constant peasant immigration from Spain to Catalunya. The torrent of peasants from Andalucía, the Levante, and Aragon toward Barcelona has given the working class movement a special character, deforming it. The proletariat has not succeeded in assimilating this flood. The great mass has smothered within itself its characteristically proletarian condition.

The proletariat in Catalunya, or, saying the same thing, the C.N.T., through its peasant influence, petty bourgeois as is natural, has been a material easily molded by the radical petty bourgeoisie. It has not succeeded in discovering itself . . .

The entire Spanish working class has, since the monarchy began to be strongly shaken, been held at the orders of the bourgeoisie through the media of social democracy and anarchosyndicalism . . .

The proclamation of the Republic was the work of the laboring class. On April 14, if the worker masses of Barcelona, in place of serving as a springboard for the bourgeoisie, had really desired to impose its triumph, victory would have been certain.

But the working class wanted no more than the bourgeois Republic. The impotence of the proletariat at this historic hour was the final result of seventy years of reformist social democracy and anarchism.

In 1930, the proletariat was on the offensive. In 1931, after the proclamation of the Republic, the bourgeoisie counterattacked, and the proletariat passed to the defensive:

The working class in this phase has been defeated because of its lack of political capacity. Anarchist trade unionism has, unconsciously, provided the bourgeoisie with its triumph. In moments of difficulty for the bourgeoisie—from September 1930 to July 1931—the revolutionary working class was strongly tied to the bourgeoisie through anarchosyndicalism, preventing the proletariat from acquiring an independent political personality with its own goals . . .

Let us suppose the working class that leads the anarchosyndicalist movement had taken part in the political conflicts directly, putting its own face forward.

It is risky to propose hypotheses. But with reference to Barcelona—the indispensable key to the vault of Spanish politics—there can be no doubt that in the elections of April 12, working-class candidates would have triumphed by a great majority.

What would have occurred on April 14? Barcelona in the hands of the workers would have meant the revolution would have extended throughout the province of Barcelona and the rest of Spain.

This failure by the working class was due to its not having understood the role of a dual power:

In the present Spanish revolution, our working class has not understood the unavoidable need to create a second power against that of the bourgeoisie. The idea launched by the 'dilettantes' of the revolutionary movement of creating soviets has encountered no echo. To propose such a thing is easy. Nobody is capable of forcing history to bring out of its bowels a new type of organization. Every country and every historical stage possesses its own characteristic forms.

The soviet is a Russian creation that has not successfully adapted itself to any other country. In Italy during the revolution of 1920, when factory committees were organized, just as in Germany in 1923, these bodies incarnated revolutionary activity and came to represent the workers. Factory committees already had existed before 1920 and 1923. The revolution did no more than transform them into revolutionary organs.

It is a question of studying whether the defeat of the communist movement in Germany, in Bulgaria, in Estonia, and in China has not been the product of an enthusiasm for stereotyping the formulae and methods of the Russian revolution.

Revolutions have great creative strength. To involve oneself in an attempt to subject them to predetermined molds is to condemn them to defeat . . .

To expect that the Spanish working class will take power only when a broad network of soviets exists, extended throughout the country, is to defer the victory of the proletariat. Power is not taken in a metaphysical way, but through the creation of the lever of a second power.

What is to be done, then?

What must be done is to take advantage of the existing material for the construction of the instrument we need . . .

The trade union and the factory committee are the real embryos of the workers' power.

The idea of taking power through the trade unions will frighten those who repetitively declaim a fossilized Marxism. To try to impose the map of Russia over that of Spain is grotesque. The Spanish revolution, while influenced by revolutions in other countries, has its own particular features. Just as there is a soviet system, there can be a union-based governing system . . .

The unions can, in the revolutionary process, take on new forms, un-suspected today. The factory councils will prove a natural derivation. Within the union form of organization there is an enormous quantity of possibilities that have not yet been tried.

What was the task of the unions? A democratic revolution, because:

Spain is one of the few countries that has not yet has its democratic-bourgeois revolution. Turkey has carried out one. And Mexico. And even China. Spain remained in an obscure corner of the map, as if history had forgotten it. But history makes exceptions for nobody.

We face a democratic revolution, in a moment when the bourgeoisie has entirely lost its revolutionary condition, and the democratic revolution is inseparable from the socialist revolution. On the other hand, the proletariat, which should have brought forward a definitive solution, is still enormously backward. It has not come to understand what its mission must be in this transcendental moment of the national destiny.

Here we have the great contradiction that gives the present revolutionary stage its character."

For this reason, "our bourgeoisie will search for a way out by means of a republican-military coup d'etat, inaugurating a bonapartist stage in the style of Pilsudski, in Poland.

All the symptoms are favorable to a bourgeois orientation in this direction.

One could not infallibly predict what would take place, but Maurín reminded his readers that:

There are three historical forces that can converge and strangle an uprising along the lines of Kornilov [a reactionary general whose threat to overthrow the Kerensky government strengthened the position of the Bolsheviks, in purported defense of the Kerensky republic, in Russia in 1917]: the pro-letariat, the peasants, and the movement for national emancipation.

The seizure of power by the laboring class, thanks to the coordination of these three forces, would signify the end of a nightmare that has gone on for centuries.

The democratic revolution would be achieved in a short time. And workers
and peasants, free, would launch themselves into the socialist revolution.

A few weeks after the publication of this book, general José Sanjurjo led
a failed military coup. The Republicans showed no alarm, although the
Bloc did.

The Hitler Victory

On January 30, 1933, the president of the German Republic, Field Marshal Paul Hindenburg, named Adolf Hitler head of government.

For the Bloc, which possessed a deeply rooted international mentality,
this fact had more importance than many things taking place in Spain; the
Bloc believed it would exercise a determining influence on the entire world,
and directly on Spain.

The seizure of power by the Nazis confirmed, in the eyes of the *bloquistes,* the correctness of the policy pursued by the Bloc. If the German
Socialists and Communists, in place of fighting among themselves, had
allied, they would not only have held back the Nazi advance, but also
would have been able to make the revolution. And a socialist revolution in
Germany, a major industrial country, would have taken primacy over the
communist movement away from the Russian Communists and would
have completely changed the situation of the workers' movement. But the
Socialists contented themselves with defending, from positions of retreat,
the Weimar Republic (which, paradoxically, inspired the Republicans in
Spain just at the time of its decomposition); the Communists, for their
part, stood with the Nazis more than once, with the aim of destroying the
Socialists. The Moscow thesis was that it was mainly necessary to eliminate
the Socialists, because they provoked democratic illusions in the German
workers. The first issue of "Rote Fahne" ("Red Flag"), the communist
newspaper, which appeared in Switzerland after Hitler's takeover of the
government, said on each page "Nach Hitler uns" ("After Hitler us.")

This position had also been defended in Spain by the official party,
following the orders of the International. The official communists did not
appreciate the German lesson. They continued saying the danger rested
with the Socialists; they saw no reactionary threat in Spain and even less
the possibility of the formation of a fascist movement in Spain.

Now that Sanjurjo's attempt to take over the Republic from without had
failed, the Bloc argued, an attempt would come from within. The Radical
party of Alejandro Lerroux, an old anticlerical demagogue turned servant
of order, allied with the right and tried to return power to the feudal forces,
to annul what had already been accomplished under the Republic, which

was very little for the workers, but too much for the bourgeoisie and the big landlords.

How to stop the advance of the Right? The Bloc, evidently, was not enough. The C.N.T. and U.G.T., anarchists and Socialists, had the majority of the working class with them. It was, then, necessary to make the C.N.T. and U.G.T. see the real character of the threat and make them accept the need to struggle unitedly against it.

Another congress of the Bloc's cadre organization, the F.C.I., held in April, launched the slogan of workers' unity against fascism. For the moment, there was no response. To propagate it, Maurín proposed a subscription campaign to launch a daily newspaper.

The international theses of the April 1933 congress, written by Maurín and Julián Gorkín, were the most interesting documents presented therein. They analyzed what had taken place in Germany, as described above, condemned the policy of both the Socialist and Communist Internationals, and demanded a union of worker forces to struggle against fascism and, for the moment, prevent it conquering new positions.

A daily newspaper began coming out soon after the congress, with 50,000 pesetas collected through public subscription. It was printed on a very old, rented press, and was titled "Adelante" ("Forward"). It was not presented as an organ of the Bloc, but as a daily newspaper for a workers' alliance. It was edited by Maurín and Luís Portela served as business manager. It had only four pages each issue. Various editors were hauled before the courts for articles and reportages published in it. The chief *counseller (conseller de gobernació)* of the Generalitat, Josep Dencàs, an extreme Catalan nationalist and head of a grouping within the Esquerra that would in time become quasi-fascist, suspended the newspaper in the middle of March 1934. All things considered, the base of the Bloc was not large enough to sustain it, and it penetrated very little into working class life.

The Trade Union Fronts

The place where the Bloc enjoyed a success that surprised even the *bloquistes* themselves was among the Barcelona white-collar clerical and sales employees.[16] The white-collar workers had never been known as combative. They are, generally, the last to organize and the first to become demoralized. They did not consider themselves to be wage workers, but part of the middle class, and they organized in centers or associations with little trade-union character.

The most important of these, in Catalunya, was the Autonomous Center of Commercial and Industrial Employees (Centre Autonomista de Dependents del Comerc i de la Industria—C.A.D.C.I.). At the same time, there were two trade unions for clerks: one, skeletal, created by the anarchists after the C.N.T. in 1932, expelled its member organization led by Arquer, and Arquer's group, which, reorganized autonomously in 1933, because the soul of the clerical workers' movement.

The Mercantile Union (Sindicat Mercantil) led by Arquer called a series of meetings with autonomous organizations of employees. Nobody wanted to hear mention of strikes. That was for manual workers . . . The members of the "Mercantil" were not discouraged. They knew that in the rank and file of these organizations there was discontent with the leadership and its conformism. Little by little, these leaders finally accepted the idea of a common front of clerical workers and of striking, or were democratically removed and replaced by others who were more combative.

Finally, in September 1933, a United Clerical Workers Front (Front Unic Mercantil) was formed with the C.A.D.C.I., the autonomous employee organizations, the union of gas and electricity workers, the Union Ultramarina (of grocery shop workers), and the union of restaurant workers (both led by *bloquistes*), the Federation of Clerks and Technicians (led by the U.S.C. which had founded it), and the Mercantile Union. A new form of struggle had emerged, imposed by the situation.

The spinal column of the new front was the Mercantile Union. The simple fact of talking about strikes among these clerical workers showed how strong the social tension had become. The Bloc had felt it and now was in a condition to lead the most important strike movement in Catalunya during the second republic, involving 80,000 workers and bringing into the social struggle a sector of the work force alienated from it until then.

On October 14, 1933, a Light and Power United Front (Front Unic de Llum i Força), set in motion by *bloquistes* headed by Miguel Tarafa, announced gains in work rules including a forty-four hour work week, sick pay, and other improvements. This encouraged the clerical workers. The governmental mixed board for commercial activities spent months discussing the new rules, along with the demands of the various organizations of the Clerical Workers' Front. On November 13, in the face of a strike brought about by the delaying tactics of the mixed board, the representatives of the employers and the workers met with the *conseller* for labor of the Generalitat. After forty-eight hours, the Front committee presented itself to an assembly and explained that the two sides, confronted with the impossibility of reaching an agreement, had decided that the *conseller* for labor, Martí Barrera, a former member of the C.N.T. who had joined the Esquerra, should arrive at a recommendation. However, the assembly was dissatisfied by the failure to obtain anything firm for the market and food store workers, who were the most exploited. And it agreed to go on strike on Tuesday, November 14.

The strike was a success. The shock groups of the Bloc (the *gabocs*) were active, since the clerical workers were little prepared for violence, although they showed great aggressivity. In order not to alienate the feelings of the Barcelona housewives, food stores were left open.

The strike was declared illegal. But it continued until Friday, when a decree of the Generalitat was published establishing the eight-hour day for the food industry, which until then had seen unlimited working hours for employees; the decree also did away with the practice of requiring the apprentices to live on the store premises, sleeping between the counters. In view of this, a new assembly of the clerical employees decided to accept the recommendation and to end the strike.

The light and power and clerical workers' united fronts had opened the way. It was necessary now to move from the union to the political terrain. The Bloc took responsibility for its completion.

The Workers' Alliance

The *bloquistes* in the light and power and clerical workers' movements had not organized their united fronts in obedience to orders from the Bloc executive committee. They proposed it on their own account, because it seemed to them to be the correct tactic and because the Bloc, already since 1932, had spoken of the need for a workers' front against the reactionary forces.

But in the political field, the initiative had to come from a political organization. The situation was worsening. The decomposition of the Republican parties was accelerating: the so-called Radical Socialist party, which was neither radical nor socialist, split. An antiworker public order law was approved, and the Right won the elections to designate members of a Tribunal of Constitutional Guarantees; following the resignation of Azaña's administration as a protest against this, Alejandro Lerroux formed a government. On November 19, 1933, the Right won an electoral majority in the Cortes, during the voting the C.N.T. carried out an intense campaign under the slogan, "Workers, Do Not Vote."

The Bloc obtained 5,745 votes in Barcelona and 24,000 in the rest of Catalunya. As an act of united front propaganda, the Bloc presented a candidacy in conjunction with the miniscule Socialist Group of Barcelona (Agrupació Socialista de Barcelona), affiliated with the P.S.O.E., which had never before participated in Catalan elections. The common slate was titled the Workers Front (Front Obrer). During this campaign Santiago Carrillo, then the general secretary of the Socialist Youth and later general secretary of the Communist Party, had a good idea: the rightist C.E.D.A. had covered the walls with election posters that said "To save Spain from

Marxism, vote for the C.E.D.A." The young socialists distributed a circular reading "To save Spain from Marxism, vote Communist."

In the municipal elections of January 14, 1934, the Catalan Left recovered their strength, but the Bloc only obtained 1,959 votes in Barcelona (the Lliga gained 133,000 and the Esquerra 162,000). In Lleida, the Bloc won 636 votes. Many who otherwise would have voted for the Bloc candidates, even knowing that they could not win, voted for the Esquerra, to stop the advance of the Lliga. The Bloc had, at that moment, 5,000 members.

Events did not cease their dramatic tempo. The C.N.T. lost a streetcar workers strike and seemed exhausted. Unemployment increased. The textile factories affiliated with the Unión Algodonera shut down, and 4,000 workers were left without jobs. In Barcelona, there were 40,000 unemployed. Various autonomous unions formed the United Front of the Textile and Clothing Industry [Front Unic de la Industria Textil i Fabril] and demanded the five-day work week, to create work for the unemployed. The number of strikes decreased, and that of strikes won fell steeply: in 1933, 40% of strikes had ended in victories for the workers, compared with only 29% in 1934.

The Esquerra was dancing on a tightrope: on one side, it adopted some measures to protect the workers and on the other Josep Dencàs, in the chief *conselleria,* began a systematic offensive against the C.N.T., which did not exclude the torture of prisoners. Maurín thus summarized the situation:

> The politico-social situation in our country could not be more grave for the working class. The reformism of the Socialist Party, the absurd ultraleftism of the F.A.I. and the blundering work carried out by the official Communist party, all of this has led the workers' movement only two steps from its complete collapse, followed by the triumph of fascism.

> The internal division of the proletariat, just as it begins to grasp the defeat of the democratic revolution at the hands of the bourgeoisie and the reactionary forces, which, left undestroyed, have proceeded to a rapid regroupment and are preparing themselves for the reconquest of positions they had lost, creates a situation propitious for fascism to first develop and then win out.[17]

What was to be done about this situation? The answer, for a *bloquista,* was evident:

> We must bar the road to fascism. How? Creating imaginary and artificial organisms in the form of 'Antifascist Committees' such as the Stalinist Communists have done in recent years? Continuing sterilely the discussion of what should or should not be done? No. Something must be done in a concrete way. A step forward. To create the bases for agreement between the existing organizations. It is necessary to invent nothing. Nor is it necessary to

keep smuggling in importations. Our proletariat, whose combative past is of the greatest importance, can and must find a new form of organization such as the circumstances demand.[18]

What could this form be? The slogan of the united front had been discredited by the actions of the official communists. After dividing the workers' movement throughout the world, the Third International had launched the slogan of a united front "from below." This signified new divisions, because to ask the workers, who had elected their union and political leaders, to rise up against them and unite with the communists, was not only absurd but divisive.

It was the policy of a phony united front that permitted Hitler's rise to power, because if in Germany a real united front had been formed, the Nazis would have been defeated. Together, Socialists and Communists would have been able to close the door to fascism.

In 1933, the situation throughout the world showed that the united front was indispensable. But in Spain, nobody talked about a united front. The Socialists continued trying, now from outside the government, to monopolize the workers' movement; the anarchists prepared new explosions; the communists insisted in their propaganda on a "united front from below" and made further efforts to divide the workers' movement, by creating their own trade union organization. In Catalunya, alongside the Bloc, there was a long list of smaller organizations: the Unió Socialista (U.S.C.), the Libertarian Syndicalist Federation (F.S.L.), the Syndicalist Party, the two latter having emerged as new anti-F.A.I. tendencies in the C.N.T. In the Catalan union movement, one found the majority of unions in the C.N.T., the minority in the U.G.T., plus those associated with the 'trentistes,' those controlled by the U.S.C., those controlled by bloquistes, and a series of autonomous unions. While the workers' movement found itself split by rivalries and resentments, the Right united (the main rightist party, the C.E.D.A., took its name from the fact of being a Spanish Confederation of Autonomous Rightists—Confederación Española de Derechas Autónomas) and strengthened itself (the Falange Española and the Councils for the National-Syndicalist Offensive (J.O.N.S.) were formed in 1933). What was necessary was that action show that the united front was possible and effective. For this reason, the bloquistes organized the United Front Against Unemployment and the two fronts based on the light and power and clerical workers, which were successful and showed results.

When Hitler took power in Germany, one of the best-known bloquistes, Dr. Tomas Tussó, who had many friends throughout the world of labor, proposed a round-table meeting between the U.S.C. and the Bloc. Various meetings took place in Tussó's house, with Maurín representing the Bloc and Joan Comorera and Joan Fronjosa for the U.S.C. The U.S.C. delegation proposed a fusion and the Bloc representative rejected it, since the U.S.C. was a cadre organization and had no rank and file, and was allied with the Esquerra as a component in the Generalitat government. It was decided that, in place of discussing a fusion, they would try to form an alliance of all the workers' organizations, and it was agreed that it would be advantageous that the call for this organization be made by a "neutral" workers' institution.

The Ateneu Enciclopèdic Popular, controlled by *bloquistes,* was just such an organism. It called a meeting, at which delegates of the Bloc, the U.S.C., the Catalan U.G.T., the P.S.O.E. of Catalunya, the *'trentista'* unions, the Bloc-controlled unions, the Communist Left (Trotskyists) and the Unió de Rabassaires participated. It was decided to form a Workers' Alliance (Aliança Obrera). Invitees who did not show up were the C.N.T. and the official P.C.E.

None of the participating organizations, nor the group of them together, could be considered the majority or of decisive influence in the Catalan workers' movement. But they formed a nucleus around which other forces could congregate in the future. They were the springboard for the united front. They showed that people with conceptions as diverse as the *sindicalistes,* the dissident Communists, and the reformist Socialists could speak together and seek a common program. Now it was necessary to broaden the alliance, to the point of including within it the C.N.T., the F.A.I., and the P.S.O.E. and U.G.T. throughout Spain. Difficult, but necessary. The facts demonstrated that the alliance was neither a political trick, nor a maneuver, but that it responded to a need. And it began to be seen that it responded also to a desire on the part of the masses. The workers, in effect, had begun to become alarmed. They showed greater wisdom than their leaders.

The document constituting the alliance in Catalunya was dated December 16, 1933:

> The undersigned entities, of diverse doctrinal tendencies and aspirations, but united by a common desire to safeguard the conquests gained until now by the Spanish working class, have constituted the Workers' Alliance, to oppose the enthronement of reaction in our country, to avoid any attempt at a coup d'etat or installment of a dictatorship if such an attempt is made, and to maintain intact and unscathed all the gains made up to the present, and which represent the most important common property of the working class.

It was signed by: Manuel Mascarell, Progreso Alfarache, Joan Peiró, for the Opposition Trade Unions ('*trentistes*'); Emili Vivas, Agustí Gabanel, for the Libertarian Syndicalist Federation; Pere Bonet, for the Federation of Unions Excluded from the C.N.T. (Bloc-controlled unions); Antoni Vila Cuenca, for the U.G.T.; Ángel Pestaña, for the Syndicalist Party; Rafael Vidiella, for the Catalan Federation of the P.S.O.E.; Joaquím Maurín, for the Workers' and Peasants' Bloc; J. Martínez Cuenca, for the Unió Socialista de Catalunya; Andreu Nin, for the Communist Left, and Josep Calvet, for the Unió de Rabassaires.

All the Catalan working class forces, except for the C.N.T. and the official Communists, were represented in the alliance. The absence of the C.N.T. was important, because it was a matter of the most powerful worker element in the country. Some personal gestures were made in an attempt to bring the organization in, but the F.A.I. people did not allow them a hearing. They were infected by a kind of pride, because they were strong—although, in 1934, their strength was less than what it was a year before—and they believed they were the sole requirement for the accomplishment of anything, beginning with the revolution. In addition, to enter the alliance would be, in their eyes, to encourage the combativeness of the political forces, which was anathema to their principles, and to accept the existence of forces whose reality they denied, such as the '*trentista*' unions and those excluded for their *bloquista* leadership. But the leaders of the alliance knew the F.A.I. leadership was composed of sincere revolutionaries and trusted in events to persuade the anarchists.

Indeed, on the side of the latter, there were various positions. In February 1934, Orobón Fernández, one of the most respected C.N.T. theoreticians, published an essay in the Madrid anarchist daily "La Tierra," titled "Trends in the Workers' Alliance" ("Directríces de la Alianza Obrera"), in which he suggested points of possible agreement and called for development of a tactical plan guaranteeing revolutionary democracy and promising immediate socialization of the means of production.

Orobón Fernández' article was a turning point in the development of the Spanish revolutionary crisis. Just after its publication, a plenum of C.N.T. regional organizations was held in Barcelona (on February 13) and agreed to "summon the U.G.T. to express what its revolutionary aspirations are," so as to be able to conclude an alliance with it. There was no answer. At this plenum the Catalan regional had raised its voice loudly against the Workers' Alliance. But on June 23, 1934, at another plenum of C.N.T. regionals held in Madrid, the Asturias regional demanded freedom to enter the alliance, which was conceded, "for reasons of local realism" in Asturias. This, on the heels of Fernández's article, was yet another turning point.

The alliance began organizing. It had an executive committee, formed by representatives of all the organizations that had joined. It met frequently and made great efforts to create local alliance committees in Catalunya and to extend their example to the rest of Spain.

The alliance leaders were particularly concerned with the position of the official Communist Party. The latter participated in two meetings of the Catalan Alliance but then broke off relations and began a campaign of defamation against the alliance, accusing it of being an instrument of the bourgeoisie, of hiding "socialist treason," and of wishing to impede, with its organization, the setting up of soviets.

To succeed in its efforts, it was not enough for the alliance to issue manifestoes; it had to join battle. In Madrid, the employers organization, encouraged by the electoral victory of the right, tried to take back the conquests of the workers. Almost all strikes were lost. Exasperated, the Madrid socialist unions declared a general strike in March 1934, and the executive committee of the alliance ordered a 24-hour general strike throughout Catalunya, in solidarity with the Madrid strikers, for the thirteenth of the month. Until then, only the C.N.T. had been able to declare general strikes in Catalunya. Would the alliance succeed in doing the same? The anarchists, and the police who in other circumstances tortured them, found themselves agreeing in their opposition to the alliance solidarity strike. But if in Barcelona it had hardly any effect, in the rest of Catalunya it was, indeed, a general strike.

The strike had echoes. The *bloquistes* of Castelló and Valencia took advantage of the situation and formed workers' alliances. The Valencia Workers' Alliance hardly set up, declared a successful general strike in solidarity with a walkout by the hydroelectric power workers. An important step came when, although the C.N.T. continued refusing affiliation to the two new alliances, the local P.S.O.E. and U.G.T. joined. This had repercussions in Asturias where the workers' movement at that time was combative and flexible. The alliance had been organized there, including not only the P.S.O.E. and U.G.T., along with the Bloc and the Trotskyist Communist Left, but also the C.N.T., thanks to the agreement at the above-mentioned June plenum. Little by little, alliance committees were formed in unexpected places. Jaén, Córdoba, Sevilla, and, finally, Madrid. But these were local committees. A national alliance did not as yet exist. The rank and file was proceeding ahead of the national leaderships, this time in the matter of organization as well as sentiment.

The alliance sought to extend itself. A delegation (Pestaña, Vila Cuenca, and Maurín) went to Madrid. It met with leaders of the Socialist Party and the U.G.T. Francisco Largo Caballero was the only one interested in the new tactics, in line with the increasingly radical position adopted by this veteran reformist union leader. A little afterward, in February 1934, Largo went to Barcelona to consult with Maurín. Their discussions were quoted in an issue of "Adelante": "No right wing solution [in government] is legally possible. Nevertheless, we must be prepared, on guard, because the reactionaries, given the difficult situation in which they find themselves, can attempt a quick success."

The Socialist Party's youth organization (Juventudes Socialistas— J.J.S.S.) and the Madrid branch of the Trotskyist Communist Left took the initiative in setting up the local Workers' Alliance (without the participation of the C.N.T., the official Communists, and Catalan groups like the Bloc, which had no Madrid branch). It was above all composed of trade unions led by Trotskyists or left Socialists. In July, Largo Caballero was elected general secretary of the U.G.T., and the national commissions of the U.G.T. and P.S.O.E. decided, finally, to support the idea of a Workers' Alliance, but still without a national character (while the C.N.T. did not accept the idea at all).

Those who persisted in turning a deaf ear to the entire project were the communists. Francisco Galán, brother of captain Fermín Galán (executed for his participation in the Jaca rising of 1930), who spoke in meetings of the Bloc in 1931, was now a Communist, and was quoted to the effect that "If I had to sit down at the same table with the Socialist leaders, I would blush like a virgin among prostitutes."[19]

While everybody else was now talking unity, in April 1934 the official Communists, imperturbably applying orders from Moscow, formed a skeletal dual union federation, the C.G.T.U. At the same time, the first congress of the official Partit Comunista de Catalunya was meeting in Barcelona, in which the Hungarian Comintern delegate Erno Gerö participated along with a delegation from the official Spanish party led by Vicente Uribe. The latter issued a report on the congress, in which he said: "Let us not forget that it is in Catalunya that the species known as the 'Workers' Alliance' has been born, with its parents including the renegades of the Workers' and Peasants' Bloc, the "*trentistes*," and the Socialists, an alliance against the United Front and the Revolution. The correct tactic of the United Front permits us to destroy the counterrevolutionary plans of the 'Workers' Alliance.'"[20]

Three months later, without anything having happened that was not predictable when this report was written, there came another report from Vicente Arroyo, commenting on an extraordinary meeting of the Central Committee of the official Spanish party, held in Madrid on September 11-12:

A single point was on the agenda: the United Front and the Workers' Alliances.

The Central Committee of the P.C.E. has discussed this question before thousands of workers and has unanimously approved the proposal of the Political Bureau to 'Join the Workers' Alliances,' with a single condition: 'The right of expression and fraternal discussion regarding all the problems of the revolution.'[21]

The official party had, then, corrected itself. And this is not because of the Spanish situation, but because from June, when the official party in Catalunya had attacked the Workers' Alliance, to September, when the official Spanish party accepted it, a turn had begun in Moscow that one year later, at the seventh world congress of the Comintern, would produce the "People's Front" tactic. Vittorio Codovilla, the Argentine-born Comintern delegate in Madrid, who called himself "Medina," visited Largo Caballero. He wanted to convince the Socialist leader that it would be convenient to substitute for the name Workers' Alliance something "more in harmony with the Russian vocabulary," Largo later recalled,[22] with the aim of facilitating the entry of the communists. But Largo refused, and the next day the communist press announced that the official party had decided to enter the alliance. The maneuver was obvious: to bring about a change in name, first to save the official party from having to join something it had attacked, and second so the public would believe the alliance, under a new name, was a creation of the official Communists.

Events showed that the organization of the alliance had been a correct decision.

In March, a group of monarchists signed an agreement with Mussolini for receipt of financial aid and weapons. In April, a gigantic mass meeting was held by the C.E.D.A. and its youth wing, the Popular Action Youth (Juventudes de Acción Popular) at the Escorial, the massive, gloomy royal complex outside Madrid that was a shrine to the Right. Its main feature was the repeated chanting of "All power to the chief!", referring to José María Gil Robles, leader of the C.E.D.A.'s main grouping, Popular Action (Acción Popular). In protest against this rightist demonstration, a general strike took place in Madrid. A new government was formed under Ricardo Samper, representing the Radical party. A farm workers' strike called by the U.G.T. was thoroughly defeated, demonstrating once again the need for action by more than a single organization in movements that hoped for a major impact. The Catalan rural landlord organization, the Institut Agrícola Català de Sant Isidre, came before the Tribunal of Constitutional Guarantees, in Madrid, to protest the new law on farm contracts adopted by the Catalan Parliament as a means of relief for the "*rabassaires*," which the tribunal duly declared unconstitutional (June 11). A new vote on the same law was taken by the Catalan Parliament. On September 8, the Catalan rural landlords journeyed en masse to Madrid to demand that the government act against the new law on farm contracts; they were greeted by a general strike ordered by the U.G.T. and supported by the C.N.T., the first time the Madrid proletariat carried out a gesture of solidarity with Catalunya. A general strike shook Asturias, declared by the Workers' Alliance, in reply to a mass meeting of the C.E.D.A. at Covadonga, and a giant demonstration took place in Barcelona under the auspices of the alliance.

In the alliance executive committee, much discussion took place. The *"trentistes"* declared themselves in favor of defending Catalan autonomy (for the first time they interested themselves in this demand, because in the end they understood it was inseparable from the rights of the workers). Nin proposed calling for the expropriation of the rural landlords. Maurín suggested they prepare for proclamation, anew, of the Catalan Republic, thus taking the initiative out of the vacillating hands of the Esquerra and putting it in those of the working class.

These differing positions led, on June 17, to the first Catalan Conference of Comarcal and Local Alliance Committees. The alliance, as a democratic organization, had to consult with its rank and file. The rank and file showed it was more moderate than the Bloc. The Bloc proposed that if the Madrid government attacked Catalunya and, therefore, a Catalan Republic was proclaimed, the alliance should aid this movement, trying to take over its leadership and guiding it toward the triumph of a Federal Socialist Republic in Spain. But the conference rejected this posture. Then, so as not to divide the alliance, the *bloquista* delegation proposed another resolution, which was approved: to await the expected reactionary attack and, when this came, to demand the proclamation of the Catalan Republic.[23]

All agreed on the need to extend the alliance throughout Spain. It was not enough to organize local alliances; an alliance or other organization was necessary at the national leadership level. The C.N.T. began to smooth over its position in the smaller Catalan towns, but in Barcelona it remained intractable. By contrast, in Madrid it participated in the general strike of September 8, because, its journal said, it could not stand to ask workers to continue on their jobs when others were on strike; but in reality it feared the movement would be taken advantage of by the Socialists to exercise pressure for their participation in government.

The *"escamots"* (action groups) of Catalan State (Estat Català), a nationalist grouping affiliated with the Esquerra, composed above all of middle class people and clerks and led by Josep Dencàs, chief *conseller* of the Generalitat, and by Miquel Badía, Barcelona commissar of public order, did everything to prevent the C.N.T. from changing its attitude of disdain for united action with the alliance and the Generalitat. The C.N.T., thanks to the policy of the F.A.I., had lost a third of its members since 1931, but remained an immense force in Barcelona, where it was still, as we have noted, considered the only organization capable of calling a general strike. The Public Order Commissariat constantly harassed *cenetistes* and *faistes*: closing union offices, suspending "Solidaridad Obrera" (three times in one year, and once for 104 days), thirty-four seizures of daily editions of this C.N.T. journal, tortures at police headquarters, constant "governor's arrests" (a police practice under the monarchy, which the republic not only did not abolish, but continued to use widely, consisting of detention for a maximum of fifteen days, without any cause, of elements considered dangerous to order, keeping them at the disposition of the provincial governor; it was not uncommon that when the moment came to free the suspect, the police would wait at the door of the prison and return the individual to detention for another fifteen days, and sometimes this practice was extended for several months.)

The Esquerra sought to weaken the alliance. The Unió de Rabassaires left the alliance, because the peasants, according to their leaders, who were from the Esquerra, were not revolutionary. "The *rabassaires* left because they wanted to make them join a strike against the Generalitat and thus separate them from the Esquerra. The peasants would not have joined such a strike, even if they had stayed in the Workers' Alliance," wrote the Rabassaire leader Nonit Puig i Vilá.[24]

The Esquerra feared undermining by the alliance, which made no secret of its tactics. Neither secret plans nor conspiracies are useful in politics. Maurín described the tactics of the alliance:

> The Generalitat could prevent the advance of the Right; if the latter advances, the former will lose everything. But if the Generalitat acts, it also fears the consequences of its gestures. For this reason, the workers' movement must remain at the side of the Generalitat to pressure it and promise it aid, without running ahead of it, and without going beyond it in the early moments. What is important is that the insurrection should begin and that the petty bourgeoisie, with its armed forces [of the Generalitat], not have an opportunity to retreat. Afterward, we will see.[25]

In the rest of Spain, the tactic would have to be different, because the parties of the petty bourgeoisie were out of power. There, the alliance would have to do everything on its own.

In October, the outbreak came. In the Cortes, Gil Robles called on Samper to resign. And Samper did so. Consultations took place. The Republican Left deputies hoped Alcalá Zamora would prevent the C.E.D.A. from entering the government; the Republican Left sought to dissolve the Cortes and hold new elections.

This was not simply another ministerial crisis; the Left, including the socialists, had indicated throughout the year their response to a C.E.D.A.

administration would not exclude armed insurrection, given that the C.E.D.A. offered no pledge of loyalty to the Republic. Finally, it became clear that Lerroux was prepared to form a government including C.E.D.A. ministers. After the failure of the coup from without, led by Sanjurjo, a coup seemed to be coming from within, supported by Lerroux.

The Alliance issued manifestoes and organized a demonstration against the threat. Dencàs did not authorize any demonstration to take place. But it did, nonetheless, on the Rambles, the Barcelona main avenue. Clashes took place with the mounted police. After October 3, the executive committee of the alliance met in permanent session and ordered all the comarcal and local committees to do the same.

October 6, 1934

The Barcelona executive committee of the alliance sent a representative to Madrid to work with the alliance in the capital, the socialists, and, if possible, the C.N.T.

On Thursday, October 4, the composition of the fourth Lerroux government was announced, including the C.E.D.A. At ten in the evening, in Barcelona, the delegates of the local alliances met in an assembly called by telephone (to pay the expenses for meetings, let it be noted, the alliance delegates had to use their own resources.)

The conclusion was obvious: if the struggle began, the alliance could gain control of the situation in all the Catalan towns except Barcelona. But Barcelona was the decisive point.

Nin and Bonet, former members of the C.N.T., met, after many attempts, with a number of F.A.I. leaders, including Francisco Ascaso, an outstanding confederal militant associated with Buenaventura Durruti, Ricardo Sanz, and Joan Garcia Oliver in a durable F.A.I. "affinity group" all of whose members, like Nin, Bonet, and many other *bloquistes*, were veterans of the "social war" in Barcelona at the beginning of the 1920s. The C.N.T. saw no necessity for either alliances or pacts; "We will meet on the barricades," they said.

Another delegation went to the Generalitat. A cold interview ensued with Lluís Companys, the Catalan president, who had been called to the meeting from a late dinner. The alliance delegates put forward the agreement they had formulated in June: if the right went on the attack—and, with the announcement of the Lerroux ministry, the attack had indeed begun—it was necessary to proclaim the Catalan Republic. On this, Companys vacillated.

The alliance delegates, after listening to reports of these two interviews, had the impression that nothing would take place without pressure. They decided to call a general strike for the next day, Friday, October 5. Maurín spoke at the close of the meeting. Referring to the crisis over Catalan land tenure as well as to the future, he declared:

> The workers demand power to organize the economy on a socialist basis . . . Either feudalism or us! Either fascism or social revolution! . . . We have invited the Generalitat government to proclaim the Catalan Republic. If it does not do so, we will do it ourselves.

> We will call a revolutionary strike. In it will participate the workers of the rest of Spain. The Esquerra has said it will not oppose a protest strike. We will give it a revolutionary character as far as the circumstances will permit us, and, if these are propitious, today's action may be the prologue for an armed insurrection.

> Each delegate will depart now, using the fastest means of transportation available. In each respective locality, the alliance committees and revolutionary committees will immediately declare the revolutionary general strike. If the municipal and other authorities belong to the Esquerra, for the moment we will carry out a joint action with them, until circumstances have changed or until the alliance establishes order. But where the local authorities belong to the Right, they must be immediately removed from office. The immediate goal is known to all: the Catalan Republic. We have to push the Esquerra to proclaim it. If it is not done, you will do it yourselves. The alliance is prepared for the march of events and will go ahead, giving the appropriate directives for the triumph of the movement.[26]

At three-thirty in the morning on Friday the 5th, all those who had attended the meeting returned to their homes. In the towns, the alliance committees, anticipating their decisions, had begun to agitate the atmosphere, to take up positions, and to collect all the available firearms, which were few.

The problem was to make the strike a general one in Barcelona, since all agreed that this would shut down the rest of Catalunya. The *bloquistes* did not have much faith in the dynamic character of the other alliance affiliates; the official Communists had not joined until the climactic meeting on the night of the 4th-5th, and everybody knew they would try to use the alliance to their own profit, but nobody was worried about that. The task of the Bloc, tacitly, was the preparation of the general strike in Barcelona.

At five in the morning of the 5th, the *bloquistes* had spread out to sites indicated in red on city maps; the shock groups (*gabocs*) to stop the streetcars from working, others without arms (since none were available), to distribute manifestoes with all speed, and to speak to groups of workers on their way to the job. Every leaflet that fell in the hands of a worker carried a giant black headline: "GENERAL STRIKE."

The strike was successful throughout Catalunya, Barcelona included.

The police did not remain neutral. It had been necessary for the strikers to burn some streetcars that had left their depots. Already, by eight-thirty in the morning, not a single streetcar was working in the city. The subways and the buses were also halted. The price: a half-dozen *aliancistes* hurt. When alliance groups went on to close the banks, which had opened up, a worker was killed. But the banks closed. The Commissar of Public Order had given the order for the arrest of all who fomented strike action and, for the first time in many months, this meant leaving the C.N.T. alone.

Indeed, at a time when in Asturias the C.N.T. was preparing to join the strike along with the other members of the alliance, in Barcelona the F.A.I. tried to convince the workers to stay on the job. As an eyewitness noted, "The major obstacle to the success of the strike was the resistance of the F.A.I. The F.A.I. members refused to strike. They backed down in some factories in the face of immediate compulsion, but they went back to work, and even with an eagerness never before seen, as soon as their adversaries had left the job. They even offered the services of the F.A.I. workers to the employers to protect factory and finance."[27]

In the town of Sabadell, the alliance isolated the guardia civil, occupied the city hall, and proclaimed the Catalan Republic; in Vilanova, a Socialist Republic was proclaimed; in Sitges, they occupied the city hall; in Lleida, the railroad workers joined the strike and, to make it more complete, derailed a freight train on the line to Madrid. There were shooting incidents with the guardia civil everywhere and the strike affected all the towns and cities of the Catalan hinterland. The C.N.T. did not actively oppose it, but, save in Asturias, did not participate.

The Generalitat had 2,500 guardias de asalto and the *Mossos d'Esquadra* (the Generalitat police body), concentrated in Barcelona, plus 7,000 *"escamots"* armed with Winchesters, and 5,000 without arms or with a pistol only. The General Captain of the Spanish army in Catalunya ordered the troops to remain in their barracks. The Generalitat police controlled the radio stations, which the alliance was not able to use even once. One could smell the odor of hesitation for fear of the workers. In response, the alliance organized a demonstration for Friday evening. At eight that night, the demonstration began marching behind a large banner reading "We demand proclamation of the Catalan Republic." Twelve thousand people arrived at the Generalitat Palace, in the plaça San Jaume at the heart of Barcelona's Gothic Quarter. A delegation entered the palace to speak with Companys. He received them in the presence of a group of Generalitat deputies. Through the windows, the multitude shouted "Arms! Arms!"

Companys insisted on the need to remain calm and to trust in the Generalitat authorities. If arms were needed, they would be there . . . The delegation answered Companys by saying the people wanted the proclamation of the Catalan Republic and arms to defend it. They did not understand the passivity of the Generalitat. In any defensive situation, the best action was an attack. Companys became angry: "We know perfectly well what must be done," he asserted.

Groups of alliance members went to the armories, prepared to seize them, but all were guarded by strong police pickets. To try to fight them would have been politically absurd, at that moment. In the morning, the walls of the city were covered with a bulletin from the Workers' Alliance, with news of the strike and from the provinces. In Lleida, a workers' militia was patrolling the streets; in Tarragona, the same; in Girona, the alliance exercised complete control; in Vilafranca, the workers had taken over the offices of the rightist parties, and a convent and four churches had been put to the torch.

At nine that night, the alliance groups requisitioned automobiles to maintain contact with the neighborhoods and the towns, since public transportation was shut down.

October 6th dawned, a Saturday. The general strike continued in Catalunya. No newspapers appeared. People learned what was happening from the radio or by reading bulletins from the alliance. The F.A.I. issued a circular ordering the workers to reopen the union halls that had been closed by the police in recent months. It did not support the strike, but sought to take advantage of it. The walls were covered with alliance posters:

> At this grave hour, energetic and decisive action is necessary. The Catalan Republic must be proclaimed this very day, tomorrow may be too late. Long live the revolutionary general strike! Long live the Catalan Republic!

In the rest of Catalunya, pressure mounted. Revolutionary committees had been organized, with the collaboration of the *rabassaires* against the orders of their leaders, and in some places with the support of the local C.N.T. The committees searched the houses of rightist elements and seized hidden weapons. The Lleida committee took over a printing office and began issuing a daily newspaper. That of Manresa called a popular assembly in the bullring. In Girona, one of the trains halted by the strike carried the French minister of foreign affairs, who was on vacation. In Palafrugell the furniture in the rightist party offices was burnt. The Generalitat demanded that the alliance executive committee order the Lleida committee to permit a cattle train to be moved. By three on Saturday afternoon, the Catalan Republic was proclaimed throughout Catalunya, except for Barcelona.

An alliance commission visited the Generalitat once more. The alliance could no longer wait, Companys was told. What happened in Catalunya would determine what happened in the rest of Spain, where the strike was becoming general. It was necessary to take advantage of the combative spirit of the masses, providing arms, surrounding the barracks. Companys spoke reassuringly, made promises, vacillated, became angry.

The *gaboc* shock groups had taken over, among other buildings, the former headquarters of the Fomento del Trabajo Nacional, the Barcelona chamber of commerce. There the alliance installed itself, very close to the Generalitat Palace. A first aid station was set up, with nurses, doctors, and a reserve of scarce ammunition.

An alliance military committee formed that morning turned the narrow street where the office was located into a center for arms instruction. Groups and sections were organized by men from the same organization, who knew each other. A machine gun company—lacking machine guns— was created under the command of a former army sergeant. Six thousand men and dozens of women participated.

At six in the evening, the alliance executive decided it was useless to continue meeting with Companys and organized a new demonstration, with a military aspect, to pressure him. Orders were given for passive resistance if the police tried to halt the march. Beneath alliance placards, the executive committee headed the files. Many people left their houses to join the demonstration. When it arrived at the Generalitat Palace, the windows were shut. The people paraded by, trying to keep step, reviewed by the executive committee, clenched fists and a single cry: "*Visca la Republica Catalana! Armes! Armes!*"

Nobody knew what effect the parade would have, watched by Companys from behind his blinds. But little time passed before there was a reply. At eight on the evening of the 6th, Companys came out on the balcony of the Generalitat Palace, and before the people in the narrow, half-filled plaza, proclaimed the Catalan State within the Spanish Federal Republic. He offered neither orders nor guidelines, but only asked that confidence in his government be maintained.

The alliance forces remained concentrated in the former Fomento building, awaiting weapons. At the C.A.D.C.I. offices, some members of an organization called Proletarian Catalan State (Estat Català Proletari)— recently set up and outside the alliance—were meeting, and from the balconies, had their rifles trained on the Naval Dockyard barracks, or Drassanes (Atarazanas), on the other side of the Rambles. The other barracks were not being watched, since the police were concentrated in their station houses and the *escamots* of Dencàs were in their own headquarters. The street belonged to those who first occupied it.

The first to occupy the street turned out to be the army. After an exchange of communications by telephone with Companys and consultations with Madrid by telex, the Captain General of Catalunya, Domenec Batet, a Catalan, ordered the troops to leave their barracks, proclaim a state of siege, and reestablish order (Batet was executed by the anti-Republican officers in Burgos in 1936).

At nine at night, cannons and machine guns were brought out of the Naval Dockyards. The C.A.D.C.I. building was subject to bombardment, with various of its defenders dying. Dencàs did not mobilize his *escamots*. By ten, the soldiers were in front of the Generalitat Palace.

On first hearing shots, many workers left their homes and ran to the offices of the alliance. The only weapons the Generalitat offered the workers were personal sidearms belonging to Companys and some deputies, who handed them over, after midnight, to an alliance militant who had served as a liaison with the Generalitat. They totalled no more than a dozen weapons ...

Members of the alliance began visiting the homes of Barcelona rightists, demanding that weapons be turned over to them. The *escamots* stayed in their headquarters, with their rifles between their legs. Food was requisitioned from those stores whose owners, according to union members, treated their employees worst.

When the sun came up, the people in the alliance headquarters began to disperse. Only the militants remained. The noise of cannon fired at the Generalitat Palace could be heard. It was answered by rifle shots. At six-thirty on the morning of the 7th, Companys decided to surrender, rather than to escape, to put himself at the head of the alliance and the *escamots,* and to flee to one of the other Catalan cities. He had made a gesture and that would suffice. Dencàs escaped through the sewers from his chief *conseller's* office in the Generalitat palace.

The surrender came without a battle. The *escamots,* the alliance, weapons, and many people were available for action. The whole of Catalunya was under the control of the alliance or the Esquerra. In the villages close to Barcelona, groups of workers and *rabassaires* had begun to mobilize, prepared to intervene without waiting any longer for orders that would not come.

They wanted to fight. If the Generalitat authorities had transferred to any town, they would have encountered mass support and combat would have begun and continued. Nobody knew, of course, what the result would be, but Catalunya would, at least, have done the same as the Asturias region, where dramatic fighting between the forces of regional "commune" and those of the bourgeois state continued for two weeks, gaining attention throughout the world.

When the radio announced the surrender of the Generalitat, the headquarters of the *escamots* emptied in ten minutes. The Winchesters remained hidden under tables. In the towns, the supporters of the Esquerra abandoned the city halls, where only the alliance partisans remained. Finally, the alliance gave the order: take the abandoned arms and return home; when repression comes, deny involvement; the important thing, now, is to save men and weapons. The struggle is over now, but will continue in the future.

A group of alliance supporters fought their way out of the central district of Barcelona, to the suburb of Gracia, and then to the towns of Sant Cugat and Sabadell. At various points, they exchanged shots with the guardia civil. In the face of the uselessness of their attempt, they finally disbanded. In the shooting, four were left dead (among them two *bloquista* women), and seventeen arrested, who weeks later were found guilty by a court martial and kept in the fortress of San Cristobal at Pamplona, in Navarra, until the general amnesty that followed the victory of the left in the elections of February 1936.[28]

With the struggle over, Patricio Navarro, of the Catalan regional committee of the C.N.T., spoke by radio from the Captaincy-General, ordering the workers to return to work.

The October events in Catalunya cost seventy-four dead (twenty-two of them members of the forces of order) and 252 wounded.[29] Aside from two Esquerra supporters dead and a dozen accidental victims, the rest were supporters of the alliance.

In Asturias, the Workers' Alliance had no hope of collaborating with the Republican authorities. The struggle went on for two weeks, and the government had to call in the Foreign Legion (the *Tercio*) to crush the uprising, which was led by the Asturian miners. Moroccan mercenaries who marched into the difficult, mountainous region with the *Tercio* accomplished a goal the Muslims had failed to achieve in their 700 years of peninsular occupation: entry into Asturias, traditionally honored by Spain's Catholics for its successful resistance to the invader by non-Asturian warriors. The Bloc participated in this heroic and far-reaching conflict, although it only had a small group in the zone. Its members were men well-known among the miners and occupied places of responsibility in the committees that organized local life during the period when the workers ruled Asturias. One *bloquista,* Manuel Grossi, was condemned to death and reprieved along with the other leaders of the regional insurrection.[30]

Asturias confirmed the correctness of the alliance position. If the alliance had not emerged in Barcelona, the initiative might not have appeared at other places in Spain. The Asturian Alliance demonstrated great imagination and initiative in organizing daily life under its control. Those who closely observed the Asturias events could predict, in a certain way, what would take place in July 1936. The militias, the collectivizations, and the committees that appeared at the beginning of the civil war were already germinating in the Asturian experiment of 1934.

Balance Sheet of October 6, 1934

The hour for post mortems had come. What caused the death of the October movement in Catalunya? A little afterward, the C.N.T. searched its conscience at a regional plenum, in which strong criticism was directed at the regional committee, which was replaced.[31]

The official Communists, for their part, tried to ascribe everything positive about the 1934 experience to themselves. To a certain degree, and particularly in foreign countries (including the United States), where Spanish labor politics were not well-known, they were unfortunately successful. For example, they stated that "in Lleida barricades were set up under the folds of our red banner," when, in reality, it was the banner of the Bloc.[32]

What was the Bloc's position? It gave its version of the facts in a pamphlet, which stated:

In the October events, there were two principal revolutionary centers: Asturias and Catalunya. Precisely in these two places, the Workers' Alliance acted with greatest effect.

In Asturias, the Workers' Alliance was complete ... The Asturias workers rose because they felt strong. And they felt strong because they knew they were united, because they marched together.

The Asturian revolutionary movement was the work of the Workers' Alliance. Its importance, its significance, its heroism all proceeded from the Workers' Alliance.

The workers' insurrection gained victory in Asturias. If then, finally, it was beaten, that was due to the workers of the rest of the Peninsula not doing the same as the workers of Asturias.

In Catalunya, the events acquired another direction because of the presence of the Generalitat and the treason that, at the last minute, was committed by the petty bourgeois parties.

The Workers' Alliance in Catalunya was incomplete. The National Labor Confederation was missing from it, something that did not take place in Asturias.

The Workers' Alliance, following an extremely correct line, considered its mission, in the first moments, to consist in pushing the Esquerra and the Generalitat to rise, since, in the final accounting, the key to the vault of the whole revolutionary movement resided in the duality of power, Madrid vs. Generalitat.

Dencàs, Companys, Lluhí (Vallescá), (Martí) Estéve, etc. (leaders of the Esquerra), seeing the working class transform the insurrection into a workers insurrection, made a rapid march backward, surrendering in cowardice and decapitating the revolutionary movement. . . .

In the rest of the country, except for some sparks in the provinces bordering on Asturias and in Vizcaya, there was no insurrection. The movement remained limited to a more or less intense general strike, where there did not reign complete normality, as happened in some places where the anarchists could make their incorrect viewpoint prevail . . .

If the Workers' Alliance had been constituted everywhere, and, as well, concentrated nationally, there is no doubt that the outcome of things would have been very different from what took place.

October constitutes, then, a formidable lesson of which we must take advantage.[33]

The C.N.T. was losing members. The small parties that made up the Alliance stagnated, with the police closing offices and the authorities shutting down periodicals. For the moment, the Right had won, although nobody believed the victory was definitive. The Right itself, from the seat of power, encouraged the Left through a series of scandals, through inefficiency, and through internal quarrels.

Some of the leaders of the revolutionary movement were arrested, but gave false names and soon escaped. From the towns, local leaders who had to hide out, having exposed themselves on October 6, descended on Barcelona. Little by little, a new "normality" returned: With halls closed, meetings were held discreetly in bars, clandestine manifestoes were circulated, and extraordinary dues were collected for the P.O.U.M. Red Aid, because dozens of the arrested would soon be sentenced.

The Bloc saw in the October process something like a general rehearsal, which afterward would bring forward a new revolution, for which the alliance would have to be prepared. There is nothing strange in the fact that, with this viewpoint, the Bloc became the only organization, in the months following October, whose membership grew numerically.

A Polemic with Santiago Carrillo

The Bloc meeting halls were closed, but this did not impede the activity of the party, whose militants came out of the October experience with an awareness of having done what was possible and a good number of whom were in prison. "La Batalla" and "L'Hora" soon reappeared. It was necessary to capitalize on the fact of having been the initiators of the Workers' Alliance. New members joined weekly in Barcelona and in the towns. The sections in Valencia and Castelló grew. In Asturias, the Bloc became better known and the Madrid Socialists began taking its existence into account.

In the unions, the *bloquistes* found a greater echo than before October, because many workers did not understand the recent passivity of the anarchists. Inside the C.N.T., discussion went on amid public silence. The anarchists did not want it said that they had sabotaged the October movement in Catalunya. They tried to emphasize their participation in Asturias—although without mentioning that it had been done in partial defiance of the C.N.T. national committee. As previously noted, the Communists tried to pass off the alliance as their own tool.

The place where discussion flourished and came before the public was among the socialists. The P.S.O.E. Right—Julián Besteiro, Andrés Saborit—began publishing a weekly, "Democracia," to which the Left, or Largo Caballero, answered with a journal, "Claridad" (Clarity), which then became a daily, and with a monthly theoretical review (already appearing before October) titled "Leviatán," edited by Luís Araquistáin, and in which some *bloquistes,* and members of the Communist Left led by Nin, collaborated occasionally.

There was great ideological disorientation among the Left socialists. They had just discovered Marxism and had the schematic attitude of the neophyte. Nobody, to them, was enough of a Marxist. In Moscow, a change was taking place that, in mid-1935, would be expressed by the passage from the tactic of "social-fascism" to that of the People's Front, and this change provoked no discomfort among the Left socialists.

The political situation continued changing. In December 1934, the government, by decree, extended the workweek in the metal industry from forty-four to forty-eight hours. In February 1935, two army sergeants who had joined the workers in Asturias were executed. In April, a ministerial crisis brought the fifth Lerroux government. In May, the sixth Lerroux government. The members of the Generalitat administration received a prison sentence of thirty years. In June, the Cortes passed a law for an agrarian counterreform. In September, Chapaprieta took over the government. There were 30,000 political prisoners.

The Communists, freed by the 1935 Seventh world Comintern congress from the straitjacket of "Social-fascism," launched themselves, with a great abundance of material means, into the task of "working on" the intellectuals, the students, the middle class, and the Socialists. They published periodicals of all kinds: film, literature, women's interests, with the aid of some Catholic intellectuals, such as José Bergamín, who from then on would remain forever in their service. They began to circulate the slogan of the People's Front, which obviously threatened to replace that of the Workers' Alliance.

Between the two concepts there were radical differences, but in the eyes of the masses it might seem that both aimed at the same thing. The People's Front was a defensive slogan tying the workers to the middle class and that proposed nothing but opposition to the advance of fascism, and when it was used by the official Communists, submitted the Spanish political struggle to the needs of Soviet diplomacy. The Workers' Alliance, by contrast, was a slogan for the offensive, which tried to gather the peasants and the nationalist middle class behind the working class, and which called for revolution.

The Bloc, in the face of this danger, tried to give new vitality to the alliance. The alliance committees began meeting again. But ideological disorientation persisted. The Socialist Youth spoke of the "Bolshevization of socialism" and found themselves ready, more and more, to accept the slogans of official Communism, without taking into account that they were the negation of the revolutionary positions the young socialists maintained, since they would tie them to the Republican parties that had failed to act in October. But at the same time, the young socialists flattered the *bloquistes* and Trotskyists, in their weekly "Renovación."

At the beginning of August 1935, "La Batalla" published an article sent by Carrillo, in which he invited the *bloquistes* to enter the P.S.O.E. to aid the Largo Caballero left wing of the party in expelling the centrist factions around Indalecio Prieto and the right-wingers led by Besteiro. This was virtually the same position taken, from exile in France, by Trotsky, and some members of the Communist Left, such as Enrique Bilbao and G. Munis (Manuel Fernández Grandizo), who left the latter organization because of its refusal to abide by Trotsky's counsels.

Maurín answered Carrillo in the same issue of "La Batalla," stating that the possibilities of the moment pointed toward a victory of the right wing of the party and that if the Bloc were to enter the P.S.O.E. it would find itself under the dominion of the socialist Right and unable to continue its task of developing Marxist unity and the unity of the workers.

The discussion continued for two months. Carrillo believed that even if the socialist Right won, the Left could separate, taking a good part of the activists with it and forming a revolutionary party, in which the *bloquistes* would play an important role. Maurín, following his tendency to examine problems in the light of international experience, believed the entry of the Bloc into the P.S.O.E. would mean the disappearance of its influence. Carrillo answered that what had happened elsewhere would not necessarily take place in Spain.[34]

Maurín, in his contribution, affirmed that what was important "was not for Communists to join with Besteiro and Prieto, but for Communists and Left socialists to meet and march together, which is not exactly the same thing."

What points would have made a unification possible and what coincidences in viewpoint would have to be sought prior to unification? Maurín enumerated them at the close of his polemic:

> From our perspective, the basic questions for a possible agreement with the socialists are the following:
>
> First. Recognition of the Workers' Alliance as an organ of struggle, for the unification of efforts in its first phases, then, as an insurrectional organ, and afterwards, an instrument of power.
>
> Second. The need for trade union unity and the formation of a single union federation.
>
> Third. The present revolution is democratic-socialist. And as a consequence, in the agrarian and national questions the classic viewpoint of Bolshevism must be adopted.
>
> Fourth. The united party would be a homogeneous whole, without factions.
>
> If the Socialist Party delivers its opinions on these points, which we consider the sine qua non, then Marxist unity will be an immediate fact.

For now, nothing more was said on this issue. The socialists did not wish to renounce what they considered to be their hegemonic position. The U.G.T. made none of the unity proposals to the C.N.T. Maurín had suggested in his polemic. Carrillo, shortly afterward, went to Moscow, where he "converted," and on returning organized a fusion of the Socialist Youth with the Communist Youth (Juventudes Comunistas—J.J.C.C.), which in reality became the absorption of the first group, who were more numerous, by the second, more disciplined and with better resources. The new organization, known as the United Socialist Youth (Junventud Socialista Unificada—J.S.U.), joined the Young Communist International, which meant submission to the orders of the Comintern. Further, had the Bloc accepted entry into the P.S.O.E. when Carrillo suggested it, its youth organization would have joined the J.J.S.S. and would have found themselves, thanks to Carrillo's trickery, converted into Stalinist youth.

As we will see, during the civil war the J.S.U. and Carrillo in particular were among the most effective tools of official Communist policy and adopted a position that was more rightist than those of Besteiro or Prieto, whom Carrillo had wanted to expel from the P.S.O.E. with the help of the Bloc.

Notes

1. Nin's correspondence with Trotsky, as cited here, appears in a mutilated, if not deliberately mendacious form, as prepared by the latter's secretariat, in Leon Trotsky, *The Spanish Revolution*, New York, 1973, pp. 369-400. The original

Nin-Trotsky correspondence was stolen by Soviet secret police agents; see Dale Reed and Michael Jakobson, "Trotsky Papers at the Hoover Institution," "American Historical Review," April 1987.

2. Humbert-Droz, op. cit., p. 409.
3. Ibid., p. 448.
4. Joaquím Maurín, *La revolución española,* Madrid, 1932, p. 117.
5. Joaquím Maurín, "El movimiento obrero en Cataluña," in "Leviatán" (Madrid), October 1934.
6. Francisco Madrid, *Film de la república comunista libertaria,* Barcelona, 1932, p. 170.
7. On the early history of the Spanish Trotskyist groups, such as that founded in Belgium in 1930 by Francisco García Lavíd ("Henri Lacroix"), as well as the activities in Madrid of Juan Andrade, see Victor Alba, *El Marxisme a Catalunya,* v. III, *Andreu Nin,* Barcelona, 1974; Francesc Bonamusa, *Andreu Nin y El movimiento comunista en españa, 1930-37,* Barcelona, 1977; and Pelai Pagés, *El movimiento Trotskista en España, 1930-35,* Barcelona, 1977.
8. Citations from the Trotsky correspondence are derived from Trotsky, *The Spanish Revolution,* op. cit. For the August 1933 circular, see ibid, pp. 198-201.
9. Humbert-Droz, op. cit., p. 457.
10. "Mundo Obrero" had begun publication in Madrid in August 1930, with 80,000 pesetas that had been advanced to it by the Cenit publishing house (which published some works of Trotsky), and 50,000 pesetas collected through a fund drive, that is to say, a subsidy from the Comintern. It was edited by a Peruvian, César Falcón.
11. This text forms a part of a book, *La revolución española,* signed by a nonexistent professor I. Kom (i.e., Internacional Comunista, or Comintern), Barcelona, 1932.
12. Joaquím Maurín, *El Bloque Obrero y Campesino,* p. 29-30.
13. Albert Balcells, *Crisis económica y agitación social en cataluña, 1930-36.* Barcelona, 1971, pp. 153-154.
14. The draft thesis on the national question, adopted almost unchanged by the congress, was published in "La Batalla," March 10, 1932.
15. Published by Edicions CIB, Barcelona, 1932. Miravitlles suddenly left the Bloc in 1934, joining the Esquerra. During the Civil War he was Propaganda Commissar for the Generalitat.
16. Observations presented here with reference to the clerical worker movement are based, in addition to the memories and personal notes of Victor Alba, on Marti Sans, *Els Treballadors Mercantils En El Moviment Obrer,* Barcelona, 1974, and on a conference given by Jordi Arquer in Paris in 1970. Both were *bloquistes* and leaders of the clerical workers' movement.
17. Mont-Fort (pseudonym of Maurín), *Alianza Obrera,* Barcelona, 1935, pp. 11-12.
18. Mont-Fort, op. cit., p. 10.
19. Cited in G. Munis (Manuel Fernández Grandizo), *Jalones de derrota, promesa de victoria,* Mexico, 1948, p. 112.
20. Published in "La Correspondencia Internacional," Moscow, June 3, 1934.
21. Published in "La Correspondencia Internacional," September 23, 1934.
22. Francisco Largo Caballero, *Mis recuerdos,* Mexico, 1954, pp. 224.
23. "La Conferencia de la Alianza Obrera de Cataluna," in "Sindicalismo," Barcelona, June 24, 1934.

24. Nonit Puig i Vila, *Que es la Unió de Rabassaires?* Barcelona, 1935, pp. 113-14.
25. Joaquím Maurín, *Hacía la segunda revolución.* Barcelona, 1935, pp. 124-25.
26. Cited in Angel Estivill, *6 D'Octubre, L'ensulciada Dels Jacobins.* Barcelona, 1935, pp. 125-26.
27. Enrique de Angulo, *Diez horas de Estat Català.* Barcelona, 1935, p. 53. Angulo was the Barcelona correspondent of the rightwing Catholic daily "El Debate," published in Madrid.
28. An account of the fighting by the Gracia group is included in a recent and important memoir by a leading P.O.U.M. militant, Carmel Rosa (Roc), *Quan Catalunya era Revolucionaria,* Salt, 1986, pp. 100-106.
29. E. Comín Colomer, *Historia del Partido Comunista de España.* Madrid, 1962, vol. II, p. 325.
30. Manuel Grossi was the author of a book, *La insurrección de Asturias,* first published in 1935 by "La Batalla," with a prologue by Maurín and an epilogue by Gorkín.
31. Diego Abad de Santillan, *Los anarquistas y la insurrección de Octubre.* Barcelona, 1935, p. 4.
32. See "L'Humanité," Paris, October 23, 1934, in an interview with leaders of the Partit Comunista de Catalunya. For a discussion of international Soviet propaganda in the wake of the 1934 events and the campaign to label the experience as a "Communist revolt," see Stephen Schwartz, *Brotherhood of the Sea*, New Brunswick, 1986, chap. 6. Also, see "Cahiers Léon Trotsky," number 20, December 1984, special issue on "L'Année 1934."
33. Mont-Fort, op. cit., pp. 22-25.
34. The articles of Carrillo and Maurín were brought together in a pamphlet, which was published in 1937 by Editorial Marxista, Barcelona, under the title *Polemica Maurín-Carrillo.*

PARTIT OBRER D'UNIFICACIÓ MARXISTA-PARTIDO OBRERO DE UNIFICACIÓN MARXISTA-

THE WORKERS' PARTY OF MARXIST UNIFICATION

3

The Formation of the P.O.U.M.

The Bloc, in arguing for the necessity of the Workers' Alliance, tried to organize it in concert with other political parties and groups; in the same way, it tried to bring about a unification of the Marxist tendencies on the Spanish scene.

Things took place spontaneously—that is, without planning, on the basis of chance personal conversations. For example, one night, while leaving a meeting of the Workers' Alliance committee in Barcelona, Maurín and Nin, the old friends, spent a little time talking together, and Nin said that, finally, the time had perhaps come for the Communist Left and the Bloc to unite.

In Catalunya, the Communist Left consisted of Nin and a dozen of his friends. But Maurín knew Nin well and knew his value. They continued discussing the matter and thought that more than a unification of just these two organizations, it would be better to try to bring in all those who considered themselves Marxists.

In March 1935, there met, brought together by the Bloc, representatives of all the Catalan Marxist groups: the Communist Left, the Socialist Union (U.S.C.), the official Communists, the Catalan Federation of the P.S.O.E., the Catalan Proletarian Party (Partit Català Proletari—P.C.P.), and the Bloc. The U.S.C. and the Bloc were the only parties worthy of the title; the rest were tiny groups.

In principle, all were in agreement on the need to unite. Various meetings were held in private houses. It quickly became clear that the Catalan P.S.O.E., U.S.C. official Communists, and P.C.P. always put forward a common viewpoint and that they had met together beforehand. The U.S.C. opposed the formation of any party that would attack the Esquerra, with which it was allied, and it feared that the greater ideological profile of the Bloc would dominate any future party, to which the Bloc would bring the only Marxist trade union force in Catalunya, something the other groups lacked. With their access to the greatest material means, the official

Communists expected to dominate the new party, and they were disposed toward unity with whoever appeared, except for the Bloc—a party of "renegades"—nor with the Communist Left, a group of "traitors." The official party delegates, naturally, did not pose the question so baldly, but they insisted that the future party affiliate with the Comintern, something that neither Nin nor the *bloquistes* would have agreed to.

Things were easy to predict: except for the Bloc and the Communist Left, all those who attended the meetings would form a separate grouping and end up dominated by the official Communists. A few days after the civil war's beginning, they formed the Unified Socialist Party of Catalunya (Partit Socialista Unificat de Catalunya—P.S.U.C.), adhering to the Third International and functioning de facto as the Catalan branch of the P.C.E.).[1]

Maurín and Nin agreed on many issues. The Bloc and the Communist Left found themselves more or less alone in the discussion of Marxist unification. By agreement with the respective executive committees of the two organizations, Maurín and Nin began discussing the bases for unification of the two entities.

We have already examined, in detail, the Bloc. What was the Communist Left? The official Communists, reproducing cliches developed in Moscow, called it "a band of traitors to the revolution in the service of international fascism." Nobody who knew anything of the rivalry between Trotsky and Stalin for Lenin's succession paid any attention to these phrases. But was the Communist Left really Trotskyist? To answer, we must examine the history of that organization.

In 1930, with Nin's return from Moscow—where, as we noted in Chapter 1, he formed a part of the Profintern secretariat, from which responsibility he was separated once he put himself firmly on Trotsky's side—he encountered in Spain some tiny groups, perhaps twenty people in all, that had declared themselves to be Trotskyists.

As we have described, he was in contact with the Catalan-Balearic Communist Federation and wanted to join the Bloc when it was first set up. Given the combination of hesitation by the Bloc, which feared the effect of Trotskyist factionalism, and the detestation Trotsky felt for Maurín, a prejudice fueled by Trotsky's lack of real knowledge of the Spanish labor movement, it was understandable that Nin would end up helping to organize a separate Trotskyist group, publishing first the review "Comunismo" and then, for a brief time, a weekly with the title "El Soviet." The latter publication, its very name reflecting the unfortunate influence of Trotsky, published virulent diatribes against the Bloc, accusing it of petty bourgeois nationalism, of vacillation, and of having little to do with communism.

But by the middle of 1932, the Spanish section of the International Secretariat of the Left Opposition had developed immense conflicts with

Trotsky over personal incompatibilities. Things became ever more embittered. In August 1933, Trotsky wrote, as noted in Chapter 2, of "the falseness and danger of the politics of comrade Nin." Finally, in September 1934, the Spanish section broke with Trotsky and his movement over the so-called "French turn."

The debate over personalities had become a debate over tactics. Trotsky, after having demanded that his followers concentrate their efforts on infiltrating the official Communist apparatus, to transform it from within, decided on a major change in the wake of the Comintern's failure to intervene against Hitler in Germany. Now, rejecting the official Communist organizations as corrupt beyond reform, by mid-1934 he was calling for entry of the Trotskyists into the socialist parties to take advantage of the radicalization visible in their ranks. From the viewpoint of sociological composition, it has been argued—by the Austrian Marxist historian Franz Borkenau and numerous others—that by this time the communist parties had largely ceased to base themselves on the working class—and had become, in the aftermath of Stalin's victory in Russia as well as the worldwide depression, parties dominated by a section of the lower middle-class intelligentsia, the "bohemia" of the great urban societies. In this regard, they resembled the fascist movements more than traditional socialist labor parties. It is worthy of remark that when, after several years of international economic crisis, the labor movement began to reassert a radical direction, in countries as different from one another as France, the country in which Trotsky's new tactical "turn" was first applied, and the United States, the earliest beneficiary of a new political interest by the laboring masses was the socialist rather than the communist movement.[2]

This situation was reflected in Spain by the very efforts of the Bloc and the Communist Left to include, consistently, the socialist currents around Largo Caballero and the magazine "Leviatán" in their unification discussions. But Nin and the Communist Left did not share Trotsky's conception of how unification with the mass of revolutionary workers in the Socialist Party was to be carried out. Trotsky, out of touch with any mass movement and surrounded by young militants who had no experience in organizing the masses, looked at the process in a mechanical way. The Communist Left—and much less the Bloc—could not simply "enter" the Socialist Party and proceed to organize a faction.

We have discussed in the previous chapter the objections of the Bloc to this conception, hinging on the real weakness of the Left within the Socialist Party, which could not be wished away by bold pronouncements. In addition, there was the problem of carrying out Marxist unification in a way that would not directly challenge the possibility of revolutionary unity with the anarchists. In the end, the Communist Left had had to adopt a virtually identical position. The refusal of Trotsky and his "center" to countenance the slightest organizational flexibility in Spain made a break inevitable.

The militants of the Communist Left knew the *bloquistes* were superior to them in numbers. But they were tired of an isolation lacking any more than occasional or exceptional contact with the masses. However much they felt they had maintained a "just position," notwithstanding its justice they had failed to produce an organization with real weight. They had little or no influence in the political life of the country or in the labor movement. On the other hand, they had managed to attract a nucleus of talented and energetic individuals, many of them with great potential but, by 1935, with great frustrations as well. Fusion with the Bloc would permit them to take part in a rising movement, which had influenced, however marginally, the march of events, and which had, more and more, penetrated the masses. For the members of the Communist Left it was not, then, difficult to decide on fusion with the Bloc.

Among the *bloquistes* there remained some mistrust. Wouldn't the ex-Trotskyists seek to apply the "French turn" program for "entryism" to the Bloc, rather than the Socialist party? On the other hand, what did the Communist Left bring with it? A few distinguished militants, who could prove useful as theoreticians, and some nuclei outside Catalunya, who could facilitate the expansion of the movement throughout the rest of Spain.

Maurín, who was interested above all in attracting Nin, for whom he felt friendship and respect, and who believed the geographical expansion of the Bloc was necessary to influence the C.N.T. and the Socialists, first convinced the executive committee and then the party rank and file of the need for fusion.

Fusion

"Negotiations were carried out by Nin and (me)," Maurín wrote to Víctor Alba, in a letter from New York dated February 29, 1972. "There were no problems. Nin had officially broken relations with Trotsky and I was persuaded that Nin was sincere and did not seek infiltration in the classic Bolshevik manner. The central topic was: international independence, no contact with Trotsky. Nin assented."

The thing that most pained the *bloquistes* was the prospect of a change in the organization's name. The Bloc's title had become popular and the *bloquistes* had a sentimental attachment to it. The name that was chosen for the new party—Workers' Party of Marxist Unification (Partit Obrer d'Unificació Marxista—Partido Obrero de Unificacíon Marxista—

P.O.U.M.)—said what it was meant to say, but sounded pretentious and did not fit with the traditional language of the Spanish labor movement.

Maurín, Nin, and some of their comrades worked together to prepare the theses on fusion, which they submitted first to discussion in the cells and then to the unification congress. Thirty-six years later, in 1971, Maurín told Víctor Alba that he felt that the fusion and the change of name of the B.O.C. had perhaps been a mistake on his part, a too-high price paid for the capture of Nin and a few of his comrades.

In a letter to the historian Pierre Broué, with a copy to Víctor Alba, dated May 18, 1972, Maurín stated:

Trotsky's assertion that 'Nin and the Spanish Trotskyists had in some degree *rallied* to (Maurín)', which (Broué) cited, is closer to the truth. . . . The only concession the B.O.C. made to the I.C.E. was the change in the name of the party. *Workers' and Peasants' Bloc* had been a temporary title, but it was felt that in adopting a new one nothing would be lost. The new name was never very fortunate: *Workers' Party of Marxist Unification*. It had, nevertheless, a double value: it made it clear that what we sought was 'unification' with another Marxist sector, which could mean nothing else but the Spanish Socialist Party (P.S.O.E.). The term 'Marxist' meant the end of the use of the description 'Communist,' which had been taken on by the Catalan (later Iberian) Communist Federation and the Communist Left . . .

I defended the fusion of the B.O.C. with the I.C.E. . . . because the important thing was to obtain cooperation with Nin, with whom we had struggled in common from 1920 to 1931. Nin, left to himself or under the influence of Trotsky—who never understood Spanish problems—was a lost cause. In the ranks of the B.O.C. he could be very valuable. The growth of the B.O.C. and its political responsibility were continually increasing, and it was necessary to strengthen the leadership. In the personal conversations I had with Nin, on leaving the meetings of the Workers' Alliance, above all beginning in 1934, both of us agreed that between our respective ways of thinking there was no fundamental disagreement. Why not, then, accept the coming together that *Nin himself proposed*?

The B.O.C. had grown and continued growing at a considerable pace. Practically speaking, the B.O.C. had made impossible the growth of the Communist Party in Catalunya. But the leading elements of the B.O.C. did not grow at the same pace as the party ranks. The reincorporation of Nin would strengthen the leadership of the B.O.C. considerably. The B.O.C., because of a series of circumstances, turned too much around the personality of Maurín, and I believed it was necessary to broaden the leadership. Further, I had never concerned myself much with the campaign Nin had waged during the years of his Trotskyist enthusiasm against the B.O.C. and myself. In a way, I accepted optimistically the idea of a *confluence*, more than that of a fusion.

Things said by Jean Rous (a French Trotskyist) regarding the acceptance of the concept of the Fourth International by 'Maurín and the Maurínists' are nonsense, to say the least. Nobody spoke in any of these conversations about a fusion of the B.O.C. and the I.C.E. with the Fourth International, which for us was an entelechy. More: the B.O.C. was a member of the international organization of independent socialist parties and groups. ... And after the fusion of the B.O.C. and the I.C.E., (the P.O.U.M.) continued to serve as a member.

(This international alignment was known as the International Bureau for Revolutionary Socialist Unity, or "London Bureau.")

The Communist Left had polled its membership by mail on the unification proposal. The Bloc held a clandestine congress. The two organizations, democratically, agreed to merge. Not all were in agreement, however. Some members of the Communist Left, obeying Trotsky's call for the "French turn," entered the Socialist party, where they soon disappeared from view: they included the veteran working-class militant Esteban Bilbao, a founder of the Spanish Communist movement, and "Lacroix" (Francisco García Lavíd), a founder of the Communist Left. At least one individual, the Mexican-born Manuel Fernandez Grandizo (G. Munis), hoped for a continuation of an orthodox Spanish "section of the International Left Opposition," although he returned to Mexico.

Within the Bloc, a group of Barcelona militants, some of them well-known, decided to leave the movement, to join other organizations, and to work within them for a broader unification. There were three leading elements in this group: Víctor Colomer, Eusebi Rodríguez Salas, and Miquel Ferrer. Virtually nobody followed them. They diffused into the other more-or-less Marxist groups and, after the commencement of the civil war, all found themselves a part of the Stalinist P.S.U.C. and obeying the instructions of the Comintern delegates. None of these individuals took part in the fusion meeting from which the P.O.U.M. emerged.

This meeting took place clandestinely on September 29, 1935, in Les Planes, close to Barcelona. It was almost a ritual act. The fusion, the new party name, and the theses approved by the cells were discussed.

A commission was set up drawn from both merging organizations, to designate the central and executive committees. This was composed of Joaquím Maurín, P.O.U.M. general secretary, Andreu Nin, Pere Bonet, Jordi Arquer, Josep Coll, Josep Rovira, Narcís Molíns i Fàbrega, and Enríc Adroher (Gironella). "La Batalla" would continue to publish weekly as the P.O.U.M. organ and with a run of 10,000 copies, which would permit it to maintain itself and even to organize a small office. "La Nueva Era," resuscitated, began appearing regularly every month, as a theoretical review.

The P.O.U.M. included nearly all the founders of Communism in Spain. All the Marxists in Spain, aside from the few who were in the Socialist Party, were found in the P.O.U.M. The party name, then, was no mere boast, although it had a provocative sound.

But the P.O.U.M. according to the theses approved by the Les Planes meeting, was only a first step. It was necessary to bring in other forces that called themselves Marxist. "The Problem of Marxist Unification" was the title of one of the theses, in which it was said that "the great revolutionary socialist party will emerge by grouping in one single unit the existing Marxist revolutionary nuclei, plus the new revolutionary generation, which is entering into action pushed by the ideal of Marxist unity, and the elements that, demoralized because of the factionalization of the workers' movement, have remained temporarily inactive."[3]

The P.O.U.M. affirmed that, at that moment, the character of the Spanish Revolution was democratic-socialist and that, to push it forward, the Workers' Alliance was necessary. Referring itself to international politics, it argued that the successive tactics of "class against class" and "social-fascism" applied by Comintern had failed and that "the line flowing from revolutionary Marxism followed during the early period (of the Third International) has broken down. It swings from one extreme to the other, in an empirical manner, entirely abandoning the essential fundamentals of Marxism."

While the U.S.S.R. had committed many errors under Stalin's leadership, the P.O.U.M. continued defending the Russian revolution, because "the most efficacious defense of the U.S.S.R. consists neither of pacts nor treaties, but the revolutionary struggle for the overthrow of the bourgeoisie in other countries.

"The P.O.U.M. considers, then, that it is an ineluctable duty to defend the first triumphant workers' republic, maintaining, nonetheless, the right to objectively criticize the positions of the leadership of the U.S.S.R. that could create problems for the U.S.S.R. itself and for the interests of the international revolutionary movement."

The P.O.U.M. did not affiliate with the Comintern or the movement for the Fourth International, but, described by Maurín, maintained its membership in the so-called "London Bureau." This body had been organized some months before, with the active participation of the Bloc, represented by Gorkin, and on the ruins of a short-lived alliance, the International Labor Community (I.A.G.), set up by a range of revolutionary socialists and dissident communist groups around the world, with the temporary help of one of the most radical of the mainstream socialist parties, the Norwegian Labor Party (N.A.P.).[4]

The London Bureau would, as we shall see, play a role of some importance in relation to the P.O.U.M. during the Spanish Civil War. Its main affiliates were the British Independent Labour Party; the French Workers and Peasants Socialist Party (P.S.O.P.), led by Marceau Pivert; the German Socialist Workers Party (S.A.P.), a left-wing split from the Social Democratic Party, to which the young Willi Brandt, exiled to Norway from Nazi Germany, belonged; the "Communist Right" group of Heinrich Brandler, and some similar groups, including the Italian Maximalist Socialists, the Greeks affiliated with the magazine "Archives of Marxism," and others. All the participants were minority groupings, which considered themselves Marxist, were directed by prestigious individuals, but without great influence among the masses, and which dissented from the positions of the second, third, and fourth internationals.

It is possible, as some Trotskyists later claimed, that Nin believed that, through the P.O.U.M., the London Bureau could be influenced in the direction of the Fourth International and perhaps used this argument with members of the Communist Left as a defense of unification with the Bloc. But we do not think so, because Nin never tried to exercise any influence in this way, either before the civil war, when it would have been difficult, or during, when it would have been relatively easy. It is easier to believe that Nin and the majority of Communist Left members were disillusioned with Trotsky and his strategy and did not consider the project for a Fourth International to be a viable one. If they thought that, they were right.

The basic positions of the P.O.U.M. were synthesized as follows in the pamphlet *Que es y Quiere el P.O.U.M.?*, published in Barcelona in 1936:

First. The Spanish Revolution is a revolution of the democratic-socialist type. The dilemma is socialism or fascism. The working class will not be able to take power peacefully, but through armed insurrection.

Second. Once power is taken, we must go on to the transitional establishment of the dictatorship of the proletariat. The organs of power will be the workers' alliances. The dictatorship of the proletariat presupposes the most broad and complete workers' democracy. The party of the revolution cannot and must not do away with workers' democratization.

Third. Need for the Workers' Alliance locally and nationally. The Workers' Alliance must necessarily pass through three phases: First, as an organism of the United Front, carrying out offensive and defensive, legal and illegal actions; second, as an insurrectional organ; and third, as an organ of power.

Fourth. Recognition of the problems of the nationalities. Spain will be structured in the form of an Iberian Union of Socialist Republics.

Fifth. A democratic solution, in its first phase, of the land problem. The land to those who work it.

Sixth. In the case of war, transformation of the imperialist war into a civil war. No hope in the League of Nations, which is the united front of the imperialists.

Seventh. The united party will remain outside the second and third internationals, both failures, and will struggle for world revolutionary socialist unity, carried out on new bases.

Eighth. Defense of the U.S.S.R., without supporting its policy of pacts with capitalist states, but through the international revolutionary action of the working class. Right to criticize the policies of the leaders of the U.S.S.R. when they are counterproductive for the march of the world revolution.

Ninth. A permanent democratic centralist regime in the unified party.

At that moment in Spain, according to the General Directorate of Security, there were 1,440,474 members of the U.G.T. and 1,577,537 in the C.N.T. The rightist parties had 549,946 members. The P.S.O.E. must have had around 100,000 members. The P.O.U.M. had 7,000 militants, which before six months had gone by had risen to 9,000, and controlled unions in which there were 60,000 workers. This was a lot compared with the 1931 figures for the Bloc, but was not enough if one took into account the ambitious goals the P.O.U.M. had chosen for itself.

The new party preserved the organic structure of the Bloc and among the rank and file rather little notice was taken of the fusion because of the small number of members of the Communist Left that had come into the new party. In the leadership, it had greater impact, because a better distribution of tasks was now possible. Nin took charge of "La Nueva Era" and the party's union work, in collaboration with Bonet, who had been responsible for unions in the Bloc. When the government, from which the C.E.D.A. was now absent, permitted a return to legality, meetings could be organized, which allowed Nin and others of his comrades to enter into contact with the party rank and file and the masses.

Workers' Alliance or People's Front?

In accord with the decisions of the fusion congress, the executive committee of the new party addressed itself by letter to all the working-class organizations in the country, proposing a meeting to study a means to oppose the approaching world war. Italy had just attacked Ethiopia, and it was feared that the League of Nations being unable to halt the conflict, its complications could lead to general war in Europe. The letter, dated October 3, 1935, stated:

Comrades,

War has just broken out [between Italy and Ethiopia . . .]

For the moment, the struggle is taking place outside Europe, but there can be no doubt that the same interimperialist rivalries, the same necessity felt by Italian fascism to provoke a European war to escape the inextricable situation in which it finds itself, and the war preparations of German fascism, can bring about in a relatively short time a world war that would be a million times more destructive and brutal than the previous one.

Our country, because of its geographical situation and in the presence, this time, of a grave problem in the Mediterranean, will only with difficulty remain at the margin of the conflict, if the working class does not energetically oppose war.

The international situation, the war atmosphere that grows more intense each day, will be the object of attempts to take advantage of it by those reactionary forces that having experienced a recent decline, are waiting for the opportune moment to impose themselves by force.

Not only these considerations, of a character we may call national, but our duty as a working class movement forming a part of the worldwide proletariat, oblige us to take a firm position, in close relationship with the workers of other countries, to oppose the forces fascism has set in motion and which they now propose to encourage and extend.

All of which leads us to the conclusion, comrades, that it is an implacable necessity that we call a meeting of delegations from all the workers' organizations, with the object of studying the means to bring about joint action against war . . .

This initiative was unsuccessful: the majority of organizations did not answer this very prescient letter. The P.O.U.M. was too new on the scene, and the Ethiopian war too far away. Events in Spain, on the other hand, were out of the ordinary: a scandal exploded, known as the "estraperlo" affair, connected with bribery in the licensing of slot machines; in it some ministers and leaders from the Radical Party were implicated. Chapaprieta once again formed a government, followed by Manuel Portela Valladares. Finally, the president dissolved the Cortes.

With these developments, the Socialists and Republicans had begun to negotiate an electoral alliance. The communists, having just been given the green light by the Comintern for application of the "people's front" tactic, participated in these meetings and obtained the adoption of the very phrase "People's Front" (Frente Popular) to designate the electoral combination outside Catalunya, where it was known as the "Left Front" (Front d'Esquerres).

This presented a problem for the P.O.U.M. Was it necessary to enter the People's, or Left Front? The party would have preferred a workers' front candidacy to that of unity between labor and the Republicans, because it believed it could win the majority and lead to a workers' government. For this reason, on November 4 it addressed a letter to the workers' parties proposing the formation of a workers' electoral front. There was no response.

The masses, agitated by the continued imprisonment of 30,000 militants arrested because of the insurrectionary events of October 1934, reacted sentimentally and not politically; the feeling was that all should unite to free the 30,000, without considering the consequences of repeating the experience of 1931. On the other hand, to remain outside the People's Front would mean to swim against the stream to no profit, to lose the possibility of gaining a parliamentary tribune, to remain without contact with the masses, and to accept isolation.

The P.O.U.M. had not been founded simply to become a sect. But there was no need to accept the People's Front blindly. Arquer published an article, "Antifascist People's Front or Workers' United Front?" in "La Nueva Era" for February 1936, in which he indicated that in the People's Front the only concessions would come from the side of the proletariat, an inefficacious tactic against fascism, and that the correct tactic would be that of the workers' front, that is, the Workers' Alliance. After much discussion of the question, the executive committee of the P.O.U.M. decided to enter the People's Front, although pointing out from the beginning that for the new party it was a circumstantial electoral pact and nothing more, and that the P.O.U.M.'s objective continued to be a national Workers' Alliance that would lead to socialist revolution.

But acceptance of the idea of the People's Front was not enough. It was necessary to participate in it as well. In Catalunya, there was no problem, for there the P.O.U.M. was strong and well-known. But the other parties refused to grant the P.O.U.M. two positions on the list of candidates, as it wished, having proposed Maurín for Barcelona and Nin for Tarragona, the province of his birth. After reaching the point of nearly abandoning the whole matter, the P.O.U.M. executive committee resigned itself to what the People's Front leaders offered them: Maurín as a P.O.U.M. candidate in Barcelona, with a promise to include Nin for Teruel and Julián Gorkín for Cádiz.

Now it became necessary to participate in the People's Front in the rest of Spain. It was a good occasion to make the party better-known nationally. Since it had nuclei in diverse places around the Peninsula, there was no reason not to recognize its involvement. But the official Communists, underhandedly, opposed acceptance of the P.O.U.M. outside the Catalan Left Front. The P.O.U.M. executive committee felt that the Socialist Party was the appropriate intermediary for correcting this and sent a letter to the P.S.O.E. executive committee on January 1, 1936. The Socialist executive answered immediately, publicly supporting the activity of the P.O.U.M. in the national People's Front, in the name of the other members. And thus, Juan Andrade signed, in Madrid on January 15, 1936, the People's Front electoral announcement while Joaquím Maurín signed it in Barcelona.

The constitution of the People's Front, using that particular title, was a success for the official Communists, although its setting up was not due to its initiatives (as it later succeeded in convincing many people). It replaced the Workers' Alliance, which the Communists detested, and gave the official party a representation on the candidates' list that was disproportionate to its real strength. It cured the official party, furthermore, of its inferiority complex, since it was the first success after a long career of failures. The only thing the official party could not obtain, throughout this maneuver, was exclusion of the P.O.U.M.

The *poumistes* considered the People's Front a step backward when compared with the Workers' Alliance. The anarchists, naturally, did not participate, and they represented the main labor movement in the country. Further, the Front electoral documents explicitly rejected the radical proposals of the Socialists. For these reasons the P.O.U.M. insisted in all their electoral propaganda on the argument that the People's Front was not a permanent organ, but only an electoral tool. The Communists, specifically, wanted to convert the Front into a governing institution and to bind to the actions of the future regime all the Front deputies who gained seats. The P.O.U.M. opposed this concept, which would submit the working class parties to the discipline of the bourgeois Republicans.

It was no secret for the *poumistes* that this was exactly what the Communists desired. It would be convenient for Moscow's diplomatic ends, at a moment when Russia did not want to frighten its temporary allies, the conservative governments in Paris (which had lately concluded a military alliance with the U.S.S.R.) and London. Suddenly, the Comintern had come to the conclusion that Spain was not ripe for the revolution that the official Communists had demanded for years, until very recently.

Trotsky, who had opposed the setting up of the P.O.U.M., strongly attacked the decision to sign the Front documents. A representative of the International Secretariat of the movement for the Fourth International, who visited Barcelona shortly afterward, showed Nin and Andrade, separately, a letter from Trotsky to his French follower Jean Rous, in which Trotsky wrote, "What is happening in Spain is a proof of the mistakes and even the treason committed by Nin and Andrade in January by their signing of the People's Front pact."

On January 22, 1936, in an article, Trotsky affirmed that "the Spanish organization of 'Left Communists,' which was always a muddled organization, after countless vacillations to the right and the left, merged with the Catalan Federation of Maurín . . . on a centrist platform." The People's Front electoral pact was described as a shameful document. And, he finished, "In Spain, genuine revolutionists will no doubt be found who will mercilessly expose the betrayal of Maurín, Nin, Andrade, and their associates and will lay the foundation for the Spanish section of the Fourth International."

The electoral campaign was brief, but very active. The two P.O.U.M. candidacies promised outside Catalunya were blocked. In Cádiz, the official Communists prevented Gorkín's appearance on the ballot, and the Republicans supported their objections. In Teruel, the Republicans opposed the inclusion of Nin, and the communists supported them. The Cádiz nomination was given to the official Communists. The People's Front central committee did not know how to or could not avoid these local breaches.

The P.O.U.M. orators took advantage of the campaign to insist on two points: the threat of a military coup and the need for a policy that would stop it—a policy that could not be simply Republican, but would have to be revolutionary. In this context, the People's Front was only a step, through which one aimed toward the Workers' Alliance, because only this could hold back the coup or cause it to abort. This position helped, in a certain way, the leaders of the C.N.T. to find justification for not carrying out a campaign in favor of their traditional abstention from participation in voting.

On January 25, 1936, a Catalan regional C.N.T. conference had approved a document supporting abstention, but never applied its conclusions. A lawyer for the C.N.T., Benito Pabón, was a People's Front candidate for Saragossa.

Elections came on February 16, and with them the victory of the People's Front. In Barcelona, Maurín won a seat, along with the other front candidates.

What did the victory of the People's Front represent? Nin explained in the February issue of "La Nueva Era" that the People's Front had gained its objective, cutting off the march of reaction and securing release from jail of the political prisoners. The victory was owed to the worker masses, not so fully represented on the ballot as they should have been. If October 1934 had not taken place, there would have been no People's Front victory. But the struggle did not end with this triumph. Now it was necessary to defeat reaction, and this would have to be the work of the working class. The new Azaña administration (which was announced two days after the elections and which immediately freed the prisoners) left the masses disillusioned. To be satisfied with the consolidation of the Republican regime, accepting a renunciation on the part of the working class of the destruction of the capitalist order such as was embodied in the People's Front manifestso, would be a crime and a betrayal. But this was what the official Communists demanded, in calling for the People's Front to be converted into a permanent institution.

The conditions were not yet ripe for the working class to take power, but preparations for power could begin. If the govenment did not act boldly, the Republican middle class and peasantry would throw themselves into the arms of the fascists and give it the social base it had previously lacked. Only a clear and decisive policy, a policy of the Workers' Alliance, could carry the masses. Thus, the slogans of the moment were: independence of the workers' movement with respect to the bourgeois Republican parties, trade union unity, a new Workers' Alliance, and the rapid formation of a broad revolutionary party.

The electoral campaign had permitted the P.O.U.M. to make itself known throughout the country. New militants flocked to the party. In July 1936, just before the military coup, the party had reached 10,000 members, that is, as many as the official Communist party in the country.[5]

Maurín in the Cortes

It was necessary to underscore the political differences on the Left. Maurín took charge of this task in the Cortes. Since his single vote could not be hoped to exercise much influence, he tried to use the parliamentary tribune as a medium of political education. In the four months he served as deputy, he spoke four times.[6] On two of these occasions, he directed questions to the government, on the bar on return to service of left-wing army officers punished for their activities during the October 1934 events, and on the reactionary members appointed to governmental commissions to select schoolteachers. The other two were political speeches. None of these commentaries was applauded, although there were what is described as "murmurs of approval." The things Maurín said shocked, disturbed, and obliged one to think. The deputies were not accustomed to this kind of dry, cutting oratory. But Largo Caballero and some of his friends showed friendship toward Maurín, for what he had to say interested them.

On April 15, 1936, with the Cortes hardly begun its new sitting, the composition of the Azaña government was presented to it. The Socialists were not represented, and, dissatisfied with the possibility of exercising bourgeois rule when proletarian revolution was already approaching, stayed out. Each of the parties explained its vote. Maurín said then, in his first parliamentary discourse:

> . . . I will begin by saying that this time the representation of the P.O.U.M. will vote confidence in the government of Sr. Azaña. Nevertheless, I must point out my disagreement with the statements made by the president of the [state] council. His excellency has said—it was the general tone of his speech—that his fundamental goal, as a leader charged with great responsibility for the future of Spain, is that calm should prevail. This desire for calm merited the applause, Sr. Azaña, of the men who sit here as representative of the "black two years" [the 1933-35 period of right-leaning government]. But the people will not maintain itself in a position of calm, there will be no calm in the

country, notwithstanding those psychological factors of which Sr. Ventosa has spoken, notwithstanding the invocation of the communist danger of which Sr. Calvo Sotelo speaks, so long as justice is not done; in this country there will be no calm so long as truth about the repression of October 1934 has not been aired, with its 3,000 dead and the 30,000 prisoners . . .

The people, the real people who suffered in October, and who still suffer cannot maintain themselves in a state of calm so long as justice is not done, and by justice we mean, señores of the right, a natural revenge, we mean an expression that you yourselves utilize, taking it from the *Bible*: we mean the law of Talion. (*Noises in the hall.*) We mean a tooth for a tooth, and an eye for an eye. And a tooth for tooth and an eye for eye, which may make you laugh, does not make the Asturias miners laugh, after losing 3,000 of their own; it does not make the men who have suffered in prison laugh. These people, intuitively, and not for simple vengeance, want to see the law of Talion applied, they want revenge, they want retaliation, they want things to balance out, and only when this natural balance has come in this country, Sr. Azaña, will there be a possibility for calm; until this justice has been effected, there will be no peace in the country . . .

I see before the government of Sr. Azaña great dangers, which nobody has pointed out, but which are floating in the air. Sr. Azaña is occupying power for the second time. We cannot say that the first government of Sr. Azaña was a complete success. The government of Sr. Azaña fell in September 1933. Every political fall, every political collapse represents, fatally, a failure. A failure caused by what? [The Azaña regime] failed because the government of the first Republican biennium did not carry out the radical policy in the social sphere that it was necessary to pursue. And it is because of that that the Right, defeated on April 12 and 14, 1931, reasserted themselves in a slow but continuous manner, and in September 1933 swept away the Republican-Socialist government and took, in a dizzying manner, power in November-December 1933.

How has it been possible to regain positions that were lost? We reconquered our lost positions thanks to sacrifice by the working class, thanks to 3,000 dead, to this pyramid of corpses, thanks to the suffering of 30,000 families. All this has permitted the existence today of the Republican government . . . But it is true, Sr. Azaña, that the experience of the proletariat, of these 3,000 dead and 30,000 prisoners, can repeat itself indefinitely? Is the proletariat a raw material for suffering cruel, iniquitous repressions, as shown by the history of our country?

. . . What, socialist comrades, did the German and Austrian Social Democrats do, believing they could establish a democratic revolution, but allowing time for the fascists to organize, so that, (the latter) preparing themselves, they could conquer state power? We will repeat the same process before the end of a year, or two, or three—I cannot say the exact date—we will have, like Italy, like Hungary, like Germany, like Portugal, like a multitude of countries, a fascist regime, which will be presided over by Gil Robles or by Calvo Sotelo or by some other aspiring 'fuhrer' or 'duce.' The great responsibility of the proletariat and of the men who represent the liberal movement is precisely to block the rising movement of fascism represented by the allied Right, and by supporting at this moment the government of Sr. Azaña, if Sr. Azaña really proposes to put into effect the [electoral program] of the People's Front.

Ah! But the truth is that Sr. Azaña finds himself unable to carry out the People's Front program.

In the government of Sr. Azaña, there are two main contradictions: the first is that in 1936, in a profoundly revolutionary period, which has terrified the men of the Right, the government of Sr. Azaña is less revolutionary, less advanced, and of a more conservative type than the government he headed in 1931-33. Within that government, there were three socialist ministers, who gave a more advanced tone than could be expected from the Republicans alone. Today, there is this first contradiction. And the second is to think that what triumphed on February 16 was a movement that was simply Republican. It was the October movement [that won] . . .

To my mind, what is happening is that those working class parties that believe in the efficacy of the People's Front (and I do not believe in its efficacy) have formed with the Republicans a People's Front government. The People's Front government will also come to ruin. . . . And then the workers will go beyond the People's Front Government; to the formation of a workers' government that will solve the problems of the Spanish Revolution.

The choice is—I repeat—fascism or socialism; we socialists naturally, pronounce ourselves for socialism. Nothing more. (*Murmurs of approval in some parts of the Chamber.*)

With the country in ferment, the right wing socialist and aspirant to the prime ministership, Indalecio Prieto, organized a maneuver to get rid of Azaña, toward which end he convinced the Cortes to declare Alcalá Zamora deposed from the presidency and to elect Azaña to this post. But the socialists refused against the wishes of Prieto, to participate in a People's Front government. In the election for the presidency, the P.O.U.M. deputy, Maurín, and those who thought similarly supported a socialist, Ramón González Peña, very popular for having been one of the chiefs of the workers' uprising in Asturias in 1934; González Peñā supported the socialist Left, although during the civil war he turned to the right wing and the communists.

Azaña assigned his friend Santiago Casares Quiroga to form a government made up entirely of Republicans; when it was presented to the Cortes on June 16, Maurín stated:

. . . I told Sr. Azaña on April 15 in this same chamber that in this government—and in that of Sr. Cesares Quiroga, the problem is even more accentuated—in this government there are two basic contradictions. And in politics, when there are fundamental contradictions, one goes nowhere, or one heads inevitably, toward failure . . .

We should not fool ourselves: between the present parliament and the real situation of the country an ever greater abyss deepens more each day. Today, parliament does not express the anxieties of the people; this parliament would represent the desires expressed by the triumph of February 16 if it had carried out one third of the platform of the People's Front; and not even a third, not even a tenth, not even a hundredth part has been put into effect. Well, then, what do you want them to think, these hundreds of thousands of peasants, of starving workers, of people vexed by the October repression, this great popular movement that has gone into action because it aspired to greater justice, and to greater economic and social well-being? Because the government, because you yourselves, because we, the majority, because we have not done, for example, a minimum part of what the government of [Léon] Blum [in France] did in the first four days of its occupation of power?

A strike movement is taking place in the country, not based on gangs, but on the mass of the citizenry, on the masses who represent the real essence of the nation.

Looking at this great strike movement, you will not be able to hold it down, either with pistols or rifles, or with other repressive measures; this strike movement, which has a reason for existing, will only be appeased if you take measures, not of a threatening character, this said for the benefit of the rightist deputies, but measures of an economic kind in the interest of the working class. The forty-hour week, a minimum wage, a guarantee that the unemployed will be provided with work, all this will bring an end to the strike movement that is now taking place in Spain. And if you do not do this, representatives of the majority, of the government, of the People's Front, the strikes will grow, there will be more unrest, and all this will make the offensive of the counterrevolution intensify, and the moment will come when, as in 1933, we will have created a divorce, an unbridgeable abyss between the will of the masses and the government of the People's Front. And I do not desire this, and because I do not desire it, I point out that, to my understanding, this must be the political road followed by the People's Front, to emerge from the present contradiction.

There is a prefascist situation in the country, it is undeniable . . .

Mussolini's fascism, at first no danger for Giolitti, was a danger for neither the socialists nor the communists. The fascists were merely terrorist gangs. Fascism assaulted the great Roman plain and made punitive expeditions, but still it did not endanger the security of the liberal state. Italian fascism, at its beginning, was made up of terrorist bands that attacked the offices of the Socialist and Communist Parties, but it still was not a movement that endangered the security of the state. Fascism, through terrorism, through action behind the scenes, and through the collaboration it offered the big bourgeoisie, prepared for a new entrance into history of big gangsters, such as the heads of the Italian and German fascist movements, who seemed to find themselves completely marginal but who nevertheless we saw later taking over power by means of a coup d'etat, supported by the big bourgeoisie . . .

To destroy fascism, coercive measures are not enough, one must also apply political measures, and one political measure, principally, señores of the

People's Front, would be for the government to respond to the demands included in the constitution of the People's Front, which would not conflict with the constitution of this government. A government that would respond now to the desires of the popular masses, and, therefore, to reality, would have to be made up, not only of the Republican Parties, but also the workers' parties, the representatives of the People's Front that believe in the policy of the People's Front.

Such a government, formed thusly, would have to nationalize the land, the railroads, heavy industry, the mines, the banks, and adopt progressive means, such as those Blum has adopted in France; this government will be able to finish with the fascist threat.

In other words, within two months we will see the counter-revolution grow more intense, and, perhaps, then it will be too late to contain the excesses of fascism, a danger far greater than perhaps we can see from these seats.

Maurín spoke of two months. At the end of a month and a day the military rising took place.

The P.O.U.M. and the Workers' Federation for Trade Union Unity (F.O.U.S.)

For the P.O.U.M., the perspective of a soon-to-come battle against fascism—although more than a mere propaganda phrase, indeed, a very real possibility—could not impede the party from continuing its normal activities.

Something that provoked concern was the union situation. The U.G.T. had become radicalized, while the C.N.T. continued under the control of the F.A.I. The latter had underhandedly counseled the workers to vote for the People's Front in February, because many C.N.T. members were imprisoned; but there remained the danger that it would launch itself into a new insurrectionary adventure, which would have provided the pretext for the Left Republicans to ally governmentally with the center, or even for the military to intervene. The unions controlled by the P.O.U.M. grew, but they remained without strength at the key point, Barcelona. However, Bonet published an article in "Nueva Era" in February 1936, "The Situation of the Union Movement in Catalunya," which summarized the problem as it was viewed by the P.O.U.M. In it he said: "These are the organizations now in existence: 1) The C.N.T., 2) the U.G.T., 3) the United Trade Union Front (Fronte Unic Sindical affiliated with the P.O.U.M.); 4) the C.N.T. "opposition unions" (the former "*trentistes*"); 5) the General Union of Workers' Unions of Catalunya (Unió General de Sindicats Obrers—U.G.S.O.), and 6) the autonomous unions . . ." What was to be done in the face of this fragmentation, which weakened the C.N.T., but which provided no perspectives for either its substitution or its reform? Bonet put forward the position of the P.O.U.M. on this matter:

> The proletariat needs union unity. The unifying movement continues to grow daily. The lessons of October have not gone by without effect. And the current favoring unification has had a new expression. That consists in the constitution in various localities of Catalunya (Mataró, Terrassa, Figueres, Reus, etc.) of Local Trade Union Unity organs (Unions Locals de Sindicats) in which the autonomous unions, 'opposition' unions, and C.N.T. and U.G.T. unions coexist. Even given their local character, these practical examples of trade union unity have great importance.
>
> The problem of unification of the trade union movement can not be resolved by entering either the C.N.T., as the anarchists claim, or the U.G.T., as the socialists want.
>
> Today then, the struggle for trade union unity, in our view, must take on greater breadth, greater transcendence. Obviously, beginning from these preliminary facts it is necessary to concentrate our efforts toward unification, with a view to the calling of a trade union unity conference in which all the unions will participate.

The panorama became more simple when the C.N.T. held its congress in May 1936 in Saragossa. The C.N.T. congress readmitted the *"trentista"* unions and adopted an ambitious political and economic program for the approaching revolution and for the organization of libertarian communism, defined as the organization's objective.

Responsibility for the trade union policy of the P.O.U.M. was taken over by Nin. Since Nin had worked so long in the Profintern, the P.O.U.M. members believed ingenuously that he could work miracles. He clearly could not. But the P.O.U.M. showed themselves to be very active in the union field. May 1, 1936 saw a conference bringing together the unions controlled by *poumistes*—i.e., the local federations in Lleida, Girona, Tarragona, and some other cities, and some Barcelona unions. They agreed to set up the Workers' Federation for Trade Union Unity (Federació Obrera d'Unificació Sindical—F.O.U.S.), of which Nin was elected secretary general with Bonet as assistant secretary. The F.O.U.S. affirmed, from the beginning, that it did not wish to be simply another little union federation, but that it proposed to work for unification with the other "centrals." It projected a union conference for autumn 1936, to try to unite the different Catalan federations and afterward to press for a unification of the C.N.T. and U.G.T. on the national level, in which all the unions outside the two main organizations would be included.

Meanwhile, the F.O.U.S. and P.O.U.M. continued setting up local Trade Union Unity organs, on the same basis as the *bloquistes*, and that created an atmosphere of cooperation necessary for any future unification. Union secretariats also were organized, to coordinate the action of all the local unions of each trade affiliated with F.O.U.S. But the *poumistes* who led unions had to attend to the immediate struggle, and this meant that the F.O.U.S., like it or not, had to function as a national federation, seeing itself opposed, on different occasions, to the C.N.T.

The F.O.U.S. had no time to solidify its ranks—which perhaps would not have solidified even if given time. It had hardly begun its organization work when July 19 came.

The People's Front in Action

The P.O.U.M. was swimming against the stream. Almost everybody had illusions in the People's Front and few saw the essential difference between it and the Workers' Alliance. The danger existed that the experience of 1931 would be repeated. The P.O.U.M. tried to avoid this loss of energy, just as the Bloc had done then. It argued that the elections of February 1936 had opened up a revolutionary period, during which the working class forces had to act with speed. On April 10, "La Batalla" criticized the aid given Azaña by the workers' parties: "Aid to bourgeois governments when the circumstances are propitious for revolutionary action, will have catastrophic consequences."

On April 24, "Mundo Obrero," the Madrid daily of the official Communist Party, denounced "the renegade Maurín, the enemy of the People's Front," and in the Cortes Dolores Ibárruri ("La Pasionaria") and Manuel Valdés, a deputy for the official party from Catalunya, attacked Maurín for having declared to some journalists that the workers' parties should leave the People's Front and form their own front. Meanwhile, with the Socialist and Communist youth organizations having unified, adopting, as we have noted, the title of Unified Socialist Youth (J.S.U.), the P.O.U.M. Youth decided to call itself the Iberian Communist Youth (Joventut/Joventud Comunista Ibérica—J.C.I.).

The P.O.U.M. refined its doctrinal positions. It had now lost all its illusions about the U.S.S.R. In Europe, using the trick of the People's Front, the communists got people to swallow nearly all their propaganda—for example, the fairy tale about the "most democratic constitution in the world" (the Soviet charter of 1936)—and to forget certain bothersome realities, such as the Siberian labor camps, the ideological colonialism of the Comintern, the deification of Stalin, and the persecution of all who showed opposition. But the P.O.U.M. in Spain saw things as they were, and understood that ideological colonialism is not an isolated fact, but a consequence and a part of an entire system of falsification of the revolution.

This was manifest in the pages of "La Batalla," "Avant," the P.O.U.M.'s new newspaper in Catalan, which began publication in December, and "La Nueva Era." The P.O.U.M. published one of the first denunciations of Stakhanovism as a system of exploitation of the workers by the bureaucracy (in an article signed by a leading P.O.U.M. militant who had come from the Communist Left, Ignacio Iglesias from Asturias). In an article by José Luis Arenillas, a well-known P.O.U.M. figure from the Basque country, on the middle class and the proletariat (published in "La Nueva Era" for July 1936), the author pointed out the importance, through the Soviet, German, and Spanish experiences, that democracy had acquired for the P.O.U.M.:

> The defense of democratic rights does not imply an accommodation with the capitalist regime. On the contrary. The defense of democratic freedoms as contained in the Constitution of the Republic and in some reforms of the past constituent assemblies, tends to break with bourgeois democracy, knocking it off its hinges, annulling it through the logical realization of its own aims.
>
> We must propagate the concept that democracy defends itself by going forward without stopping. Because if it does not go toward socialism, it is destined to move backward toward fascism. For this reason, the working class must be inspired by the following principle: If to defend and install proletarian democracy it is necessary to struggle against capitalism, it is necessary to defend what remains of democracy. To educate and organize the broad masses, a minimum of liberty is needed. And it is obvious that we do not exclude, by saying this, the need for underground work, necessary and very useful at every moment but especially during periods of repression . . .
>
> Against utopian and vague solutions we must present concrete and easily realizable solutions taking, every day, more positions from the bourgeoisie. Because what we must do is instill in the consciousness of the middle class the awareness that the social transformation they desire cannot be realized without a structural change and that, consequently, every demand will be complicated by the needs of capitalism, and will not be practicable if the working class does not grasp political power.

The masses showed that they had a better memory than their leaders and that they remembered the deception of 1931. They were skeptical of the new government. The peasants occupied the land. The workers declared strikes. The workers' organizations began organizing militarily. Demonstrations by the members of the fascist Falange Española in dark blue shirts, those of the J.S.U. in light blue, and the blue work shirts of the P.O.U.M., like the French "bleu de travail," crossed each others' paths in the streets on Sundays, leading to fistfights and exchanges of shots. In the universities, Falangist and leftist students battled it out. Politics became more and more a matter of shouting slogans. There were constant clashes between workers and the police, peasants and the civil guard. There were arrests, deaths, offices of the Right and the workers' movement closed down, and censorship.

The P.O.U.M., in the face of all this, insisted on a return to the Workers' Alliance, but giving it a national character. In March it unsuccessfully proposed its reestablishment.

The economic situation worsened. The rich exported capital as in 1931. Many landowners left their fields fallow. In the construction industry, there was 11% unemployment. Throughout the country, the proportion of unemployed was 5.6% of the work force, which seems small compared with today's endemic unemployment of 15-20% in Spain as well as in Belgium and other Western industrial democracies, but which was a large figure at the time. On the stock exchange, the average share price had fallen from 167.7 pesetas in 1929 to 91.1 in 1936.

At that moment, there were 970,000 workers in Catalunya, among them 390,000 in agriculture, 73,000 metalworkers, 73,000 in construction, and 180,000 in the textile industry. The cost of living index was rising: from 102.7 in 1931 (1913 = 100) to 184.8 in June 1936. Wages did not increase, but rather tended to fall, thanks to unemployment.[7]

Gil Robles, head of the C.E.D.A., said in the Cortes, on June 17, that

> From February 16 to June 15, a numerical summary shows the following data: Churches totally destroyed, 160; attacks on churches, extinguished fires, vandalism, and attempted attacks, 251; dead, 269; wounded of varying gravity, 1,287; personal attacks, frustrated or whose consequences were not reported, 215; robberies carried out, 138; attempted robberies, 23; political party and private buildings destroyed, 69; attacks on the same, 312; general strikes, 113; partial strikes, 228; newspaper offices totally destroyed, 10; attacks on newspapers and attempts at assault and destruction, 33; bombings, 140; bombs placed without exploding, 72.

Nin wrote in the issue of "La Nueva Era" that came out at the beginning of July, "For the democratic bourgeoisie, the revolution is over. For the working class, this is only a stage of development . . . Each step backward by reaction, each advance of the revolution is a result of the extra-legal action of the working class."

Events began accelerating. The extreme Right saw more clearly than the Republican rulers and even the working class leaders. In Madrid, rightist gunmen avenged an earlier death by killing José Castillo, an officer of the guardia de asalto; José Calvo Sotelo, one of the leaders of the Right, was assassinated in turn by guardias de asalto.

In the May issue of "La Nueva Era" Maurín had explained the causes of a situation so tense and so charged for the future, and pointed out what that future must be:

> Everywhere the problem may be considered, we come inevitably to the conclusion that to escape from the present morass there is no other viable perspective than to fully enter into measures of a socialist type.
>
> But as the Republicans, the liberal bourgeoisie, cannot escape from their own shadow, the failure of their action will be as inevitable as during the first period of their rule: 1931-1933.
>
> If the Spanish proletariat had a great revolutionary Marxist Party, we would probably already have seen the takeover of power by the working class.
>
> The seizure of power by the working class will mean the realization of the democratic revolution the bourgeoisie cannot complete—liberation of the land, of the nationalities, destruction of the Church, economic emancipation of women, improvement of the material and moral situation of the workers—at the same time beginning the socialist revolution, nationalizing the land, transport, mines, heavy industry, and the banks.
>
> Our revolution is democratic and socialist at the same time, since the triumphant proletariat will have to carry out a good part of the revolution and tasks corresponding to the bourgeoisie and, simultaneously, begin the socialist revolution. The transcendence that the taking of power by the workers in our country will have in the whole world is incalculable, it will inaugurate a period of great revolutionary movements, of the overthrow of fascist regimes, and of a sweeping push by the enslaved peoples in pursuit of their liberation.

The murder of Calvo Sotelo on Monday, July 13, made it inevitable that the Right would take the initiative when the workers movement was not yet prepared.

On Thursday, the 16th, the P.O.U.M. executive committee met and examined the situation. It expected a coup at any moment. It agreed that Maurín and Nin should meet with Companys, Generalitat president. At ten in the evening, Companys told them that he knew that in some barracks in the city there had been agitation, that he tried to communicate with Madrid, but was unable to.

The executive decided, then, that Maurín should leave for Madrid the following day, Friday, and that once there he should decide, according to the news of the moment, whether to go to Galicia, where a P.O.U.M. group in Santiago de Compostela had organized various propaganda events.

Once in Madrid, Maurín spoke in the corridors of the Cortes with various politicians, among them Lana Sarrate, a deputy for Huesca and personal friend of Azaña. He told him that some hours before he had spoken with the president of the Republic, who had affirmed to him that *"this week nothing will happen; next week, we'll see."* Maurín was doubtful, but finally, believing the information from Azaña, and pressed by the spirit of the party he took the train for Santiago.

Saturday, the 18th, in the evening, he was speaking at the Casa del Pueblo in Santiago when the news of a military uprising arrived. On Sunday, the 19th, in many cities fighting had begun, transportation was paralyzed, and it was impossible to get to Barcelona, where Maurín would have wanted to be. He went to La Coruña and spoke to the governor. On Monday, the 20th, at two in the afternoon, the troops in La Coruña rose against the republic.

The Spanish Civil War had begun.

Notes

1. For the minutes of the two meetings, see "Documentos: El Proceso de Unificación Marxista, 1935," in "Tribuna Socialista." (Paris) Oct.-Dec. 1976.
2. On the change in the composition of the Comintern parties, see Franz Borkenau, *World Communism*, Ann Arbor, 1962. A classic exposition of the role of the "armed bohemian" in modern politics and of the similarities between the German C.P. and the Nazi party is Konrad Heiden, *Der Fuhrer*, New York, 1944.
3. The theses approved by the fusion congress were published in the pamphlet *¿Que es y Que Quiere el Partido Obrero de Unificación Marxista?*, Barcelona, 1935.
4. On the I.A.G., see Robert J. Alexander, *The Right Opposition*, Westport, 1981, and Stephen Schwartz, *Brotherhood of the Sea*, op. cit.
5. In the official *Historia del Partido Comunista de Espana* it is claimed that on July 18, 1936, the official party had 100,000 members. Informed observers (Gerald Brenan, Franz Borkenau, Walter Krivitsky) attribute to it only 3,000. We believe that is too small a number and that 10,000 is the appropriate figure. But taking into account that, as we have pointed out, the C.N.T. then had two million adherents and the Socialist Party and trade unions, together, about the same, even 100,000 members of the official party would represent only 2.5% of the organized workers and hardly justifies the sixteen communist deputies (out of 452) gained by the party not through its own efforts but thanks to the People's Front electoral slate.
6. Maurín's parliamentary speeches were published, naturally, in the "Diario de Sesiones" of the Cortes, and were reprinted in a pamphlet published by Editorial Marxista, Barcelona, in 1937: *Intervenciones Parliamentarias*, by Joaquím Maurín.
7. Balcells, op. cit., pp. 24, 40-41, 242.

4

Revolution

On July 18, Companys spoke by radio, advising the people to go to bed, because, he said, in Catalunya nothing had happened or would happen.

But the worker militants did not go to bed. *Cenetista* groups concentrated in the neighborhoods of the barracks and at some strategic intersections. The P.O.U.M. executive committee met and charged Josep Rovira with the immediate tasks of organizing the militants for the struggle. A military committee consisting of Rovira, Andreu Capdevila from the Barcelona local committee, Carmel Rosa ("Roc") from the youth organization, and two others, had been set up to direct the action of shock groups based on the *gabocs*. It was obvious fighting would take place, and, remembering the events of October 6, 1934, nobody had confidence in the actions of the Generalitat. A manifesto was printed—the only one in those days— to be distributed at daybreak, July 19. It was decided to immediately demand the reconstitution of the Workers' Alliance. But none of the leaders stayed in the party offices. The truth is that apart from the C.N.T. and P.O.U.M., everybody slept.

Late the night of the 18th, Josep Coll and Julián Gorkín went to the Generalitat, demanding arms. They were told that such action was superfluous, that all necessary measures had been taken. It seemed certain that the experience of October 6 would be repeated.

Two more manifestoes were composed: one from the J.C.I., the P.O.U.M. youth organization, addressed to the soldiers and calling on them to desert, and another from the party itself, calling for a general strike. Continuous efforts were made to set up the Workers' Alliance. This time it was possible to talk with some official Communist leaders as well as some *cenetistes*. The first said the People's Front would suffice for the mobilization of the masses, and the second repeated what had often been said before: "We will meet on the barricades."

This time, the promised meeting took place. In the early hours of Sunday, July 19, the battle began. P.O.U.M. groups fought, above all, in the

111

plaça Catalunya, at the center of the city above the Rambles, at the nearby plaça de l'Universitat, and at the barracks of the Naval Dockyard, the famous Drassanes (Atarazanas). Germinal Vidal, general secretary of the Bloc youth (Joventuts del Bloc) since 1932, and then head of the P.O.U.M. Youth, and his comrade Batista, fell at the plaça de l'Universitat. (Germinal Vidal was succeeded as youth leader by Wilebaldo Solano.[1]

The executive was meeting in a private house, in the center of the city, receiving news from throughout Barcelona. Those at the meeting had the same idea in their minds, between the arrivals of fresh bulletins: regret that Maurín was not there. Militants, out of breath and excited, came in with news from all the points of contact: The air force had not joined the coup, the soldiers had been held back by barricades on the Paral.lel, near the França railroad station the workers had created improvised tanks by loading rolls of newsprint on trucks. Companys had addressed the police, calling for the loyalty to the Republic, the Telefonica building commanding the plaça Catalunya had been taken, lost, and retaken by the workers, *poumistes* and *cenetistes* had opened the doors of the armories with gunfire. On the radio, the public was informed that Azaña had called on Martínez Barrio to form a government and that the latter had tried to negotiate with the coup leaders, until General Emilio Mola, the intellectual leader of the anti-Republic conspiracy, hung up the telephone on him. Better, the P.O.U.M. leadership believed, to risk everything under fire than to surrender without a struggle.

At midmorning on Sunday, the possibilities for victory had been clearly affirmed. By noon, the battle was over in Barcelona. Columns of smoke rose from many churches and convents, set ablaze by the enraged masses. The police, in their station houses, distributed arms to the same workers that days before they arrested.

The P.O.U.M. requisitioned, at the bottom of the Rambles, the Principal Palace Theatre. A first aid station had been set up in a night club in the lobby. The Hotel Falcón, on the other side of the Rambles, was requisitioned for the use of the exhausted militants and for the delegates who had already begun coming in from the outlying towns, where *cenetistes* and *poumistes* had formed committees, which had seized the town halls.

In the Generalitat Palace, the situation was chaotic. Three leaders of the F.A.I. visited Companys, who said to them that, if they wished it, power was theirs. They did not wish it. Later, they would say they had refused to take power because they did not want to install their own dictatorship. But it is more probable that, accustomed to criticizing all politics and all power, the possibility of actually taking and exercising it never entered their heads. Companys, with his little speech in private, put them between a rock and a hard place: either to accept responsibility for governing or let the Esquerra, which until two days before had persecuted the C.N.T., continue governing ("Solidaridad Obrera," the anarchosyndicalist daily nicknamed "La Soli," came out on the morning of July 19, still bearing the white spaces that were the mark of the censorship).

The fears of the P.O.U.M. were confirmed: the anarchists rejected the seizure of power. They left Companys and the Esquerra in the government. But without the *cenetistes* neither Barcelona nor Catalunya would have been saved from the coup.

The Committee for Militias

On July 20, two of the three conditions for the victory of a revolution, cited by Lenin in his famous critique of Left Communism, were present in Barcelona: the privileged classes could no longer rule in the old way, and the masses had shown their unwillingness to continue living in the old way. In every locality where the republican authorities had armed the people, the coup had failed. Where the authorities refused the distribution of arms, the officers' insurrection succeeded.

But the third, "Leninist" condition was lacking: there was no single revolutionary organization leading the masses. The C.N.T. could have been such an organization had it freed itself in time from its antipolitical prejudices; the Socialist Party also, if its radicalization had been more extensive and prolonged and if it was not prone to retreat in the face of the Communists. The P.O.U.M., because of its youthfulness and its limitation to Catalunya, was not yet the great revolutionary party its militants dreamed it would become. The most positive alternative would have been a coalition of the C.N.T., the socialist Left, and the P.O.U.M. And this would have had to occur when the enthusiasm of the masses was still at white heat.

In July 1936, Catalunya and much of Spain faced a situation any Marxist would have considered ideal: There was a working class with a high level of class consciousness, which wanted power. This was what Marxists always dreamed of but seldom attained. And this situation, which went beyond those considered the high points of the twentieth century socialist struggle—Germany in 1919 and France in 1936, where Marxists were the dominant trend—was centered in Catalunya, where Marxism was a minority viewpoint and was represented exclusively by the P.O.U.M.; and all this at a moment when the international workers' movement found itself in crisis, moving backwards, suffering the rot of Stalinism and the weakness of reformism. This highly conscious working class, which wanted to rule, was, finally, organized in a movement that rejected and feared power.

In the P.O.U.M. executive, the lack of a real political leader was felt. Maurín, who would have filled the need, was in Galicia, isolated, perhaps executed, for Galicia was entirely in the hands of the military. Nin was excellent as an official and a functionary, but he had neither the capacity nor the experience to be a real leader, and the other elements in the executive were yet his inferior in this regard.

At that moment, the vacillations of the revolutionary leadership in Barcelona had an unexpected effect. The middle class, which sensed the Esquerra would not be able to continue defending its interests, began to believe in the P.O.U.M. as a counterforce to the C.N.T., seeing in the P.O.U.M. a sensible, "respectable" party. A good part of this feeling must have derived, curiously, from the differing language politics of the two revolutionary tendencies: The C.N.T. rejected use of Catalan as a middle-class characteristic, since a great part of the Barcelona proletariat, having emigrated from Andalucía and Murcia, spoke Castilian. But the radical intelligentsia and many workers in Barcelona, as well as the majority of the working class in such areas as Lleida, to whom the P.O.U.M. actively appealed, spoke, read, and wrote Catalan. Whether their motivations, it is more interesting to note that those petty bourgeois who entered the P.O.U.M. at this time, under probational membership, became real *poumistes* and did not abandon the party when the hour of persecution came. The 10,000 members of the party rose to 30,000 in two weeks.

On July 21, a Committee for Militias (*Comité de Milícies*) was formed, charged with organizing the columns that would leave Barcelona for Saragossa and other places, and in which all the parties and unions were represented. Soon, the Committee for Militias had begun acting as the real government, since the Generalitat had no strength. The P.O.U.M. appointed Josep Rovira as its delegate on the committee.

The P.O.U.M. executive committee asked French comrades from the Marceau Pivert group to make efforts through the French foreign ministry to see if that country's consul in Galicia could find out anything about Maurín, who was married to a French subject. The Quai d'Orsay demonstrated a negligent attitude and did not succeed in turning anything up. Meanwhile, it was necessary to find someone to replace Maurín. Nin was named political secretary for the party (leaving Maurín his post as general secretary).

For Nin, the situation was not an easy one. The *bloquistes*, who made up the immense majority of the P.O.U.M., had felt a special warmth for Maurín. Whoever occupied his post would encounter resentment and coldness.

Notwithstanding all this, Nin succeeded in establishing good relations with the militants. But he was never able to become a leader capable of guiding the party. The P.O.U.M. would suffer, throughout the civil war, from Maurín's absence.

This does not mean that, had Maurín been in Barcelona, things would have occurred differently. It was the masses, in the beginning, with their spontaneous reactions—much more sensible than anybody would have expected—that made decisions, often without being aware of it. Maurín could not have ignored or opposed these decisions, supporting a desire to on his part.

One thing the executive and the militants understood: if the C.N.T. did not take power in Catalunya, no genuine revolution could take place. But the C.N.T. did not desire power. They believed power over the economy would suffice, and they presented their renunciation of state power as a gesture of generosity, when in reality it reflected a surrender to ideological prejudices.

But power remained, in disintegration in the Generalitat Palace, and in potency in the Committee for Militias. While vacillating over this fundamental question, the Committee for Militias organized the first columns for the march toward the fascist-occupied sector of Aragon, around Saragossa, long the cynosure of the anarchosyndicalists in their hopes for expansion. The first columns included 13,000 volunteers from the C.N.T., 3,000 from the P.O.U.M., 2,000 from the U.G.T., and 200 from the forces of the Generalitat.[2]

All the organizations were carrying out requisitions. The P.O.U.M. was not particularly greedy about this, and that explains why it had to content itself with the old printing presses used by the reactionary daily "El Correo Catalan," for the printing of the now daily "Avant." Notwithstanding what the communists later claimed, the P.O.U.M. requisitioned rather little, not out of scruple, but because of disinterest.

Similarly, the *poumistes* took little part in the atrocities and brutalities that were then commonplace as the angry populace vented its rage on suspected counterrevolutionaries. This was not to say they considered themselves to be purer or superior, since they did nothing to stop these injustices or to withhold support for them, at least until Andreu Nin, who would become Generalitat *conseller* of justice, acted to curb the excesses of popular revenge. This is also not to say they did not commit some themselves. Certainly, in outlying areas of Catalunya, where the party had more power, they did more to halt atrocities than where they were a second- or third-ranking organization. And this was not because they were better than the militants of other organizations, but because the education they had received made them more concerned for political questions than for spectacular manifestations of a power the workers did not really exercise and for which, in a certain way, they compensated by dramatic acts.

Political questions were not lacking. The parties that chose not to join the Bloc in the P.O.U.M., (the U.S.C., the official Communist Party of

Catalunya, the Partit Català Proletari, and the Catalan Federation of the Socialist party) in great haste organized a new party, the Unified Socialist Party of Catalunya (Partit Socialista Unificat de Catalunya—P.S.U.C.), which immediately joined the Comintern and whose general secretary was Joan Comorera, the U.S.C. stalwart who had served as a *conseller* in the Generalitat administration in alliance with the Esquerra.

On March 26, Comorera had declared to journalists, about the negotiations toward formation of the new party, that he was in favor of joining the Comintern, *although this could only be decided by a fusion congress.* This support was the price he paid for the general secretaryship, because Comorera was one of the most moderate members of the very moderate U.S.C., particularly during his periods as *conseller*, and he had no ideological reason for desiring that the new party belong to the third rather than the second international. Nominally, the P.S.U.C. was an independent Catalan party, with a direct relation to Moscow. In practice, it followed the directions of the official Spanish Communist Party. Ernö Gerö (Pedro), the Hungarian sent by the Comintern to run the official Spanish party, had the same mission with regard to the P.S.U.C., but at the orders of a *troika* sent to Spain after the outbreak of the civil war, consisting of the Argentine Vittorio Codovilla, who had been in Madrid since 1931, the Italian Palmiro Togliatti (Ercoli), and the Bulgarian Stoyan Minev (Stepanov), assisted by various other agents of the Comintern and the Soviet secret services, of whom the most important was an Italian from Trieste, Vittorio Vidali, alias "Carlos Contreras," who had previously operated in sinister fashion in Mexico and the United States under yet another name, Enea Sormenti. At its formation, the P.S.U.C. had 5,000 to 6,000 members, but by November it had reached 42,000.[3]

On July 21, the delegates of the fusing parties met, and, on the 22nd, the constitution of the P.S.U.C. was announced, with neither a congress nor an assembly. The adherence to Moscow was, then, decided by a few leaders. As late as the 1970s the P.S.U.C. had never held a congress. For the P.O.U.M., the P.S.U.C. represented a double problem: a political problem, which they already understood, because they saw little difference between the Catalan branch of the official party and the P.S.U.C., and because, for the moment, they felt greater strength and more sympathy from the public. The psychological problem was less simple, because in the parties that made up the P.S.U.C. there were former *bloquistes* who had left the Bloc when the P.O.U.M. was set up, with whom the *bloquistes* had coexisted for years, whom they still considered friends, and whom they now saw prepared to become their rivals.

But all this—requisitions, popular excesses, the P.S.U.C.—was anecdotal. What was decisive to the P.O.U.M. was the question of power.

Finally, the P.O.U.M. executive opened its eyes and ears: late, but before the leaders of other organizations. It understood the will of the party rank and file as it reflected the will of the worker masses, not only the militants, but also the workers in the unions and even those unorganized.

The atmosphere among the workers can be simply summed up: They desired to be masters. They did not desire it because the unions or parties told them to, but spontaneously. It was not the unions that ordered the formation of control committees in the factories whose owners had fled, were in hiding, or were dead—it was the workers themselves.

Naturally, the majority of members of these committees came from the C.N.T., but there were also P.O.U.M. members and some P.S.U.C. and Esquerra followers, as well as unaffiliated individuals, among them. Only after days had passed did the unions occupy themselves with coordinating and representing these committees. But the committees emerged spontaneously. Problems came up and among the different alternatives the workers chose the one that expressed their aspirations. Clearly these aspirations where the product of many years of working class—especially anarchosyndicalist—propaganda. Utopia had become reality, not by the will of those who preached, but of those who believed. In the development of this phenomenon of spontaneity, the overall political environment of the country had considerable influence. The officers who participated in the coup movement affirmed their desire to defend public order and avoid a revolution (only after some weeks had passed did they begin to talk very much about a communist threat). Events induced people to believe that, had the military rising not taken place, sooner or later there would have been a workers' insurrection. The struggle against the coup was, in fact, a workers' insurrection.

It was not the leadership of the C.N.T., P.O.U.M., or P.S.U.C., who told the workers of the towns and neighborhoods to form committees and occupy the city halls. The committees were formed the night of July 19-20 on the initiative of the local militants, for the requisition of weapons and buildings, control of automobile traffic, and vigilance at boulevards and barracks. At some locations, where the P.O.U.M. had strength, the committees were made up exclusively of worker representatives. In others, Esquerra elements also were admitted. In Lleida, where the P.O.U.M. was the main force, the committee included the P.O.U.M., the C.N.T., and the P.S.U.C. The president and commissar of public order in Lleida was a P.O.U.M. member.

If the unions succeeded in quickly taking over the factory committees, which was necessary, they never succeeded in completely controlling the town and neighborhood committees. Each organism acted on its own. There was an element of anarchist distrust of authority in this, as well as an enjoyment of power, and a rank-and-file suspicion about the leaders, a fear that in Barcelona the leadership would allow itself to be pacified by the republican politicians. If the politicians had been more clever, the coup could have been avoided; one could not expect to leave them in a government they did not know how to protect or defend.

Outside Catalunya, in the province of Castelló the regional governing committee was formed exclusively by the C.N.T., P.O.U.M., and socialists, with no republican participation. In Valencia, the comparable body included all the parties and unions, the P.O.U.M. included. Everywhere the P.O.U.M. was accepted, no matter how small its local organization. Two P.O.U.M. members held high posts in the Basque country, where there was virtually no P.O.U.M. organization. In Madrid, the P.O.U.M. published a weekly and organized a column of militia that advanced toward Siguenza and took, lost, and retook this town.[4]

At the end of the first week following the coup attempt, things began to be seen clearly, at least in Catalunya. The Committee for Militias was a parallel power that was not daring enough to resolve the dual-power situation by taking over all power for itself. The anarchists believed the important thing was to arm the militias and control the economy. They did not see that the Generalitat had already begun reasserting its control over the latter through a series of measures it had adopted: suspension of exchange transactions, a bar on withdrawals from current accounts "by persons who had participated in the coup attempt," creation of a regulatory office to handle the payment of wages (facilitating credit for those factory control committees that found the factory safes empty). Two powers really did exist. One of them, that corresponding to the workers, had the strength but not the will to rule; the other, the petty-bourgeois republican force, lacked strength, but possessed a clear will to recover power. During the year that followed, from mid-1936 to mid-1937, the political life of Catalunya would revolve around this contradiction.

The masses, instinctively revolutionary, spontaneously interested in power, remained as if paralyzed by the ideological and tactical confusionism of the C.N.T. and F.A.I. leadership. For the P.O.U.M., the first year of civil war would bring constant, and, in the final analysis, sterile efforts to bring to the C.N.T. masses a consciousness of the need to hold power. Seen retrospectively, one may say it was an effort wasted from the beginning. But everything seemed possible in those days—an atmosphere of revolutionary optimism powerfully described by writers like Andre Malraux, who wrote perhaps somewhat floridly, of the "apocalypse of brotherhood." George Orwell, although he arrived some months later, when the grand moment was waning, nonetheless captured the exhilaration of this unique collective experience, when he described Barcelona as the first town where he had ever had the sense "that the working class was in the saddle."

The P.O.U.M. Position

In a revolutionary situation, what perspectives faced the P.O.U.M., a revolutionary party?

Beginning in October 1934, the Bloc—the basic force of the P.O.U.M.—had said the democratic revolution, which the bourgeoisie could not complete, would have to be carried out by the workers, and that the workers then would have to prepare themselves to move from the democratic to the socialist revolution.

Ignacio Iglesias, who had come to the P.O.U.M. from the Trotskyist I.C.E., has described the political continuity of the party in the following terms:

> It was during this period [from fusion to civil war] that the P.O.U.M. laid down the general lines of its policy ... which determined its later attitude during the civil war ... All the political positions of the P.O.U.M. during the civil war may be implicitly found in those that the party adopted during the period from October 1935 to July 1936. This was true to such an extent that the P.O.U.M. did not change its attitudes with respect to the People's Front, the People's Front administrations, the communists, the struggle for socialism, etc.[5]

It was unthinkable, then, that the members of the P.O.U.M., educated in the hope and will to create the socialist revolution, would renounce it when the conditions for it were favorable. Perhaps, if Maurín had been in Barcelona, he would have evaluated the situation differently than the P.O.U.M. members did, and would have said, along with the anarchists, that the taking of power was not desirable, that the P.O.U.M. could not take power alone, and that for these reasons it was necessary to exercise pressure so the civil war might effect the democratic revolution, and nothing more.

But the *poumistes*, or better said, the *bloquistes*, had been brought up with the constant task of influencing the C.N.T., which they considered the great revolutionary force in the country. Only after October 1934 did they decide to organize their own trade union federation and look with less skeptical eyes at the left wing of the socialists, led by Largo Caballero. Perhaps Maurín would have reinforced this change, which had hardly begun. But it is not certain, indeed far from it, that Maurín would have reacted in such a way, because everybody who lived through the weeks at the beginning aof the conflict knew that such a position, in Catalunya, would have left the P.O.U.M. in total isolation.

We emphasize that the P.O.U.M., like all the other working class organizations, vacillated following July 19. But the workers did not vacillate. The P.O.U.M. executive adopted its own policy, which reflected what the rank and file of the party, through the local committees, had done spontaneously, without receiving orders from Barcelona. Nin, Bonet, Arquer, Rovira, etc. did not determine the line of the P.O.U.M.; rather it was the party members themselves, who, with their actions, dictated the line of the executive.

It is worth recalling, fifty years later, some facts that are nowhere in print, but which every P.O.U.M. member knew at that time. The first is that the executive served as a brake, where it could, on the most radical and sharp positions of the local committees, especially those in Barcelona and Lleida and in the party youth organization—in all of which *bloquistes* dominated. The second is that it was the former *bloquistes* that held the most radical positions. Those P.O.U.M. militants who came to the party from the Communist Left—a small minority—held more moderate positions and, above all, were more obsessed with the fear of losing a contact, always precarious, with the C.N.T. We must underscore this point, because many people, historians included, have commented on the supposed 'Trotskyism' of the P.O.U.M., a fallacy brilliantly disposed of by George Orwell, in his classic work on the Spanish Civil War, *Homage to Catalonia*. While it may be argued that some of the former Trotskyists, including Nin, remained Trotskyists in a limited, personal sense, although outside the discipline of and without political loyalty to Trotsky's own movement, they had relatively little influence over the party's line.[6]

What was it that the rank and file dictated to the executive? A reading of the P.O.U.M. press from the first days shows what happened. Proof of the vacillation of the executive is given by the fact that, in place of immediately transforming "La Batalla" into a Castilian-language daily, given that this was the political language of the worker masses throughout Spain, the party began publishing "Avant" as a daily in Catalan, with which it continued until the beginning of August. The executive let itself be dazzled by the attitude of confidence in the P.O.U.M. held by many middle-class groupings, which had not yet discovered that the official Communists of the P.S.U.C. were a more reliable bulwark against the revolutionary impatience of the C.N.T. masses. And the middle class was *catalanista*.

On July 20, the first issue of "Avant" appeared, a single, one-sided sheet printed in headline type. The executive did not yet know, nor did anybody else, what was happening outside Barcelona. "Avant" came out with directives that had nothing revolutionary about them: "Slogans of the moment:

Organization and maintenance of the workers' militias; jailing and immediate trial for the reactionary officers who have joined the rising; unity of action of all the workers for the imposition of these slogans; general strike until the rising is definitively defeated throughout the peninsula."

On July 21, the delegates of all the local committees were called on by radio to meet that evening in the Principal Palace theatre. The F.O.U.S. ordered its unions to enter into contact with those of the C.N.T. and U.G.T. to help set up factory committees, which the workers were creating on their own. "Avant" said, "The revolutionary alliance is the guarantee of victory. The only guarantee of victory is that the revolution not stagnate." It published an announcement on militia enlistment.

On the 23rd, now with eight pages, "Avant" informed its readers of the departure for Saragossa of the first militia columns. There was a call to the clerical employees to return to work, so weekly wages could be paid out. "Let the Generalitat supply cash to the businesses that do not have cash. Control of the banks and transport. Workers' control of production. Pensions for the families of coup victims."

July 24: A list of demands presented by the P.O.U.M. executive committee, still very timid—a 36-hour work week, a 10% increase in salaries of less than 500 pesetas monthly; a 25% cut in rents; wage payments for strike days, unemployment insurance; control of production by the factory committees; division of the properties of the big landlords; revision of the Catalan autonomy statute in a progressive direction; purge of the armed forces and police, and selection of police chiefs and military officers by the rank-and-file soldiers and guards; maintenance of the militias; an immediate trial of the heads of the coup attempt. This program was submitted to the other organizations as a proposed basis for joint action. Its perspectives were indeed modest, for within two days the Generalitat had reduced the workday to seven hours and had cut rents.

The same issue of the daily stated that on Monday, the 20th, Companys, as president of the Generalitat, had invited the P.O.U.M. to take part in the liaison committee of the Left Front (as the electoral People's Front was known in Catalunya) which was conceived of, without doubt, and without saying so publicly, as a counterweight to the C.N.T. The P.O.U.M. delegate declared that participation in the front would not mean losing its independence as a party.

On the 22nd, in a further meeting, Comorera, from the P.S.U.C. and undoubtedly under orders from Gerö, asked the P.O.U.M. to leave if it could not agree to abide by the discipline of the liaison committee. To this argument, the P.O.U.M. replied with a letter:

We are ready to establish contacts in moments of danger. However, we do not believe these contacts have to be transformed into a permanent organic link, and even less can we accept that (the liaison committee) should be converted into a conglomeration of parties that would reduce to nothing the indispensable independence of political organizations, converting itself in fact into a party organization.

Soon, the executive had discovered that in Catalunya nobody called themselves communists, but they had the perspicacity to see that the communists, through the P.S.U.C. and by using Companys (who in these things was ingenuous enough), were trying to apply a tactic that years later they would employ with success while taking over the nations of Eastern Europe, and which the Hungarian communist dictator Matyas Rakosi called the "salami tactic": since the Left Front was already in place, the communists would use it while slicing off and consuming or destroying its constituents, one at a time. Naturally, the communists were convinced they would control the front. The P.O.U.M. spoiled the maneuver and its letter exposed the situation for the benefit of the other parties.

The same July 24, "Avant" announced the departure of a second P.O.U.M. militia column for the front: 1,500 men. And it published a giant headline: "Do not act on your own. Mind the slogans of the Party. Discipline is an element as necessary as courage."

July 30: A manifesto from the F.O.U.S. calling on the workers to struggle for the unity of the two main union federations. Meanwhile, it was necessary to "maintain trade-union cooperation. The F.O.U.S. is ready to defend with energy the rights of its organization." The same day, a conference of delegates from local P.O.U.M. committees was held.

July 31: The P.O.U.M. daily spoke of terrorism and established the distinction between revolutionary and counterrevolutionary terrorism. "The P.O.U.M. is an enemy of individual actions, uncontrolled shootings, robbery, and vandalism. Those who commit such acts dishonor and endanger the revolution. To avoid them we must take extreme measures, without wavering." The headline read: "Dissolution of the permanent army and substitution of the militias for the army."

August 1's headline read: "We must set up a revolutionary tribunal." This was directed against the action of those who were now referred to as the "uncontrolled." Commenting on the new Generalitat administration, headed by Joan Casanoves, "Avant" said, "By its composition, it is a thousand miles from present reality and does not respond, to say the least, to the present stage of our revolution."

It stated that the P.O.U.M. had been invited to enter the Generalitat and had declined, because it was opposed to participating in any government that did not have a clearly proletarian makeup. But it would "aid any progressive people's government. The one that has been set up inspires little confidence. It is further down [in society] that we must concentrate our attentions, from below that new institutions will emerge. Everything done outside the creative action of the masses is artificial and ephemeral. At the top we see ministerial crises; at the bottom, the revolution continues."

It also informed its readers about the efforts of the P.O.U.M. to form a Revolutionary Workers' Alliance. Before July 19, it had held three interviews, without result, with the C.N.T. and with the parties that would make up the P.S.U.C. On July 27, the party's representatives made a new visit to the P.S.U.C., with a proposal for a liaison committee of workers' parties and organizations. At a further meeting, the now-indoctrinated P.S.U.C. members demanded, as a condition for continued negotiation, the entry of the F.O.U.S. into the U.G.T. and a renunciation by the P.O.U.M. of all propaganda work outside Catalunya. Naturally, the P.O.U.M. could not accept.

The same day, "Avant" noted that a public P.O.U.M. meeting had been held the day before, the first by any organization since July 19. At the meeting, it was pointed out that whenever the republic was in danger, the workers had saved it so that afterward the republicans, once their position was secured, could persecute the workers. This must not be repeated. "We have to go forward to a socialist republic of Iberia."

Nin affirmed that the fascist coup had been turned into a working-class insurrection, which was now turning into a socialist revolution. But for victory, power must be taken. Catalunya could not hold back while waiting for the proletariat in the rest of Spain to follow its example. The people had resolved the problems of the democratic revolution. The peasants had seized the land, the workers had destroyed the church and the army, Catalunya had affirmed its identity as a nation. It was necessary now to go on to the socialist revolution. Only with enthusiasm and the unity that could be forged by the socialist revolution alone could the war be won.

The ex-communist and outstanding scholar Franz Borkenau was present at a similar meeting on August 6. He wrote:

> The P.O.U.M. is weak. The speeches were not very interesting. On my way home, a young intellectual from the P.O.U.M., a German refugee with a good Marxist education, explained to me: 'You see, it is quite obvious that neither the Generalitat nor Madrid really want to win; proof of it is the stalemate on the Saragossa front . . . and the hesitations as to the bombardment of Oviedo. They fear the revolution will evolve, with military successes. They will try to make the civil war a failure, in order to prepare a settlement with Franco, at the expense of the workers.' This is not an official P.O.U.M. opinion; it only approximately reproduces the trend of ideas among the P.O.U.M.[7]

The P.O.U.M., like the other main organizations, grew. Some came to it out of desire for an endorsement or a party card. Many came because of the contagious enthusiasm of the moment. Others came because, as we have noted, they thought the P.O.U.M. would come out against C.N.T., a force of which the middle class was enormously fearful. This is easy to understand, given the tension between *cenetistes* and *poumistes*, which had been expressed at times in shots no less than shouts. The C.N.T. could not forget that Nin was a friend of Trotsky, the man who had drowned in blood the anarchical rebellion of the Kronstadt sailors, in 1921, as well as the libertarian movement of the Ukrainian peasants led by Nestor Makhno. But young people, who had discovered the lure of revolution, preferred the theoretical rigor of the P.O.U.M. to the rhetoric of the anarchists, and the P.O.U.M. youth organization also grew.

This growth was manifest in the press. Beginning August 2, "La Batalla," in Castilian, replaced the Catalan journal "Avant" as the party daily, with a press run of 20,000 copies. The J.C.I., the P.O.U.M. youth organization, published "Juventud Comunista," while in Madrid "El Combatiente Rojo" began to appear—both were published in Castilian. "Combat" in Catalan and "Adelante" in Castilian came out in Lleida. "L'Espurna" in Girona, "Front" in Terrassa, and "El Plá de Bagés" in Manresa appeared in Catalan. A bulletin for militia members at the Aragon front, "Alerta," was in Castilian. A publishing house, Editorial Marxista, began issuing pamphlets and books after some months.

August saw the arrival of the first among a legion of foreigners whose participation in the struggle of the P.O.U.M., further examined in Chapter 7 of this work, would, through the power of the pen that many of the foreign volunteers used with skill, record for non-Iberians the truth of the party's role and program. Because the P.O.U.M. was a member of the London Bureau, members of other parties affiliated with the bureau naturally flocked to the party, some as journalists, others as political leaders, to express their solidarity, and still others to fight. These last were especially useful because many of them had served in the First World War, and had a better knowledge of the use of arms than the militiamen. The Hotel Falcón, where they were billeted, was a Babel.

An Italian Trotskyist, Nicola de Bartolomeo, known as Fosco, in Spain since May 1936 and a participant in the July fighting, was charged by the P.O.U.M. with handling the party's relationship with antifascist refugees. A dissident member of the Italian extreme-left Bordighist movement, Enrico Russo, soon became a militia chief. Pavel Thalmann, a Swiss former Comintern functionary, had also come soon after July, following his companion Clara Ensner, came before hoping to compete as a swimmer in the Barcelona antifascist olympics held as a counter to the 1936 Berlin games.

Others included a Hungarian comrade of Bela Kun in that country's short-lived 1919 revolution, Doctor Mina, who stopped at the Falcón on his way to the front. Michel Collinet and his comrade Simone (the ex-wife of the surrealist poet André Breton), from the left-wing socialist group led by Marceau Pivert, were among the first to come from France.

The surrealist poet Benjamin Péret also arrived from France. An Argentine, Hipólito Etchebehere, and his comrade Mika, entered the militias immediately, with Hipólito soon killed in battle. Mika Etchebehere would arrange the arrival in Spain of one of the best-known foreigners, the Austrian ex-Communist Kurt Landau, who came with his wife Katia (Julia). From the Anglo-Saxon world came Mary Low, born in England, and a Trotskyist sympathetic to the P.O.U.M., in the company of an energetic Cuban Trotskyist, Juan Breá.

Lois Cusick, an American woman, and her husband Charles Orr, arrived from the United States. A few months afterward, they were followed by a former Comintern operative turned Trotskyist, Russell Blackwell, who spoke perfect Spanish and used the name Rosalio Negrete; Negrete, curiously enough, would arrange for the return to Barcelona of a Catalan member of the Bloc, Josep Escuder, who had gone to New York, where he became well-known in the world of that city's metropolitan daily journalism in the earlier part of the decade, and who had resumed his New York residence after a short visit to Barcelona late in 1935. Escuder would take over the management of "La Batalla."

Marcel Ollivier, a French proofreader, an Italian who used the name Martini and who later became a parliamentary deputy in his country, and many more found lodging in the Falcón. Leaders who visited from abroad included Henrik Sneevliet, a founder of the Comintern and workers' leader in Indonesia and the Netherlands, who would be executed by the Nazis in 1942 (and honored as a national hero in Holland); John McNair and Fenner Brockway of the Independent Labour Party in Britain; Heinrich Brandler, one of the founding leaders of German Communism, expelled as a rightist, and Bertram D. Wolfe from the similarly "rightist" Communist Opposition led by Jay Lovestone in the United States.

Among the younger foreigners were Willi Brandt, decades afterward prime minister of West Germany, and Bob Edwards, a young British trade unionist who later became known as a national union leader and Labour member of the British House of Commons. But the foreign volunteer whose fame would prove most lasting was Eric Blair, the young English writer who used the name George Orwell. Although he arrived relatively late, in December, he would come to profoundly grasp and faithfully express the ideals and aspirations of the P.O.U.M.

None of these foreigners carried any weight in the development of the P.O.U.M.'s political line, although Landau was a valued collaborator. In reality, the P.O.U.M. exercised a determining influence on the other parties of the London Bureau, through its press and its reports.

When the foreigners arrived, the situation had already polarized in such a way that little room for maneuver was left. It was the official Communists who took responsibility for provoking this polarization.

Two Opposite Strategies

Maurín, years later, noted that a revolutionary movement may enjoy great impact on its epoch either because of its mission, its history, its successes, its influence in the trade unions and with intellectuals, its numerical strength, its parliamentary activity, or its leaders. The civil war surprised the official Communists at a moment in their history that Maurín went on to characterize as follows:

> This is what the Communist Party was in the middle of July 1936: 1) Mission: To convert Spain into a Russian dependency; 2) History: lamentable and negative; 3) Successes: none, except for the People's Front, which was a purely electoral one; 4) Trade union influence: Nil. The C.G.T.U. was a complete failure, and, to camouflage its burial, the party claimed that it fused with the U.G.T.; 5) Influence among intellectuals: Nil; 6) Proportional strength in the working class: 2.5%; 7) Parliamentary representation: 16 deputies out of a total of 452, or 3.5%. Under an electoral system based on proportional representation, the number of its deputies should have been 1; 8) Leaders: Humbert-Droz (Swiss), Codovilla (Argentine), Rabaté (French), Stepanov (Bulgarian) . . . Otherwise, nothing. A little later, José Díaz, Dolores Ibárruri, and others.

> Until July 17, 1936, the Communist Party of Spain was more fictional than anything else. And the major proof of this is that Sevilla, which was the communist *fortress* par excellence—'*Red* Sevilla,' as the communists themselves said, was taken by General Queipo de Llano without any great difficulty. Where were they and what did they do, the communist warrior hosts of '*Red* Sevilla' on July 18-19, 1936? The socialists saved Madrid and Bilbao; the anarchosyndicalists and the P.O.U.M., did the same in Barcelona; the socialists and the trade unionists together saved Valencia. The fifth city in Spain, in rank of importance, after Madrid, Barcelona, Valencia, and Bilbao, is Sevilla, which the Communists lost to the coup.[8]

In the first days following the military uprising, the communists kept quiet. They did not know what position to adopt. They had no influence in the street and contented themselves with capitalizing on the situation to reinforce their ranks—something they were able to do above all in Madrid, where they set up the "Fifth Regiment," a politicized military body that functioned as a police and Soviet espionage agency in the republican regime.[9]

The official party's intellectuals, headed by the poet Rafael Alberti (a good man gone wrong) and with the support of the Catholic writer José Bergamín (a bad man gone worse), set up writers' organizations and began publishing "El Mono Azul," ("Blue Overalls"). They spoke of saving democracy, but they adopted positions that were unclear.

In Catalunya, the P.S.U.C. also suffered confusion, occupied as it was with organizing itself and bringing in new elements. But at the beginning of August, orders had already come from Moscow, along with more Comintern agents, who installed themselves in Madrid and Barcelona. It was then that one began to discern the role the official party hoped to play in the situation: To convert itself into the party of order, and avoid, if possible, the consolidation of the gains already achieved by the people themselves and the indigenous revolutionary organizations, with the overall goal of infiltrating, capturing, and exercising a one-party dictatorship over the republic. An important element in this situation was the failure of many critics of the communists to understand the motivations that threw them into alliance with the bourgeoisie; not concern for the preservation of capitalist democracy, but interest in assuring that capitalist democracy should be guarded against working-class democracy until the moment could come when democracy could be abolished altogether, or replaced by "Soviet democracy." Obviously, the communist "revolution" in the interest of a totalitarian party-state would, in the end, find easier adversaries among the old bourgeois politicians, in the ultimate sharing out of power, than in the combative ranks of the anarchosyndicalists, socialists, and P.O.U.M. However, many anti-Stalinists at the time did not clearly see this Muscovite goal and simply attacked the communists as "traitors" allied with the bourgeoisie. This perception was partially supported by clear indications that Moscow's final concern in Spain was to assure France, its ally by treaty since 1935, and Britain, its probable ally in a war with Germany, alarmed at the events in Spain, should not be allowed to blame the Spanish revolution on Moscow and the Communists. But to gain the control essential for such a "pacification," a communist dictatorship was necessary. Thus a complicated game of camouflage came into being.

Further, there was no worker constituency available to the communists, since the workers were practically all already organized, some in the C.N.T., others in the U.G.T. (where the communists, for the moment, enjoyed very little influence), others in the Socialist Party, and still others in the P.O.U.M. But there were two kinds of people to be found, adrift and available: the republican middle class, which had lost confidence in the parties that permitted the outbreak of the military coup, and people who sympathized with the Right and who now found themselves without a party, undefended, demoralized, and frightened.

The communists sought to serve as a shelter for these centrists and rightists who were now without leadership. The Catalan U.G.T., controlled by the P.S.U.C., and which at the beginning of the civil war had fewer members than the F.O.U.S., admitted the Associations and Entities of Small Merchants and Industrialists (Gremis i Entitats de Petits Comerçants e Industrials—G.E.P.C.I.), mostly as a trade association of small shopkeepers, which had 18,000 members. Cells of the P.S.U.C. soon swelled with people who had been able to find no other refuge and who could not obtain a card from the other parties and unions. It also attracted some moderate intellectuals, who could not see themselves in the C.N.T. and who held the Esquerra in contempt as vulgar. The U.G.T. used them to set up a union of artists and writers that produced a vast quantity of P.S.U.C. propaganda, of which the best-known items are their posters.

None of this happened either by chance or because the P.S.U.C. or the official Communist Party of Spain openly courted these masses in political widowhood. The political positions of the party forced these masses through the door the communists held open.

On August 8, 1936, one of the communist leaders, Jesús Hernández declared, "We cannot speak of proletarian revolution in Spain, because the historical conditions do not permit it . . . we want to defend small-scale industry, which finds itself under pressures as bad or worse than those of the workers."

José Díaz, general secretary of the official party, affirmed "We only desire to struggle for a democratic republic, with a broad social content. We cannot speak now of either the dictatorship of the proletariat or of socialism, but only of democracy in struggle against fascism." Nothing, then, about Revolutionary Workers' Alliances, but only the submission of all to the People's Front.

By mid-August, there was no longer room for doubt: the republican zone had divided into two great camps: that of those whose slogans counterposed fascism and the republic (the communists, the republicans, and the right wing socialists), and those who opposed fascism with social revolution (the C.N.T., F.A.I., P.O.U.M., and Left Socialists).

At the moment of Spain's deepest revolutionary crisis, the confrontation in Catalunya worked a transformation not only on the communists, but on the P.O.U.M. as well. During the movement for a Catalan Republic in 1934, the Bloc had allied closely with the Esquerra and the Generalitat, a bourgeois regime, in a situation where the worker masses of the C.N.T. maintained an attitude of opposition to which the Esquerra, in the subsequent period, reacted with repression.

As we have noted, the P.O.U.M. in the first days after July 1936 pursued a seeming policy of *Catalanisme* and attracted some people who saw in the party a bulwark against the C.N.T. The anger of the *cenetistes* at the memory of their recent treatment at the hands of the Esquerra certainly contributed to the polarization between the republican and revolutionary camps. Had the P.O.U.M. been the kind of opportunist party it was labeled by, notably, Trotsky and his followers, it might have maintained its links with the Esquerra and acted against the C.N.T. But the P.O.U.M. looked to the future of the revolution, rather than the past of its participation in the Catalan Republic movement of 1934. It sided firmly with the C.N.T., its former competitor and even its former adversary, on the platform of proletarian solidarity, rather than with its friends in the Generalitat, on the platform of Catalan nationalism.

But if the republican Right was aggressive, the Left was hesitant. The Left Socialists had no concrete program. The C.N.T. tried to make revolution without seizing power; the P.O.U.M. found no way to get closer to the Left Socialists, with whom they had only sporadic contact through certain top leaders, nor with the C.N.T., which considered the P.O.U.M. to be Marxist, naturally, and which for that reason saw it as an opponent.

It should be emphasized that the C.N.T. did not lack for responsibilities in the polarization against the P.O.U.M.. It was in the trade union arena that the anarchists contributed to it most decisively. Although the C.N.T. remained weak outside Barcelona city, the small C.N.T. affiliated unions in the Catalan provinces grew in the wake of July 19. This added to the impression that the F.O.U.S., the P.O.U.M. union federation, was superfluous, although the F.O.U.S. continued to dominate union activity in Lleida and Girona and had considerable strength in Tarragona.

At the same time, the Catalan U.G.T. was now organizing local unions, supported by the resources of the official Communist network, in places the U.G.T. had never before existed. The anarchist press began stating that the P.O.U.M. unions, being Marxist, should join the U.G.T., with the libertarian organizations remaining within the C.N.T. and opposing any union remaining outside the two main federations. In putting the problem thusly, the C.N.T. helped the communists.

The C.N.T., then, forced the F.O.U.S. into the U.G.T. The F.O.U.S. secretariat proposed to its corresponding U.G.T. body a collective entry into the latter, when, as previously noted, the F.O.U.S. had more members than the Catalan U.G.T., but it was also plain to see that the U.G.T. was growing speedily. For the P.O.U.M., an entry into the U.G.T. also presented the possibility of gaining influence within it and even of conquering it and taking it out of communist hands. But the leaders of the Catalan U.G.T., all members of the P.S.U.C., were late to reply, because they thought, correctly, that the F.O.U.S. would lose influence, and, in any case, could not grow, thanks to the C.N.T.'s refusal to acknowledge its existence.

On August 10, 1936, the Generalitat published a decree establishing obligatory trade union membership. The following day, a C.N.T.-U.G.T. liaison committee was set up, without the F.O.U.S. The F.O.U.S. remained condemned to disappear. Thanks to the sectarian attitude of the anarchists, the P.S.U.C. had won the battle. And the F.O.U.S. adopted the only possible decision in such circumstances: it ordered its unions to join the U.G.T., since, labeled as Marxists, they would not be allowed into the C.N.T. Thus, the F.O.U.S. unions found themselves, for the moment, led locally by the P.O.U.M., but under the overall control of a Catalan leadership in communist hands. Little by little, the local P.O.U.M. leaders were eliminated through bureaucratic maneuvers. The P.O.U.M. found itself, then, two months after the beginning of the revolution, without a base in the unions. The party had undergone a disastrous repetition of the experience at the beginning of the year, which had convinced the P.O.U.M. to set up its own union federation: that of the impossibility of acting within the C.N.T. thanks to anarchist sectarianism.[10]

In the countryside, similar events took place. The P.O.U.M. had strength among the peasants of Lleida and Girona, and the Esquerra among the *rabassaires* of Barcelona province and Tarragona. To maintain its influence, the Unió de Rabassaires set up the Federation of Agricultural Trade Unions of Catalunya (Federació de Sindicats Agrícoles de Catalunya). The C.N.T., which had never organized farm workers in Catalunya, created a Union of Agricultural Trade Unions of Catalunya (Unió de Sindicats Agrícoles de Catalunya). The P.O.U.M. unions and those of the former U.S.C. fused in a Union of Peasant Trade Unions (Unió de Sindicats Camperols), which joined the U.G.T. and from whose leadership the P.S.U.C. members quickly eliminated the *poumistes*. The P.O.U.M., in this way, also lost its base among the peasantry.

Notwithstanding all these problems, the P.O.U.M. membership viewed the situation optimistically. Compared with the march of events in Russia, as seen through a Bolshevik glass, the Catalan situation seemed superior. On September 6, in a meeting, Nin declared "the July 19 rebellion provoked a proletarian revolution more profound than the Russian revolution." And Wilebaldo Solano, a P.O.U.M. youth leader, later recalled that Nin "was surprised that in the early days after July everything continued functioning. It seemed incredible to him, remembering what he had seen in Russia, that trains, streetcars, factories continued working. This indicated, he believed, a greater level of political maturity in the Catalan and Spanish proletariat."[11]

Even Trotsky, in his later book *The Lessons of Spain: The Last Warning*, and notwithstanding his general ignorance of the Spanish situation, was aware of this, and wrote, "In its specific gravity in the country's economic life, in political and cultural level, the Spanish proletariat found itself, not below, but above the Russian proletariat at the beginning of 1917."[12]

It was not only thanks to individual initiative that everything worked, but also the coordinated wishes of the workers that things should go better, rather than orders from new "rulers." This was manifested in the Committee for Militias. Already on July 25, "Avant" said the committee was a "second power today; the only, revolutionary power, tomorrow."

In the same September 6 meeting, Nin explained how the P.O.U.M. saw the workers' power: "the dictatorship of the proletariat is the workers' dictatorship as exercised by the entire laboring class, without any exception." And he said to the C.N.T.: "We are going forward to the installation of this workers' democracy. Here and away from here our party is ready to struggle with the comrades of the C.N.T. and with the entire working class against any attempt to convert the dictatorship of the proletariat into a party dictatorship or a personal dictatorship. The dictatorship of the proletariat now exists, in fact, in Catalunya. The F.A.I. said in a manifesto that it opposes the dictatorship of any party. We are in agreement with this. The dictatorship cannot be exercised by one or another sector of the working class, but by everybody together."[13]

As we have seen, during August the position of the P.O.U.M. was clarified. It was clear that fascism was growing in Europe, that the countries that could aid the republic were not socialist, but capitalist, that the People's Front, victorious in France and with a government under the presidency of Léon Blum, showed itself to be little ready to give aid, and that none of this offered favorable perspectives for a revolutionary victory. But the *poumistes* sought to apply in this situation the position they defended from the period before October 1934 and that Maurín had set out in writing many times: the need to pass from a bourgeois democratic to a socialist revolution. In many places, the *poumistes* were the local power or formed part of it; what they had dreamed of, without finally believing it was possible, was now within reach. They did not want to miss the opportunity. The executive could do nothing but reflect this sentiment on the part of the rank and file.

The Moscow Trials

One question on which the ranks of the P.O.U.M. were undivided was that of the Moscow trials. From August 19 to 23, 1936, in the House of Trade Unions in the Soviet capital, court was in session, with Lev Kamenev, Grigory Zinovyev, and other comrades of Lenin accused as fascist agents. Nin had known some of the accused during his Profintern work ten or more years before. Obviously, he believed neither the accusations nor the bizarre confessions that were delivered in court.

The "witch trials" in Moscow, as the Austrian socialist Friedrich Adler called them, elicited condemnation from around the world, but in general it may be said that the reaction was slight, compared with the crime. The "blackmail" of the international labor movement by the People's Front functioned well, and many kept silent for fear of "harming antifascist unity," as if such unity was not threatened by the trials themselves. The P.O.U.M. did not fall into this trap. The executive explained to the militants the sense of the trials: the desire of Stalin to eliminate any possible rival and, at the same time, to present to the Russian people scapegoats for the errors of the regime.

The first trial was barely covered by the Spanish and Catalan communist press. The republican and C.N.T. publications published the news but added no comments. "La Batalla," by contrast, explained the trials at length, and the rest of the P.O.U.M. press did the same, not because of a decision of the executive, but because of the local committees, which controlled the party publications. The local committees decided to speak out on the trials, because they saw in them the best way to convey to the people what the P.S.U.C., which continued to grow, could one day do. In addition, the *poumistes* knew the real history of the Russian revolution and refused to accept that Lenin's comrades could have become fascists. There was no way to escape reacting.

On August 27, news came of the execution of Kamenev, Zinovyev, and other old Bolsheviks. The editorial in "La Batalla" said at that time: "We are revolutionary socialists, Marxists. In the name of socialism and the revolutionary working class, we protest against the monstrous crime that has just been perpetrated in Moscow."

And since the trials had come to turn on Trotsky's figure, the editorial went on to say: "Trotsky is for us, along with Lenin, one of the great figures of the October revolution and a great revolutionary socialist writer. Insulted, persecuted, we express our solidarity with him, without hiding, at the same time, our disagreement with some of his opinions."

It was in the face of this reaction by the P.O.U.M. that the P.S.U.C. press began discussing the first Moscow trial. The P.S.U.C. journalists, almost all of them coming from bourgeois parties and newspapers, who felt no personal solidarity with the victims, followed orders.

It fell to the P.O.U.M., which faced a very difficult situation, to have the honor of having been the first workers' organization apart from the Austrian socialists, to react in the face of the Moscow trials and to refuse to accept the blackmail of "antifascist unity" to cover up the crime. Among the first and the few in the world, in Spain they were alone. The C.N.T., the socialists, and the republicans did not comprehend the significance of what was happening in Moscow, published little and said less. The C.N.T., which should have seen a warning in the trials, treated them as a family quarrel.

If there were no differences among the P.O.U.M. membership regarding this affair, the same could not be said for its international allies, including those in the London Bureau. Those who made the greatest efforts to persuade the P.O.U.M. not to criticize the trials were the Germans, particularly the "communist rightist" Brandler, and the S.A.P. youth leader Willi Brandt. They convinced nobody in Barcelona.

Other foreigners, with a very different mission, were in Barcelona at the same time: Palmiro Togliatti, whom Nin had met during the latter's travels in Italy for the Profintern in the 1920s; Stoyan Minev (Stepanov), with whom Nin had organized a conference in Moscow of Latin American communist parties and who had participated in the Trotskyist movement in Russia; and another former Trotskyist and comrade of Nin in Russia, Vladimir A. Antonov-Ovseyenko, Soviet consul in the Catalan capital. Although Nin knew Antonov, the diplomat affected not to recognize him when they met at public functions. Nin, for his part, took advantage of Antonov's clouded past: he found and translated a pamphlet by Antonov, in which the latter argued that worker militias are a more effective fighting force than regular armies; Editorial Marxista published it just when the communists were defending the need to transform the militias into a regular army.

State or Committees?

There were more pressing problems to worry about than these unwelcome guests. Who must control the economy? The C.N.T. wanted it to be the trade unions, which had already begun coordinating the factory councils. But as in the case of the Committee for Militias, where there were representatives of other, nonunion organizations, the committee took the initiative, on August 11, of forming a Council on Economy, in which the same organizations that made up the Committee for Militias were represented.

This seemed to be a victory of the Militias over the Generalitat and would have been so, had the committee dared to become a government. But the C.N.T. still feared the word "government," and the P.S.U.C. insisted that the committee limit itself to military questions; for the rest, they said, the Generalitat suffices. And the masses became accustomed, little by little, to again accepting the Generalitat as the government.

"La Batalla" greeted the creation of the Council on Economy with enthusiasm. It had already signaled the danger of creating a "trade union capitalism, even with, as it noted, the factory councils functioning: 'We have avoided disorder, and the upheavals of disorganization, in a word, all this revolutionary chaos that until today was considered inherent in great social convulsions.'"

Proof of the importance the P.O.U.M. gave to the Council on Economy was that its delegate to the council was no less than Nin himself. But the individual who actually took charge of this work was J. Oltra Pico, from the factory city of Sabadell. After commanding a militia column on the Aragon front, he went on to organize a technical advisory staff for the P.O.U.M. to help those who had to occupy themselves with the economic affairs of the towns, factory committees, and unions.

In September, an important step was taken toward "normalization"—meaning, of course, a return to a prerevolutionary situation. Companys, now over the terror he felt on July 19, forgot what he had told the anarchists at that time. They had left him in his position as Generalitat president, and it was logical for him to wish to preside over something more than a title. To preside over a government made up of republicans, as he did between July 19 and September, meant not much more; indeed, even to preside over a government of the Esquerra and the P.S.U.C. was, at that time, to turn one's back on reality.

Companys was an excellent politician and knew the anarchists very well; he did not like the idea of remaining a prisoner of the P.S.U.C. while the C.N.T. dominated the Committee for Militias, which was outside the game he was trying to direct. For this reason, at the beginning of September, he launched the idea of forming a Generalitat administration based on the organizations in the Committee for Militias and substituting its authority for that of the latter. The Council on Economy would become an institution of the Generalitat, and with it the weapons and factories now controlled by the unions would come under the Generalitat's control.

For the anarchists, this involved, above all, a question of principle: how could they, as anarchists, participate in a government? Antifascist unity and the war finally convinced them. The C.N.T. took an important step: it chose to enter. Diego Abad de Santillán, the main theoretician of the F.A.I., dissented, calling for "strengthening the Committee for Militias . . . its security was in its power, which was that of all the people . . . In this interpretation I found myself isolated and opposed by my friends and comrades," Abad de Santillán wrote.[14]

For the P.O.U.M., the question was not one of principle, as far as government per se was concerned. As a Marxist party, it believed in the necessity of taking power. But would entry into a Generalitat administration be the same as taking power? Could it be considered a revolutionary power, once the C.N.T. and the P.O.U.M. entered it?

When the negotiations reached a certain point, the P.O.U.M. executive took up the question of entry into the Generalitat and accepted it, with two votes against. The executive then called a meeting of the central committee, composed of the members elected at the meeting at which the party was set up, but with others co-opted to substitute for those who had fallen in the struggle or who were now at the front. Its members remained in permanent contact with the rank and file. War had not slowed down the democratic mechanisms of the party. It was the only party in Catalunya for which this was true. The P.S.U.C. simply followed the orders of its leaders. The C.N.T. followed the directions of the F.A.I., and the meetings of its unions, in truth, were only attended by the longstanding activists.

The P.O.U.M. central committee accepted entry into the Generalitat administration. Some pointed out that a *conseller* named by the P.O.U.M. would have to enforce bourgeois laws. But when they saw that this point of view found few supporters, they suggested that, at least, a militant of the second rank should be named as the party's *conseller*, to express the lukewarm position of the party regarding the Generalitat. Almost nobody supported that argument, however. What convinced the central committee was fear that if the party refused it would find itself isolated, because the masses would not understand why, with the C.N.T. having entered the government, the P.O.U.M. would not do the same, and the C.N.T. would interpret the action of the P.O.U.M. as an implicit criticism, which would make it more difficult to expand the P.O.U.M.'s influence over the C.N.T. Further, should the P.O.U.M. refuse, such an act would neither save the Committee for Militias nor avoid the formation of a new Generalitat administration. It simply would have kept the P.O.U.M. on the margin.

How to present this new P.O.U.M. position to the masses? By saying that "the new government will have a working class majority" (and to accept this one would have to agree that the P.S.U.C. was a workers' party, something very doubtful from an objective point of view) "but with some representatives of the petty bourgeoisie."

"La Batalla" affirmed that the new government represented "an original, and not long-lasting, kind of revolutionary transition, which will be surpassed by the total seizure of power by the working-class organizations." "Juventud Comunista," the organ of the P.O.U.M. youth, which did not view the situation very enthusiastically, nonetheless explained it with greater sincerity: "Our party has agreed to enter the Generalitat because it has not wanted to go against the stream in this extremely grave moment and because it considers that the socialist revolution can be pushed ahead through the Generalitat."

The real question was not whether it was correct to enter the Generalitat administration, but whether this should replace or be replaced by the Committee for Militias as an organ of working-class power. But with nobody outside the P.O.U.M. viewing the problem in these terms, the P.O.U.M. had no recourse but to accept the false dilemma of entry or nonentry. Once it was accepted, the answer, for the reasons we have explained, had to be what it was. It should be noted that Trotsky accused the party of "entering a bourgeois government that had as its aim to destroy all the conquests, all the points of support for the nascent socialist revolution."

The P.O.U.M. central committee, in its resolution ("La Batalla," September 18, 1936), affirmed that the government must be made up only of workers' parties and trade union federations, but added:

> "If this point of view is not shared by the other organizations, we are ready to leave this question in suspense, above all because the Esquerra has a profoundly popular nature, with the peasant masses and working class sectors that support it unmistakably evolving toward revolution. The important thing is the program and the hegemony of the proletariat, which must be guaranteed. The new government must declare that it seeks to transform the impulses of the masses into revolutionary legality leading toward socialist revolution. With regard to the hegemony of the proletariat, the majority that is enjoyed by the working-class representatives will make it certain."

The negotiations continued. Nin participated for the P.O.U.M. On September 25, he informed the executive that the agreement had been signed. La Batalla, reporting on the new administration, declared,

> We are in a transitory situation, in which the force of events has obliged us to collaborate directly in the Generalitat council alongside the other revolutionary organizations. But the direct representation of the proletariat must come from the workers' committees.

The new Generalitat administration was made up of three members from the Esquerra, including the chief *conseller* and head of the cabinet; three from the C.N.T.; and one each from the P.O.U.M., the P.S.U.C., the U.G.T., and the Unió de Rabassaires, plus a military officer as *conseller* for defense. The C.N.T. representatives were all of the second rank in their organization. Those from the other parties were much more prominent figures.

The following are the most important points in the declaration of principles of the new Generalitat government:

> ... The immediate program of the council is as follows:
>
> a) Concentration of the maximum effort for the war, not sparing a single measure that can contribute to its rapid and victorious end. A unified com-

mand, coordination of all fighting units, creation of drafted militias and strengthening of discipline.

b) Economic reconstruction of the country, to which end the program of the Council on Economy created by decree the past August 11, which specifies the following, must be immediately applied:

1. Regularization of production in accord with the needs of consumption.

2. Control of foreign trade.

3. Collectivization of large scale rural properties and respect for small agrarian land ownership.

4. The partial devaluation of urban properties through cutting of rents or establishment of corresponding taxes when it is not suitable to aid tenants.

5. Collectivization of heavy industry, the public services, and transportation.

6. Seizure and collectivization of properties abandoned by their owners.

7. Support for organization of cooperatives in the distribution of consumer goods and, in particular, the development of cooperatives on the premises of large stores.

8. Control of banking activities including nationalization of banks.

9. Workers' control in private industries.

10. Active reabsorption by agriculture and industry of the unemployed, a return to the countryside of workers that can be absorbed by the new organization of agricultural work, creation of new industries, complete electrification of Catalunya, etc.

11. The rapid suppression of the different indirect taxes, as quickly and to the extent possible.

c) Elevation of popular culture, in all its many aspects, under the sign of the New Unified School (Escola Nova Unificada—E.N.U.) which will make it possible that, in addition to the privileges available before now, every gifted child will be able to go on from primary school through secondary studies, with support for all cultural manifestations . . .

The council declares that it will respect and aid the efforts of the productive Catalan trades, and, directing itself particularly to the peasantry, it declares that their work will be supported, and they have no reason to fear for the plot of land they own and cultivate with the sweat of their brows, that the new order of things will respect the fruits of their labor, while it will mercilessly attack the latifundium through expropriation of the big landlords who are enemies of the regime, and will annul all the duties and services which now weigh on the rural population.

Nin in the Generalitat

On September 8, Nin declared that in Catalunya the dictatorship of the proletariat already virtually existed. On September 27, "La Batalla" demanded that power devolve to the workers' committees. On October 9, the Generalitat dissolved the committees. These three dates indicate the psychological and political problems the P.O.U.M. had to deal with.

Andreu Nin was named *conseller* of justice in the new administration. Nin found himself practically alone in the government. The three C.N.T. representatives, who voted with him many times, were not strong personalities and often let themselves be held back by a desire for "respectability." In any case, Nin and the three C.N.T. members were almost always in a minority and thus had to give tacit approval, with their presence, to measures of which they disapproved.

In the *Conselleria* of Justice Nin carried out many good works: He broadened the scope of the people's tribunals, adding to their jurisdiction military crimes of a political character; he also reorganized the people's tribunals, particularly in Barcelona where a gang of lawyers created all kinds of problems under revolutionary pretexts. Nin gave the people's tribunals a new structure (a president and a career prosecutor along with a judge for each of the revolutionary organizations and parties). He created a judicial body to examine death sentences and to propose, where appropriate, their commutation to the Generalitat president (who thus was provided with a prerogative that had previously been exclusive to the Presidency of the Spanish Republic); he established eighteen years as the age of adulthood, and he formulated very simple rules for adoption, with the goal of facilitating such relationships for war orphans. He also legalized marriage services performed before union officials and militia leaders.

But the P.O.U.M. had not entered the Generalitat to concern itself with the minutiae of judicial reform, no matter how progressive, but to bring about the adoption of measures that would widen the revolution and, with it, bring victory in the war. On this terrain, the government was not what the *poumistes*, admittedly without much optimism, had hoped it would be.

The first public ceremony of the new government involved an act of political juggling: a reception for the first Soviet consul there had ever been in Barcelona, Vladimir Alyeksyeyevich Antonov-Ovsyeyenko. Nin, who spoke Russian, was given the task of delivering a short welcoming speech. Antonov, as previously noted, acted as if he had never seen Nin before.

A few days later, the Soviet consul visited the C.N.T. leaders: "I remember that poor Antonov began his relations with us saying that Stalin was deeply disgusted by the presence of Nin in the Generalitat," recalled Abad de Santillán in a letter from Buenos Aires to Víctor Alba, dated January 19, 1972. "This alone was enough for us to want to demonstrate in every way our friendship with [Nin]," Abad de Santillán added.

His reference to "poor Antonov" recalls the fact that the consul was recalled to Moscow in 1937 and executed, along with the first Soviet ambassador to Spain, Marcel Rosenberg.

But the sympathy of the C.N.T. for Nin was sterile; the government of the Generalitat, which was supposed to be proletarian, was, in reality, petty bourgeois. To call the P.S.U.C. a workers' party was only a rhetorical exercise. The C.N.T. *consellers* and Nin proposed, for example, a Catalan government monopoly on foreign trade. The P.S.U.C. was opposed and the Esquerra as well voted against it. The Generalitat remained, therefore, without its only possible source of foreign exchange.

The C.N.T. *consellers* and Nin were united on another important question. They proposed a law legalizing the collectivizations that gave the unions fundamental economic functions. The P.S.U.C. proposed a counterdraft that in fact put the collectivized entities under the control of the state and left the door open so that, in the future, the former owners could recover their enterprises and be indemnified.

The C.N.T. representatives and Nin, to avoid the adoption of this cynical product of P.S.U.C. maneuvering, threatened to quit the administration if it was even discussed. In its final, approved form, a draft proposed by the Esquerra was adopted, in which the C.N.T. *consellers* and Nin obtained the elimination of indemnification of former owners; but they did not succeed in adding a clause that would have established fifty employees as the minimum number for an enterprise to be legally collectivized. The adopted draft set the limit for collectivization at 100, although businesses with fewer employees were still subject to workers' control.

This was not an ideal law, because it reduced the independence of the collectivized enterprises and the trade union involvement in the economy. Nevertheless, the law counted some advances: it established the collectivization of all enterprises that had more than 100 employees, while until then only those enterprises whose owners were absent were collectivized. It also established control over the banks (although not their nationalization, which the P.O.U.M. proposed). On the other hand, it established that an intervenor from the Generalitat should be appointed for each business, and it accepted indemnization in principle (although only for foreign citizens.) As a complement to this law, the C.N.T. and P.O.U.M. proposed the setting up of a bank that would provide credit for the collectivized enterprises, but the Generalitat majority voted for the establishment of a savings bank that would tie the collectivized enterprises to the Generalitat, and this at the expense of the enterprises themselves, which would be obliged to put up the bank's capital.

Two weeks after its formation, the new government agreed, on October 9, to dissolve the people's committees and to bring back the former municipal administrations, without the members elected before July 19 but with representatives of the parties and unions in their places: three delegates for each organization for each representative of the organization in the Generalitat; the P.O.U.M. thus received three representatives in each town hall, independently of the strength it had in the locality.

The people's committees had the same relationship to the town halls that the Committee for Militias had to the Generalitat. Once it was accepted that power should pass from the Committee for Militias to the government, no argument could be made that the same should not be done with the other committees.

But the ranks of the P.O.U.M. did not resign themselves to this situation. They were the main force in some places and they could see coming a time when they would find themselves converted into a minority in every town hall. The C.N.T., by contrast, accepted the change because it gave them a strength in the towns that they had never had outside the city of Barcelona. The *poumistes* in Lleida, the majority force in the province, protested to the party executive. They had already been warned that if the P.O.U.M. entered the Generalitat they would have to accept such measures; indeed, such measures would have had to be accepted whether the P.O.U.M. was in the government or not.

Nin accepted responsibility for settling the situation in Lleida and went there with a government commission to convince the Lleida P.O.U.M. to accept the decree. They received the delegation weapons in hand, but when they found Nin among the group, they accepted party discipline and agreed to the division of power. This was, unquestionably, a low point for the party.

On November 16, with all resistance now vanquished—and there had not been much—the Generalitat decreed the suppression of three thousand official posts in committees, people's tribunals, commissions, etc., the majority of them held by workers. The structure of working-class power was, thus, eliminated.

The Activity of Party Members

Aside from a half dozen militants who worked with Nin in the *Conselleria* of Justice, the *poumistes* had no official relationship with the Generalitat. There were other fields of action that better fitted their manner of being. While Nin attended meetings of the government council and worked on decrees, the rank and file of the party went to meetings of the Council on Economy, the factory control committees, the town halls, and at the front where they were fighting. The real history of the P.O.U.M. comes from the activities there, rather than in the Generalitat.

The P.O.U.M. had grown, but in a lesser proportion than the other organizations, because, as happened with the Bloc in 1931, it could neither offer protection nor satisfy ambitions, being a minority. By spring of the following year the P.S.U.C. had reached 42,000 members and the official Communist party had enlisted 200,000 affiliates throughout the Republican zone, but already in October 1936 the P.O.U.M. had risen to 40,000. Apparently the respective forces were roughly balanced, although the P.S.U.C. could also call on the ranks of the Catalan U.G.T., which it controlled, while the P.O.U.M., as we have seen, lost its trade union base.

The P.O.U.M.'s activities branched out. For example, groups for Marxist education were set up for new members. In the Virreina Palace, in the middle Rambles, the war wounded worked cataloguing books under the direction of Joaquím Maurín's brother Julià (Julián) and made plans for a museum of the revolution, all under the umbrella of a Maurín Institute. The women's section organized courses in childcare, nursing, and military instruction, the latter of particular significance since the Spanish revolution and civil war was the first modern conflict in which large numbers of women played an active role as combatants. The P.O.U.M. Red Aid (Socors Roig) created an information service on wounds and first aid at the front and established a tuberculosis sanatorium in a requisitioned castle in the Pyrenean town of Alp. Like the other organizations, the P.O.U.M. had a radio station in Barcelona and one in Madrid, with foreign language services in which many foreign volunteers worked. But there were suspicions that the radio broadcasts had little effect.

The P.O.U.M. exercised influence in some organizations that could be considered marginal. For example, they played a major role in the cooperative movement, which they tried to radicalize. There were also prominent P.O.U.M. members in the directing committee of the New Unified School (E.N.U.), where they worked, at times in collaboration and at times in rivalry, with the C.N.T., to oppose communist infiltration in the schools.

Although responsible posts were taken by militants from the period before July 19, in all these activities members who had joined after that date also participated. Very little friction between the old and new militants seems to have existed.

The P.O.U.M. had no time to carry out an effective municipal policy. The city halls saw themselves limited to immediate problems—which were often considerable—because the war and the scarcity of the work force and of materials, did not permit them to undertake public works, build more schools, do away with the difference between working class and bourgeois neighborhoods, and socially homogenize the city districts so that all of those inhabited by workers would be well equipped for services and comfortable residentially.

It was possible to take a decisive step forward in only one area: that of housing. Many apartments remained abandoned, and many rental properties no longer had landlords, who had fled. Many whole buildings, the famous "torres" of Barcelona, were requisitioned. This not only allowed the workers' organizations to install themselves in much larger quarters, but also to find new places to live for slum-dwellers—who for the first time lived in comfortable sites—and, later, to help the refugees who came by the thousands to the cities from towns the enemy army had conquered.

The Generalitat established a Housing Commissariat that administered apartments and houses that were without owners. This could not be considered a solution, because it did not extend to all housing, but only to that which was abandoned. In some places, on the initiative of the P.O.U.M., the municipal administration took over control of housing (such as in Badalona), and the system functioned efficiently. The place where problems had the greatest impact was Barcelona.

The P.O.U.M. was represented on the Barcelona municipal council by three members. The nine C.N.T. council members called for trade union control over housing in Barcelona, meaning the liaison committee of the C.N.T. and U.G.T. construction unions should become the administrator of apartments and houses. The P.O.U.M. councillors considered the housing problem to be not only the concern of the construction workers, but of all the city's inhabitants, and for that reason believed that housing should belong to and be administered by the whole population, through municipalization; the unions should intervene in the administration of housing, because they knew the people's needs, but they should be neither owners nor administrators of properties. The city councillors for the P.S.U.C. and Esquerra desired that, as in previous debates, the right of indemnization for the owners of houses be recognized. C.N.T. and P.O.U.M. members were not able to get their recommendations accepted, and they only succeeded in prolonging the affair, to prevent approval of the principle of indemnization; thus, throughout the war, the provisional system of the Housing Commissariat was maintained.[15]

A question that did not come to be debated, but which had to be resolved in the interest of the war effort, was that of the public services. The unions of streetcar, subway, and bus workers, through a control committee, administered urban transport, but without representation by the using public. The technical problems created by the war and bombardments notwithstanding, urban transport generally functioned well.

The same question should have been put forward, in the long term, with regard to the other public services, such as water, gas, electricity, and the telephones, that is, it should have been decided whether the unions could be considered representatives not only of the workers, but also of the users of these services, or if it was necessary to find some way to give a voice and vote to the latter in the administration of these services.

Another area in which the P.O.U.M. intervened was that of police activities. Josep Coll was named General Secretary of the Commissariat of Public Order in Barcelona and P.O.U.M. representative to the Council for Security, which was set up immediately after July 19 to supervise the forces of order, including a new, revolutionary organism, the Control Patrols, with a composition similar to that of the Committee for Militias. But the P.O.U.M. did not succeed—even in Lleida—in really changing the police. While the local committees called on militants to enter the service, very few were persuaded.

The relations of the P.O.U.M. members in the Commissariat of Public Order were good with the C.N.T. and the Esquerra and bad with the P.S.U.C. Since neither the *cenetistes* not the republicans wished to work with the P.S.U.C., whom they suspected of using the police bodies in the interests of their own party, the P.S.U.C. began, little by little, to form police groupings completely controlled by them, which later provided them the opportunity to use the public security organs as a party agency. Disguised P.S.U.C. members infiltrated police groups led by *cenetistes* and *poumistes*—following orders from the foreign police experts who worked with the Soviet advisers—and this further helped the P.S.U.C.-controlled police when the period of repression came.

The Economy

Much more important for the P.O.U.M. was the economy. It was there that they tried to play a major role. Given their limited forces, there was no way they could claim a directing role, but they still helped set policy.

The anarchists had a certain advantage in this field over the other working-class sectors, because, being great enthusiasts for the planning of an ideal society, they had developed an idea, although vague, of how they wanted to organize it. Facts did not correspond to this idea, but little by little the idea influenced the facts. In the face of the reality of workers' control committees in the factories—which, as we have seen, were organized in a spontaneous way—they tried to give these institutions a structure that would support their idea of what "their" society should be. In the case of rural property, things were dealt with more directly, because in the areas where the C.N.T. militia columns were active—Aragon and a part of Valencia—they organized the life of the peasants in accordance with the models they derived from readings in the extensive anarchist literature. The P.O.U.M., by contrast, had to elaborate their economic program while it was under way, as a reaction to events.

We may distinguish three stages in the economic thinking and activities of the P.O.U.M.: that of workers' control, when they wanted to avoid, by such a measure, bourgeois sabotage of the war effort (and when they still did not see clearly that they were living through a revolution); that of collectivizations, putting the economy in the hands of the workers (once they had come to understand that a revolution was taking place and that they had to utilize the forms they had spontaneously adopted); and that of socialization, to set up a new society on the basis of the means of production (when it was seen that the collectivizations had proven insufficient to give an effective leadership in the economic sphere).

But there was a gulf between these stages and political reality. The stage of workers' control followed the action of the workers themselves. The stage of collectivization coincided with the action of the workers, but did not anticipate what they would have to do next. The stage of socialization, beginning in 1937, emerged when the forces opposed to the revolution were on the rise and there were no longer political possibilities for applying socialist measures and almost no space for saving the collectivizations without forfeiting their revolutionary character.

The phase of workers' control was expressed by the P.O.U.M. slogans in the first week of civil war, including the premonitory demand for collectivization, in the debates in the Council for Economy and the Generalitat administration on the collectivization law, and—in a merely theoretical way—in the resolutions of the P.O.U.M. central committee passed in January 1937.[16]

With respect to agrarian policy, the P.O.U.M. had a clear position. It approved the Generalitat decree of August 27, 1936, which established the obligation of all the peasants in each town to join and maintain independent local unions. But, as we have noted, polarization in the union field also penetrated the countryside, where three federations, one for the Esquerra, one for the C.N.T., and one for the U.G.T., were set up, eliminating the P.O.U.M. union influence among the peasants. As in other instances, this problem was felt most acutely in Lleida, where the party had enjoyed virtual hegemony over the peasant movement.

If the P.O.U.M. had been able to choose, it probably would not have carried out the collectivization of industry along the lines that were adopted, for it would have allowed itself to be influenced, doubtlessly, by the Russian experience after 1917 and would have sought a more direct control over the collectivizing process.

The workers themselves, giving the collectivizations a form of their own, saved the P.O.U.M. from this misstep and gave it, at the same time, an opportunity to prepare its theoretical position with regard to socialization. This was implicit in the education of the militants and in the Marxist conceptions that inspired them. The public point of departure for this theoretical process was a note in "Avant" on July 29, in which the fear was visible that the seizure of the industries by the workers would lead to disorder. The note counseled the workers to apply the social legislation then in effect and to make sure the technical personnel in the enterprises worked with the same zeal they had previously shown: "the responsible personnel, supervisors, section heads, and foremen should enjoy the same prerogatives they have always had, on the condition that they take into account that they are now working for the benefit of the enterprise as a whole and not for the boss. The workers' committees will prevent and will energetically punish any act of sabotage and will stimulate the employees to demonstrate that proletarian order is superior to that of the bourgeoisie."

This advice came late, for the workers had begun to organize production in their own way. For a month, the C.N.T. decided everything in this field, but by asking for credit from the Generalitat for the enterprises whose owners had left them without funds. This gave the Generalitat the power to influence the future of the collectivizations. We have already dealt with the debate that took place with regard to the collectivization law. The area in which the P.O.U.M. showed the most resistance involved the indemnization of former owners; these "could hope, at the most, to obtain work in their former businesses, in the same conditions as those of any other worker that was employed there," said "La Batalla" on October 25, 1936.

There was discussion in the P.O.U.M. regarding the future of small business. Many enterprises with fewer than fifty workers were, in fact, collectivized. Oltra Pico complained about this, because, he argued, "with the petty bourgeoisie, more important than dispossessing them of their businesses was their removal from power; by contrast, their economic power was taken away while they were left with their political power, with which, as is logical, they attempted to recover the first thing and to put obstacles in the way of the revolution."[17]

The P.O.U.M. leader of the printing workers union, Adolfo Bueso, in a radio speech (published in "La Batalla," November 19, 1936), affirmed that it was necessary "to finish with all of petty industry and to socialize production in a clearly socialist way that would end the contradictions of the capitalist system." Bueso undoubtedly was influenced by the fact that in his trade, where the majority of the enterprises were very small, the employers had always shown an exceptionally harsh face.

The collectivization law did not satisfy the P.O.U.M. members. "Front," published in the factory city of Terrassa, and the P.O.U.M. periodical that most concerned itself with economic questions said after adoption of the decree that "in reality it has the primordial aim of fostering a complex of capitalist egoisms among the workers, of making each factory belong exclusively to its workers, in place of satisfying collective needs."[18]

The collectivization decree had another failing: "The problem of competition must be resolved. While the unions may want a regularization of prices, their efforts will be useless if we allow the regime of private economy to be maintained between the [collectivized] enterprises."

To prevent this, it was necessary to go on to the organization of trusts in the various industries that would coordinate production (for example, spinning, fabric-making, and garment finishing) on the basis of an industrywide, or, in the Spanish vocabulary, a "vertical" structure. "Slowly, perhaps, but surely we will have to study the organization of industry on an economywide ['horizontal'] system."

The fragmentation of the collectivization system brought grave inconveniences, including that of the differences in salary and available positions in the various industries. While the workers in the garment industry were paid no more than 70 pesetas per week, streetcar drivers received more than 100 and workers in the Barcelona theatre and entertainment industry received 150. In the textile industry, the scarcity of raw materials had brought the reduction of the work day (and the daily wage), to contend with rising unemployment. These problems could only be resolved through solidarity between the unions, which should have been institutionalized in place of leaving it to the good will, not always secure, of the workers. The problem was aggravated by the existence of two competing union federations, each of which had its own attitude about the solutions to be employed.

Questions came under discussion that the Generalitat decree did not resolve and that the P.O.U.M. considered important: it was necessary to go toward a leveling of salaries, not an absolute, but a general one, because "if we wish to create an era of social justice, we have to begin by settling our differences"; it was necessary to dictate norms for the standardization of accounting, without which any planning would be impossible; in the area of accounting, certain sections had to be annulled, such as those involving dividends that were undistributed, loans to absent persons (owners that fled), industrial obligations and mortgages; the taxation established by a Generalitat decree for collectivized enterprises had to be applied equally to private businesses under workers' control (those with fewer than 100 employees).

The collectivizations brought forward, further, a problem of political psychology. Obligatory trade union membership, decreed by the Generalitat—which the P.O.U.M. looked upon with distrust and the C.N.T. with applause—involved a danger that the unions would turn into simple bureaucratic organisms and that, given their direction of the collectivizations, the latter too would produce a mere bureaucracy. Obligatory union membership could end up eliminating the influence of the more conscious workers—those who had been union members before July 19—submerging them in an indifferent or little-interested mass.

These dangers, "La Batalla" wrote on November 19, could only be avoided by "limiting the leading role in the revolution to the parties and specific organizations that fulfill the same role as parties." This was a reference to the F.A.I., which did not want to be called a party. That is, it was necessary to "deunionize" the revolution, returning the unions to their old role as defenders of the workers and giving them a new role as coordinator of collectivizations, but leaving to the parties decisions about the economic policy that should be followed.

This was viewed as a condition for workers' democracy, since neither of the two union federations permitted the existence of differing ideological factions with proportional representation in the leadership.

Another problem, at the same time economic, political, and psychological, was that of the work day. During the phase of workers' control, the P.O.U.M. had demanded a 36-hour week and the Generalitat established a variable standard of 35 hours. But with the coming of the war, it was necessary to increase production. Was it necessary, then, to temporarily increase the work day? The question was discussed, but not very much; the answer was almost automatic: yes. Nobody thought of searching for methods that would immunize the economy against the risk that, once the special circumstances of the war were past, new ones would be invented to justify the increase in productivity on the basis of longer working hours. Nobody could say what would have happened if the war had been won. In this as in many other questions, the answer would have depended on whether the political system would have been limited to a single party or would have allowed political pluralism.

To summarize, the collectivizations were not the solution for the problem of property, but a step toward a solution. "La Batalla" for October 27 wrote:

> The spontaneous movement for collectivism has clearly demonstrated the socialist direction in which the masses are moving. But it is necessary to avoid deviations that have emerged and been manifested in the masses themselves. We have had occasion to see how, in certain working class sectors, the collectivization of a factory or an industry consists only of appropriating it without worrying about its needs and those of production in general, as a whole, nor whether the raw materials it consumed were needed more in other branches of production. There have been unions that have believed collectivization consisted in appropriating to themselves the private property of an enterprise. And this is a grave mistake, which we must denounce and underscore. The seizure or socialization of an industry should never be carried out in

order to enrich either a single union or working class sector, but to create wealth for the entire proletariat.

To pose the problem in this way was the same as to say that it was necessary to go beyond the phase of collectivization. The P.O.U.M. began to say this at the end of 1936, when political conditions were not favorable for this step forward, and when there were signs that steps backward would soon be taken.

Socialization was not proposed simply as a matter of dogmatism. The collectivizations, at the same time as they resolved some problems, brought others to light, which could only be resolved in one of two ways: either submitting them to the arbitration of the state, which was not seen as under the control of the workers, or going on to the phase of socialization, which clearly would have to be carried out by a worker-controlled state. Therefore, further steps toward socialization were conceivable only if power was taken by the working-class organizations. And since the C.N.T. still refused to call for a seizure of power, to speak of socialization was to engage in a mere theoretical exercise. Socialization signified "the disappearance of the interest of the isolated enterprise and its fusion into the general interest . . . the complete rationalization of industry . . . the disappearance of irritating differences in pay and working conditions that are produced between enterprises in the same branch of industry and between different branches of industry . . . situating the economy on a level of development and its products on a level of economic equality."[19]

In Catalunya, there was a lesser proportion of small property than in the rest of Spain, the small and middle property owners and lessees were organized, and their conditions were less difficult. During the phase of workers' control, the P.O.U.M. called for redistribution of the properties of the big landlords among the poor peasants and "the annulment of all the duties that weigh on the tenant farmers, who should have title to the land so long as they work it" (according to a manifesto published by the P.O.U.M. executive on July 24). On August 5, the executive declared that the agrarian reform laws and laws on cultivation contracts had been surpassed and that the big landlords must be expropriated and the land divided between peasants and rural workers. In reality, the town committees had given ownership of the land to the peasants, following orders from nobody; in some places the *cenetistes* initiated the organization of agrarian collectives and the *poumistes* set up cooperatives on large holdings that it was considered uneconomical to break up.

But the P.O.U.M. did not seek a forced collectivization of agriculture. Nin said clearly in a meeting, "We aspire to the socialization of land, the same as with the rest of the instruments of production; but we understand that an immediate and general socialization in the countryside would not presently be beneficial. What is taking place is the beginning in the countryside of the realization of collectivization, establishing collective use of the big properties and estates that must be expropriated; but completely respecting the work of the small producer, who must be won over to the collectivist cause in a patient manner and taking account of the advantages of socialization. Acting this way will seal the revolutionary union of the peasants and the proletariat to carry out the socialist revolution" ("La Batalla," October 27, 1936).

On November 15 an agrarian conference of P.O.U.M. met and declared:

> 1. All rural property must be socialized.

> 2. The application of this socialization process must be put in the charge of agricultural trade unions, through their general and representative bodies.

> 3. Socialized land must be distributed for use according to the needs of the peasants who work it.

> 4. Current small proprietors can continue in the usufruct of the lands they cultivate. Nevertheless, no peasant should have more land than he and his family can cultivate.

> 5. Crops should belong to the cultivator. Unions and cooperatives will be the only intermediaries between the producer and the consumer.

> 6. The collective use of the land must be supported through supply of all necessary technical and economic aid.

> 7. With an understanding that the collective use of the land implies, to a great extent, a process of education, model farms should be created, which, being provided with all the advances of modern technique, will demonstrate to the peasant that with less effort than he has expended on individual use, a larger yield may be obtained.[20]

In the towns where the C.N.T. predominated, the tendency was toward forced collectivization, although it was disguised as a voluntary action, and this exasperated many peasants, who did not have a collectivist outlook and who, once they had obtained land, felt their demands to have been satisfied and considered the revolution to have ended.

The P.O.U.M. daily newspaper warned of the dangers of this contradiction between the state of mind of the peasants and the C.N.T. attitude—which in impoverished Aragon found a welcome and, overall, was successful, but which in Catalunya went against the grain of the country people. The P.O.U.M., recalling the lessons of forced collectivization under Stalin, did not want any repetition in Catalunya of the terrible effects of the Russian collectivization. To collectivize the land while techniques of cultivation could not be industrialized would be counterproductive. "The peasants, alarmed by impositions, will refuse to sow crops and will end up turning against the revolution they now support."[21]

In sum, for the P.O.U.M., the local agricultural trade union should possess the land and share it out among the peasants. The peasant who had land for cultivation with his family and without exploiting labor should keep it and should pay no rent if he was a tenant farmer, but should pay to the town authorities a proportional tax based on his harvest. If he had excess land, if he had to hire workers to cultivate it, the excess share should pass to the union, which would give it to a rural worker. The small proprietors could, on their own, form production cooperatives whose leaders must be elected by all the members. Large farms, which were worked by hired labor, should not be broken up, but should also pass into union hands, to be organized cooperatively by all those who were involved in the process of production on the farm. In every agricultural union, then, there should be a section of small proprietors and a section of cooperatives or communities; between them a union leadership should be elected, which would coordinate the administration of the agrarian collectivity.

The small proprietors should in no way be obliged to enter a cooperative, nor should they even be invited to do so; the process would have to wait until the peasants themselves asked to enter. The *poumistes* in the countryside were intransigent on the subject of the voluntary character of collectivization at the same time as they carried out a constant propaganda to convince the peasants that collective land use would be more profitable.

The Militias

The militias in the Spanish Civil War have been idealized by a few commentators and denigrated by others. The P.S.U.C. chief, Comorera, with an air of racism, referred to them as "the tribes." The P.O.U.M. saw in them "the guarantee of the revolution." In discussing the militias, it is difficult to separate myth from reality. In this book, we base our opinion of the militias mainly on the personal recollections of Víctor Alba, on his correspondence with Manuel Grossi, a P.O.U.M. militia commander, and on interviews with some officers and militia rank-and-filers.

On July 24, the first militia contingents came together and headed for the front in Aragon. They were sure they would reach Saragossa within a few days. The preparation of the columns was inconsistent, because almost nobody in the workers' movement had military experience and they did not trust those professional officers who had not been arrested for complicity in the coup. The first columns were made up of 2,800 P.O.U.M. members, commanded by Jordi Arquer and Manuel Grossi, 1,200 of whom were armed; there were no machine guns. The P.S.U.C. fielded

1,200 volunteers, under the official Communists, José del Barrio and Manuel del Trueba. The C.N.T. brought together 4,000 *milicians*, as well as members of the Generalitat police body, the *Mossos d'Esquadra*, and some guardias de asalto, all under the orders of the charismatic Buenaventura Durruti. In Lleida, a non-P.O.U.M. column assaulted the local jail and killed all the prisoners, which made the advance into Aragon difficult, since the columns were now preceded by a terrorist reputation.

Lleida also was the site of the first conflict over the distribution of arms. The city committee had collected a considerable quantity, and there were disputes and divisions over how they should be divided up; the C.N.T. column ended up with most of them. Durruti, during these discussions, affirmed several times that "the C.N.T. is enough by itself to win the war, without any other forces than its own." When he was told joint action was necessary, he answered "in the end, this will all be discussed after we have won. And believe me, we will know how to be tolerant."

The Lleida revolutionary committee, controlled by the P.O.U.M., provided the columns with trucks, and by the 26th they had reached Monzón, and by the 27th Barbastro. A certain colonel Villalba, who had been arrested in the latter city, was released, and named military chief of the Aragon front, establishing a command post in Barbastro, although this did not become a general staff headquarters.

On July 27, the columns marched to the front. The P.O.U.M. Maurín column advanced toward Barbagal and Sariñena. In the towns they passed through, they met with the inhabitants, called on them to elect committees, and distributed the land, but did not impose collectivization, leaving the latter option to the initiative of the peasants themselves. This caused incidents when the C.N.T. columns arrived in the vicinity and tried to force collectivization. Finally, to avoid shooting, the *poumistes* resigned themselves to the collectivization of the land in "their" towns, without the will of the peasants being taken into account. It must be said that, in a short time, the laboring peasants showed themselves to be relatively satisfied with the results of collectivization. Although some sections of the P.O.U.M. were organized, the Aragon Council, the regional government established in the middle of October, was made up entirely of *cenetistes,* headed by Joaquín Ascaso, brother of a fallen F.A.I. hero, Francisco Ascaso.

There were things that were more urgent, for the moment. On August 1, 300 poumistes from the Maurín column occupied Grañen during an advance by a P.S.U.C. column toward Tardienta. From Grañen, they went on to Robres, where they first faced members of the fascist Falange Española, in their dark-blue shirts, then to Alcubierre, where they found, in the plaza, the bodies, still warm, of a group of executed peasants.

The P.O.U.M. established its command center in the town and set up a hospital. On August 5, they took Leciñena, quite close to Saragossa, and received orders from Barbastro to go no further. This halt permitted them to organize themselves under a general staff and to receive groups that came from the towns to voluntarily join the forces.

The militia was impatient for activity. They sought to organize guerrilla warfare, infiltrating behind the enemy lines, but Barbastro refused to permit it. This was the state of mind Franz Borkenau encountered among the P.O.U.M. forces when he first visited Spain. He told Grossi that his forces were the most disciplined he had seen, but he wrote in his book as follows: "August 14 . . . Lecinana (sic), the center of the larger of the two P.O.U.M. columns on the Aragon front. We were received with great friendliness by its leader, Grossi, and offered every chance to see what was going on."

A meeting of the column discussed relieving the guards in the most advanced positions. Grossi "himself led the relief and stayed out with them for a whole night . . . Grossi is a type somewhat crude, but *au fond* is very appealing and certainly possesses the personal allegiance of his column. He is evidently brave . . . but he is deficient as an organizer and has no idea of the job of warfare. There is an obvious rivalry between him and his military adviser."[22]

Borkenau, although an acute observer, lacked a good deal in the way of accurate information. For example, he was one of the first to refer to the P.O.U.M. indiscriminately as "Trotskyists." He also stated that Alcubierre was taken by the Catalans, failing to specify that it was by a P.O.U.M. column, lost, and then retaken, when in reality it was only taken once and did not fall into enemy hands so long as the P.O.U.M. defended that sector.

In Leciñena, in September, a P.O.U.M. newspaper for the fighting forces, "Front," began appearing. In the middle of the month, Leciñena was attacked by the fascists, probably as a diversion. Ammunition was short for the rifles, and there was none for the few available machine guns, notwithstanding insistent demands addressed to Barbastro. The P.O.U.M. militia began to suspect that certain interests wished to leave them aside and would even look with pleasure at whatever retreat they might suffer, so as to accuse them of negligence and indiscipline. Josep Rovira, the P.O.U.M. representative in the Committee for Militias, visited the front several times to calm the militia.

In the Zuera sector, on the right flank of the Tardienta sector, was a small P.S.U.C. column commanded by an old communist known because of his dark complexion by the nickname of "The Negus" (a widely used title for the emperor of Ethiopia, Haile Selassie). He went to Leciñena and proposed to the P.O.U.M. command that the task of guarding the front lines between the positions of the two columns be shared. The *poumistes* answered that they could not accept the suggestion because they lacked sufficient arms. However, the same "Negus" had seen shipments of supplies arrive in Barbastro! He went there and, after much shouting, obtained thirty rifles and three small-calibre mortars, which allowed the P.O.U.M. militia to garrison their section of the line. Later, this action caused Trueba, the head of the P.S.U.C. column, to accuse "The Negus" of aiding the P.O.U.M. and to eliminate him.

In reality, these arms had been sent to the front in preparation for an attack on Perdiguera. On September 11, the Catalan *diada* or national holiday, the order to attack was given, with whatever arms were available. It was a rout. Excellent militants died after reaching the outskirts of the town, because the lack of ammunition prevented reinforcements from reaching them in time. Furthermore, this defeat was used by the P.S.U.C., which presented it as "proof" that the P.O.U.M. was helping the enemy. The English communist poet John Cornford participated in this attack as a member of the P.O.U.M. militia.

The P.O.U.M. militia was disheartened. They knew the arms that had been sent to the front were all diverted to Tardienta, where the P.S.U.C. was stationed. They had learned from the local peasants that the fascists were concentrated in Perdiguera and Ziera. They warned Barbastro. But Barbastro neither took precautions nor sent arms, and, three weeks later, Moroccan colonial troops and regulars of the fascist forces attacked Leciñena. Among those who lost their lives in the attack were fourteen P.O.U.M. youth members from the town of Sitges, who had just returned from an unsuccessful expedition against the fascist-held island of Mallorca, led by a regular army captain, Alberto Bayo Giroud. Bayo would later become known as an international authority on guerrilla tactics and as an adviser to Fidel Castro's Cuban revolutionary army. The Mallorca expedition included 300 members of the P.O.U.M. along with *cenetistes* and some 2,000 members of Estat Català.[23]

The fascist attack on Leciñena involved tanks, which the militia had to face for the first time. Leciñena was lost. Naturally, this was also used by the P.S.U.C. in its propaganda against the P.O.U.M.

All this is anecdotal. The front was small, the forces reduced, arms scarce, and fighting intermittent. In Aragon, no great battles took place; this reflected the caution of the fascists in attacking what they considered to be the final, irreducible redoubt of the republican cause, backed up as it was by Catalunya and Barcelona. They knew the Aragon front could not be easily taken; and, indeed, they not only gained no territory there for most of the war, but they also held off their final assault until the end of 1938, almost three years later. When the Aragon front fell, it was no longer defended by the militias, but by regular forces, many of them under communist control.

Command procedures were refined. In Sietamo, a P.O.U.M. general staff was set up with Josep Rovira as chief and Joan Vila, from Sabadell, as political commissar. With foreign volunteers who were now arriving (many of whom would be sent by the parties affiliated with the London Bureau), an international column was organized, named after Lenin, and conducted itself very well. Some of the shock troops were German refugees and French and Belgian workers, but there were many more Italians. Unlike the "International Brigades" organized by the Comintern, these foreigners had not awaited orders from Moscow to join the struggle. Such "premature internationalists" were also to be found in the C.N.T. columns.

Had a regular army existed, these foreigners might not have been welcomed. But the communists, with the support of the republicans, carried on a persistent campaign in favor of converting the militias into a regular army. The P.O.U.M. desired that the militias be preserved and to support its position published the previously mentioned pamphlet of Antonov-Ovsyeyenko, as well as the *Red Army Manual* written by Trotsky. On September 29, two levies of soldiers were drafted to fight the fascists (until then the militias had been entirely voluntary) and this was used to present as inevitable the transformation of the militias into a regular army.

In October a political commissariat was set up for the forces, with a pro-communist member of the Socialist party, Julio Álvarez del Vayo, as its head (in December he was replaced by the communist Antonio Mije, who was in turn replaced by another communist, José Hernández. The troops on the Aragon front were reorganized as the 25th, 26th, and 28th divisions (C.N.T.), the 27th (P.S.U.C.), and the 29th (P.O.U.M.). There were now 22,000 fighters at the front, of which 4,000 were guardias de asalto, 13,000 C.N.T., 2,000 P.S.U.C., and 3,000 P.O.U.M. The latter made up a brigade and two batallions (later two brigades, the 128th and 129th). Josep Rovira commanded the 29th division. The officer positions went almost entirely to P.O.U.M. members, especially youth members.

From time to time, a shipment of arms would arrive. They had been bought secretly in France by the P.O.U.M. and likewise secretly transported, with the help of some socialists in the French customs service. To pay for these arms, the P.O.U.M. used money obtained in the requisitions of the July days. Since the Paris brokers paid a higher rate for the fascist Burgos peseta than for republican money, rubber stamps were made up and the money was stamped as if it had come from Burgos, rather than Madrid, boosting the amount of money available for arms purchases.

There was little activity at the front after the first weeks. The communists continued to use this as a pretext to ask in their press, insidiously, why Saragossa had not been taken. "El Combatiente Rojo," the "organ of the militia, soldiers, and antifascist police" published by the 29th division, answered that question with an article signed by Narcís Molíns i Fábrega: "Those whose situation would allow them to aid the advance toward Saragossa are those who are putting obstacles in its way and, at the same time, dare to demand further responsibilities from others."

He pointed out that much of the armaments sent to the republic had been held up in their passage across the Mediterranean from Russia, where it was hoped that an arms blackmail would bear results, forcing the C.N.T. and P.O.U.M. to submit to the P.S.U.C.; the longer their delivery by ship was delayed, the worse was the danger of their being lost to the torpedoes of Italian submarines, which had begun an undeclared war on all shipping that called at republican ports.

"Is the problem that there can be no attacks on the Aragon front until one or another group has renounced the postulates of the proletarian revolution?" Molins ended his article. Arms promised to the front arrived as if from an eye-dropper, along with many new soldiers lacking training.

The International Situation

There were many things in the politics of the P.O.U.M. that enraged the official Communists, aside from the fact of their existence, which exasperated the Communists enough.

One thing was the international position of the P.O.U.M. and the echo it found outside Spain. As we have already explained, the P.O.U.M. was a member of the so-called "London Bureau" of International Revolutionary Socialist Unity. Moscow could not tolerate the existence of an international grouping of parties that called itself revolutionary but did not accept the orders of the Comintern.

The bureau, as might be supposed, became more active with the beginning of the Spanish conflict, not only because this was a motive for the movement to throw all its forces into the struggle, but also because the P.O.U.M. provided it with great resources and advantages. (It may be remarked that the C.N.T.-F.A.I. played the same role with the worldwide network of anarchist and syndicalist groups known as the International Workers' Association.)

Although, as we have noted, the P.O.U.M. did relatively little requisitioning, what it did was sufficient to enable the party to extend material support to some small revolutionary parties, such as the Revolutionary Socialist Workers' Party (R.S.A.P.) led by Sneevliet, which stood in the Dutch 1937 elections, but without much success.

From October 31 to November 2, 1936, an international congress against war and fascism and to aid the Spanish revolution was held in Brussels, organized by the London Bureau. The congress approved various resolutions, supporting the positions of the P.O.U.M., condemning the communist attacks on the party—which had not yet reached the virulence that would characterize them a few months later—and putting forward an international working-class line that escaped the straitjacket of the Comintern's slogans.[24]

The following organizations belonging to the bureau participated in the congress: the P.O.U.M., represented by Gorkín, the British I.L.P., the German S.A.P., the Italian Maximalist Socialist Party, the Independent Socialist Workers Party of Poland, the Revolutionary Socialist League, and the R.S.A.P. from Holland. Others who participated in the congress included the following organizations, none of which was very important at the time: from Britain, the War Resisters League, "No More War," the Movement for Colonial Freedom, and the Revolutionary Socialist Party; from France, the group that published the journal "Que Faire?," the revolutionary Left in the French Socialist Party (S.F.I.O.), the teachers' union and lay instruction movement known as "L'École Emancipée," and the Vigilance Committee of Antifascist Intellectuals; from Italy, the Italian League for the Rights of Man (in exile); from Sweden, the Socialist Party (not the larger, moderate Social Democratic governing party); from Belgium, the International Socialist Anti-War League; from the United States and Canada, the Revolutionary Workers League, an extreme faction that had split with the Trotskyist movement under the leadership of Hugo Oehler; from the Jewish areas in Palestine, Left Poale Zion and Kibbutz Artzi, as well as the Marxist Circles and the "Antifa" antifascist defense organization; from Greece, the grouping around the journal "Archives of Marxism," known as "Archiomarxists." Also, naturally, the International Revolutionary Youth Bureau, the London Bureau's youth arm, was represented.

Altogether, these groups did not command masses of followers, but the P.O.U.M. felt that, bringing the word of the Spanish revolution and defending it, these parties could strengthen themselves and grow.

The Brussels congress launched the aforementioned calls for solidarity, but also approved some theses that reflected the thinking of the P.O.U.M. and that tried to combat the ideological confusion then present in the workers' movement. Fenner Brockway, an I.L.P. leader and secretary of the London Bureau, argued that the cause of this confusion was the abandonment of the principle of class struggle. However, he declared that "from the events in Spain, where fascism and socialism are struggling, will come the forces that will build a New Revolutionary International."

The congress decided to meet again in Barcelona in spring 1937, and to examine the conditions that would permit the formation of a truly revolutionary international.

It is easy to imagine how unsettling the latter decision was to the Spanish communists as well as to Moscow. They could hardly have been pleased to learn what the congress said about the decision of the U.S.S.R. to join the international committee on nonintervention in Spain, set up by the major powers with the aim of quarantining the revolution; this, the congress said, "reflected the policy of the Soviet government in recent years." The congress condemned the Moscow trials (at the same time as it called for the defense of the U.S.S.R. against imperialist aggression) and demanded an impartial international inquiry on the accusations against the old Bolsheviks. Solidarity with the U.S.S.R., another resolution said, could be expressed in no better manner than through the opposition of the working class of each country to the local ruling class; neither the politics of "national union," nor the acceptance of fascist and nationalist tendencies into the anticolonial struggle, both of which the communists sought, could be considered revolutionary. The discussion regarding the U.S.S.R. was long, because there were delegates to the congress who believed that any criticism of the U.S.S.R. would help fascism.

The international situation confronted the P.O.U.M. with this same problem, not with regard to the Moscow trials, in which, as we have seen, its position was sharp, but in relation to Soviet aid and the diplomatic maneuvers undertaken by Moscow in the matter of nonintervention.

One of the arguments most often employed against revolutionary measures in the Spanish conflict was that these would impede the granting of international aid to the republic. The C.N.T. leaders justified their acceptance of a policy of restricting the collectivizations by calling on such arguments, as Joan García Oliver would clearly state only a few months later. In a visit by Gorkín to Largo Caballero, after the government of the latter had been moved to Valencia, the P.O.U.M. leader stressed that the sacrifices of the workers were motivated by love neither for the Republic as such nor for the People's Front, and the head of government replied, "I already know that the militias are fighting for much more, but we cannot forget the international situation."

Gorkín answered that it was unthinkable that the foreign powers could be deceived. It was enough to read the big newspapers from London and Paris to see that the governments of those countries knew that the victory of the Spanish Republic would be a victory for socialism.

One issue that complicated the international relations of the republic was that of the Spanish possessions in Morocco. As George Orwell and other argued, had the republic declared that Morocco would henceforth be free of its imperialist interference, there was hope that the fidelity of the Moroccan colonial troops to the fascist generals would be undermined. Given the crucial role of the Moroccan *banderas* in the offensive against the republic, this was much more than a matter of radical political theorizing. Indeed, today, after forty years of "decolonization" and "anti-imperialism" in the history of the European powers, it should be clear that such an action would have had an immense, worldwide impact. But the P.O.U.M. was the only Spanish political organization that demanded Moroccan independence; indeed, this was an item in the program produced by the 1935 fusion that created the party, and it had been adopted by the B.O.C. as early as 1932. Narcís Molins i Fábrega, a close collaborator of Nin who came to the party with the Communist Left, had served in the Spanish Army in Morocco, where he had left a number of friends. According to notes furnished to Víctor Alba by Molins, in 1955, when he was in exile in Mexico, once the war began Molins received messages that put him in contact with the Moroccan nationalist movement. He met with a Moroccan representative in Paris, who asked for money for arms and promised to quickly organize an insurrection in the Spanish zone of Morocco, where the situation, thanks to the war, was favorable for such an enterprise. In exchange, the republican regime would recognize Moroccan independence. The P.O.U.M. brought this proposal to the attention of Largo Caballero, who rejected it for fear of provoking a conflict with France, the main colonial power in Morocco, whose own People's Front government showed obvious anxiety over the possibility of a rebellion in the Spanish zone spreading to the French zone and thence, perhaps, to the rest of French North Africa. In the end, the republic found itself bereft of much French military aid, at the same time as its rulers had foregone the possibility of unleashing a rebellion that almost certainly would have weakened the fascists.

It should be noted that, while Moroccan colonial mercenaries supported the coup against the republic, Arab revolutionaries from Algeria fought in the ranks of the militia, most of them members of the North African Star movement led by Messali Hadj, which had links with the London Bureau.

The P.O.U.M. shared certain illusions about international aid. On October 7, the Soviet government declared that if violations of non-intervention procedures by the fascist powers, Germany and Italy, which were directly aiding the republic's enemies, did not cease, the U.S.S.R. would consider itself free of any obligation to honor nonintervention promises. "La Batalla" declared that the possibility of the U.S.S.R. breaking with non-intervention "will have extraordinary political consequences. It is probably the most important political event since the beginning of the civil war."

A few days later, on October 11, the same daily affirmed that "if France does not send [us] arms, Blum will be discredited. We do not believe Blum would commit such a colossal error." But the U.S.S.R. could neither destroy the nonintervention committee nor force it to honor the principles on which it had been set up, nor was Blum able to avoid the colossal error that "La Batalla's" writer felt was impossible.

The P.O.U.M. lost its illusions about nonintervention faster than the other organizations, and a month after the incorrect predictions just described, it began to express distrust over the possibility of foreign help. This was first produced by the situation with the Soviet Union. Only the U.S.S.R., Mexico, and to a small extent France provided weapons to the republic. Soviet arms had hardly begun to arrive in October, when the opportunity for quickly winning the war was already lost, and they never came in sufficient quantity to make a decisive difference in military operations. This produced the dilemma for the P.O.U.M. of either telling the truth and denouncing the Soviet arms blackmail, or of acting as the other organizations did and accepting it, submitting to the demands of the communists and abandoning the conquests of the revolution. But the arms thus obtained would never suffice to win the war and, in exchange, would be paid for by a political retreat that would demoralize the militia and the rearguard. These arms could have no other effect than that of simply prolonging the war, which was clearly the interest of Muscovite diplomacy, which, as we now know, came in 1938 to the position of seeking a pact with Hitler, with the fate of republican Spain as a part of the deal.

The P.O.U.M. decided to speak the truth, because it believed that only if they knew the truth would the workers be able to resist communist pressure and put Moscow in the position of having to choose between giving real aid and declaring itself openly against the revolution. In their hearts, the *poumistes* did not wish to renounce their hope in the U.S.S.R. as a socialist and revolutionary power.

On November 15 "La Batalla" commented on the decision of the Soviet Union to support the Republic:

> What brought this change about? Perhaps Stalin understood the error he committed over the past two and a half months and has wanted to rectify it? That it was an error is proven by the simple fact of the rectification, the change. But the most important real factor that has dictated this change is the discovery by Stalin that Franco, with the open aid of Hitler and Mussolini, could triumph in the civil war, which would reinforce the political and strategic positions of Hitlerian fascism that Stalin considers his mortal enemy. The rectification of the error has not come from a desire to serve the interests of the Spanish revolution—Lenin would not for a single moment have declared himself neutral about this—but from foreign policy worries, from an instinct to conserve the relationship of international forces. In a word: what interests Stalin is not the fate of the Spanish proletariat but the defense of the Soviet government according to a policy of pacts between opposing groups of states.

Nine days later (November 24), the same daily said that Soviet aid to the republic was used by the communists to exercise pressure against revolutionary measures, and added: "It is intolerable that, while lending us a certain aid, one would attempt to impose on us particular political forms, pronouncing vetoes and in fact directing Spanish politics."

The communist press immediately attacked the P.O.U.M., accusing it of "playing the fascists' game." The barbs in "La Batalla" must have stung deeply, for at the end of twelve days and probably after receiving orders from Moscow, the Soviet consulate in Barcelona published a note that constituted the first open act of intervention in the internal affairs of the republic and that broke with all norms of diplomatic conduct. This note, distributed to the press by the Propaganda Commissariat of the Generalitat, in which government the P.O.U.M. was represented, said:

> One of the maneuvers of the press in the pay of international fascism consists in the calumny that the representatives of the Soviet Union accredited to the Government are who in fact direct the foreign policy of the Spanish republic. The aims that motivate the servants of fascism to circulate such an insinuation are clear enough. They wish, in the first place, to undermine abroad the prestige of the republican government of Spain; in the second place, to weaken the sentiment of fraternal solidarity that is increasing every day between the peoples of Spain and the peoples of the Soviet Union, the principal moral base of the antifascist struggle; in the third place, to support and reinforce the tendencies toward a disorganization undermining the Republican United Front exhibited by various uncontrolled and irresponsible groups. And now among the organs of the Catalan press there is to be found a sheet that has undertaken the task of supporting this fascist campaign. In its issue of November 24, 'La Batalla' has tried to add support to the indicated fascist insinuations. The consulate general of the U.S.S.R. in Barcelona rejects with contempt the lamentable inventions of this sheet. For the consul general of the U.S.S.R. in Barcelona: the Press attache, Korobizin.

The P.O.U.M. and C.N.T. press reacted to this note by pointing out its significance, but the republican and socialist press remained silent, the first for fear of angering the P.S.U.C. and the second for fear of interfering with Soviet aid. It may be said that the toleration of this note gave carte blanche to the Soviet diplomats to further inject themselves into the internal affairs of the republic.

It is interesting, regarding this problem, to examine the idea that if the communists were criticized, aid would have been suspended. From what we know of Stalin, it is possible he would have said "without obedience, no arms." But it is also possible that he would have taken other factors into account. A former Stalinist, who has become a theoretician of "Eurocommunism," Fernando Claudín, has discussed the issue as follows:

> Refusal to help the Spanish proletariat, given the tremendous sympathy its

fight would arouse even in the Social Democratic labor movement, would have dealt a heavy blow to the standing of the U.S.S.R. among the workers throughout the world. And although Stalin's international strategy was based fundamentally on using the contradictions between the imperialist powers, and not on the world revolutionary movement, it could not do without the support of the international labor movement. It needed that, even for only exploiting interimperialist contradictions—to ensure, for example, the alliance with France, and to bring about an understanding with Britain, the 'pressure' in this direction exercised by the respective working classes of those countries was needed.

A Spanish socialist republic of the type described—that is, one independent of the Comintern and the U.S.S.R., and it was only conceivable as such—would command the weapon of open criticism, the possibility of denouncing frankly before the proletariat of the world the conduct of the Moscow government, should the latter refuse to help the Spanish revolution. It is not absurd to suppose that, faced with this danger, 'Moscow would have been forced to supply arms, and possibly at more reasonable prices,' as Trotsky said. If, however, we look at this problem in the light of subsequent events, and in particular of the German-Soviet pact and of the abandonment of the Yugoslav revolution in 1948, it is not absurd, either, to think that Stalin would have reacted by denouncing our hypothetical heterodox Spanish communists for their alliance with the Anarcho-Syndicalists, Caballerists, and P.O.U.Mists, as a sinister provocation (organized by the Gestapo under the guidance of Trotsky) against the U.S.S.R. and the Western democracies, in order to prevent them from coming to the help of the Spanish Republic, that legal, constitutional, parliamentary, etc., institution.[25]

The Antonov-Ovsyeyenko Crisis

Beginning in November, a paradoxical situation existed. The P.S.U.C., C.N.T., and P.O.U.M. were, all three, in the government of the Generalitat. But the P.S.U.C. attacked the C.N.T. and the P.O.U.M and these organizations criticized the positions of the P.S.U.C. The P.S.U.C. could not carry the struggle to the terrain of ideas, because its position was weak and because the mass it wished to neutralize, the members of the C.N.T., would not have accepted their positions. It was necessary, then, to put the struggle on the personal level, that of contempt and insult. Moscow, with its trials of the old Bolsheviks, had provided the example. For the official Communists, it should not have been a difficult one to follow, because they were already accustomed to it, but for the former *bloquistes* who had joined the P.S.U.C. the matter was not so simple. The truth was that if it was costly to adapt themselves to the positions of their leaders, they did not show it and, docilely, they followed orders and did not waver in echoing the insults and defamations against those whom, only a few months before, had been their comrades.

There were doubts within the P.O.U.M. about whether it was appropriate to remain in the Generalitat regime. The fact that Nin was a *conseller* had proven of little use, not even in bringing up the problem of confidence in him and of deciding whether the attacks of the P.S.U.C., or at least the tone it employed, would cease, or whether the administration would leave office. Nin's appointment had not even helped the P.O.U.M. militias gain arms.

It was also of no use in protecting the P.O.U.M. members outside Catalunya. In Madrid, a Communist veto prevented the P.O.U.M. from obtaining a seat in the Defense Council for the capital. Manuel Albar, from the Socialist Party, told Enrique Rodríguez, of the P.O.U.M. local committee, "Ambassador Rosenberg has vetoed your involvement. It is unjust, obviously, but we understand it; the U.S.S.R. is powerful and between depriving ourselves of the support of the U.S.S.R. or the support of the P.O.U.M. there is no possible choice."

The council refused arms to the P.O.U.M. militias, suspended publication of the party's Madrid daily, "El Combatiente Rojo," and refused permission to reestablish "La Antorcha," which had a long history in the working class movement, as the P.O.U.M. journal. This order was received just when the news was received that Jesús Blanco, secretary of the P.O.U.M. local committee in Madrid, had been killed at the front. Finally, the council closed the P.O.U.M. offices, those of its Red Aid organization, and its radio station. In the face of all this, when at the end of the year the immediate danger to Madrid from the fascist offensive had passed, the P.O.U.M. executive ordered party members in the capital to move to Barcelona, where they could function as militants, rather than remaining in Madrid, exposed to persecution and impotent because of their reduced numbers. The P.O.U.M. militias at Madrid joined a C.N.T. column where, at least, they ran no risk of attack from the republican side.

While all this was happening, the official Communists had begun a "law and order" campaign. The official party organized radio broadcasts directed to the offspring of the bourgeoisie and the aristocrats on the other side of the trenches, calling on them to cross over to the republican lines (something they evidently did not do). Constancia de la Mora, granddaughter of an old monarchist politician and wife of Ignacio Hidalgo de Cisneros, a communist who ended up as head of the Republican air force, took charge of the censorship in Madrid; she not only prevented publication of criticism of the communists, but also personally censored the correspondence of Largo Caballero, who had become the head of the republican government in August 1936.

Jesús Hernández called for the reopening of churches in the antifascist zone, a move that was proudly reported by the French communist deputy Gabriel Péri in the Paris communist daily "L'Humanité," on April 19,

1937. José Díaz, in a meeting, stated that "fascism, Trotskyism, and the uncontrollables are the three enemies of the people." The sons of Alcalá Zamora (the latter having installed himself in modest circumstances in Buenos Aires), led workers' delegations to the U.S.S.R.

The Soviet press envoy, Mikhail Koltsov (who Stalin had executed when he returned to the U.S.S.R.), wrote in his diary, for August 9, 1936:

> The P.O.U.M. is playing a role of provocation and demoralization. It was formed, immediately after (sic) the coup, on the basis of two parties: the Trotskyist group of Nin and the Maurín organization, constituted by rightist renegades of the Bukharin tendency, excluded from the C.P. Maurín is stuck in fascist territory and Nin has assumed the leadership of the united Spanish Trotskyists-Bukharinists. The P.O.U.M. have their newspaper, which offers the anarchists blandishments agitating them against the communist workers, demanding a broad and immediate social revolution in Spain, and speaking with repugnant demagoguery against the Soviet Union. On the practical terrain, they are much more reasonable: they have taken over the best hotels and most aristocratic buildings in Barcelona, controlling the most expensive restaurants and places of entertainment.[26]

What was behind this campaign was obvious: the interest of Moscow not only in eliminating a party that criticized it, but also in making it seem that outside the U.S.S.R. there existed the same supposed organizations of fascist agents disguised as revolutionaries as they claimed were linked to the old Bolsheviks. The P.O.U.M. seemed ready to be turned into an "example," and the Spanish situation lent itself to such a development.

But there were other motives, which a U.S. journalist, Louis Fischer, then sympathetic to the communists, explained much later: "bourgeois generals, politicians, and many peasants who approved the Communist Party's policy in protecting small property holders have joined . . . essentially, their new political affiliation reflects a despair of the old social system as well as the hope to salvage one or two of its remnants."[27]

It should not be forgotten that, in August, communists such as Santiago Carrillo had dared to say that "in fighting fascism we are not struggling for a socialist revolution, but for the democratic republic," and that on August 3 "L'Humanité" in Paris published a communiqué by the French Communist Party in which it reported that "the central committee of the Spanish Communist Party has asked us to announce to public opinion, in answer to the tendentious campaigns and fantastic reports of certain press organs, that the Spanish people, in their struggle against the rebels, are not trying to establish the dictatorship of the proletariat, but that they have a single aim: the defense of republican order and respect for property."

It was just this that gained the P.S.U.C. and the official party throughout Spain the strength that turned them into an effective instrument of Soviet diplomacy for the first time in the party's history. A socialist who in those moments was on the left and who then passed over to the party right, stated years later:

> The republican middle class, surprised by the moderate tone of communist propaganda and impressed by the unity and realism prevailing in the party, increased its ranks by a great number ... The army officers and functionaries, who had never even glanced at a Marxist propaganda pamphlet in the past, became communists, some out of calculation, others because of moral weakness, others still inspired by the enthusiasm that animated the communist organization.[28]

What position did the C.N.T. adopt in the face of the campaign against the P.O.U.M., which argued that it was only the first step in a campaign against the C.N.T.? (In August, Jesús Hernández had declared to "Paris-Midi": "The anarchists prefer the rearguard to the firing line ... After the victory we will correct them.") Some anarchist sectors took account of the significance of the campaign; for example, in September, at a meeting of regional delegates from the C.N.T., a line was approved that was not much different from that of the P.O.U.M.: that a national defense council be formed, made up of the trade union federations and left parties, which would eliminate the vestiges of the bourgeois republic, create a national workers' militia, and call an international conference of antifascists.[29]

The C.N.T. needed to extend its influence and revolutionary measures beyond Catalunya, Aragon, and the Llevante, because in Andalucía, Murcia, and the Central region the situation was less dynamic, and popular initiative had been channeled by the communists and socialists; in Euzkadi, to which the Cortes had, finally, given an autonomy statute, the Basque nationalists, supported by the communists, opposed any social changes. In reality, when treating the Spanish revolution, it would be more accurate to speak of the Catalan revolution, because only in Catalunya was there the action of a revolutionary will; in the rest of the republican zone the will existed, but was passive or without sufficient strength to impose itself. Throughout the previous decades, Catalunya had been the bulwark of progress and advanced ideas in Spain, as reflected in its art and its literature, as well as its politics. That the P.O.U.M. was largely limited to Catalunya reflected organic problems in Iberian society rather than any erroneous policy of the party. Catalunya had produced great artists, such as Antoni Gaudí, Pablo Picasso, and Joan Miró; it had been the stage for the most progressive national liberation movement in Europe; it had maintained the most revolutionary labor movement of contemporary times, the C.N.T.; and it had seen the rise of the P.O.U.M.

In the Center (Madrid), where already in October 1934 there was a current in the C.N.T. favorable to the Workers' Alliance, the P.O.U.M. position was better understood. The newspaper "C.N.T." invited the Madrid P.O.U.M. to present its viewpoint in its columns. And on October 30, the same journal affirmed that the C.N.T. "in order to win the war is ready to collaborate with anybody in a directing body, whether it is called a council or a government." This was a step the C.N.T. had taken in Catalunya with respect to the Generalitat, but which it still did not dare to adopt regarding the Madrid regime.

When, on November 5, the C.N.T. decided, finally, to enter the Largo Caballero administration, with four ministers (two syndicalists and two anarchists), "Soli" in Barcelona justified the action with arguments that seemed the same as those of the P.O.U.M. in explaining its own entry into the Generalitat: "The government, as much as an instrument of control as a state organism, has ceased to be a force for oppression of the working class, in the same way that the state is no longer a force that divides society into classes. Both will oppress the people even less now that the C.N.T. belongs to them."

It is interesting to compare this argument with that employed by the anarchists to explain their failure to take power on July 20. For example, the F.A.I. theoretician, Diego Abád de Santillán, in his book *Porqué Perdimos la Guerra* (Buenos Aires, 1940, p. 76), said that "we could have stood alone, imposing our absolute will, declaring the Generalitat meaningless and instituting in its place a real people's power; but we did not believe in dictatorship when it was exercised against us, and we did not desire it when we could have exercised it against others."

Joan García Oliver said, in his book *De Julio a Julio* (Barcelona, 1937, p. 26), that the following dilemma had emerged: "Either libertarian communism, which is the same as an anarchist dictatorship, or democracy, which means collaboration . . . The C.N.T. and F.A.I. decided in favor of collaboration and democracy, renouncing revolutionary totalitarianism . . . They believed in the word and the person of a Catalan democrat and maintained and sustained Companys in the presidency of the Generalitat."

The P.O.U.M. began to ask themselves if it was not the petty bourgeoisie that had taken the initiative and power, and Ignacio Iglesias started writing a pamphlet on the middle class,[30] which showed that the P.O.U.M. tried to analyze the situation and did not accept mere slogans.

It was common to think that the petty bourgeoisie feared the revolution, and the help offered to it by the P.S.U.C. seemed to bear this out. The theses of Iglesias were different: the petty bourgeoisie, in crisis, can be revolutionary, if the revolutionaries know how to speak a language that does not frighten it and can put itself on the side of the workers, to gain its own ends, naturally, on the condition that there exist worker organizations that take advantage of this possibility and that do not become bogged down by measures that add nothing substantial to the revolution and that, by contrast, can separate the middle classes from the revolution. It was, obviously, a cry of alarm to the P.O.U.M. and C.N.T.: *Attention*! If the middle classes follow the P.S.U.C. it is because the former parties have not known how to attract them; it is necessary to bring them over to the revolutionary side, and there is still time to do it. Implicitly, Iglesias said that a new initiative would have to be made.

It was the P.S.U.C. that put forward the key question: since the petty bourgeois was really ruling, why maintain worker elements in the government? They should be displaced or invited in from time to time to offer their advice on what the petty bourgeoisie—for which read the P.S.U.C.— would decide. The cleanup should begin, naturally, with the weakest, the P.O.U.M. Further, this would satisfy the demands of Soviet foreign policy. Two birds would be killed with a single stone.

During this period, Nin committed a major tactical error. As early as August he had proposed to the P.O.U.M. executive that, since Trotsky was in exile in Norway and had nowhere else to go, having been rejected by many countries, the P.O.U.M. should suggest to the Generalitat that he be offered asylum in Catalunya. His military experience could be useful, it was argued. This was the worst kind of foolishness. Perhaps Nin felt impelled to commit it because of his friendship (now cooled) with the old Bolshevik, who, as we have seen, had violently attacked the party; perhaps he wanted to demonstrate that notwithstanding the attacks, he, Nin, had put aside personal resentments in the interest of solidarity, something Trotsky himself would certainly never have done. Uneasily, the executive accepted the suggestion, not without some pointing out that they saw no reason to invite Trotsky, since he had, as far as they knew, done nothing to put himself at the disposal of the Spanish revolution, as dictated by proletarian internationalism and as so many others had done. The thing could appear a provocation, had not the communists sought the skin of the P.O.U.M. no matter what they did. But the idea of offering asylum to Trotsky helped the communists to make people believe the myth that the P.O.U.M. was a "Trotskyist" party. When Nin made the proposal to the Generalitat, Comorera opposed it and the rest said they would have to study it calmly—a way of rejecting it without dirtying their hands. Antonov-Ovsyeyenko spoke to Companys and told him that if Trotsky was given asylum, the U.S.S.R. would suspend its aid to the republic.[31]

It was not the P.O.U.M.'s suggestion, obviously, that put the communists on the offensive. But they had been given a good platform from which to launch it, after having prepared it for some time.

Comorera had various meetings with Companys. The latter saw that, from the point of view of middle class politics, the time had come to "domesticate" the C.N.T., but he did not wish to destroy it, because it was convenient for him to keep it as a counterweight to the P.S.U.C., which was stealing his support. The C.N.T. was already in the government of Largo Caballero and could not be eliminated from it, but it was possible, because the C.N.T. was in the government, to "correct it." For this, the P.S.U.C. was necessary. The Esquerra was now no more than a name; its party organization had collapsed, it had almost no militia, and thus, on its own, could not beat the C.N.T.

On November 9, Companys made some declarations to the press: "It is in the interest of all to save the honor and glory of the revolution ... Councils and little councils, commissions, committees, and initiatives exist in excess ... There are more than a dozen reasons obliging us to set up a strong government, with full powers, that will impose its authority."

The Generalitat administration did not resign from office. That was not even mentioned. On December 12, Companys received a C.N.T. commission and dined with the Soviet consul and with Josep Terradelle (head of the Generalitat administration and leader of the Esquerra). At the close of the dinner, Terradelle told some journalists who had been waiting for the meal to end, "It is useless to deny that a political problem has come up." Antonov had not asked that the dinner be kept secret; on the contrary, now that he was sure of getting what he wanted, he wanted it to be known, and that it begin to be understood that it was no longer possible to maintain attitudes disagreeable to Moscow. Much more than gold would have to be paid for Soviet weapons.

On the 13th, "Soli" accused the communists of being responsible for the emergence of a political crisis and argued that the entire antifascist movement should continue to be represented in the Generalitat. But the time had already passed—and it was very brief—in which an editorial in "Soli" counted more than the maneuvers of the P.S.U.C. and the declarations of Companys.

"La Batalla" commented on the 13th, "The rupture [in the government] could not be avoided, because of the intransigence of the P.S.U.C., which was not content to demand our elimination, but which looked forward to the pure and simple annulment of all the revolutionary conquests of the working class, something we will never permit." But was the fact that the P.S.U.C. could achieve this not proof that the P.O.U.M. and C.N.T. were not in a situation to prevent such an outcome?

Comorera allowed part of the truth to get out. When a journalist asked him why the P.S.U.C. demanded the removal of the P.O.U.M. from the government, this man who had been known since the days of the U.S.C. for his anti-Sovietism replied, "The indescribable anti-Soviet campaign [of the

P.O.U.M.] . . . to combat the U.S.S.R. at this time is to commit treason. And we are against traitors."[32]

The P.S.U.C. did not give in. It wanted another government, and Companys agreed. The C.N.T. accepted the elimination of the P.O.U.M. from the government and the replacement of the Commissar of Public Order, an Esquerra member, by someone from the P.S.U.C. The communists, then, would have control over the government and the police.

"Treball," the P.S.U.C. organ, commented triumphantly, "We are struggling against provocateurs with the same tenacity and for the same reasons that we fight the fascists."

On the evening of the 14th, the crisis took on an official and public character. Immediately another government, not particularly strong, was formed by the C.N.T., the U.G.T., the Esquerra, and the Unió de Rabassaires (a trade-union government was how it was described, although the Esquerra represented the middle class). While the representative for the U.G.T. acted, in reality, on behalf of the P.S.U.C., the imaginary removal of the official Communists, demanded by the C.N.T., had taken place. Comorera became *conseller* of supplies and the economy, replacing a C.N.T. member; that is, he was given power to apply the collectivization decree, or, rather, to stulify what had been taking place under the control of the unions, and, therefore, the power to undermine the C.N.T. On January 12, it was seen how far he dared to go, when a decree was published establishing governmental control over the economy, creating new taxes, and fixing norms for the indemnification of expropriated businessmen. Rafael Vidiella, ex-anarchist, ex-socialist, and a vegetarian, succeeded Nin in the *Consellería* of Justice. Nin refused to participate in a ceremony marking his surrender of powers. Vidiella, misunderstanding the situation, said before the high functionaries of the *Consellería*, "In me you have a comrade. You can count on me."

"But not on me," Nin answered. "What is going on when every day you call us agents of fascism?"

The Spanish revolution had begun its phase of open counterrevolution.

Notes

1. A vivid eyewitness description of the fighting at the plaça Catalunya and the plaça de l'Universitat is included in Carmel Rosa (Roc), op. cit., pp. 147-149.
2. D.T. Cattell, *Communism and the Spanish Civil War,* Berkeley, 1956, p. 47.
3. Ibid., p. 49.
4. An English-language narrative on the P.O.U.M. that includes a description of fighting at Siguenza is Mary Low and Juan Brea, *Red Spanish Notebook,* San Francisco, 1979. Mika Etchebehere and Pavel and Clara Thalmann have also contributed accounts, in French and German. On these writers, see chapter 7.

5. Letter from Ignacio Iglesias to Víctor Alba, July 1, 1973.
6. George Orwell, *Homage to Catalonia,* London, 1937. An article that places Nin, but not the P.O.U.M., in the overall tradition of Trotskyism is Stephen Schwartz, "A la Memoria de Andreu Nin," in "Cuenta y Razon" (Madrid), September-December 1985.
7. Franz Borkenau, *The Spanish Cockpit,* Ann Arbor, 1963, p. 85.
8. Joaquim Maurín, *Revolucion y contrarrevolucion en España,* Appendix, p. 288.
9. A thorough analysis of the role of the Fifth Regiment as an agency of Communist influence on the Republican side is included in Burnett Bolloten, *The Spanish Revolution,* Chapel Hill, 1979, one of the most comprehensive works on the Spanish Civil War.
10. This discussion of the fate of the F.O.U.S. is based on conversations between Víctor Alba and Pere Bonet, assistant general secretary of the F.O.U.S. and trade union secretary of the B.O.C. from its foundation on.
11. Wilebaldo Solano, in La Revolution Espagnole, "Etudes Marxistes," Paris, 1969, p. 36.
12. Trotsky, op. cit., p. 322.
13. This and other speeches of Nin, with some of his writings from this period, are included in *Los Problemas de la revolucion española,* Paris, 1971. This speech appears beginning on page 175.
14. Diego Abad de Santillán, *Porqué perdimos la guerra,* Buenos Aires, 1940, p. 70.
15. Information based on a letter from Pere Bonet in Paris to Víctor Alba, August 18, 1972.
16. A good summary of the successive positions of the party in this area is included in a university thesis by Pelai Pagès and Xavier Virós (still unpublished), "El P.O.U.M. ante la revolución española," Barcelona, 1971.
17. *La Guerra i la Revolució a Catalunya en el Terreny Economic,* a collection of articles that originally appeared in the P.O.U.M. newspaper "Front" (Terrassa), written by Oltra Pico, and to which he attached a prologue when they were published in pamphlet form (Barcelona, 1937). See p. 17.
18. Ibid., pp. 16, 22, 28.
19. Ibid., pp. 3 and 6.
20. "La Batalla," November 17, 1936.
21. "La Batalla," November 19-20, 1936.
22. Borkenau, *The Spanish Cockpit,* pp. 105-106.
23. See John Cornford, "Diary Letter from Aragon," in Valentine Cunningham, *The Penguin Book of Spanish Civil War Verse,* Harmondsworth, 1980, an important and honest account of the attack on Perdiguera. On the Mallorca expedition, see Manuel Cruells, *L'Expedicio a Mallorca.* ANY 1936, Barcelona, 1972, p. 145. On Bayo, see Stephen Schwartz, "On Revolutionary War," in Stephen Schwartz, ed., *The Transition,* San Francisco, 1986, pp. 92-93.
24. The resolutions of this congress were published in a pamphlet titled *A Lead to World Socialism,* London, 1937.
25. Fernando Claudín, *The Communist Movement,* Part One, New York, 1975, pp. 239-240. The Trotsky citation is Trotsky, op. cit., p. 319.
26. Mikhail Koltsov, *Diario de la guerra de españa,* Paris, 1953, p. 13.
27. Cited in Felix Morrow, *Revolution and Counter-revolution in Spain,* New York, 1938, pp. 67-68.
28. Antonio Ramos Oliveira, *Politics, Economics and Men of Modern Spain.* London, 1946, p. 294.

29. Stanley Payne, *The Spanish Revolution,* New York, 1970, p. 249.
30. Ignacio Iglesias, *El Proletariado y las clases medias,* Barcelona, 1937. When it was published, the situation of the P.O.U.M. had changed, but the pamphlet continued to be relevant. Iglesias was a clerical worker from Asturias who had taken refuge in Barcelona after October 1934 as a member of the Communist Left and who returned to Asturias, on order of the P.O.U.M. executive, at the beginning of 1937.
31. According to a letter to Victor Alba from Ignacio Iglesias (July 1, 1973), the P.O.U.M. executive agreed to ask the Generalitat to grant asylum to Trotsky at the beginning of August. In a letter of Trotsky's to Jean Rous, the former commented on the possibility, but the letter was intercepted by fascist agents and never reached its destination. See Trotsky, op. cit., p. 239.
32. "La Noche" (Barcelona), December 14, 1936.

5

Defamation

The dangerous turn of events, both for the P.O.U.M. and for the Spanish revolution in general, was quickly perceived by the P.O.U.M. itself, and soon, as well, by a part of the C.N.T. and some foreign organizations. But the P.O.U.M. could not resign itself to the situation. It had to react and try to change the direction of developments, not only in the interest of its own security, but also because it did not accept the idea of the revolution being beaten. It did not suffer the pretension of thinking that it, as a party, was in itself the revolution; i.e., it did not allow itself to be misled by the Bolshevik example that identified the party with the revolution. In Spain, the future of the revolution, for reasons we have described, depended to a great extent on what took place in Catalunya, and what happened in Catalunya depended on the C.N.T.

"La Batalla" commented on the Generalitat crisis in its December 15 issue:

> The P.S.U.C., in its press organ, and from the public tribune, has initiated an entire campaign of insults and calumnies against our party, a campaign that has had no other object than to prepare what they have already demanded: our elimination from the [Generalitat] council. We have carried out every kind of effort against a break in unity of action at moments like these, not because we have either greater or lesser attachment to governmental positions, but because we would consider such a break to be something that only would benefit fascism. Other organizations have made efforts, at the same time, to avoid a rupture, and in the very first place the C.N.T.

"Soli" seemed to be aware of the significance of the crisis, although the C.N.T. had accepted the situation with little comment. The same day, December 15, it commented, "The war cannot be separated from the revolution." But it insisted that the C.N.T. "has such an elevated conception of individual and collective freedom that we do not desire the triumph of a

171

proletarian economic policy at the cost of imposition of a dictatorship of the working class."

"Treball," the P.S.U.C. daily, on the same day, published a blessing on itself:

> Our attitude toward the P.O.U.M. is not . . . as some seem to think, a partisan posture. We struggle against provocateurs with the same tenacity and for the same reason as against the fascists. The whole world knows our work in favor of unification; the whole world knows that we were its initiators and that we have been and will continue being its most fierce defenders.

Within twenty-four hours of taking position of his new post as *conseller* of supplies, Comorera made declarations affirming that the food ware-houses were empty and that the C.N.T. member who occupied the post before him was an incompetent. It seemed not to matter that these state-ments pushed prices up and activated the black market. What was impor-tant was to turn the anger of housewives at scarcities against the C.N.T.

The Communist Offensive

While to P.O.U.M. members this campaign still "seemed a lie," an en-larged central committee plenum met from December 12 through 16 and occupied itself with topics of the moment and others that were not so pressing: measures to pass from the collectivization to the socialization of the economy, for example. The reading of the central committee resolu-tions[1] gives the impression that the P.O.U.M. was not aware that its exit from the Catalan government was not a mere accident. In any case, the central committee meeting had an air of normality that the situation did not justify. The plenum opposed the formation of a regular army, which was already taking place, because "the working class cannot permit that under pretext of military necessity, an army will be rebuilt that tomorrow will be an instrument to destroy it." But since the militias were already disappearing, it proposed that a revolutionary Red Army be formed.

The central committee condemned the Moscow trials and affirmed that "the best way of defending the Russian Revolution, of which from the beginning we have been the most enthusiastic defenders, consists in push-ing to the end the socialist revolution in our country. For this reason, we must not submit ourselves to any international, because the second and third internationals are not and cannot be the instrument of the world revolution. Nor can it be the fourth international founded by Trotsky, without a base in the masses because of its sectarian character."

The central committee decided to organize for February 15, 1937, a

P.O.U.M. congress, and dedicated part of its agenda to discussion of the problems for the party created by its leaving the Catalan government and by the P.S.U.C. offensive. The reaction, almost unanimous, was toward the radicalization of the P.O.U.M.'s positions. It was necessary to accentuate the revolutionary character of the war, not to be limited to a defense of conquests already achieved. The resolution on internal policy said:

> The revolution is undergoing a critical moment. The bourgeoisie is trying once again to raise its head . . . The war and the revolution are inseparable, and if we permit the triumph of the counterrevolution, the war will be lost. If fascism did not triumph, it was because of the action of the proletariat. It exercised absolute power, in the first months following July 19 . . .

> The most efficacious means to consolidate the conquests of the revolution and to push the revolution forward consists in utilizing the bodies that express the aspirations of the working class. To maintain the bourgeois parliament is an anachronism that could be fatal . . . In its place, a constituent assembly must be formed, elected by the committees of workers, peasants, and soldiers, the factory committees, etc., and from which a workers' and peasants' government must come . . . The indispensable condition for the victory of the revolution is a vast and profound workers' democracy that would protect the revolution from any attempt at a dictatorial hegemony on the part of a given party or organization . . .

The members of the central committee knew that none of this could be put into practice without the action of the C.N.T. and that it would be more difficult now than some months before, before the dissolution of the committees by the Catalan government, of which the P.O.U.M. was a part.

For political motives—and also, later, for psychological and even for personal security reasons—the P.O.U.M. had to get closer to the C.N.T., to dialogue, if possible, with its leaders and militants, trying to create in them the awareness that the question of power was fundamental. This had to be done rapidly, before the counterrevolutionary offensive gained positions that would make it unbeatable and rebound to make the fascist enemy unbeatable.

This necessity would determine the policy of the P.O.U.M. in the first half of 1937. If the P.O.U.M. launched itself energetically to this task, the people in the street also understood that the P.O.U.M. was no longer a party of the future. In a meeting in January 1937, in which Nin exaggerated to the point of saying that "there can be no government without the P.O.U.M. and even less against the P.O.U.M.," Borkenau, who at this time had returned to Spain for a second visit, had the impression that the P.O.U.M. was "in obvious decline," along with the Esquerra; he noted that "the P.O.U.M. was liked by nobody, being overbearing and claiming with its small forces leadership over the old established mass organizations, both anarchist and socialist. All through the time of their supremacy, the anarchists had handled the P.O.U.M. rather rudely, but this time they felt that they were themselves concerned in the attack" of the P.S.U.C. on the P.O.U.M.[2]

The aggressiveness of the P.S.U.C. and the official Communist Party throughout Spain grew. Even in places where the P.O.U.M. had never existed and where nobody knew anything about it, the communist press dedicated an immense space to attacking it, with great confusion among its readers. Now they spoke not of the P.O.U.M., but of the "Trotskyites," which bothered the P.O.U.M. even more than the attacks themselves.

"La Batalla" declared on January 27:

> Stalin knows perfectly well that with the exception of one or two of the defendants [in the Moscow trials] the rest are not Trotskyists ... They also accuse us of being Trotskyists. We are not. ... They call the Moscow defendants Gestapo agents. They say the same about us. ... Fortunately, Spain is not Russia, but an attempt is being made to place Spain under Russian domination, which we will oppose with all our energy.

The communist slander campaign for the moment found no echo in the rest of the left-wing press, but only the anarchosyndicalist journals and those sympathetic to Caballero in the Socialist Party (reduced to two) condemned it. The campaign was not in vain. Pressure was brought on the authorities to take advantage of any pretext to harass the P.O.U.M., and when such took place, they took the measures as a proof that what the lie campaign claimed was true. For example, when the Madrid Defense Council suppressed the P.O.U.M. press in the capital, following communist pressure (which was irresistible in Madrid), the communist periodicals said the decision of the council demonstrated that the P.O.U.M. was fascist, else why would its journal have been suppressed?

The weakness of People's Front elements around the world, who in the name of not helping fascism kept quiet about the Moscow trials, was repeated in Spain; with the pretext of not helping the enemy, the communist calumnies and insults against the P.O.U.M. were tolerated.

In January, the periodical of the P.S.U.C. Karl Marx Division published a cartoon of Nin in comradeship with Franco, with an article stating, "Nin has never worked, because he has always lived off money from Hitler."

In a meeting of the P.O.U.M. Youth on January 30, Nin referred satirically to this personal attack: "My friends could consider themselves to have been cheated, and demand part of my income." He went on to say:

> When people go to such extremes, what we feel is sorrow for the calumniators. And it is sadder still when we take into account that the poor fool

who has written this is the person who least believes it . . . If the slanderers who accuse us of being Franco's accomplices believe these accusations, let them call us before the people's tribunals, which I established, and we will see what happens.

But obviously it was not before the people's tribunals that the P.O.U.M. would be called by the communists, at least not until the masses could be convinced to accept an image of the P.O.U.M. that was very different from reality.

For four months, the P.O.U.M. dedicated itself to sounding the warning that the anti-P.O.U.M. campaign was the first step toward the elimination of the C.N.T. The *cenetistes*, fooled by their own numerical strength, still so believed in their power that they were very late in taking reality into account. They were in the government and did not believe it could function without them. For that reason, they considered things like the following, published in "Frente Rojo" in Valencia on February 6, as family quarrels:

> At the present time, the rag published in Barcelona under the title of 'La Batalla' defends itself with arguments as inconsistent and comical as the following: Referring to the [Moscow] trial of the Trotskyites, it calls it an 'unjust farce,' and in the line just afterward it recognizes that the ambassadors of France and the United States were present. That is, a trial that has developed before hundreds of foreign journalists, before the diplomatic corps, with juridical guarantees for the defendants that do not exist in any other country, for the P.O.U.M. deserves to be described as a farce. Naturally, their Spanish accomplices are not going to recognize the justice exercised against a gang of murderers. The day the Trotskyites are judged in Spain— because we, like our fraternal colleague 'Mundo Obrero' demand that a people's tribunal judge the fascist cadres of this organization—their accomplices from everywhere else in the world will say that the justice meted out by our people has been an 'unjust farce.'

The official Communists were thus preparing the terrain for a move from the harassment of the P.O.U.M. to its direct repression. It was not enough to silence a voice of criticism directed against the Moscow trials; we now know, from the testimony of Soviet defectors such as Walter Krivitsky, that Stalin sought above all else a repetition of the Moscow trials in at least one Western country, and more if possible, so as to silence the wider chorus of disbelief in Soviet justice. Such an attempt took place in Czechoslovakia, notably, as well as in Spain.[3]

In one area, the P.O.U.M.'s link with the C.N.T. had begun to show a certain success: the P.O.U.M. Youth (JCI) and the Juventudes Libertarias (J.J.L.L.) formed a Revolutionary Youth Front (Front de la Joventut Revolucionaria—F.J.R.), in which they were joined by such other organizations as the Juventudes Cooperativistas, and the anarchist Agrupación de Mujeres Libres (Grouping of Free Women) the latter an outstanding example of revolutionary feminism. The agreement setting up the F.J.R. was signed on February 11, 1937, and three days later was presented to the masses in an enormous meeting in the plaça Catalunya. The agreement found support in Madrid, where a congress of the Central regional J.J.L.L. affirmed that the war aimed not at democracy, but at revolution. The J.S.U., controlled by the official Communists, was undergoing a crisis. Various of its elements who came from the Socialist Party did not accept Carrillo's definition of the J.S.U. as non-Marxist. Rafael Fernández, secretary of the Asturias J.S.U., quit his post in the J.S.U. national committee and signed an agreement with the J.J.L.L. setting up an Asturian F.J.R. Jose Gregori, Llevante regional J.S.U. secretary, also resigned. Carrillo accused them of "letting themselves be manipulated by the Trotskyites."

The activity of the J.C.I. enraged the communists. Carrillo affirmed that "the enemies of unity are the Trotskyite elements, who have done everything they could to prevent this unity from being carried out. Once union was effected between the socialist and communist youth, they created an Iberian Communist Youth that, maneuvering in the name of Lenin and the Russian Revolution, hoped with trickery to attract the youth. But its maneuvers past and present have served it for nothing. What has become clear is the treasonous role the Trotskyites play. What has made it manifest is that when the Trotskyites fight against the J.S.U., the Communist Party, the People's Front, the unity of the antifascist popular masses, in reality they do nothing but play the sad role of agents of international fascism."

The pamphlet publication of this diatribe then adds that, on hearing this, "the public rises and sings 'The International.'"[4]

The F.J.R. began planning a meeting for Valencia, in May, in which the Revolutionary Youth Front would be constituted nationally, and it established contacts with more former socialist youth members discontented with communist rule over their organization, and who proposed to return to a separate socialist youth organization.

On March 2, the government fined "La Batalla" 5,000 pesetas for having published news not submitted to war censorship. The official Communist Party celebrated an expanded plenum of its central committee in Valencia, beginning March 4, in which José Díaz presented a report on what the Communist Party considered indispensable for winning the war: army unification (that is, in fact, communist control of the army) and elimination of the P.O.U.M. The plenum documents showed an aggressive posture and determined the tone of communist propaganda in the months to follow. It is worth reading from the resolution in question:

> The expanded plenum of the central committee of the Communist party of Spain has come to the following conclusions:

Educating the people in hatred and intransigence toward the enemy. Against open enemies and against hidden enemies. To educate the people in hatred and intransigence to the point of extermination against national and foreign fascism invading and razing with arms our country and which carries out treason in the rearguard, but also against its agents disguised as 'revolutionaries' who work in the ranks of the antifascist organizations.

We must struggle to end the tolerance and the lack of vigilance of certain proletarian organizations that establish links of convenience with counter-revolutionary Trotskyism, with the P.O.U.M. gang, considering it to be a section of the workers' movement. Trotskyism, nationally and internationally, whatever the mask it hides behind, has been revealed to be an organization that is 'counterrevolutionary and terrorist, in the service of international fascism.' We must bring into the heart of the worker masses, to educate them in fierce struggle and hatred against their enemies, the just position of our party, of refusal to participate in any organization or event in which the Trotskyites are involved. Trotskyism is, with its high-sounding and pseudo-revolutionary verbiage, the inspirer of the 'uncontrollables,' encouraging the action of those who want to act outside the democratic law established by the People's Front Government, and, with its venomous intrigues, creating difficulties at the front and in the rearguard, putting at risk the results of our struggle.

We must fight until we achieve the elimination of fascism, Trotskyism, and the 'uncontrollables' from the political life of our country.[5]

In the March 14 "La Batalla," Nin, in a long article on "The Marxist Conception of Power and the Spanish Revolution," tried to dispel the fears of the anarchists regarding this topic: "If the conquest of economic power is not crowned by that of political power, the consequences will be disastrous. On July 19, it was enough to wish it for the remains of bourgeois power to have been eliminated."

He believed it was easier to make the C.N.T. workers understand the need to participate in a revolutionary workers' government than in a petty bourgeois government. "If the C.N.T., the F.A.I., and the P.O.U.M., among which there now exist views in common of the greatest importance, dedicate themselves to an agreement on this essential base (the need for a revolutionary government) the revolution could save itself, because the workers have not yet been disarmed and still hold important strategic positions."

But there was no time to waste. If the opportunity for its emancipation and for a powerful advance of the world revolution was not seized immediately by the Spanish working class, it would be too late. "We must strike while the iron is hot."

But those who had a grasp on the iron were the communists. On March 17, they succeeded in forcing the Generalitat administration, which included the C.N.T., to suspend "La Batalla" for four days, for not having observed the rules of censorship. The paper came out under another name, just as Lenin's "Pravda" in the days leading up to the October Revolution was forced to invent a new name for itself each day, following new suppressions. The F.J.R. and the J.J.L.L. protested, the C.N.T. became aware that it had made a mistake, and at the end of two days the suspension was lifted. But shortly thereafter, the P.O.U.M. radio station was confiscated and, since it was less prominent, no protests took place and the P.O.U.M. remained without a radio, a matter of little immediate importance, since few people listened to the party's broadcasts.

The Dilemma of the C.N.T.

The P.O.U.M. was aware that alone they could not respond to the communist attacks and that these were provocations aimed at forcing them to react in a way that would justify a broader repression. There were moments, however, when exasperation threatened to explode. The P.O.U.M. local committee in Barcelona, for example, proposed a return to the policy of organizing people's committees to take power immediately.

On March 21, P.O.U.M. meeting was held to answer the communist campaign. The speech Nin delivered carried the following subheads, which summarized his remarks:

> To hold back the advancing counterrevolution. In July, power was in the street. They wish to reconstitute the bourgeois state. The government in Valencia (where the central government had fled from Madrid) against Catalunya. The counterrevolution in the public order. Nobody will suffocate the voice of our party. Nin states that the revolution has gone backward under pressure of communist reformism, which is a political current not working-class, but petty bourgeois. If, on July 20, the P.O.U.M. had the strength of the C.N.T., things would not be as they are, for we would have taken power. The C.N.T. must examine its conscience, going beyond theoretical prejudices. There is still time to form a workers' and peasants' government.

But the recommendations of the P.O.U.M. in this direction gained no hearing among the C.N.T. masses. Nevertheless, the Generalitat administration resigned on March 27, because its C.N.T. *consellers* refused to support decrees reorganizing the police, with the aim of depoliticizing the forces of order.

The P.O.U.M. central committee, which was in session, supported the C.N.T. position in this matter and suggested that in each *consellería* there should be a commission made up of representatives of all the Left organizations, to avoid the use of any *consellería* for political ends. "This is not a true Generalitat administration," the central committee declared, "because it does not reflect the situation created on July 19."

It was necessary, then, to form a government with representatives of all the working class organizations and with a precise program. "La Batalla" for April 4, reporting on the central committee discussions, outlined what this program should be:

> The P.O.U.M. central committee, meeting last Sunday, made public a note respecting the crisis of the Generalitat council, bringing together in thirteen concrete points the program that, in agreement with the aspirations of the masses and the needs of the revolution, a government of all working-class political and union forces must apply, as the sole rational, logical, and viable solution to the crisis. We reproduce those concrete points for the interest they have at these moments:
>
> 1. Socialization of the major transport industries.
>
> 2. Nationalization of the banking system.
>
> 3. Municipalization of housing.
>
> 4. Formation of an army controlled by the working masses.
>
> 5. Constitution of a single internal security body, based on the control patrols and on the investigative office created by the revolution and with the incorporation of the former organs that have demonstrated their loyalty to the working class.
>
> 6. An immediate offensive in Aragon.
>
> 7. Reduction of large salaries.
>
> 8. Monopoly of foreign trade.
>
> 9. Creation of a powerful socialized and rigorously centralized war industry.
>
> 10. Nationalization of the land, turning it over in usufruct to those who work it, granting them the necessary credit. Collective exploitation of the big estates and economic relief to those enterprises of a collective character created during the course of the revolution and that have demonstrated their vitality.
>
> 11. An implacable struggle against profiteers and speculators through an extremely rigorous and direct control of the distribution and the prices of subsistence goods.
>
> 12. A rapid and efficient organization of air and maritime defense of the entire territory.
>
> 13. Convocation of a congress of delegates of the unions of workers, peasants, and soldiers, which would establish the fundamental bases of a new regime and elect a workers' and peasants' government that will be the most democratic ever known in that it will express unequivocally the will of the immense majority of the country and will have total authority to secure the new revolutionary order.[6]

This program was an excellent one for the continuation of the revolution, but not for its defense against powerful and ruthless enemies. It was not even certain that a government organized on this program would express the will of the immense majority of the country. In the rest of the republican zone, outside Catalunya, there is considerable evidence of the minority position of the genuinely revolutionary forces, which were, in any case, less explicit about their demands than those in Catalunya. In Catalunya itself, nobody could say whether, once the enthusiasm provoked by July 19 had passed, the majority favored the revolution.

The nearly sterile effort to win over the anarchists continued. On March 23, "La Batalla" had published another long article by Nin in which he explained that the dictatorship of the proletariat the P.O.U.M. called for was not like that of the U.S.S.R., which was based on a single party. "We have a system of workers' democracy with parties, unions, publications. For this reason, there are no soviets in Spain. In Russia, there was a tradition neither of democracy, nor of proletarian organization and struggle, things that would make impossible the dictatorship of a single revolutionary organization."

The latest crisis of the Generalitat lasted a month, ending on April 26, with an administration of the same composition as its predecessor, but which accepted that the police should continue to be made up of individuals named by the organizations and parties (except those who were police before July 19). The C.N.T. had, then, held off the blow, for the moment and only on one issue.

At the same time as the P.O.U.M. found itself in debate with the C.N.T., it also found it necessary to publicize its differences with the official Trotskyists. First, they had to answer (to the extent possible) the falsifications of the communists, but also, a tiny Trotskyist grouplet, the Bolshevik-Leninist Section of Spain (Seccion Bolchevique-Leninista de Espana—S.B.L.) had tried to infiltrate the party's ranks, mainly through some Italian members of the P.O.U.M. militia, to excite the rank and file against the leadership.

The S.B.L. consisted almost entirely of foreigners. At the beginning, the Trotskyists had been mainly led by Fosco, the Italian Trotskyist charged with relations between the P.O.U.M. and the antifascist refugees, and had managed to establish fairly good relations with the party, thanks to the flexibility and enthusiasm of such individuals as Pavel and Clara Thalmann, Mary Low and Juan Bréa, and Lois and Charles Orr (whose work is described in greater detail in chapter 7), along with other foreign volunteers—including another Italian, Domenico Sedran (who used the name "Adolfo Carlini"), a young Frenchman, Robert de Fauconnet, and a young German Jew, Hans Freund, known as "Moulin."

Although frank about their loyalty to Trotsky, these individuals won respect among the P.O.U.M. ranks by their courage and dedication. But the situation grew complicated, thanks to factional intrigues within the Trotskyist movement. Fosco was aligned with a minority tendency led by one Raymond Molinier, a French activist. Jean Rous, who soon arrived on the scene representing the majority (anti-Molinier) tendency, attacked Fosco's line of working within the P.O.U.M., supporting his criticism with violent anti-P.O.U.M. statements by Trotsky himself. The effect of this was only to vitiate the goodwill the Trotskyists had built up in the early stage of their participation.

In November 1936, a new, "cleansed" group, the S.B.L., appeared, on a frankly anti-P.O.U.M. program. Fosco was declared outside the Trotskyist movement. The head of this "official" grouping was G. Munis (Manuel Fernández Grandizo), a young member of the former Communist Left who had gone to Mexico, where his family lived, just before the revolution, and only returned after the passage of some months.

Munis had been active as a factional leader against Nin as early as 1932. A writer and theoretician of some talent, Munis was nonetheless a rigid and dogmatic adherent of Trotsky's. His grouping, the S.B.L., never gained more than thirty members; the most prominent, aside from Munis, were Moulin, Carlini, who became a militiaman, and a republican soldier, Jaime Fernández Rodríguez (later known as "Costa"), the only republican hostage to escape from the fascist-held Alcázar in Toledo. Although other Trotskyists stayed outside it, the Munis-Carlini-Moulin group obtained the official sanction of Rous and Trotsky, the latter still occupied, for the greater part of the time he spent writing on Spanish questions, with his war on the P.O.U.M. The French surrealist poet Benjamin Péret, who had acted briefly as Rous' second in dealing with the P.O.U.M., also ended up associated with the S.B.L.[7]

On April 24, Gorkín reported in "La Batalla":

> With the outbreak of civil war, we have seen manifested once again the sectarianism of Trotsky. The current representative of the Fourth International [Jean Rous], two hours after his arrival [in Barcelona], and after conversing with us for fifteen minutes, brought out of his pocket a program prepared in advance, offering us counsel on the tactic that we should apply. We told him in a friendly way that he should take a walk around Barcelona and study the situation more closely. This citizen is a perfect symbol of Trotskyism, of sectarian doctrinarism, of great smugness, certain that he possesses the philosopher's stone of the revolution.

In theses Nin had begun to prepare for the P.O.U.M. congress on "The Problem of Power, the Petty Bourgeoisie, and the Revolution," he wrote:

> The imperious duty of the moment is the conquest of power by the pro-

letariat, allied with the peasantry, which can be accomplished peacefully, and the consequent formation of a workers' and peasants' government, alone capable of organizing, in accord with the needs of the population and the war, the disturbed economy, and establishing revolutionary order in the country ... The most considerable obstacle opposed to the advance of the proletarian revolution is reformism ... whose most characteristic exponent is the Communist Party ... which has definitely abandoned revolutionary class politics ... Naturally, this can only be carried out by an alliance of the P.O.U.M., C.N.T., and left wing of the P.S.O.E. ... The communists have abandoned the Leninist theory of the state and have fallen into the utopia of a democratic state above classes ... with the aim of mystifying the masses and preparing the pure and simple consolidation of the bourgeois regime.[8]

In reality, the country was speaking in a less and less revolutionary way with the passage of each day. The apparatus of communist propaganda became tremendously efficient. It did not succeed in making people enthusiastic about its slogans, but it was able to suffocate the slogans of others. On April 4, "La Batalla," in its column entitled "Of the Day" ("Del Día"), had said, with regard to this:

The theoretical degeneration of 'official' Communism produced justly unexpected surprises. During the first years of the republic, they agitated with the demand of a Soviet republic ... without soviets. That was during the bourgeois-democratic stage. Now, in the middle of a socialist revolution, they waste their energy trying to go back to the bourgeois-democratic republic.

But there is something still more monstrous than all this. Concentrating their interest on the fact of the invasion by the German and Italian armies—something that corroborates the class character of our civil war—they pluck the strings of their hearts when they talk about the independence of 'our' fatherland. They refer to the Napoleonic invasion, while some—the better educated—speak of the Arabs overrunning Spanish soil. [The Spanish patriotic figures] Pelayo, el Cid Campeador, Mina, el Empecinado, Velarde, and many others are the heroes of the hour. Thus they justify our movement backward, and, what is worse, they claim these figures as their personal property. The so-called reconquest prevented the Arabs from extending their superior civilization throughout the peninsula and the war of independence liquidated every possibility of the vivifying wind of the French Revolution from entering our country. But this attitude is a hundred percent in the interest of patrioteering Stalinism.

Andrade wrote on April 15 in "La Révolution Espagnole," the P.O.U.M. international organ in French, "It can be affirmed that the future of the Spanish revolution absolutely depends on the attitude of the C.N.T. and F.A.I. .... The possibility of the P.O.U.M. turning into a great mass party that could acquire hegemony in the revolution is limited by the existence of anarchism." And confronting the foreign Trotskyists, he continued: "Those that have a narrowly sectarian, schematic conception that a minority with correct politics can rapidly turn itself into a determining force, will receive necessary lessons from Spanish events."

But if it was not possible to quickly create a great mass party, this difficulty could be resolved by setting up a revolutionary united front between the C.N.T.-F.A.I. and P.O.U.M.. "The problem consists, for the Marxists, in aiding [the C.N.T.-F.A.I.] to overcome its prejudices and to give itself a new orientation."

On April 25, in a speech, Nin tried once again to dissipate the hesitations of the anarchists. "The formulae of the Russian Revolution, mechanically applied, will lead us to the defeat of Marxism. From the Russian Revolution, we have to take, not the letter, but the spirit, the experience ... In Spain, the existence of an anarchist movement presents new problems ... The C.N.T. is a potentially revolutionary organization, notwithstanding its prejudices and its mistaken positions ... The vacillations of the C.N.T. are due to the lack of a theory of power ... But the P.O.U.M. is a thousand times closer to the C.N.T. and the F.A.I. than to the P.S.U.C." He ended by affirming that "the proletariat can still take power without violence, but if the counterrevolution advances further, it will have to take power, through violence."[9]

The situation was becoming more and more tense. The communists believed the moment for action was approaching. The anarchist leaders felt the nervousness of their militants. And the communists kept up their pressure.

Of the P.O.U.M. press outside Catalunya, "El Comunista" in Valencia was the only periodical that could continue to publish. "Juventud Roja," the P.O.U.M. youth organ in Valencia, was suspended because the censorship had left its pages almost completely blank. On a petition of the P.S.U.C., the P.O.U.M. Red Aid was suspended from the Catalan Committee for Aid to Madrid. The campaign kept coming closer to the C.N.T.: "Nosotros," an outstanding organ for the most active anarchists, published in Valencia, was suspended, along with the journal "C.N.T." in Bilbao, where the Northern Regional Committee of the C.N.T. was arrested, and the Euzkadi government turned the C.N.T.'s printing shop over to the Communist Party. The Madrid anarchosyndicalist papers "C.N.T." and "Castilla Libre" were suspended for several days. Each time, "Soli" protested, stating that its patience was becoming exhausted, but the four C.N.T. ministers in the central government remained at their posts, incapable of halting the communist offensive.

Dolores Ibárruri had written in "Frente Rojo" on February 4, "There can be neither compromises nor dealings with them [the 'Trotskyites of the P.O.U.M.'] ... We must always remember that between ourselves and the Trotskyites there is an abyss filled with blood."

The attacks on the P.O.U.M. reached the front in Aragon. On February 23, an operation by the P.O.U.M. 29th Division in the direction of Vivel del Rio, under orders from Barbastro, saw the P.S.U.C. 27th Division refuse to support the P.O.U.M. attack by flanking action, leading to defeat. It was for having denounced this that "La Batalla" was, as we have noted, suspended. "El Leninista," the internal bulletin of the P.S.U.C., announced that the P.S.U.C. cell in the Servicios Eléctricos firm had been able to eliminate the P.O.U.M. from the control committee of the enterprise: "Presently, in this building, among more than seven hundred employees, there is not a single P.O.U.M. militant."

In March, a speech by José Díaz added fuel to the fire: "Our enemy is fascism ... but our hatred, with the same degree of concentrated strength, is directed also against the agents of fascism, the P.O.U.M., the disguised Trotskyites, who hide themselves behind supposedly revolutionary slogans with the aim of carrying out their main mission as agents of our enemy." In one thing the plan failed: They could not drive a wedge between the P.O.U.M. leaders and the militants. The Russian journalist Koltsov had already prepared the ground, declaring that there were "P.O.U.Mists of good faith," but that "Nin followed the orders of Trotsky."[10]

During the same month of March, "Soli" affirmed that the attacks on the P.O.U.M. were dividing the antifascist front. Immediately, "Pravda," on March 22, in an article signed by N. Olivier, replied under the title "The Intrigues of the Trotskyite Agents of Franco"; the Communist Party circulated a translation of this article among its propagandists, as an inspirational document:

> The central organ of the anarchists, 'Solidaridad Obrera,' which is published in Barcelona, on March 16 threatens the Soviet press with insulting attacks. And in a special way, the author judges the articles by Soviet correspondents, regarding the counterrevolutionary attitude of the Trotskyite P.O.U.M. organization, as a harmful tactic whose aim is to sow discord among the 'antifascists of Spain.'

> This filthy little article, which defends the Trotskyite traitors, is created by obscure elements who have infiltrated the ranks of the anarchosyndicalist organization. These are former collaborators of Primo de Rivera, of the Falange Española, and Trotskyites ...

The anarchist figure who best understood the position of the P.O.U.M. was the Italian Camillo Berneri, who stated in an article, "If the P.O.U.M. was a predominant political force, there would be a basis to criticize it. But today the P.O.U.M. is a considerable force in the antifascist struggle and in the resistance to the strangling of the revolution, and for that reason the theoretical differences between us and them are a small thing compared with the present and possible convergences on the field of action. Many critical themes and many agitational formulae of the P.O.U.M. reflect reality and strengthen the development of the Spanish social revolution . . . We must say very publicly that whoever caluminates and insults the P.O.U.M. and demands its suppression, is a saboteur of the antifascist struggle and this cannot be tolerated . . ."[11]

Although the campaign against the P.O.U.M. satisfied the P.S.U.C.'s base of frightened petty bourgeois, the latter party responded to orders from much higher up. Stalin himself decided the position of the Spanish and Catalan communists. In a personal letter to Largo Caballero, dated in Moscow on December 24, 1936, Stalin told him that parliamentary action could be, in Spain, more efficient than what had taken place in Russia, and gave some "friendly advice." It included the proposal that Largo's government attract the urban petty and middle bourgeoisie to its side, "protecting them from any measure of confiscation and assuring them freedom of trade"; Stalin also advised Largo to declare that the government of Spain would not "tolerate anybody threatening the property and legitimate interests of foreigners in Spain, of citizens of countries that are not helping the fascists."[12]

The Comintern, obviously, echoed Stalin's arguments, not only transmitting orders to the previously mentioned *troika* of its chief agents in Spain, but also putting their positions in documents. In these, however, it seldom mentioned the P.O.U.M. by name, but referred to it as a "Trotskyite organization."

In a December 1936 letter, the Comintern executive committee said it considered "correct the struggle of the Spanish Communist party, supported by other People's Front organizations, against the Trotskyites as fascist agents, who in the interest of Hitler and General Franco try to break up the People's Front, sustaining a campaign of calumnies against the U.S.S.R. and utilizing all means, all classes of intrigues and demagogical tricks to impede the defeat of fascism in Spain. Given that the Trotskyites, in the interest of fascism, will carry out their subversive work in the rearguard, the Presidium approves the policy of the Spanish party directed to the complete and definitive destruction of Trotskyism in Spain, as something essential for the victory over fascism . . ."[13]

Koltsov, the journalist, gave a literary form to the campaign and added elements typical of a novel. In his diary, he wrote on January 21, 1937, as follows:

> What has ruined things for [the P.O.U.M.] and led to their failure has been that their own leader has imposed on them obligations that are in truth unspoken and that cannot be complied with in any way. In the country where

the People's Front is leading the armed struggle for freedom and independence, in the country where a man from the Soviet Union is literally surrounded by general veneration and affection, Trotsky has given to his partisans two orders: first, to attack the People's Front, and second, to attack the
Soviet Union.[14]

At times, curious coincidences existed, such as when Winston Churchill,
wrote in his diary of the P.O.U.M. as "a sect achieving the quintessence of
fetidness." Churchill later commented in horror on the "success of the
Trotskyist and anarchist forces," which he did not consider impossible.[15] A
Franco victory did not seem to him to be contrary to British and French
interests.

Nin said, in a meeting on April 10,

> There are those who think of the revolution as a train that comes into the
> station punctually and that the stationmaster then says, 'Gentlemen, we have
> arrived at the social revolution.' The revolution is not and cannot be this. It is
> a violent, harsh cause, filled with horrors and uncontrolled groups. We have
> inevitably to pass through all this to create a new order. We understand that
> the shopkeepers and young Christians are frightened. We have no fear.

The Events of May 1937

Not everything was propaganda. There was also action, sometimes
bloody. At the end of January, in Fatarella, a real battle took place between
the partisans and the adversaries of agrarian collectivization. On February
17, a C.N.T. member was killed by U.G.T. supporters in Barcelona. On
February 26, shooting broke out between *cenetistes* and *ugetistes* in the
city of Manresa, and one person was killed. There was shooting as well in
Vilanova. In Centelles, the local president of the J.J.L.L. was assassinated,
and his corpse was mutilated. In Barcelona, a police demonstration against
the C.N.T. police commissioner Eroles was organized behind the scenes by
the former *cenetista* and *bloquista* Eusebi Rodríguez Salas, known by the
nickname "One-Arm" ("El Manco"), and now a member of the P.S.U.C.,
functioning as head of the Commissariat of Public Order. On March 5,
twelve tanks were stolen from war materiel stocks in Barcelona, by
P.S.U.C. members who faked the signature of the C.N.T. member in charge
of war supplies, Eugenio Vallejo. In Reus, a committee of the J.J.L.L. and
the J.C.I. organized a collection of food and arms for Madrid and Rodríguez Salas sent four truckloads of guardias de asalto to take over the collected supplies, which he did not permit to be sent on. On April 25, in
Molíns de Rei, Roldán Cortada, a member of the U.G.T. central committee, who opposed the pogrom politics of the moment, was murdered. His

funeral, at which delegations from the C.N.T. and P.O.U.M. were present, was "a plebiscite for unity" according to the P.S.U.C. organ "Treball," and a "counterrevolutionary demonstration," according to "La Batalla."

On April 27, a profoundly disturbing incident took place, which illuminated the dangerous situation in Catalunya. Shooting broke out in the village of Bellver de Cerdanya, some distance from the town of Puigcerdá on the French border, between the C.N.T. members who controlled the border and Catalan nationalist and P.S.U.C. elements among the local peasants. Antonio Martín, a prominent C.N.T. militant who had supervised the border force, was killed. Martín had been the object of a virulent press campaign by the communists.[16]

Seven *cenetistes* were arrested in the murder of Roldán Cortada, although the death of Martín was left uninvestigated. From April 26 through 28, Rodríguez Salas and Eroles exchanged notes in the press, the first claiming an attempt had been made on his life, the second pronouncing this attempt imaginary. During the nights of April 28, 29, and 30, the police were ordered to remain in their headquarters.

On April 26, a new Generalitat administration was finally formed, after a month of crisis, with Esquerra member Artemi Ayguadé as chief *conseller*. The Generalitat council suspended its meeting of April 29, because, according to a press note, "it could not continue its tasks under the pressure, the danger, and the disorder supposed by the existence of groups that in some places in Catalunya try to impose themselves by threats and to compromise the revolution and the war."

Ayguadé, who had manipulated local quarrels such as those at Bellver de Cerdanya and Puígcerdá against the anarchists, gave twenty-four hours for all arms in private hands to be turned over to the police. "Solidaridad Obrera" answered that "the proletariat in arms is the guarantee of the revolution."

Some P.O.U.M. leaders met with some from the C.N.T. and asked them if they were ready to definitively free themselves from communist pressure. The answer expressed wavering; the C.N.T. sought nothing more than the removal of Ayguadé and Rodríguez Salas.

May 1, the international workers' holiday, was not to be celebrated in Barcelona, and a planned joint demonstration by the C.N.T. and U.G.T. was called off, because everybody feared it would end in shooting. George Orwell, who had come to Barcelona on leave from the Aragon front, commented on the "queer state of affairs. Barcelona, the . . . revolutionary city, was probably the only city in non-Fascist Europe that had no celebrations that day. But I admit I was rather relieved. The I.L.P. contingent was expected to march in the P.O.U.M. section of the procession . . . The last thing I wished for was to be mixed up in some meaningless street fight. To be marching up the street behind red flags inscribed with elevating slogans, and then to be bumped off from an upper window by some total stranger with a submachine gun—that is not my idea of a useful way to die."[17]

That day, as it had for a week, "La Batalla" published notices warning the workers that the P.S.U.C. was preparing a provocation and calling on them not to let themselves be fooled by it, since the moment for struggle should be decided by the workers and not the provocateurs.

On May 2, "Soli" published a giant headline: "Workers, do not let yourselves be disarmed for any reason. This is our slogan: Let nobody let himself be disarmed."

"La Batalla" continued warning the workers not to be provoked. But the hour had come when the provocation could no longer be held off. To understand what took place, one must know how the situation developed in the Commissariat of Public Order. This was described in detail to Víctor Alba in an interview given in 1971 by Josep Coll, who, from July 1936 on, was general secretary of the Commissariat, representing the P.O.U.M.

After July 19, the police remained disorganized. By decision of the Committee for Militias, a security council (consell de seguretat) was then formed, made up of representatives of the same organizations that belonged to the Committee for Militias.

Josep Coll served in the council for the P.O.U.M. The council's secretary and effective head was Aurelio Fernández, from the C.N.T. The council controlled almost all the police bodies in Catalunya. The Public Order Commissar in Barcelona was Andreu Reverter, from the Esquerra, whose power went to his head. He gave so many orders for arrest and execution—among them that of his mother-in-law—that those ordered to make arrests took the suspects to a building and guarded them, hoping that the furies of Reverter would pass. When this latter worthy ordered the arrest of the C.N.T. representative and council secretary, Fernández, the group around Reverter became alarmed and warned Companys. The Generalitat president gave an order to the president of the provincial appeals court that Reverter should be arrested; Reverter was immediately tried and executed.

The new commissar was a Cortes deputy for the Esquerra, Martí Rouret, whose weak character was not adequate for the job. In view of this, Comorera suggested to Companys that the Esquerra and P.S.U.C. posts in the police should be exchanged, and this was done. Rodríguez Salas thus found himself catapulted into the commissar's position. To achieve control over the police, it was necessary to diminish the authority of the C.N.T. representatives. To this end, Rodríguez Salas underhandedly counterposed the guardia de asalto to the revolutionary Control Patrols, gaining the support of the former. The C.N.T. accepted all of this, but when in March it was proposed that a decree remove the political character of the police, the C.N.T. consellers, as we have seen, refused to accept it, provoking a crisis.

The C.N.T. prevented the adoption, for the moment, of this proposal, which, in fact, would have put the police in the hands of the P.S.U.C. under a nonpolitical pretext, similar to that used by the communists in calling for a single command in the army.

These were the individuals who occupied the front positions in the provocation the P.S.U.C. had prepared. It exploded on May 3, 1937. It could have begun a few days before or later. Seen in historical perspective, it was inevitable.

The building owned by the Compañía Telefónica and housing the Barcelona telephone exchange was then the tallest in the city, located on southeast side of the plaça Catalunya only a few hundred yards from the head of the Rambles. It had cost a number of lives for it to be taken and retaken, on July 19. Those who held the Telefónica controlled all telephone communications between Barcelona and the rest of the world.

It had been held, since July 19, by the C.N.T. union that represented the company's workers, although the enterprise control committee included a Generalitat delegate. The P.S.U.C. claimed that this allowed the C.N.T. to listen to telephone conversations between the governmental authorities; the truth was that this could be done from many other places, apart from the central exchange, and that the role of the Telefónica was mainly that of a political symbol.

Rodríguez Salas arrived at the Telefónica, leading a group of police, in the afternoon of May 3, a Monday, and told the guard at the door that he was there to take charge of the building in the name of the government. The Resistance came when the police occupied the lobby. They were unable to go any farther than the next floor, and during the following week the building was divided between C.N.T. members on the upper floors and police downstairs.

When the news that the police had attacked the *cenetistes* in the Telefónica circulated through the city, a general strike broke out spontaneously. No C.N.T. committee had to give the order. Immediately, militants set up positions in front of the police stations and P.S.U.C. offices. The P.S.U.C. was isolated in its buildings, as was the Generalitat.

That night, the population relived the experience of July 19, this time out of desperation rather than with a feeling of victory. Politically, the struggle had come down to the P.S.U.C. versus the C.N.T., but the real fighting took place between the C.N.T. and the police, since the P.S.U.C. left up to the government the job of "pacifying" the streets.

The streets, however, took six days to "pacify," and when "order" was finally restored, it was thanks not to the action of the police but to the speeches of the C.N.T. leaders who ceaselessly called on the workers to return to work and lay down their arms.

Was it possible for the workers to take power? The P.O.U.M. membership thought so, but had little real hope. They knew they were faced with a provocation and that if the general situation had been favorable to the workers, no such provocation would have taken place. The communists now controlled a good part of the army. In many places, communists ran the police. Still, the Left Socialists were the real masters of the U.G.T., and the C.N.T. remained powerful. Largo Caballero was head of the Valencia government. The Esquerra and the other bourgeois republican parties were a negligible factor, since they drifted in the direction of those who appeared to be the winners and could not exercise a definitive influence over the struggle. In terms of indigenous strength, then, the communists remained the weakest. But they depended on the Soviet arms blackmail, threatening that if the C.N.T. and Left Socialists took power for themselves, the deliveries of Russian weaponry would cease, as well as on the fear the C.N.T. leaders had of taking power.

If the C.N.T. had taken power in Catalunya—where it could have done so, had it wanted to, in less than twenty-four hours—the situation would have changed in the rest of the republican zone. It would have put Moscow before the dilemma of abandoning the Spanish revolution or of aiding it notwithstanding the fact that it would be freed of communist control.

Further, it is very possible that Largo Caballero, exasperated with the communists as he was, would have taken advantage of the new situation in Catalunya to reorganize his government and give it a more dynamic policy that would inspire enthusiasm in the masses and thus bring about the possibility of military victories.

This was the reasoning of the P.O.U.M.

With the C.N.T. militants now in the street, the leaders of the anarcho-syndicalist movement, disorganized and caught by surprise, the P.S.U.C. carrying out provocations, and the Largo Caballero government trying to find a way out with neither winners nor losers (as if this were possible), what position could the P.O.U.M. adopt? It could only put itself at the side of the masses. If now, when playing their last card, the workers did not find the P.O.U.M. at their side, what authority would the party have later to get the masses to listen to it? The P.O.U.M. adopted this position, although its members immediately knew that if they did not attain the seizure of power, the bill would have to be paid politically, so to speak, by they themselves, as the weakest force on the scene. To stay out of the struggle, calling it a provocation and declaring that the P.O.U.M. did not wish to let itself be provoked, would eliminate neither the waverings of the C.N.T. leaders nor the repression the P.O.U.M., if the party's tactic was unsuccessful, and furthermore could reduce the possibility of victory.

In sum, by going into the streets, the P.O.U.M. had nothing to lose; remaining out of the struggle, it would lose what it had and the few possibilities remaining for it in the future. These considerations did not even take account of something that for the P.O.U.M. was not rhetorical, but a vibrant reaction: solidarity with the workers in struggle. Now they could repeat to the C.N.T. what they had been told by the anarchosyndicalists on October 6, 1934, and on July 19, 1936: We will meet on the barricades.

They met there. In the towns, unity of action emerged spontaneously, and P.O.U.M. and C.N.T. members, in many places, carried out a preventive occupation of P.S.U.C. buildings. In Lleida, they took control of the city. In other places, they forced the former guardia civil to turn over arms to them.

The night of May 3-4 was spent taking and fortifying positions. Rifles were not in abundance, but there were enough pistols and hand grenades. There was a kind of truce, while the C.N.T. leadership made efforts, eventually successful, to have Rodríguez Salas and Ayguadé removed. Companys, who was in Benicarló with Azaña, rapidly returned to Barcelona and at 8:00 the evening of May 3 met with the C.N.T. leaders.

The P.O.U.M. regional committee met that night with its C.N.T. counterpart. "We set the problem out in concrete terms," Gorkin explained later. "Either we must put ourselves at the head of the movement, to destroy the enemy within, or the movement will fail and the enemy will destroy us." But the C.N.T. regional committee did not wish to adopt a definite position.[18]

On Tuesday, May 4, the city began to be covered by barricades. "La Batalla" stated:

> The proletarian answer could not be more striking ... The barricades of freedom have returned throughout the city. The spirit of July 19 has taken Barcelona anew. The majority of towns in Catalunya have echoed the events in the capital. The working class is strong and will know how to smash any attempts at counterrevolution.
>
> We must remain alert with rifle in hand. We must maintain this magnificent spirit of resistance and struggle, the guarantee of our triumph. And we must prevent the counterrevolution from raising its head again.
>
> For this reason we demand:
>
> Dismissal of Rodríguez Salas, the Commissar of Public Order who bears direct responsibility for these provocations.
>
> Annulment of the public order decrees.
>
> Public order in the hands of the working class.
>
> A Revolutionary Workers' Front of the organizations that struggle for triumph over fascism at the front and victory of the revolution in the rearguard.
>
> Creation of Committees for the Defense of the Revolution in every neighborhood, in every town, and in every workplace.

These slogans did not reflect the totality of what the P.O.U.M. desired. But the executive did not dare go further than the C.N.T., for fear of remaining in an exposed position. This note in "La Batalla" was written shortly after the P.O.U.M. had been told by the C.N.T. regional committee that "we are happy the workers are showing their teeth . . . Companys will realize, now, that he must change the composition of his cabinet . . . With Artemi [Ayguadé] and El Manco [Rodríguez Salas] gone, we will be satisfied."

The day went on with continued discussion as well as shooting. From Valencia came García Oliver, Largo Caballero's justice minister and a F.A.I. leader; at eight-thirty in the evening he spoke by radio, recommending that the struggle be ended. The C.N.T. radio station ceaselessly repeated, "Put down your arms, embrace as brothers." Nobody complied. The antiaircraft batteries on Montjuïc, controlled by the C.N.T., fixed their aim on the Generalitat Palace. But no serious attempt was made to storm the Generalitat, for this would have meant resolving the dilemma, which the C.N.T. leaders did not really wish.

On Wednesday, May 5, a new anarchist organization made its voice heard: the Grouping of the Friends of Durruti (Agrupación de Amigos de Durruti), affiliated with the F.A.I. and led by a Catalan journalist and editor of the C.N.T. journal "La Noche," Jaume Balius. The Friends of Durruti sought to provide leadership for the spontaneous movement of the C.N.T. ranks. They called for the formation of a revolutionary junta: "The revolution before all else: We must not give up the streets," said one of their manifestoes. "We salute the comrades of the P.O.U.M. who have fraternized with us."

In "La Batalla" for March 4, Nin had commented enthusiastically on an editorial in "La Noche" calling for resistance to the counterrevolutionary turn of events, and Juan Andrade favorably reviewed the group's demands in the paper's May 1st issue. Although rumors describing the Friends of Durruti as a group under the influence of the P.O.U.M. or of "Trotskyists" have been taken up by many historians, there is no evidence that the Friends was anything but a spontaneous offshoot within the C.N.T.[19]

Largo Caballero was afraid the events in Barcelona would be used by the communists to get rid of him, since they wanted someone more docile in his place. He called in the C.N.T. ministers and told them that Ayguadé had asked for the dispatch of 1,500 guardias de asalto from Valencia to Barcelona; Largo did not want to do it, because "this would give strength to elements that could have provoked the incidents." But he asked the C.N.T. ministers to go to Barcelona and end the fighting there.

García Oliver, again on radio, engaged in sentimental blackmail: "Think of the anguish of the antifascist workers in the zone of Spain dominated by

Hitler and Mussolini . . . when they learn that in Catalunya we are killing one another . . . Let everybody stop fighting, even if people interested in preventing a solution of the situation provoke them . . ."

Marià (Mariano) Vazquez, the leader of the Catalan regional C.N.T., also called for a truce. A radio speech by the anarchist minister of health in Largo's cabinet, Federica Montseny, another outstanding C.N.T.-F.A.I. leader, obtained no results, any more than a joint C.N.T.-U.G.T. note declaring that "the conflict has been satisfactorily resolved" and that the workers "should return to their regular jobs."

When the C.N.T. ministers returned to Valencia, the communist ministers, in a meeting of the cabinet, threatened to leave the government if the central authorities did not order the military occupation of Catalunya. For four hours, Montseny argued with the communists and republicans. Finally, a vote was taken. The C.N.T. and Largo Caballero lost; the government would order the takeover of Catalunya.

At noon on May 5, a new Generalitat administration was presented to the public: four *consellers* would represent the C.N.T., U.G.T., Esquerra, and the Rabassaires. This was called a trade-union government. The U.G.T. representative, Antoni Sésé (a former *bloquista* who had joined the official Communists in 1932) was on his way to the Generalitat in his car when it was fired on after it passed a barricade without halting. Sésé was killed.

That day, police agents searched the house of Camillo Berneri, the Italian anarchist whose journal, "Guerra di Classe," had become a tribune of the forces that favored prosecution of the social revolution. A few hours later, Berneri and his comrade Francesco Barbieri were arrested. Their corpses were discovered the next morning.

Within the month, the Italian communist organ in France, "Il Grido del Popolo," which Berneri had criticized in his article defending the P.O.U.M., commented that Berneri, "one of the leaders of the 'Friends of Durruti' group that . . . provoked the bloody uprising against the People's Front government in Catalunya . . . got his just deserts."[20] The death of Berneri, a widely respected and loved figure in anarchism, was a great shock in Barcelona and internationally.

On Thursday, May 6, Largo Caballero named General Sebastián Pozas, a professional officer, as military commandant of Catalunya (in which post he exclusively helped the communists) and gave him orders to shift 5,000 guardias de asalto to Barcelona. Largo did not realize that the heads of this body were almost all communists.

On the barricades, wavering had begun. Some returned home, although the strike continued, except in the food stores. Shooting broke out again. At seven-thirty in the morning a radio statement declared that the Generalitat council had met and demanded compliance with its orders to "locate the provocateurs." This phrase gave the game away. The communists realized that they could not yet completely eliminate the C.N.T., but they believed they could at least lay the "blame" for the events on the P.O.U.M. and use this opportunity to "legally" liquidate the party. A meeting of U.G.T. leaders named José del Barrio, an old communist, as Sésé's successor in the post of U.G.T. secretary for Catalunya. Further, the U.G.T. regional committee for Catalunya unanimously agreed on the immediate expulsion from the union federation of "all P.O.U.M. leaders."

Republican and foreign naval maneuvers were observed off the entrance to Barcelona harbor. At three in the afternoon of May 6, the Valencia government took over the control of public order in Catalunya. Thanks to the intrigues of the P.S.U.C. and the Esquerra—in common with Estat Catala whose orientation toward fascist Italy led the C.N.T. to accuse its May opponents of a conspiracy that included Mussolini—the Generalitat had lost control of the regional police forces. From then until the end of the war, when it was forcibly suppressed by Franco, the Generalitat of Catalunya was no more than a cultural and even folkloric body.

In a teletype sent by García Oliver in Valencia to Federica Montseny, we read the following:

> It is indispensable that [the guardia de asalto sent by the government] reach their goal, to relieve the police . . . that are inflamed by the conflict . . . It is imperative that you understand this . . . and that you make the comrades in the towns, through which these impartial—strictly impartial—forces must pass, understand. They are strictly impartial, because the government knows that otherwise the conflict will extend throughout Catalunya and the rest of Spain and will have as its result not only a political failure, but also a military defeat.[21]

The same day, May 6, "La Batalla" published an editorial:

> The P.O.U.M. immediately joined the movement spontaneously unleashed by the working class of Barcelona. As an antibourgeois, antireformist, eminently revolutionary party, it could not fail to do so. Its place was in the street, alongside the proletarians in struggle.
>
> Undoubtedly, the latter have obtained an important partial victory. They have routed the counterrevolutionary provocation. They have achieved the dismissal of those directly responsible for the provocation. They have delivered a serious blow to the bourgeoisie and reformism. They could have attained more—much, much more—if those who held the leadership of the hegemonic organizations of the working class in Catalunya had known how to rise to the level of the masses.
>
> Under the repeated urging of their leaders, the masses have begun a retreat

from the struggle. In this they show proof of a great spirit of discipline. The proletariat must remain, nevertheless, vigilant. It must stand guard, weapon in hand. It must watch the movements of the bourgeoisie and of reformism, ready to crush its counterrevolutionary maneuvers . . .

On Friday, May 7, the guardia de asalto sent from Valencia entered Barcelona without immediate incident, protected by García Oliver's teletype. The C.N.T. members on the barricades, seeing their arrival, shrugged their shoulders and remained silent. If the leaders they believed in were not at their side, what was the use of fighting on? New leaders capable of replacing them had not come from the masses. The movement had come into being decapitated. The P.O.U.M., which did not desire the movement and which warned of the dangers of a provocation, did not try to take over the leadership of the street because the C.N.T. masses, rather than seeking power, had gone to the barricades in defense of their own organization and would not allow the movement to be led by those who did not spring from the confederal movement.

Numerous workers had gone home, taking their weapons with them. But there was nothing of the feeling after October 6, 1934, when it was a matter of a first round. Now, the revolution was over.

There were in the P.O.U.M. small groups that wanted to continue the struggle and proposed the organization of a central committee of barricade representatives. But the barricades were being abandoned. When the P.O.U.M., realizing that its orders would count for nothing, called for a withdrawal from the fighting, the Barcelona local committee criticized the executive, accusing it of capitulation.

"*Els fets de Maig*" ("the May events"), "the tragic week in May," "bloody May," as the experience would come to be called, had taken at least 500 lives, with 1,500 wounded. The police had arrested 206 people. After Friday, when people returned to their homes, more deaths followed, caused not by the open fighting, but by the secret operations of the communists and their police allies, who, once the danger had passed, lost their heads and abandoned the relative moderation forced upon them during the barricade struggle.

The list of the murdered is long. Following Berneri and Barbieri, the body of Alfredo Martínez, secretary of the J.J.L.L. and a member of the main anarchist leadership team in Barcelona during the events, was found after a few days. Two young men who had worked in the P.O.U.M. radio station and who were taken to the P.S.U.C. headquarters in the landmark building by Antoni Gaudí, the "Pedrera" on the Passeig de Gracia, were killed in a torture chamber in the building's cellar. Twelve young anarchists were killed in the P.S.U.C.'s Karl Marx Barracks and taken by ambulance to the outskirts of Sardanyola, where their bodies were dumped.

By noon on Friday, May 7, the streetcars had begun to run again. The police occupied the barricades. For a week, young P.S.U.C. members, many of them small girls, worked to dismantle the barricades, their pictures appearing in the newspapers. The Valencia guardias freed the 206 people arrested during the fighting. The C.N.T. issued a manifesto expressing its willingness to collaborate in "the reestablishment of order."

Some further data should be noted on these events, during which the workers, replying to a provocation and finding themselves without a leadership, saw the revolution's agony on the barricades. For example, Willi Brandt, who had been replaced in the youth arm of the London Bureau by Peter Blachstein (later a Social Democratic deputy to the West German parliament), found himself in Barcelona during the events. The youth bureau had met in Barcelona only a little before the explosion. Various members of the German S.A.P. were arrested after the May events; Brandt escaped by ship, but Blachstein continued to work with the J.C.I. Both participated in the ensuing international campaign to defend the P.O.U.M.

In Barbastro, at the Aragon front, contingents from the C.N.T. and P.O.U.M. Divisions met to monitor the movements of the P.S.U.C. troops, since they feared they would abandon the front and attack the C.N.T. and P.O.U.M. forces. No section of the front garrisoned by P.O.U.M. or C.N.T. troops remained unprotected.

The communists accused the C.N.T. and P.O.U.M. of leaving the front, although one battalion each from the communist-controlled XIIth and XIIIth International Brigades were moved from the trenches to the town of Tortosa, a center of C.N.T. resistance, a few days after the events in Barcelona. The order to shift these two battalions was given by communist commanders and not by the heads of the brigades. When the Italian republican Randolfo Pacciardi, chief of the XIIth I.B., learned of the action, he went to Tortosa and prevented the two battalions from carrying out a massacre.[22]

A detailed version of problems at the front was issued by a "Judicial Adviser of the Aragon Front" (Asesoría Jurídica del Frente de Aragón), on orders from the commanding general of the Eastern Army, Pozas. This typewritten document, dated May 15 and 17 but unsigned save for the title "The Judicial Adviser" ("El Asesor Jurídico"), was seized by the Franco forces at the end of the civil war and has come to light with the opening of official archives since Franco's death in 1976.

As an anonymous document composed at a time when communist and other elements in the army were notoriously free with the assignment of authority both formal and informal for the pursuit of political interests, the report is naturally suspect. However, it outlines a number of occurrences of interest at the front.

On May 5, the document claimed, between 1,500 and 2,000 members of the C.N.T. Red and Black Column under the prominent anarchist militant Miguel García Vivancos, affiliated with the C.N.T. 28th Division, and P.O.U.M. 29th Division troops under Josep Rovira, left the front near Huesca for Barcelona, heavily armed. In Lleida, where some of them were disarmed by ground troops of the republican air force, they met with higher officers and then returned to the front. C.N.T.-F.A.I. militants from the comarca of Binéfar took over military supply dumps at Monte Juliá. Local incidents involving conflicts over collectivization were included in the report, which ended dramatically with the charge that peasants, exasperated by collectivization, "speak with persistence, too much persistence, of burning the harvests."

A postscript to the report stated that a batallion of the C.N.T. 25th (Jubert) Division had left the front, heading in the direction of Tortosa. The same postscript reported coordination between Joaquín Ascaso, anarchist head of the governing Council of Aragon, Antonio Ortíz, head of the 25th Division, Saturnino Carod (misspelled as "Caroz"), the division's political commissar, and representatives of the C.N.T. 26th (Durruti) division, to prepare resistance to Valencia forces at Teruel. Obviously, none of these occurrences can be said to involve endangerment of the front by either the P.O.U.M. or C.N.T.[23]

Perhaps the most famous commentator on the May events in any language is George Orwell, whose eyewitness account recounts his participation in the fighting. In the aftermath of the conflict in the streets, Orwell grasped the power of totalitarian propaganda to alter people's understanding of contemporary as well as past history, as he reviewed the lies about the clash retold in the communist press. The communist handling of the May events would thus become a classic and justly famous example of what today we call "disinformation."

Most importantly, Orwell detailed the truth about P.O.U.M. responsibility in the incidents, showing that, rather than provoking or leading the battle, as the Communists charged, the P.O.U.M. had held back.

Another noncommunist observer was John McNair, a comrade of Orwell's, who communicated with Fenner Brockway, I.L.P. member of the British House of Commons and head of the London Bureau. Brockway published an account noting that "The P.O.U.M. hoped the action of a constituent assembly would be vigorous enough to force the government to submit to it, but it also considered that an insurrection would be wrong in the face of the fascist menace. In the ranks of the P.O.U.M. there were divergences regarding whether the party should or should not participate in the insurrection, but the executive was opposed."[24]

The communist description of the events differed according to the improvisations of its many and various propagandists. The "Daily Worker" of London, for example, admitted on May 11 that the fighting had begun when police tried to disarm the Telefónica security force. However, on May 29, "International Press Correspondence," the official Comintern news organ, claimed the events began when the police tried to disarm elements of the P.O.U.M.. These versions may be compared with that of another Englishman, the writer Ralph Bates, who stated:

> Some anarchist extremists were dissatisfied, and they—as much as ignorant groups of the C.N.T.—were influenced by the counterrevolutionary propaganda of the Trotskyite P.O.U.M. . . . Demoralized by Trotskyite propaganda, a small number of members of the C.N.T., Libertarian Youth, F.A.I., and P.O.U.M. rose on May 6 (sic), 1937 in Catalunya, notwithstanding the appeal to reason of the leadership. This counterrevolutionary revolt was rapidly suffocated.[25]

More discreet, but no closer to reality, was the version put out by the bourgeois republican press. Companys first called the men on the barricades "uncontrolled elements." Afterward, he said it was an uprising smashed by the Generalitat's own forces. Azaña was even less informed, and, since he hated the anarchists (as he had proven many times during his tenure as head of government), he allowed himself to be convinced by communist propaganda and even included in his diary some of the lies the communists broadcast, taking them as good coin. On May 20, that is, quite a bit after the events, he wrote from his residence at La Pobleta: "In the rebellion, the most active part was taken by the P.O.U.M., Estat Català (sic), the libertarian *ateneus*, and C.N.T. elements although not all of them or even very many of them . . . some C.N.T. columns abandoned the front and headed for Barcelona to help the rebels."[26]

No less influenced by communist propaganda was the U.S. ambassador on the scene, Claude G. Bowers. Bowers stated in his memoirs that "In early May, the loyalist government moved against (the anarchists) with cold steel. A crisis had been provoked by the anarchists and the P.O.U.M., which was composed of Trotsky communists. It was generally believed that many of these were Franco agents. In factories, they were urging the seizure of private property and strikes, to slow down production in the midst of war." (Bowers' memoirs are of interest to historians only as a curiosity, reflecting their author's superficiality and ignorance. He never mentions the persecution of the P.O.U.M. and fate of Nin, and ascribes Largo Caballero's resignation from the chief executive post in the republican government, which took place soon after the May events, to the socialist leader's "high blood pressure"!)[27]

The anarchists, for the moment, had relatively little to say about the May days. Later, in exile, Abad de Santillán, confessed that:

We have been accused of having been the main cause of the ceasefire [in May]. Not with pride, but with repentance, because to the degree that we stopped the shooting by some of our own, we saw a redoubling of the provocations from the few centers of communist and Catalan republican resistance . . . We did not lack material strength . . . But we lacked confidence in those who had erected themselves as representatives of our movement; we did not possess a nucleus of men of firmness and prestige who could be called upon to stand behind us in any emergency situation. What, then, could we do? Disgusted as we were at seeing the attitudes of the very comrades who exercised leadership functions, it was not possible to remain with our arms crossed.

Accompanied by the J.J.L.L. leader Alfredo Martínez, he met with Vázquez, Montseny, and García Oliver.

I told them that once we had gone into the street, our error consisted in stopping the shooting without resolving the still-existing problems. For our part, we regretted what had happened and believed there was still time to recover what we had lost. It was impossible to reach an agreement. We were told that we had done exactly right in halting the fighting and that there was nothing to do but to await further events and adapt as well as possible to them. Then we withdrew, doubly beaten.

This quotation will help the reader comprehend the impossibility of the task faced by the P.O.U.M. and the distance from reality involved in any hope of convincing the C.N.T. that it should take power.

A final note on the May events should be added here. As noted by Orwell, the tiny official Trotskyist cell, the S.B.L. led by Munis, participated in the events on the side of the workers, distributing a leaflet on the barricades. Munis was just then in France, and the main activity of the group in the events seems to have been carried by Moulin. Beginning with the American Trotskyist Felix Morrow (who never visited the country and whose *Revolution and Counterrevolution in Spain* is based exclusively on notes amassed by Charles and Lois Orr), it has been the fashion among historians of a Trotskyist sympathy to hail the S.B.L. as a leading actor in the events, even echoing Stalinist charges that the group "inspired" the Friends of Durruti.

The truth is that the S.B.L. was too small to play any but a marginal role in the events, and Munis has admitted that the group did not even know of the existence of the Friends of Durruti until the events took place.[28]

The Question of Power

But was there still the possibility of the workers' taking power? Reasoning coldly, the P.O.U.M. understood that the moment for taking power was

July 19, 1936. But they knew they could not do it, for lack of sufficient strength.

As on October 6, 1934, they found the situation depended on the decision of another organization; then, it had been the Esquerra, which did not dare to carry its rebellion to its logical consequences, and now it was the C.N.T., which did not dare to take power. July 19 had been a military victory, but a political defeat. Whatever was done afterward, the fault was irreparable.

Beginning in September, the forces of "order," having recovered their position, counterattacked. The May days, in, reality, were not a revolutionary offensive, but a defensive condemned to failure. Now it was too late to take power. The political drama of the Catalan Marxists—as they well understood—was that at three decisive moments (April 14, 1931, October 6, 1934, and July 19, 1936) they had not had enough strength to give battle on their own, and others were unwilling to give it for the goals of the Marxists. The anarchist tradition of the Catalan proletariat had kept it immobile on April 14, made it follow behind the Esquerra on October 6 and had made it turn its back on power on July 19.

For the P.O.U.M. to accept that power could not be taken was to accept losing the war, because without the revolutionary upsurge that a workers' takeover of government would generate in the masses, the war was lost; and no P.O.U.M. member wanted to accept that the war could not be won. Furthermore, the *bloquistes* and then the *poumistes* had dreamed of seizing power, struggled to create the conditions that would make it possible, and prepared themselves for the opportune moment. When it finally came, they could not take advantage of it because they were not yet the great revolutionary party they wanted to be.

The May events, for the P.O.U.M., were a communist provocation; notwithstanding all that, if the C.N.T. learned the lessons of May, it might still be possible to take power. The P.O.U.M. knew it was not, but believed it was. It was thus with diminished enthusiasm that the P.O.U.M. went into the streets, so as not to become distanced from the rank and file of the C.N.T. If the executive had not given the order, the militants would have still turned out, either way.

Nin had expressed these hopes, against all political reason, when on March 14 he wrote in "La Batalla":

> The working class is not yet disarmed. It retains strategically important positions. Its specific weight is enormous. Nothing can be done without it. And, if you wish, nothing can be done against it. Although not so favorable as in the first months of the revolution, the correlation of forces is such that the proletariat, in the present circumstances, can take power without recourse to

armed insurrection. Enough that it put all of its organized strength into play with the unbreakable decision to carry the resolution to its last consequences.

This was objectively true. But it was not so in the mind of the masses or of the anarchist leaders. Still, the P.O.U.M. persisted in believing that the C.N.T. would open its eyes, however much they had witnessed the ideological disintegration of the old union federation. Gorkín, years later, described the moment as follows:

> We were watching a double phenomenon: the C.N.T. ministers in the central government were given the task of imposing prudence and moderation on the C.N.T. *consellers* of the Generalitat. But the C.N.T. ranks did not go along with this swindle. Although lacking political education, the C.N.T. militants—the real, authentic militants—possessed a magnificent class instinct, a heroic fearlessness, a spirit of sacrifice up to any test. With real leaders and with correct thinking and a constructive program, this mass would have accomplished marvels. The divorce between the ranks of the C.N.T. and its ministers and *consellers* were already visible. The latter, apolitical until very recently, had suddenly turned, perhaps for this very reason, into heavyweight politicians. The ranks saw that, with the collaboration of its men, the revolution was turning into a charade, the conquests of the heroic days were being taken back, and they themselves were being reduced to impotence.
>
> Their irritation knew no limits. Their leaders said, 'We are opportunists for the moment. We will compromise with the demands of the communists. Later we will let them feel our claws.'
>
> 'Later will be too late,' we replied.[29]

On May 11, the P.O.U.M. expanded central committee met. However crucial the events, the P.O.U.M. continued holding central committee meetings at least every three months, as dictated by its statutes. The party leadership expounded, in four points, on its position, which was published in "La Batalla" on May 13:

> 1. The constant provocations of the counterrevolution, incarnated in the reformist parties of the P.S.U.C. and the petty bourgeoisie, provocations that in the field of economy, war, and public order have tended to liquidate the revolutionary conquests gained by the working class on July 19, with arms in hand, and that culminated on May 3 with the attempt to take over the Telefónica, brought about the armed protest of the proletariat.
>
> 2. The political position of the P.O.U.M. can be nothing other than active solidarity with the workers who spontaneously declared a general strike, raised barricades in the streets of Barcelona, and knew how to defend, with exemplary heroism, the threatened conquests of the revolution.
>
> 3. With the workers who fought in the streets lacking concrete goals and a

responsible leadership, the P.O.U.M. could do nothing other than to order and organize a strategic retreat, thus winning over the revolutionary working class and avoiding a desperate action that could degenerate into a 'putsch,' resulting in the total defeat of the most advanced section of the proletariat.

4. The experience of the 'May days' shows, in an unequivocal manner, that the only progressive way out of the present situation is a seizure of power by the working class, and for this it is unavoidable that the revolutionary action of the worker masses be coordinated through the constitution of a Revolutionary Workers' Front, which will bring together all the organizations ready to fight for the total destruction of fascism, which can take place only with a military victory at the front and with the triumph of the revolution in the rearguard.

The expanded central committee believes the line followed by the party during these events has been completely just, and it entirely solidarizes with the executive committee, convinced that it has understood how to defend the interests of the revolution and of the broad working masses.

Nin edited a long manifesto, signed by the central committee, in which, according to the custom in the workers' movement, he drew lessons from the events:

FIRST LESSON. All the profuse propaganda carried out in recent months by the petty bourgeoisie and the reformists in favor of antifascist unity, had no other aim than to speculate on the unity sentiment of the working masses and its hatred for fascism to strangle the revolution and reestablish the bourgeois state machinery.

SECOND LESSON. The campaign carried out under the slogans 'first win the war, afterward revolution,' and 'Everything for the war effort,' hid a real attempt to undermine the revolution, the indispensable premise for a free hand to negotiate peace. The continuous suppression of the revolutionary conquests, the threat of foreign intervention, which was on the point of becoming reality when foreign warships arrived at the port of Barcelona, the rumors, every day more insistent, of a possible 'embrace of Vergara' (i.e., a nonpolitical truce), coinciding with the May 3 provocation, constitute manifest proof of this.

THIRD LESSON. There is only one progressive way, for the proletariat and for military victory, out of the present situation: the conquest of power. During the May days, it was in reach of our hands. If it was not taken it was, fundamentally, because the traditional organizations, inspired by the anarchist doctrine, did not put forward the problem and because our party, which had ceaselessly brought it up throughout the course of the revolution, is a minority and a youthful organization, without yet having sufficient strength to take for itself the responsibility of orienting the struggle in this direction.

To prepare the necessary conditions to take political power away from the bourgeoisie is the immediate and fundamental mission of the proletariat. For this, it is necessary to set up a 'Revolutionary Workers' Front,' that is, to bring together with the aim of coordinated action the worker organizations that are ready to set up obstacles to the advance of the bourgeois counter-revolution and to push ahead the proletarian revolution.

One of the concrete forms of this Revolutionary Workers' Front can be revolutionary defense committees, which should immediately be set up in every workplace, in all the neighborhoods, and in all the towns, and which should coordinate their action through a central defense committtee expressing the will of all the committees.

FOURTH LESSON. The victory of the working class is impossible without a responsible leadership, which will know what it wants and where it is going and will coordinate the struggle. The Revolutionary Workers' Front can be the basis for this indispensable leadership.

FIFTH LESSON. The conduct of the Communist party of Spain and its branch, the P.S.U.C., in Catalunya, during the May days, has come to demonstrate that these parties do not represent a mere reformist tendency in the workers' movement, but constitute the vanguard and the tool of the bourgeois counterrevolution. For this reason, if a united front with these parties, as well as with the petty bourgeois organizations, is well-nigh indispensable for the military struggle against fascism, any possibility of common action on the political field must be discarded. The representatives of the revolutionary proletariat and of the executioners of the working class cannot sit at the same table. For this reason, the Antifascist People's Front, synonymous with class collaboration and with a counterrevolutionary policy, must be opposed by the Revolutionary Workers' Front . . .

The working class cannot allow itself to be fooled, but, rather, with the same heroic impulse that led it to victory over fascism in Madrid, Valencia, and Barcelona on July 19 and to generously sacrifice its blood on the battlefields, will defend the conquests already gained and will take power, persuaded that only the triumphant proletarian revolution can carry the war to its ultimate consequences: the destruction of fascism and the establishment of socialism.

What further could the P.O.U.M. recommend? To go underground, which it predicted would be necessary, but did not really much believe in? Such a thing would not be discussed in a manifesto. Accept communist arguments and, having lost the revolution, concentrate on the war? But the P.O.U.M. believed the war could not be won without completing the revolution.

A Maurín would have been necessary to remove the problem from the area of phrases and to outline the situation crudely and directly, to address the question of a postwar Spain, regardless of the war's outcome. But Maurín, at that moment, was thought to be dead in the enemy zone.

Everybody knew that persecution would be unleashed against the P.O.U.M. For this reason, the central committee ordered the party members to prepare for it and for underground work. But, in the depths of its being, the P.O.U.M. continued thinking the persecution would continue being more verbal and even legal than physical, and after the passage of some weeks the precautions and illegal measures would relax. Proof of this is that the same central committee decided that the party congress, which the May events had prevented from being held, would meet on June 18, 1937.

Preparing the Repression

At the moment, everything seemed to have returned to normality. The most normal phenomena were the attacks on the P.O.U.M. The Catalan U.G.T. committee met and gave the press the following bulletin of its decisions:

> 1. To characterize the movement beginning on May 4 as a counterrevolution-ary movement, aiming to deepen the disorganization and indiscipline of the rearguard and to break the Aragon front. To consider that a rapid and ener-getic policy of public order throughout Catalunya is needed, to reestablish the normality that today is only a matter of appearances, finishing with the activities of the uncontrolled elements and the Trotskyist provocateurs who still persist and maintain intact cadres and arms . . .

> 3. To affirm that there can be no equal treatment between the men or organi-zations that rose against the government and those that, on the other side, defended the cause of antifascism, so that while ratifying its agreement to expel the members of the P.O.U.M. from the U.G.T., it further demands the dissolution of that party and a declaration of its illegality, the suspension of the daily 'La Batalla' and all its press, and the seizure of its printing houses, radio, etc., doing exactly the same to organizations of the type of the Friends of Durruti, which has been disauthorized by the C.N.T. regional committee.

This was, simply put, the official "program" of the Communist party against the P.O.U.M., announced, according to custom, not by the party itself but by an organization in appearance—very superficially—neutral. Immediately a chorus began acclaiming these decisions.

Jaume Miravitlles recounts an anecdote that shows to what point the communists encountered allies in this campaign. The London "Daily Worker" for May 7 published the "news" that the monarchist flag had been raised alongside those of the P.O.U.M. and F.A.I. above the town halls taken over by the latter forces. Julio Alvarez del Vayo, an unprincipled communist puppet within the Socialist Party, went to Paris to try to con-vince his brother-in-law, the socialist intellectual Luis Araquistáin, then serving as Spanish ambassador to France, to circulate this "news" to the French press. Araquistáin refused, but Alvarez del Vayo arranged for some-one on the embassy staff to distribute the press release, and the ambassador saw himself obliged to deny a "news release" issued by his own embassy.[30]

As masterfully described in Orwell's *Homage to Catalonia*, the main weapon of the communists in their conflict with the P.O.U.M. was the outright lie. Orwell eloquently answered the absurd stories about monarchist flags, as well as pointing out the contradictory accounts that blossomed in the communist press as the weeks following the May fighting went by. Most alarmingly, however, the lies of the Stalinists met with either acquiescence or silence in the broad ranks of the People's Front movements around the world; although independent voices were raised in defense of the Spanish revolution, a great many supporters of the Left seemed indifferent to the possible untruthfulness of communist propaganda. It may be that, by 1937, the old proletarian morality of the international socialist movement had been nearly entirely replaced by the intellectual nihilism of the new, middle-class Left, a Left that accepted propagandist lies as a necessity of the struggle.

Against this, the P.O.U.M. could do little. What did it matter that, at the beginning of 1937, the P.O.U.M. executive had adopted a suggestion made public by Victor Serge in Paris, to form an international commission of inquiry that would investigate the accusations made against the P.O.U.M. (reported in "La Batalla," January 7, 1937)? The executive even proposed that the commission be made up of delegates of the second, third, and fourth internationals, along with the International Workers' Association (the anarchist international), and the London Bureau. What did it matter that the executive presented a libel suit, which had no success, against three communist journals ("La Batalla," May 16)? The P.O.U.M. would have to wait for Orwell's book, which they had no idea was even in the writing, for the public outside Spain to be given an impartial source of information, since the majority of foreign correspondents on the scene had adopted the communist version of events, quoting it in their dispatches as their own and authentic.

This was, as Orwell himself ascertained, an ominous turning point for the Left as well as for political morals in the democratic nations. Indeed, after the Spanish Civil War, the international Left would never succeed in reviving its old proletarian ideals or in ridding itself of a reputation for such "Leninist" duplicity.

The communists worked without a break. They decided it was necessary to eliminate Largo Caballero before beginning a military offensive in Extremadura, which had been prepared and which could have been successful, because this success would have bolstered Largo's position as head of government. In a meeting on May 9, José Díaz accused the P.O.U.M. of being Franco agents and demanded the party's dissolution.[31]

On May 11, the Valencia socialist newspaper "Adelante," associated with Largo, criticized the communists as follows:

> If suppressive measures are applied [against the P.O.U.M.] in the way de-
> manded by the organ of the Spanish section of the Communist International,
> the government would become like that of Gil Robles or Lerroux, the unity
> of the working class would be destroyed, and we would be exposed to the loss
> of the war and the defeat of the revolution. A government composed in the
> majority of elements drawn from the workers' movement cannot employ
> these methods, which are reserved to reactionary and fascist-type regimes.

In Barcelona, the walls began to be covered by a P.S.U.C. poster showing a mask with a hammer and sickle—indicating the P.O.U.M.—behind which lurked a horrible face with a swastika.

On May 14, Soviet ambassador Marcel Rosenberg visited Largo Caballero and demanded the dissolution of the P.O.U.M. The signal had already been transmitted: the communist head of the republican airforce, Hidalgo de Cisneros, had told Largo that "his" planes would not partici-pate in the Extremadura operation.

On May 15, the council of ministers met. Largo explained his decision to submit Catalunya to martial law, saying the conflict there was not with the government, but was between the two union federations. The communist ministers demanded the dissolution of the "Trotskyite P.O.U.M." Largo Caballero recounted, "I argued that nothing could be done legally, that if the P.O.U.M. had violated the law, the tribunals would judge them."

Montseny, one of the two F.A.I. ministers, supported Largo. Then the communist ministers, Vicente Uribe and Jesús Hernández, withdrew. Largo Caballero sought to continue the meeting, but Prieto objected that, with two ministers having resigned—this was how he interpreted the com-munist withdrawal—the government should be considered to have re-signed. Largo answered, "All the other ministers have remained silent. Nobody has supported me, although they all call themselves democrats."[32]

Largo Caballero visited Azaña, president of the republic, to present his resignation. Azaña recounts the experience as follows:

> He spoke against the communists, saying that the latest reason for his hos-
> tility was that he, Largo, had refused to dissolve the P.O.U.M., as they de-
> manded, because of the events in Barcelona. 'I am a man of ideas . . . and I
> cannot use violence in this way. Even if the investigations turn something up,
> and no matter what people say, I will refuse to take any measure anywhere
> near what the communists desire. If I had satisfied them, this would not be
> happening.'

Azaña, in his diary, adds no comment; the president of the republic abstained from demonstrating confidence in the possibility of the re-publican justice system clarifying responsibilities for the May events. A little afterward, two republican ministers, José Giral and Carles Esplá, visited him and told him that during the council meeting, "Largo

Caballero called the communists slanderers and liars, that there were six hours of unusual violence and foul language."[33]

Consultations began. Largo was charged with forming a new government, but had to refuse, since the republicans would not accept his formula of a government with representatives of the two union federations but without the communists. Finally, maneuvers by Prieto and the communists were successful and Juan Negrín, a right-wing socialist and minister of the interior under Largo, was named as the new head of government.

Negrín had been responsible for the secret shipping to the U.S.S.R. of the gold reserve of the Bank of Spain, to pay for arms which had yet to be delivered. His cabinet was made up of right-wing socialists, republicans, and communists, without any representatives of the two union federations.

"La Batalla" had called for a C.N.T.-U.G.T. government. It put itself at Largo's side when it was already too late and without a single word of sympathy for his personal position, when he had refused to dissolve the P.O.U.M. "Soli," which had also called for a government of the two union federations, said on May 18, "A counterrevolutionary government has been established."

The same day, Largo Caballero made a speech in Valencia explaining the causes of the crisis: "The demand for dissolution of the P.O.U.M. was only a pretext, because the campaign against Largo Caballero had already begun."

When they asked him to dissolve the P.O.U.M., "I told them that having been persecuted many times, I had not entered the government to serve any of the political factions that made it up, that whoever wanted to should denounce criminal acts or errors to the justice system and that the latter authority, should they consider it appropriate, would dissolve the guilty organizations, but that Largo Caballero, as President of the council, would never dissolve any of these organizations."[34]

The communists, in discussing the crisis, did not speak of the P.O.U.M., but of the desire to form a government "capable of winning the war."

To summarize, then, the May events had considerable consequences. Catalunya lost not only the state functions it had gained after July 19, but also the control of public order; the collectivizations had lost their revolutionary character; the control patrols were dissolved; a regular army organization was imposed in place of the militias; the Esquerra had become an appendix of the P.S.U.C.; the Extremadura offensive, which could have changed the course of the war, was frustrated; the Negrín government was set up, which further trimmed the rights of Catalunya and which openly annulled the working class conquests after July 19.

The communists had gotten their way. But to be considered victorious in Moscow, they still had to get rid of the P.O.U.M.

Notes

1. The resolutions of the meeting were published in a pamphlet: *Resoluciones Aprobadas en el Pleno Ampliado del Comite Central del P.O.U.M.*, Barcelona, 1937.
2. Franz Borkenau, op. cit., pp. 177-182.
3. See the special issue of "Cahiers Leon Trotsky" dedicated to the Moscow trials and their echoes around the world, "Les Procés de Moscou dans le Monde," July-September 1979.
4. Speech by Santiago Carrillo, secretary of the J.S.U., in the Teatro Apolo in Valencia, December 16, 1936, pp. 12-13.
5. *Pleno Ampliado del C.C. del Partido Comunista de Espana*. Valencia, 1937, pp. 11-13.
6. The twenty-seven resolutions of the central committee were published in "La Batalla" for March 30, with a commentary by Nin.
7. On the S.B.L., see Stephen Schwartz, "A La Memoria de Andreu Nin," op. cit., and articles by various authors, "Cahiers Leon Trotsky," July-September 1979, and June 1982. Also, see Pierre Broué, ed., Leon Trotsky, *La Revolucion Espagnola* (1930-40), Paris, 1975, pp. 624-628, reprinting from Fosco, "L'Activité des B.L. en Espagne et ses Enseignements," "Bulletin Interieur d'Information du Parti Communiste Internationaliste" (Paris), October 15, 1938. Munis, op. cit., is interesting on some aspects of the revolution and has been taken up as a major source by such historians as Bolloten, Broué, and Paul Preston (*The Coming of the Spanish Civil War*, London, 1985) but offers very little on the real history of the Trotskyist groupings in the conflict. Of greater interest are Low and Breá, op. cit.: the Russell Blackwell (Rosalio Negrete) correspondence with the American Trotskyist leader Hugo Oehler; Domenico Sedran, "Memoires d'Un Prolétaire Révolutionnaire," in "Cahiers Leon Trotsky," March 1987, and the memoirs of Pavel and Clara Thalmann; on some of these writers and on Péret, see chapter 7.
8. Published in the mimeographed "Boletin Interior" of the P.O.U.M., Barcelona, April 5, 1937.
9. "La Batalla," April 27, 1937.
10. M. Koltsov, "The Trotskyist Criminals in Spain, in "International Press Correspondence," March 30, 1937.
11. Camillo Berneri, "In Difesa del P.O.U.M.—Noi e il P.O.U.M.," in *Scritti Scelti, Petrogrado 1917-Barcellona 1937*, Milano, 1964, pp. 231 and ff. This was probably the last article Berneri wrote before his death. It was published in anarchosyndicalist periodicals around the world.
12. Cited in *Guerra y Revolucion en Espana*, Moscow, 1965, vol. II., pp. 101-102.
13. Jeanne Degras, *The Communist International*, London, 1963, vol. III, p. 398.
14. Koltsov, *Diario de la Guerra de Espana*, pp. 311 and ff.
15. Winston Churchill, *Step by Step*, London, 1939, pp. 72 and 120.
16. The Puigcerdá incident has been one of the most controversial for writers on the Spanish Civil War. Although guardias de asalto and the Catalan *Mossos d'Esquadra* were implicated in the overall conflict in the region, the shooting that produced Martín's death seems to have been provoked by local tensions over collectivization. For an account by a C.N.T. activist of Martín's death, see the interview with Mariano Puente, in Nancy Macdonald, *Homage to the Spanish Exiles*, New York, 1987, pp. 171-189. For the opposing point of view,

see Francesc Viadiu, "Los Communistas Aprovecharon Su Oportunidad," in "Historia" (Madrid), April 1977.

17. George Orwell, op. cit., p. 116 (Penguin edition).
18. Documentation furnished by Burnett Bolloten.
19. Aside from recent Spanish reprints of their journal "El Amigo del Pueblo," the most comprehensive information on the Friends of Durruti is contained in two non-Spanish publications, Georges Fontenis, *Le Message Revolutionnaire des 'Amis de Durruti'* (*Espagne* 1937), Cangey (France), 1983, and Paul Sharkey, *The Friends of Durruti—a Chronology*, Tokyo, 1984.
20. "Il Grido del Popolo" (Paris?), May 28, 1937, cited in Sharkey, ibid.
21. Documentation furnished by Burnett Bolloten.
22. Verle B. Johnston, *Legions of Babel*, University Park, NJ, 1967, p. 198.
23. "Informe que emite la asesoría jurídica del frente de Aragón en virtud de orden telegráfica del General Jefe del Ejército del Este," May 15 and 17, 1937, Servicio Histórico Militár, "Documentación Roja," Madrid. Copy provided to Stephen Schwartz by Burnett Bolloten.
24. Fenner Brockway, *The Truth About Barcelona*, London, 1937, p. 11.
25. Ralph Bates, introduction to *Unidad Proletaria U.G.T.-C.N.T.*, Mexico, 1938, pp. 11-12 (in Spanish only).
26. Manuel Azaña, "Memorias Políticas y de Guerra," in *Obras Completas*, Mexico, 1969, vol. IV, p. 582.
27. Claude G. Bowers, *My Mission to Spain*, New York, 1954, p. 356.
28. G. Munis, in conversation with Stephen Schwartz, 1979; also see Sedrán op. cit.
29. Julián Gorkín, *Canibales Politicos*, Mexico, 1941, pp. 68-69.
30. Jaume Miravitlles, *Episodia de la Guerra Civil Espanyola*, Barcelona, 1974, op. cit., p. 172.
31. The details of how this decision was arrived at by the Communist Party is to be found in Jesús Hernández, *Yo fui un ministro de Stalin*, Mexico, 1952, p. 84.
32. Largo Caballero, op. cit., p. 4.
33. Azaña, op. cit., pp. 595-596.
34. *Largo Caballero Denuncia*, Valencia, 1937, pp. 12-13.

6

Persecution

Twenty-nine days went by before the communists felt they could begin the open repression of the P.O.U.M. It was a month during which the P.O.U.M. recovered its confidence and believed the communists, notwithstanding all that had happened, would not dare to launch themselves into the physical extermination of dissidents. Measures to organize the party underground were downgraded. If the number of P.O.U.M. members, which had climbed from 10,000 to 30,000 in the first weeks of July, and had then risen to a possible 70,000 by December, had now fallen back to 40,000, the figure in October 1936, the P.O.U.M. nonetheless remained a force.

Nin edited a draft political thesis for the congress which it was hoped would be held on June 18, in which he insisted on the central theme of P.O.U.M. propaganda: the need for the working class to take power, to form a workers' and peasants' government, and to move forward toward setting up a socialist regime.[1] He also insisted that the dictatorship of the proletariat did not mean a party dictatorship. The thesis proposed a Revolutionary Workers' Front of the C.N.T., the F.A.I., and the P.O.U.M. (they still did not take into full account the Socialist Left, perhaps reflecting a Catalan bias), to bring about "a program of clear and concrete realizations—today perfectly possible" (although they did not say what they would be) "which would determine a fundamental change in the correlation of forces and would effect a powerful push on the revolution."

In the face of this, Nin warned of the danger of a foreign capitalist intervention.

> If the decisive factor was technological superiority, the victory of the proletariat could be discounted. But there is a real factor that is infinitely more important: the expansive strength of the revolution. Triumphant in Spain, it would have immediate repercussions in other countries, and particularly in Germany and Italy, to whose fascist regimes it would deliver a mortal blow.

This was dreaming, many P.O.U.M. members thought. The thing to be done was not to insist on revolution when the counterrevolution was advancing, but to maintain positions and await an opportunity. Yes to a Revolutionary Workers' Front, but as a defensive rather than an offensive action.

The degree to which Nin's position lacked realism became clear to Gorkín when he visited Brussels, where he was welcomed by Victor Serge. Serge had been personally close to the Catalan anarchists, having participated in the 1917 revolutionary attempt in Spain, which he described in his novel *Birth of Our Power.*

The Belgian-born nephew of a famous nineteenth century Russian revolutionary, the terrorist Kibalchich, Serge had gone to Russia after the October revolution and worked in the Comintern alongside Boris Souvarine, Franz Borkenau, and others. He had become a friend and comrade of Nin in Moscow and had functioned as a leader of the Trotskyist Opposition. Banished to a Central Asian "isolator", he was released from the U.S.S.R. thanks to the success of his novels and reportages in France combined with pressure by French leftist intellectuals, particularly André Gide. By 1936, Serge was firmly on the side of the P.O.U.M. against all critics, including Trotsky.[2]

In Brussels, Gorkín met with the leaders of the Socialist International and the International Federation of Trade Unions, to ask them to set up an international commission of inquiry on the case of the P.O.U.M. He was told that the social democratic organizations did not wish to intervene in "quarrels between antifascist brothers."[3]

But how could the P.O.U.M. leaders have thought that these bureaucratized folk—who in the case of the I.F.T.U. were then flirting with the communists on the presumption that the Russian governmental "trade unions," with their considerable financial resources, might affiliate with them—would support a genuine revolution in Spain?

The slanders did not cease. The communist press "reported" that Gorkín had attended a meeting in Freiburg, Germany, with agents of the Nazi Gestapo. Gorkín, by agreement with the party executive, filed a suit over this incident but it was rejected by the judicial authorities on the pretext that the P.O.U.M. had not filed a copy of its statutes. On the other hand, the same Gorkín, as editor of "La Batalla," was tried for a May Day editorial advising the workers to hide their weapons.

Public interest—even that of the workers—in political questions continued lessening, and rationing, with goods very scarce, was a bigger worry than any of the ideological disputes, but the campaign against the P.O.U.M. saw no quarter. The P.C.E.'s José Díaz affirmed in a meeting of his party's central committee, "The P.O.U.M. must be eliminated from the political life of the country."

The communists took advantage of the fact that in its first weeks the

Negrín government encountered a boycott by the working masses, to obtain for itself the key positions, and not necessarily those that would make for brilliant careers. Colonel Antonio Ortega, a communist, for example, was named General Director of Security, and from that moment on, the socialist Julián Zugazagoitia, minister of the interior, completely lost control of the police.

The P.C.E.

What, in reality, was this official Communist party that, in 1937, carried out in Barcelona and Valencia operations similar to those that would be undertaken a decade later in the countries of Eastern Europe? We have noted the difficulty some historians have had in understanding "communist conservatism" in the Spanish revolution. This phenomenon may be partially explained by tactical opportunism. But it is also clear that the political culture of the communist state as it later existed in Eastern Europe (in some cases ruled by veterans of the International Brigades in Spain) is a profoundly reactionary one. There is no mystery in "communist conservatism" in Spain: it was simply a faithful expression of the communist goal—a military-police dictatorship ruled by a single party.

It has been claimed that the official Communist Party rose from 100,000 members in 1936 (clearly an exaggerated figure) to 249,000 in March 1937 and 310,000 in June, when, through Negrín, it gained power over the republican government. From then on, its ranks did not increase much, notwithstanding the numerous means of pressure put into practice—especially in the army—to obtain recruits.

According to Comorera, the members of the P.S.U.C. rose from 6,000 in July 1936 to 42,000 in March 1937. The P.S.U.C. may have reached 60,000 by the May events, and hardly grew thereafter. The Basque Communist Party had 22,000 members in March 1937 (compared with 3,000 in July 1936, when it was still a section of the Spanish party). In toto, then, the communists had at most 400,000 members, fewer than the U.G.T. or the C.N.T., but more than the P.S.O.E. and many more than the F.A.I. or the P.O.U.M., to say nothing of the other republican parties.[4]

What was the social composition of this party? According to statistics from the party itself, in March 1937, 35% of its members were, by origin, industrial workers, crafts workers, or small proprietors, 30% peasants, 25% agricultural day laborers, 7% middle class, and 3% intellectuals and professionals. On the other hand, of its overall membership, only 8% were women and a remarkable 53% were military (soldiers, officers, commissars). Any observer of events can confirm that the majority of the new members, beginning in March 1937, belonged to the middle class. For the P.S.U.C., this last point was obvious beginning in July 1936, and, perhaps for that very reason, the P.S.U.C. never published statistics on its composition.

Although officially independent and directly affiliated with the Comintern, the three parties—Spanish, Catalan, and Basque—formed a single unit, whose leaders were never elected, but rather named by other bodies, themselves unelected, and they never decided questions of importance. The decisions were adopted by the *troika* of Soviet advisers Togliatti, Codovilla, and Stepanov for approval by the local leaders. At the beginning, the Soviet embassy and consulate also exercised influence in the *troika*, but with the return of Rosenberg and Antonov-Ovsyeyenko to Russia, and their liquidation, the *troika* worked directly under Moscow, probably because with Negrín in power it was no longer necessary to observe diplomatic forms. At the same time, the power of the Russian military officers increased (no regular Soviet troops served in Spain).

Many of the Russians who served in Spain were naturally unable to give testimony on their actions, because when they returned to the U.S.S.R. they disappeared, as in the case of the two diplomats mentioned above. Antonov-Ovsyeyenko, a notable Bolshevik hero who appears in the final scene of Sergei Eisenstein's film *October* (playing himself), was rehabilitated during the Khrushchev era, and his son Anton Antonov-Ovsyeyenko has written brilliantly on Stalinism. General Yan K. Berzin, head of Red Army Intelligence (G.R.U.), and an outstanding military figure apart from his tenure as head of the Soviet military mission in Spain in 1936-37, was shot on his return to Moscow, as was an International Brigades commander, "Kléber," the Austrian-born Manfred Stern.

Others who perished in the Stalinist purges included Artur Stashevsky, the commercial attache who worked with Negrín on the transfer to Russia of the gold reserve of the Bank of Spain, and the journalist Koltsov. Berzin and Koltsov were both rehabilitated under Khrushchev. A German communist, Hans Beimler, was killed in Spain and proclaimed a combat martyr and hero, although there have always been rumors that he was eliminated as a purge victim.

Officers in the service of the Comintern in Spain who survived the purges of the 1930s included a number who went on to distinguished careers in the Second World War and in the postwar Soviet and Eastern European defense establishments. They included Soviet Marshal Rodion Y. Malinovsky (known as "Manolo" in Spain), and Admiral N.G. Kuznetsov. The Polish general Karol Swierczewski, known as "General Walter" when he commanded the 35th Division of the Spanish Republican Army, was prominent in Poland after 1945. Lúdwik Svoboda, a Czechoslovak who fought in Spain, shared the leadership of his own country in tandem with the ill-fated Alexander Dubcek in the year 1968; because General Svoboda had also led a detachment of Czechoslovak volunteers in the Soviet Army during the Second World War, he was spared the humiliation inflicted on his associates in the reformist leadership of the "Prague Spring."

Czechoslovak veterans of Spain fought as far afield as China, where they served in the local Red Army. The Spanish veteran Ferenc Munnich was Hungarian head of state from 1958 to 1961. Another Hungarian, Erno Gerö, known in Spain since the early 1930s (and who used the pseudonym "Pedro" during the war), the de facto head of the P.S.U.C., survived to play a less than honorable role in 1956, in his own country, when he called on the Russians to send tanks into Budapest. Less than twenty years before, he had been the architect both of the Telefónica provocation and of the recalling to the Soviet Union of Antonov-Ovsyeyenko. After the Hungarian Revolution, Gerö fled to the Soviet Union. He died in Budapest in 1980. Spanish veterans also have been prominent in the governments of East Germany and Bulgaria.[5]

Some communists active in Spain and prominent in Eastern Europe after the Second World War were tried and executed in the wave of anti-Semitic show trials held in the "people's democracies" in the late 1940s and early 1950s. The victims in this hecatomb include a whole generation of communist leaders; Spain had been a training ground where many communists of the 1930s were blooded. Among the most prominent figures in the trials was Laszlo Rajk in Hungary, who had fought with distinction in Spain and has been fully rehabilitated. One of the most famous and feared Soviet agents in the West, Otto Katz, who used the name Andre Simone, was a star performer in the Prague show trial of Rúdolf Slánsky, testifying to having been a "Trotskyite agent" beginning in Spain, where, in reality, he and his cohort dedicated themselves to ruthlessly vilifying and exterminating, where possible, the P.O.U.M. and other dissidents. In Albania, Spanish veteran Koci Xoxe was executed in the wave of 1940s-1950s purges, while another participant in the Spanish war, Mehmet Shehu, was murdered in the final phase of the Enver Hoxha regime, thirty years later.

Many Spanish veterans have occupied posts as lower functionaries in the Soviet and Eastern European regimes, but the single example of a country where the "Spaniards" maintained themselves as a compact power center, extending from the highest party posts downward, is Yugoslavia.

The "Spaniards" in Yugoslavia included, by association, Marshal Tito himself, since he worked as a recruiter for the International Brigades, although he was never himself on Spanish soil. Tito's immediate leadership circle in the 1941-45 Yugoslav partisan war against the Germans, and in the period of resistance to the Soviet Union beginning in 1948, was headed by a communist veteran of Spain, Koca Popovic. The Spanish experience of the Yugoslav communist leaders is only one expression of a strong strain of "nostalgia for modernity" in the elite of this mountainous country, so recently won from Austrian and Turkish domination—many of the "Spanish" group, including Popovic and others, were poets of a surrealist persuasion before becoming revolutionary soldiers in Spain. Yugoslavia remained one of only two countries in the world—the other being Mexico—that had no diplomatic relations with Spain so long as Franco remained alive. (It should, perhaps, also be noted that Croatian and other nationalist groups in Yugoslavia have criticized the long-time concentration of power in the hands of the "Spaniards" in the Yugoslav political leadership.)

The Soviet political police, today known as the K.G.B. or Committee for State Security, was then known officially as the N.K.V.D. (People's Commissariat of Internal Affairs), and, by common usage among many, as the G.P.U., its former title (State Political Administration). It had a limited number of active agents in Spain, organized in a highly disciplined task force or *spetsnaz*.

The task force in Spain was directed on the spot by Aleksandr Orlov, according to numerous observers, although Orlov, who fled Europe and broke with his masters in 1938, claimed for many years that he was only responsible for the organization of espionage in the fascist zone. In evaluating the role of Orlov, one enters a twilight zone of intelligence activities, where the verification of data in a form acceptable to historians becomes nearly impossible. Suffice it to say that in the academic and intelligence communities alike, Orlov, who had now been dead for almost a decade, has both defenders and detractors. It is perhaps worth recording that the outstanding eyewitness historian Burnett Bolloten, who saw Orlov many times in Spain, has never believed Orlov's version of events.[6]

Walter Krivitsky, a senior officer in the Soviet secret police who visited Spain several times and who, having defected, published a book, *In Stalin's Secret Service,* also described Orlov as one of the heads of the N.K.V.D. in Spain. A colleague of Krivitsky, Ignace Poretsky, known as Ignace Reiss, a revolutionary of Polish extraction who with him coordinated N.K.V.D. activities in Europe and the United States, learned early in 1937 of the impending attack on the P.O.U.M. and, horrified, defected from the G.P.U. and attempted to warn the P.O.U.M. leadership through Sneevliet. But he was too late, making contact with Sneevliet only a week before after the party leaders had been arrested.

Slutsky, head of the foreign section of the Soviet secret police, retained overall responsibility for all these agents. Krivitsky wrote of him:

> Sloutski, chief of the Foreign Division of the Ogpu, had been ordered from Moscow to inspect the secret police, which was modeled on that of Russia.

He arrived a day or two after my departure. The Ogpu was then blossoming out all over loyalist territory, but concentrating on Catalonia, where the independent groups were strongest and where also the real Trotskyists had their party headquarters.

'They have good material over there,' Sloutski told me when he returned to Paris some weeks later, 'but they lack experience. We cannot allow Spain to become a free camping ground for all the anti-Soviet elements that have been flocking there from all over the world. After all, it is our Spain now, part of the Soviet front. We must make it solid for us. Who knows how many spies there are among those volunteers? And as for the anarchists and Trotskyists, even though they *are* anti-Fascist soldiers, they are our enemies. They are counter-revolutionists, and we have to root them out.'[7]

This throng of agents—political, military, diplomatic, police—conducted themselves with an exalted and dictatorial manner, to such a point that in 1937 one of the better of them, Berzin, became alarmed, according to Krivitsky, warning that Soviet secret police agents were "compromising the Soviet authority in Spain by their unwarranted interference and espionage."

José Díaz saw how in the meetings of the P.C.E. political bureau, in which the *troika* was present, its special friends—Ibárruri, her lover Francisco Anton, etc.—did not even bother to discuss the matters at hand, but simply declared that "Togliatti has said that . . ."[8]

No less tragic than that of their counterparts in Hungary and Czechoslovakia was the fate of some indigenous agents of the Comintern, once the war had ended. Joaquím Olaso, a former *bloquista* who, having gone over to the P.S.U.C., played a prominent role in denouncing members of the P.O.U.M. to the police in Catalunya during the period of repression, was apparently murdered in 1954 in France along with his companion, after having been expelled from the party (although there have been suggestions that he committed suicide).

Joan Comorera died in prison in Spain, the country to which he returned once his comrades in the P.S.U.C. had thrown him out of the leadership. While Comorera hoped to gain control over some cadres of the underground party, what he found instead was a denunciation to the Franco police by his own "friends" and the publication of a letter from his daughter denouncing him as a traitor.

Between the end of the Spanish war in 1939 and the end of the Second World War, most of the former *bloquistes*, members of the Unió Socialista, and Catalan P.S.O.E. members who had joined the P.S.U.C. in 1936 had left the party. Some defended Tito and, later, others departed from the fold with the events in Hungary in 1956 and in Czechoslovakia in 1968. Some who had fled to Russia left the party as soon as they were allowed out of the

Soviet Union. But there were those who could not save themselves. Llíbert Estartus, a former B.O.C. leader who joined the P.S.U.C. and who later participated in the French resistance—and who had always demonstrated independence of mind—was murdered in France by the communists in 1944.[9]

Of the three individuals who made up the famous *troika*, Palmiro Togliatti and Vittorio Codovilla became the heads of the Communist Parties in, respectively, Italy and Argentina, while Stepanov (Stoyan Minev) went on to a career as a minor figure in communist East Europe. Of their aides, the notorious Vittorio Vidali ("comandante Carlos Contreras") became head of the Communist Party in the city of Trieste on the Italian-Yugoslav border, later serving as a vice president of the Italian senate, while André Marty, known as "the butcher of Albacete" for his ruthless purges in the ranks of the International Brigades, ended up expelled from the leadership of the French Communist Party in the early 1950s.

The case of the P.O.U.M. has continued to haunt the leaders of the Spanish Communist Party. By the mid-1970s, Santiago Carrillo had published a statement admitting that Nin was murdered; on the fortieth anniversary of the May events, a largely unrepentant Rafael Vidiella, although defending the campaign carried out by his party, the P.S.U.C., nonetheless tried to cite Andreu Nin as a personal friend. By 1987, Gregori Lopez Raimundo, leader of the P.S.U.C., was prepared to disclaim any P.S.U.C. involvement in the more distasteful aspects of the anti-P.O.U.M. onslaught.[10]

There can be no doubt that the attitude toward the P.O.U.M. became, with the passage of time, an internal infection in the ranks of the official party and of the communist generation of the civil war. The Catalan communist writer Teresa Pamies, who was an adolescent when the civil war took place, has written that she is "aware that sooner or later, the communists will have to take up again the file on the P.O.U.M., the death of Andreu Nin" (she was not ready yet to call it a murder) . . . "It is not a matter of bending the knee, but of beginning to clarify the things that took place." In her memoirs, she wrote "we still don't know what was done with Nin," thus ignoring the revelations of Jesús Hernández, the former communist leader, and goes on to say that "If someone had asked those of us who were militants (of the P.S.U.C.) if it was necessary to execute Andreu Nin, leader of the 'Trotskyite-fascist putsch,' we would have answered 'Yes.' And that is the lesson that must be remembered."[11]

The ex-Communist screenwriter and novelist Jorge Semprún was more blunt. As this book was in its final editing, Semprún commented, at an event celebrating the 50th anniversary of the 1937 antifascist writers' congresses held in Spain (about which see further below), "Perhaps the moment has come to recall Andreu Nin, whom we ourselves tortured and murdered." A few weeks later, Rafael Ribó, current secretary-general of the P.S.U.C., described the crime as "one of the characteristic injustices that demonstrates the aberrant quality of the Stalinist system." Ribó went on to call for the "indispensable . . . revision of our (i.e. the P.S.U.C.'s) *official* historical versions." Ribó was the first P.S.U.C. leader to *officially* use the words "they kidnapped him, they killed him, they murdered him" in speaking of the Nin case.[12]

Since everything the Spanish communists did—however accompanied by enthusiasm on their part—was done on Moscow's orders, and since in Moscow it was Stalin who gave the orders, it is clear that Stalin was the gravedigger of the Spanish revolution, just as he was that of the Russian revolution.

In this sense, the Spanish communists, if they were successful in the mission assigned to them by Stalin (that of digging the grave in which the Spanish revolution was to be interred), nonetheless failed historically, because nobody believed, among those who knew what was going on, the accusations against the P.O.U.M., and nobody believes them today. Indeed, while the reputation of Nin as a literary and political figure has grown in Catalunya since his death, the *Catalanistes* of the P.S.U.C. clearly have passed nothing to later generations in the way of a cultural and political heritage. The memory of their treatment of the P.O.U.M. is an albatross around the necks of the official Communists in Spain today. Indeed, it is only fit that in anarchist publications on post-Franco Spain, the conflict between Francoists and communists has been described as one between "the murderers of Garcia Lorca and those of Andreu Nin."

The Trotskyists

In one thing, however, the official Communists were truly successful: in making people believe the P.O.U.M. was a Trotskyist movement. Not that there is anything criminal in being a Trotskyist. But the historiography of the Spanish Civil War so abounds in errors on this point that it is necessary to underscore the question: was the P.O.U.M. Trotskyist?

The communists claimed it was. Their publications and correspondents proclaimed it to the world. It was easy to explain complex matters with a single adjective.

Perhaps the best proof of the enormous effectiveness of the communist propaganda apparatus is that professional historians as well as journalists and others whose training supposedly obligates them to genuinely investigate a situation, have used the same adjective. To enumerate all their names would be extremely tiresome, and unfortunately would include many who attach nothing pejorative to it; indeed, some firm friends of the P.O.U.M., including C.N.T. members after the May events, called the P.O.U.M. 'Trotskyist.' Borkenau was another friend of the P.O.U.M. who described it this way. Orwell declared that the P.O.U.M. could only be called Trotskyist in the broadest sense of "one who, like Trotsky, advocates 'world revolution' as against 'socialism in a single country.' More loosely, a revolutionary extremist." But that was precisely the way the term came to be used by the intelligentsia of the democratic West in referring to the P.O.U.M.

Obviously, few of the authorities who have erroneously expatiated on the P.O.U.M.'s "Trotskyism" can have taken much time reading either the P.O.U.M. press or Trotsky's own writings on the subject. To their credit, some outstanding historians of the conflict in Spain have endeavored to establish the truth of the matter. One such is Burnett Bolloten, who worked with Jordi Arquer in assembling his authoritative account, *The Spanish Revolution: The Left and the Struggle for Power.* Another is Pierre Broué, himself a Trotskyist who has scrupulously examined the P.O.U.M. counter-position to Trotskyism in books and articles, and through the work of the Institut Léon Trotsky at Grenoble.

Unfortunately, though, authors like Hugh Thomas are still more widely read on the subject. Hugh Thomas, in later editions of his book *The Spanish Civil War,* has repaired some of the more egregious errors of his earlier work, but his treatment of the P.O.U.M. was originally very bad, aside from the errors abounding in the overall work. Since his book was developed under the inspiration of Juan Negrín, on whose papers he depended, neither his errors nor his echoes of the Stalinist chorus against the P.O.U.M. should perhaps surprise anybody.

"The bigger the lie, the easier to make it believable" has generally been considered a Hitlerian principle, although in the case of the P.O.U.M., and elsewhere, it has been used by Soviet-inspired leftists. It exasperated the P.O.U.M. Had the P.O.U.M. been nothing more than a shadow of Trotsky, its conduct from the beginning would have followed the rigid slogans of that personality's followers, and the P.O.U.M. would have acted the same as the official Communists did in the relationship the latter had with Stalin.

But the P.O.U.M. was different. It was a party rooted in the reality of the Catalan working class movement and with ramifications in the whole experience of the Spanish revolution. Nobody gave orders to the P.O.U.M. They had said what they said and had done what they had done on their own initiative, in every case; demanding the right to have their strengths and weaknesses considered in a balanced way, as well as the proven valor and tenacity, the fidelity to certain basic principles, they knew was theirs. For this they paid a heavy price.

The falsity of describing the P.O.U.M. as Trotskyist is also proven by a simple examination of the history of the real Trotskyists during the civil war. Regardless of their personal esteem for Trotsky, P.O.U.M. leaders such as Nin and Andrade, who continued to share some Trotskyist views, refused to break the discipline of the party by forming a "Trotskyist" faction. Thus, as we have said, they can be considered "Trotskyists" only in their personal being, and not in a truly political way. Finally, as we noted in Chapter 4, they did not have a determining influence on the party line. The idea that the 200 or so former members of the Communist Left could handily direct the 10,000 or so former *bloquistes* in the party, with all the political sophistication of the latter, was laughable, and besides, the former B.O.C. members were generally more radical than those of the I.C.E.

The real Trotskyists on the scene after July 1936 were in the Bolshevik-Leninist Section, eventually headed by Munis, which is described in Chapter 5. Some Spaniards, including Munis himself, had remained outside the P.O.U.M. when the Communist Left agreed to a fusion with the Bloc; but they had no strength. Some simply joined the Socialist Party. As we have noted, Munis himself returned to Mexico and was late in returning to Spain. In truth, the Bolshevik-Leninist Section remained little more than a name.

The official Trotskyists wasted more ink and saliva attacking the P.O.U.M. than they did the official Communist Party. Furthermore, the unceasing character of the criticism had, truth to tell, something in common with the Stalinist method. Jean Rous criticized the P.O.U.M. at the moment when it was most persecuted (although he later recognized that this criticism was formulated in "excessively sectarian terms.")[13] About Victor Serge, his friend, who was in Paris working to defend the P.O.U.M., Trotsky wrote that he was "in a hurry to compromise himself by a frivolous attitude."

In the ranks of the Trotskyist Fourth International, the Belgian group in particular came out against the sectarian attacks on the P.O.U.M., and its leaders were driven away from the international. It became known some twenty years afterward that the sowing of discord between Trotsky, on the one side, and the Belgian Trotskyists and Dutch R.S.A.P. leader Sneevliet on the other, over the P.O.U.M., was a task performed by one of the most infamous Soviet secret police agents, Mark Zborowski ("Etienne").

Zborowski, agent provocateur, has become a figure of true horror to scholars as well as partisans of the Trotskyist tradition. In his twenties, a refugee from the Ukraine, he studied anthropology in Paris. There he met and befriended Lev Sedov, Trotsky's son, and infiltrated the very heart of the Trotskyist international organization, to a point where Sedov trusted Zborowski to collect and read his mail.

Within months of the suppression of the P.O.U.M., Zborowski provided his co-agents with the address of the N.K.V.D. defector Ignace Reiss, and the latter was shot down in Switzerland. When Orlov defected, he tried unsuccessfully to warn Trotsky of "Etienne's" activities. Pierre Naville and Gérard Rosenthal, two French Trotskyist intellectuals, were particularly suspicious of Zborowski. But it was already too late. In 1938, six months before Orlov's defection, Sedov had died, under very suspicious circumstances, following a medical operation. It has been claimed that Zborowski killed Sedov with a poisoned orange.

Zborowski operated in conjunction with a network in France headed by Sergei Efron, a long-term Soviet agent who, married to the exiled Russian poetess Marina Tsvetayeva, posed as an anti-communist. The network under Efron carried out the murder of Ignace Reiss, as well as participating in the killing of Lev Sedov and engineering the "disappearance" in Paris of a leading member of the Fourth International, Rudolf Klement. The Efron-Zborowski ring worked closely with the task force in Spain that organized the "disappearance" of Andreu Nin and others, and coordinated plans for attacks on Victor Serge and Sneevliet.

Zborowski was not exposed until the 1950s, at the time of the breakup of the Soble ring of Soviet agents in the United States, where Zborowski had settled, pursuing the profession of anthropology. Yakov Sobolevicius, known as Jack Soble, and his brother Ruvin (Robert Soblen), had long histories as Soviet infiltrators in the Trotskyist movement, originally having been known under the revolutionary pseudonyms of "Senin" and "Roman Well." Much of the Sobles' spying in the United States was directed at Russian Mensheviks and at the Trotskyists. The Soviets unsuccessfully tried to get the Sobles and Zborowski to return to Russia after Stalin's death. Zborowski was tried and served a short prison term in the United States. At the time of this writing, he lives in retirement in San Francisco.[14]

But if the Trotskyists were largely blind to the maneuvers of Soviet agents like Zborowski, they were proud of their purported acuity when it came to their political differences with the P.O.U.M. The brunt of Munis's book *Jalones de derrota, promesa de victoria* is a ferocious attack on the P.O.U.M.:

> It may be seen that the idiosyncratic characteristics of the B.O.C. were also present in its successor, the P.O.U.M. In the politics of the first is to be found all the politics of the second. The blunders and capitulations of the P.O.U.M. during the civil war are far from being circumstantial . . . And if one wanted to provide a frightful and ugly example . . . of worthless practical leadership, of sluggishness in movement and failure to take advantage of opportunities, the [Spanish] Communist Left would provide the most obvious one . . . The Bolshevik-Leninist Section was founded too late, with the civil war already

begun, to be able to conquer a preponderant position in the short time available.[15]

In the following decades, Trotskyists have applied the same language to the P.O.U.M.; this is true of British, French, and U.S. Trotskyists, as well as the Spanish-speaking variety, such as Munis. They have attacked it for its relations with the London Bureau, which the Trotskyists called "pacifist and parliamentary scoundrels"; they attacked it for having signed the People's Front declaration in 1936, for having entered the Generalitat, and for not taking power in 1937, as if all these decisions were not determined by the relationship of forces in Spain. Trotskyists furthermore exaggerated the success of the official Communists in suppressing the P.O.U.M., fostering a legend that the P.O.U.M., unable to defend itself (presumably because it lacked the Trotskyist program), was entirely annihilated. In reality, the P.O.U.M., with its strong local roots, and thanks to the solidarity of the C.N.T., defended itself amazingly well against both Stalinist repression and that carried out subsequently by Franco.

The extraordinary thing about these criticisms is not their Stalinist tone or their lack of contact with reality, but the fact that the Trotskyists have never, in any country or at any time, succeeded in doing what they reproached the P.O.U.M. for not doing: becoming the leading party of the revolution. In the three countries where Trotskyism achieved a status comparable to that of the P.O.U.M.— Vietnam (while under the French), Sri Lanka, and Bolivia—they achieved not more, but very much less than the P.O.U.M. In Vietnam, they were destroyed by the Stalinist forces of Ho Chi Minh. In Sri Lanka, they ended up identifying with Sinhalese nationalism in its oppression of the Tamils and entered a succession of bourgeois governments. In Bolivia, they resemble nothing more than a provincial curiosity. Even the record of the P.O.U.M. in resisting totalitarian attacks has never been equaled by a Trotskyist organization. Trotskyism was wiped out in Russia, where it was close to the center of power; its fate in Vietnam, as noted, was ignominious; likewise, in Mao's China and Castro's Cuba, it was suppressed, and in revolutionary Nicaragua, where its partisans played a significant role in the struggle against Somoza, it was swept aside. The Trotskyist movement has come to support Stalinist-style dictatorships in the nearly fifty years since its founder's death, and it has tended to remain silent about the fate of its militants in countries like Vietnam, China, Cuba, and Nicaragua.

But what was the position of Trotsky himself, in relation to the Spanish Civil War and the P.O.U.M.? We discussed in Chapter 3 the evolution followed by Trotsky and his Spanish friends and how nearly all of them broke with him in 1934. It must be said that Trotsky himself was mainly responsible for the lack of influence of his movement in Spain, because in his writings he demonstrated an ignorance of Spanish reality and a schematism that is surprising even in someone so famous for dogmatism.

Obsessed by the Bolshevik experience, he systematically tried to superpose a Russian model on Spain. It was specifically the ex-Trotskyists in the P.O.U.M. who tried to point out to him the differences between Russia—without democratic traditions and a powerful workers' movement—and Spain, which possessed both things. But Trotsky never understood these distinctions. For him, whatever was possible in Russia in 1917, and, specifically, the seizure of power by an audacious minority with "the right line," must also be possible in Spain.

In 1931, Trotsky believed the monarchy in Spain "would maintain itself until the proclamation of the proletarian dictatorship." The workers should therefore prepare for the conquest of power. In 1936, he criticized the People's Front because, he said, it "turned the workers into victims of the Stalinists." But he argued for the Trotskyists to enter the Socialist Party, one of the initiators of the People's Front, while calling the Front's electoral manifesto "a shameful document" which, by their signing it, "turned the old 'Left' Communists into the tails of the Left bourgeoisie. It is difficult to imagine a more humiliating fall," he added.

In April 1936, he stated that the P.O.U.M. was "in no way better than the socialist and 'communist' traitors," and told the few official Trotskyists remaining in Spain that "Marxist action in Spain can begin only by means of an irreconcilable condemnation of the whole policy of Nin and Andrade, which was and remains not only false but criminal."

After the May events, in an article written when, Trotsky said, he still had only limited information, he argued nothing less than that "It seems very probable that this impressive experience will provoke a split in the P.O.U.M. The elements that excluded the Trotskyists ... will definitely betray the revolution by seeking the mercy and then the favor of the Moscow bureaucracy. On the other hand, the revolutionary elements must understand that there is no intermediary between the Fourth International and betrayal."

In a polemic with the Belgian and Dutch sympathizers of the P.O.U.M., the old Bolshevik claimed that (in May 1937) "the bourgeois reaction would not have found two regiments to defend it in the entirety of Spain," and this when the regular army was under complete communist control.

When, early in 1939, Barcelona fell to the Franco forces, Trotsky wrote that the revolution had been "brought to ruin by petty, despicable, and utterly corrupted 'leaders'," and later accused the P.O.U.M. of having "dragged at the tail of the C.N.T." He went on to accuse the P.O.U.M. of wanting "to participate in the Republican government and to enter as a loyal, peace-loving opposition into the general bloc of ruling parties; and on the other hand to achieve peaceful, comradely relations at a time when it was a question of implacable civil war."

In the febrile mind of Trotsky, the P.O.U.M. had become "the principal obstacle to the creation of a revolutionary party" in Spain.

Trotsky's representative, Jean Rous, eventually recognized the tremendous error of this sectarian approach and admitted that Trotsky had been unjust in his treatment of the P.O.U.M. Trotsky himself implicitly admitted it, writing as early as August 1936, and in apparent self-contradiction, that as regards relations between the Trotskyists, the P.O.U.M., and even the anarchosyndicalists he loathed, "It seems to me it would be extremely dangerous to let oneself be guided *exclusively* or even *primarily* by doctrinal considerations."

A year later, he declared:

> When Andreu Nin, the leader of the P.O.U.M., was arrested in Barcelona, there could be not the slightest doubt that the agents of the G.P.U. would not let him out alive . . . Quite apart from the differences of opinion that separate me from the P.O.U.M., I must acknowledge that in the struggle that Nin led against the Soviet bureaucracy, it was Nin who was right. He tried to defend the independence of the Spanish proletariat from the diplomatic machinations and intrigues of the clique that holds power in Moscow. He did not want the P.O.U.M. to become a tool in the hands of Stalin. He refused to cooperate with the G.P.U. against the interests of the Spanish people. This was his only crime. And for this crime he paid with his life.[16]

But clearly, the attacks of Trotsky, the arguments of the P.O.U.M. members, and the reality of things did not weigh much against the enormous avalanche of communist propaganda. This was so intense that in less than a month the necessary atmosphere was created for a passage from verbal persecution to physical repression.

The Arrests

The Negrín government took charge of the repression.

On June 14, Gorkín visited the Valencia office of interior minister Julián Zugazagoitia, whom he had known in the past as editor of the newspaper "El Socialista" in Madrid, to ask that a suspension decreed against "La Batalla" be lifted.

Zugazagoitia told him, "I would very much like to authorize the publication of 'La Batalla' as early as tomorrow, but I am afraid the order would be ignored."

Gorkín, acting surprised, asked, " But what government is this that does not act in accordance with the orders of its ministers?"

"You know as well as I," was the reply.

Gorkin's companion, a P.O.U.M. member from Madrid, protested against the persecution of the P.O.U.M. in that city and asked if they were protected by republican legality or if their lives were in danger.

"The P.O.U.M. affair has become poisoned. I don't know if I will be able to do anything," the minister averred.

Finally, "Zuga," as he was known, promised to bring up these questions in the meeting of the council of ministers set for June 18 and to issue a written account of the ensuing discussion. As he showed them to the door, he said, "Between now and then, I hope nothing happens to you."[17]

Either the minister was a good actor, or he was minister in name only, because before the 18th of the month, something happened to the leaders of the P.O.U.M.

On June 16, 1937, the party executive met, as it did each morning, in the Virreina Palace, a historic building in the middle Rambles that had been taken over by the Institut Maurín, and where there was more quiet than in the party headquarters nearby. The P.O.U.M. congress was scheduled to begin two days later. Questions of detail on the congress were taken up as well as the matter of what Gorkin would say at his trial as editor of "La Batalla," which was scheduled to begin the same day.

It was agreed that he would take advantage of the opportunity to denounce the communist campaign. It was believed that the people's tribunal would clear him.

Finally, details of the conference of the London Bureau, to be held in Barcelona on July 19, 1937, the first anniversary of the beginning of the revolution, were brought up. Some members of the executive feared the government would prevent the London Bureau conference by refusing visas to foreign delegates. But nobody anticipated any obstacles to the holding of the party congress on June 18. The communist campaign was fierce, but the P.O.U.M. members had grown used to it, and the repetition of the same litany of insults had begun to tire even the socialists and republicans.

When the meeting of the executive ended, some of the participants went to the party headquarters and others dispersed to carry on their activities. A comrade from the headquarters guard came to the group and told them that some time before a military man, who claimed to be a P.O.U.M. sympathizer, had stopped at the door and said the police had orders to arrest the members of the executive. They shrugged off this report. Nobody would dare, here in Barcelona, in the full daylight of the Rambles. Not even Nin, who had personal knowledge of the Soviet police, paid attention to the warning of this anonymous friend.

Within minutes, a car filled with police had arrived at the headquarters building. The agents asked for Nin, arrested him, and placed him in the car, which drove off. It was one in the afternoon.

As the car holding Nin left, the comrades in the other offices, having learned the news, grabbed the telephones and began advising the other party offices and searching for the other members of the executive.

A little later, the "La Batalla" editorial staff was visited by police, who occupied, as well, the remaining party offices in the city. Soon the Hotel Falcón, where all who were found were arrested, was transformed into a jail. These arrests were carried out by "secret" agents from Madrid, i.e. communists, since the Madrid police was completely in communist hands.

The evening of June 16, the following members of the executive had also been arrested: Gorkín, Arquer, Andrade, and Bonet. Escuder, the managing editor of "La Batalla" recently arrived from New York, David Rey, who had been imprisoned for seven years under the dictatorship, and Josep Coll, recuperating in a hospital, were also arrested. Josep Rovira, head of the P.O.U.M. 29th Division, was detained under the pretext of an order from higher up in the army and following pressure by the communists. Others numbering up to two hundred were arrested immediately. The members of the executive were taken by car to the headquarters of the Dirección General de la Seguridad, in Valencia. There they encountered, already arrested, several comrades, including Sixto Rabinat, secretary of the Valencia provincial council, and Luis Portela, a founder of the Communist Party in Spain. Portela was the first defendant sentenced to death by the bourgeois regime for his participation in the 1934 events (and then held "in perpetuity" in Pamplona prison), editor of the Valencia P.O.U.M. organ, "El Comunista," as well as being a member of the party executive. Eduardo de Sirval was arrested; he was the brother of Luis de Sirval, a leftwing journalist killed by the military in Asturias in the aftermath of 1934 whose case was a cause celebre. Within a month, the number of the arrested would reach nearly a thousand.[18]

On June 18, that is, the date when the P.O.U.M. congress was scheduled to begin (it did not take place, because the delegates had been advised from Barcelona by telephone or personally that they should not come into the city, so as to avoid the trap), the press provided the first news of the arrests with a simple announcement from the Commissariat of Public Order: "An important espionage service has been uncovered, in relation with which a considerable number of arrests have been carried out, among which we must point out those of a very dangerous contingent of foreign citizens and of personalities from a certain political party."

Not a single name was given. It was necessary to wait until June 24 for the newspapers to declare that "the principal accused in the espionage service discovered in the past few days are the leading circles of the P.O.U.M., with Andreu Nin and other well-known persons under arrests."

On June 22, two days before the release of the names of the arrested, the government announced the creation of a special tribunal for espionage, obviously intended for the trial of the P.O.U.M. leaders.

On June 25, Koltsov noted in his diary, in an entry that is very thorough although utterly lacking in truth or objectivity, the substance of what was appearing in the Spanish press:

> The republican police have long hesitated, indecisively, and have spent a long time haggling with the minister of justice, Irujo; finally they could not contain themselves any longer and began to eliminate the most important nests of the P.O.U.M., having arrested the Trotskyite leaders . . .

> In the little hotel where the P.O.U.M. central committee was installed many financial assets and eight million pesetas in money have been found. (In Barcelona, during the entirety of the past month, the population has suffered from the lack of money for making change) . . .

> The arrest of the Trotskyites was a matter on which above all the Madrid police insisted. In it there are socialists, republicans, and non-party people who, until now, felt that the struggle against Trotskyism was a special affair of the communists . . .

> In Madrid, a new organization for fascist espionage has been uncovered, with traces leading to Barcelona. The arrested spies possessed a radio transmitter that secretly transmitted to Franco data regarding the disposition and regroupment of the republican troops . . .

> In the espionage organization, along with members of the old reactionary aristocracy and of the Falange Española, the P.O.U.M. leaders were active. Apart from their espionage work, it was a matter also of preparing for a particular moment an armed fascist rising in the streets of Madrid . . .

> In one of the spies' nests a map of Madrid has been found, and on its reverse the police have discovered a document written in invisible ink. The message has been examined, and the text reads as follows:

> To the Generalissimo, personally:

> 'I communicate: We are in a condition to communicate everything we know about the placement of Red units. The latest data, sent through our transmitter, demonstrates the real improvement of our information service.'

> The rest of the document was in code. There was no way to decipher it. The police had no answer. The examining magistrate had the idea of checking with the General Staff office. There he found code books captured from the Franco forces. One of them exactly corresponded to the letter. The continuation of the letter said:

> 'The grouping and accumulation of forces in the rear guard for the moment is

going slowly. We now have 400 men ready to act. Being well armed, in favorable conditions, they can serve as shock troops for the movement. Your order regarding the infiltration of our men into the ranks of the extremists and the P.O.U.M. has been successfully carried out. We need a leader in the propaganda field who can begin working independently of us so as to act with less risk. In compliance with your order, I have been in Barcelona visiting N, a leading member of the P.O.U.M. I told him of your orders. The lack of a contact between you and he was caused by some problems with their transmitter, which began working again while I was there. You have probably already received his answer regarding the basic problem. N insisted greatly to you and to our foreign friends that I should be the only individual maintaining contact with him. He has promised to send new people to Madrid to reactivate the work of the P.O.U.M. Thanks to these measures, the P.O.U.M. will become in Madrid what it is in Barcelona, a real point of support for our movement. The data transmitted through B are no longer good. In a short while, we will communicate new information. The organization of support groups is accelerating. The problem of organizing operations in the south remains unclear.'

This police operation was possible because Negrin paid with it for communist help in becoming head of government. Zugazagoitia went along with it because it was unavoidable, once the imbecility of naming colonel Ortega head of security had been committed. Both, however, knew that the accusations against the P.O.U.M. were false and said nothing. It would not be until the end of the war, when they no longer needed to pay for communist favors or otherwise submit to them, that some would speak, although still with much reticence.

Negrín would write to Herbert L. Matthews, the pro-Communist correspondent for "The New York Times," that the P.O.U.M. "was controlled by elements highly allergic . . . to anything that would mean a single and supreme leadership for the struggle under a common discipline."[19]

Zúgazagoítia affirmed that the P.O.U.M. "paid for the windows that the F.A.I. had broken. The conviction I had and that no later information ever shook was that the insurrection [in May 1937] was fomented by the anarchists."[20]

Thus, Negrín allowed the P.O.U.M. to be persecuted and killed because they did not accept his single leadership, and Zugazagoitia allowed it to happen because someone had to pay for the broken windows.

On June 16, 1937, a new epoch began for the P.O.U.M. militants, which would continue until the end of the war, and for which there seem to be few historical precedents. If they fell into the enemy's hands, they would face the possibility if not the probability of death, and if they did not keep an eye on their "friends," the same thing would take place. If the war was lost, they would be persecuted, and if it was won, the persecution that had already begun would continue (indeed, there was the distinct chance that a republican victory would result in a second civil war between the communists and C.N.T.).

The P.O.U.M. members could not trust those comrades of the recent past who had gone over to the P.S.U.C., and if they saw them on the street they would have to change direction, because they never knew if the other person would say hello or pretend not to have seen them, or if the encounter would lead to denunciation and arrest.

From the beginning of the civil war, private life had ceased to exist. In many cases, the way the P.O.U.M. members earned their living was linked to their political activity, either as committee members, militia officers or simple soldiers, or because they worked for a party organization or union. Suddenly, this means of earning a living disappeared and it was not easy, in the middle of the war and a fierce persecution, to find another.

They needed, like everybody—and now more than everybody else, in order to escape the communist police—a union card, but the U.G.T. leaders had expelled them and given their names to the press, so as to help the work of the police. In the villages, where everybody knew them, the situation became even more difficult, and very often a P.O.U.M. member had to leave for Barcelona or some other place where their politics were not well-known. Many had to leave their families and hide out by changing their residences.

"Las Noticias," the newspaper of the Catalan U.G.T., was the first to explain, after a fashion, the causes of the repression:

> A few days ago, the police uncovered in Barcelona an organization of enormous importance dedicated to espionage in various countries of the world and that has placed in Spain, because of the war, many of its agents. The most elementary caution in such causes obliged us, at the beginning of the discovery of this case, to remain silent about this important activity of the police, because it could have redounded against the total success of the operation; but now, with some days having passed, of which the agents in charge of this affair took magnificent advantage to find out the least details and to jail the guilty, we can explain to our readers some information about this vast espionage organization which had its most important elements infiltrated into the Workers' Party of Marxist Unification (P.O.U.M.).
>
> As a first measure, the police proceeded to detain all the leading members of the P.O.U.M. and a great number of foreigners of both sexes, who appeared to be the persons in direct relation with the espionage service.
>
> Then, the brigade in charge of this affair having continued with its inquiries, it went on to the arrest of other elements that seem to have also been found to be implicated. Presently it is calculated that the number of arrested is some 300 . . .
>
> In searching the buildings used by this party, documents of great importance

have been found that have a direct relation with this *affaire,* to a point where the guilty have no way of denying their culpability.

In an apartment house in the San Gervasi district, owned by Bertran y Musitu, and where the P.O.U.M. had installed a headquarters, thousands of supply kits for soldiers were found. The police also carried out a search in a property in the carrer Hostafrancs, seizing there twelve new rifles, four old ones, seven bombs, and a large quantity of cartridges . . . Also, more weapons and ammunition have been found in other P.O.U.M. buildings. The investigative brigade headed by Gómez Serrano yesterday seized everything in the Hotel Falcón. Five six-ton trucks were loaded with seized goods, including a great quantity of silver objects, whose weight came to many kilograms, and clothing for soldiers, as well as bedsheets and other supplies.

The reports published abroad were hardly better. The news agencies picked up stories from the local papers, and almost the only ones that wrote in detail on the arrests were the communist journals. The communists claimed that no fewer than 200 of the arrested had made "detailed confessions."

The truth is that nobody confessed to anything, because there was simply nothing to confess. Not a single arrested P.O.U.M. member surrendered to the threats, the tortures, the offers—running the full gamut—that were intended to elicit confessions of things that had never happened. The rank and file militants as well as the leaders conducted themselves far better than the old Bolsheviks in Russia. There were some defections (a head of the P.O.U.M. Red Aid, Maruny, the former union activist Ramon Magré, and, later, the agrarian leader Santiago Palacín) and some who solicited membership in the P.S.U.C. and published articles condemning the P.O.U.M., but even these did not speak of "traitors" or "spies" but only of political differences. The few who joined the P.S.U.C. were old militants; among the new members who had joined since July 19, there were some who withdrew from party activity, hiding in their homes or elsewhere, but none of them did the bidding of the P.S.U.C., and many members continued working for the party.

Obviously, most people who knew anything did not believe what was said about the P.O.U.M., but to go from not believing to publicly declaring that they did not believe was a long step, which few dared take. In private, naturally, they demonstrated personal sympathy for the persecuted, hiding them at times or helping them, but in public, nothing. If not for its strong local base and, above all, the action of the C.N.T., the P.O.U.M. might have been exterminated. The C.N.T. unions gave membership books to P.O.U.M. members so they could work, and the C.N.T. militia brigades saved the lives of many, admitting P.O.U.M. militia members into the ranks of both soldiers and officers. P.O.U.M. militants who passed through the militia recruitment offices had to make sure they would be sent to C.N.T. units, for if they found themselves in a communist unit, it was almost certain they would end up being identified and, in no few cases, murdered, with the excuse given that they had deserted or gone over to the enemy.

The reaction of the C.N.T. was rapid. Within days of the arrests, Juan López, until very recently C.N.T. minister of commerce in Largo Caballero's cabinet, sounded the alarm to the confederal militants in the pages of the Valencia F.A.I. daily "Nosotros":

> "If we put in the balance the leaders of the Communist Party, on one side, and those of the P.O.U.M. on the other, in order to weigh the quantity of revolutionary dignity in each of the two parties, I am absolutely sure that the greatest weight would be with the P.O.U.M. . . . Who are these terrible individuals of the P.O.U.M. that the communists present to us each day as elements in touch with Hitler and Mussolini? . . . Nin . . . one of the most prescient Marxist minds in Spain . . . Who is David Rey? There are many snot-nosed kids who today pass themselves off as leaders of parties 'that are always right' who were still in their mothers' wombs when this working class militant was already exhausted from his sufferings in prison and his persecution by the reactionary governments of the monarchy . . . In the same place we put Nin and David Rey are all the rest of the list [of arrested], some young and others older, but all of them at the same level."

On June 28, with no published reports as to the whereabouts of the P.O.U.M. leaders, the C.N.T. national committee directed a long statement to the chief executives of the republic, the Cortes, and the government, the ministers of justice and the interior, and the leaders of the various party and union organizations, in which we find the following remarks:

> Are there agents of Franco, spies, and provocateurs, hidden in the ranks of the P.O.U.M.? Then let them be arrested, let them be tried with guarantees that there will be no deception, and let them then be shot. But only the agents, spies, and provocateurs. Not the members of a party that someone wishes to destroy and to eliminate first by putting it outside the law and then by annihilating its representative leaders, men who, through their long history, have acquired prestige among the masses. Nobody can convince us that Nin, that Andrade, that Gorkin, that David Rey are traitors, agents of fascism, spies, etc., etc., unless it can all be proven. We need proof to believe it . . . And proof must be given in a clear and categorical manner, not behind closed doors, which remind us too suspiciously of procedures imported from other countries.

The Murders

In Valencia, the arrested members of the executive were set free by the judge, who found no reason to try them. But the police arrested them at the gates of the jail and took them to Madrid, from where Gorkín succeeded in sending a note to Zugazagoitia: "On June 14," he wrote, "you made me a promise in the office of your ministry. On the 16th, we were arrested like vulgar criminals. Put at liberty in Valencia, we were kidnapped at the door of the Model Prison. We are being kept in an uninhabitable basement, sleeping on the dirt floor. Is this the treatment deserved by lifelong revolutionary militants? You will have to provide explanations for it to the Spanish and international proletariat."[21]

At the end of four more days, they were taken out of the basement of the house, which had been turned into a Communist Party private prison or *cheka* (a usage originally applied to these sites by the anarchists, in recollection of the original title of the Soviet secret police), and they were taken successively to the Atocha district *cheka,* the San Anton jail, and, finally, at the end of a week, were returned to Valencia, because the minister of justice had demanded it and had sent an inspector to collect them. It seemed that, finally, members of the government had become alarmed.

There was reason for alarm. Negrín and his justice and interior ministers had begun receiving telegrams from abroad. The C.N.T. press and what remained of the Left socialist press protested. The Madrid C.N.T. daily "Castilla Libre" was even suspended for this reason. Most importantly, nobody seemed to know what had happened to Andreu Nin. To be able to answer the protests from abroad, an investigation on the whereabouts of Nin was ordered. None of the ministers, aside from the communists, had expected things to go so far. To arrest, try, and even sentence was one thing, since plenty of people disliked the P.O.U.M.: but to the communist police and their Soviet controllers that was not enough. How to satisfy Moscow, the protestors, and one's own conscience? Negrín would have no answer.

An idea of the atmosphere at that moment is given by the fact that, while the arrested members of the executive were in Madrid, five corpses were found on a highway, disfigured, and those who learned of this immediately feared that the victims were the P.O.U.M. leaders. "Treball," the P.S.U.C. daily, published issue upon issue with special notices calling on its readers to denounce the P.O.U.M. members they knew to the police or to the P.S.U.C.'s cells, and printed lists of P.O.U.M. militants expelled from the U.G.T., to aid the police in searching for them. The fate of the *poumistes,* during these weeks, was determined by the fact that the police ordered to find them were from Madrid rather than Barcelona, and did not know the city. It was for that reason that informers were needed.

It has never been possible to compile a complete list of those arrested in the first weeks of repression nor of those murdered at that time. We calculate that a thousand were arrested and at least fifty killed. However, some cases should be recalled, so as to help the reader imagine the ambience of the moment. (More detailed information was published at the time by the British I.L.P. and by Editions Spartacus in Paris.)

The foreigners were, for the moment, those who were treated the worst, because they were immediately suspect as spies. Although most of them succeeded in leaving the country, under expulsion orders, some did not meet such a relatively happy fate. Kurt Landau, the Austrian dissident Marxist who had come to edit the German P.O.U.M. bulletin, went underground when his companion Katia was arrested: she was conducted to a *cheka* in the portal de l'Angel in Barcelona, and remained imprisoned for some time. He was finally captured, months later, and disappeared, his body never found. Robert Smillie, son of a prominent British labor leader, and delegate for the I.L.P. youth in Spain, was arrested and taken to Valencia where, following an appendicitis attack, he was denied hospital treatment until it was too late; his death is memorialized in Orwell's *Homage to Catalonia*.

Some who disappeared in the Stalinist repression had no connection with the P.O.U.M. Such was the case with José Robles, a professor at the Johns Hopkins University who had been on the staff of a Russian officer; his son was imprisoned in the fascist zone. Robles disappeared; his close friend, the American novelist John Dos Passos, came to Spain to investigate the case and learned nothing.

But the Soviet terror net concentrated on dissident Marxists. Erwin Wolf, a Czech married to the daughter of a Norwegian socialist deputy, had been a secretary of Trotsky and was a political adversary of the P.O.U.M. Arrested, then freed, he disappeared, with the Spanish Republican embassy in Prague assuring his family that he was free.

Another such case was that of the Trotskyist Moulin, who had been photographed during the May events distributing the S.B.L.'s leaflets and who used his contacts in the C.N.T. to find refuge in the countryside. He was arrested and vanished.

Mark Rein, the son of the exiled Russian Menshevik Rafail Abramovich, disappeared from the Hotel Continental while on assignment as a journalist for a Scandinavian socialist daily. French prime minister Léon Blum personally intervened with the Spanish Republican embassy in Paris but learned nothing. Blum asked that, at least, Rein's body be returned, but he received no answer.

A French subject, Nicholas Sundelevich, was arrested because he was found with two P.O.U.M. stamps that a friend, Max Petel, had left with him, and was accused of nothing less than the preparation, from Barcelona, of an assassination attempt on Stalin. He and another Frenchman, Gaston Ladmiral, were finally freed, thanks to the intervention of the French consul. U.S. citizens Charles and Lois Orr and Wolf Kupinsky

(Harry Milton) were arrested; Kupinsky was able to return to the United States, and the Orrs were saved from the Soviet secret police by the action of another American, Russell Blackwell (Rosalio Negrete) acting in concert with America Escuder, wife of the managing editor of "La Batalla." Negrete was arrested in turn, and freed following pressure from the United States.

Many foreigners were accused, once they were arrested, by Lev Narvich, a Soviet secret police agent who had visited the P.O.U.M. executive offices in Barcelona several times, claiming to be a pro-P.O.U.M. commissar from the International Brigades. Narvich met with Andrade and Nin, fraternized with people coming through the building, and, according to a document probably written by Andrade, used his "magnificent camera" to photograph Nin, Landau, and numerous other comrades, on the pretext of collecting souvenirs. On June 17, 1937 Katia Landau notified the party leadership that the police who had arrested her had a copy of Narvich's photograph of Kurt Landau.

While in jail in Valencia, the imprisoned leaders found a newspaper picture of the Stalinist officer Líster's general staff, in which Narvich was to be found. Narvich had previously carried out a spying operation on the Madrid P.O.U.M. branch, and in September 1937 was reported in Paris, where he sought out Narcís Molins i Fàbrega, the only major party leader free. Narvich then unwisely returned to Barcelona, and in early 1938 he was killed and his body dumped in Horta, on the outskirts of Barcelona. Julián Gorkin, in his book *Caníbales Políticos,* accepted responsibility for this action in the name of the P.O.U.M.'s self-defense groups.

Narvich's name turned up when, in 1938, Munis and two comrades, Domenico Sedrán (Carlini) and Jaime Fernández Rodríguez, were tried by the republican government as heads of the Bolshevik-Leninist Section. The charge that they had liquidated Narvich, identified as a "Russian captain," was prominent in the proceeding, but went unproven.

Over forty years later, Narvich turned up yet again in the published memoirs of Kirill Henkin, a former Soviet agent turned defector. Henkin, who was active in Spain, describes Narvich as "a young Russian Jew from Paris" who had belonged to the Union for Repatriation of Russians Abroad, a Soviet-controlled agency dedicated to capturing White Russian exiles. The union was the center of the Efron-Zborowski ring's intrigues. Henkin notes, regarding Narvich, that "the Trotskyists" hunted him down in a dark alley in Barcelona, and Khenkin was told that "a hero had fallen gloriously in combat."[22]

It appears that in the prison at Valencia there came to be 150 arrested foreigners and when an international delegation, in November 1937, obtained permission to visit the Model Prison in Barcelona they found in it prisoners from a dozen countries.

At the same time, "purges" were taking place in the International Brigades where the combined impact of the Moscow trials and the repression against the P.O.U.M. had sown doubts. Some I.B. soldiers were arrested, others executed for "treason," and others killed and then labeled as deserters. There were several prisons for I.B. suspects, including one in Horta, where 265 prisoners were held, and others at Castelldefels and in the province of Castelló.[23]

Those who were arrested during this phase reported the existence of torture, and when they did not suffer it themselves, saw it applied to others. The worst treated were the women. Their supervision was entrusted to a Soviet agent of Austrian birth, Leopold Kulcsar, who died insane; his wife, Ilse, later married a Spanish writer who died in exile.[24]

There were cases of prison deaths, aside from that of Bob Smillie. In the detention camp at Omells de Na Gaia, headed by a communist, Astorga Vayo, J.C.I. militant Francesc Pina was shot without trial, on a disciplinary pretext. In the Model Prison in Barcelona Manuel Maurín, brother of Joaquím, was left untreated and died a few days after entering the hospital.

Faced with the impossibility of making up a complete list of the P.O.U.M.'s victims of the various kinds of repression as well as the war, "La Batalla" in exile, after the Second World War, put together a symbolic list, on which figure the names of those dead because of communist repression, repression in the Franco zone, at the front, during the anti-Hitler resistance of the Second World War, and murdered by the communists at the end of the latter conflict.

This list reads as follows:

- Andreu Nin, political secretary, assassinated by the communists almost certainly in June 1937.
- Germinal Vidal, secretary general of the J.C.I., died in the street fighting in Barcelona, July 19, 1936.
- José Luis Arenillas, member of the central committee, secretary of the Euzkadi regional party organization, medical services director of the Republican Army of the North, executed by the fascists in Bilbao in 1938.
- Luis Rastrollo, member of the central committee, secretary of the Galicia regional organization, executed by the fascists in 1936.
- Miquel Pedrola, of the J.C.I. executive, killed at the Huesca front in 1936.
- Felipe Alutiz, member of the central committee, secretary of the party in Pamplona, executed by the fascists in 1936.
- José Rabassa, member of the central committee, secretary of the Valencia regional organization, executed by the fascists in 1939.
- Jesús Blanco, member of the J.C.I. central committee, killed at the Madrid front in 1936.

- Luis Grossi, member of the J.C.I. central committee, killed at the Oviedo front in 1936.
- Armand Cahué, brigade commander of the 29th Division, killed at the Aragon front in 1937.
- Manuel Fernández Sendón ("Fersen"), secretary of the party in La Coruña, executed by the fascists in 1936.
- Marcià Mena (Marciano in Castilian), from Lleida, executed by the communists in 1937.
- Jaume Trepat, teacher, murdered by the communists in 1938.
- Josep Hervas, teacher, murdered by the communists in 1938.
- Luis García, secretary of the Centro Obrero in Gijon, killed at the Oviedo front in 1937.
- José Alcantarilla, J.C.I. secretary in Valencia, killed at the Aragon front in 1938.
- J.C. Herrera, secretary of party in Sevilla, executed by the fascists in 1936.
- Josep Vilar, head of the Tarragona provincial party committee, killed in Dachau, probably in 1943.
- Joan Farré Gassó, of the executive, secretary of the Lleida provincial party committee, murdered by the communists in France in 1944.
- Antoni Franquesa, killed by the guardia civil in Barcelona in 1947.

The cases of Marcià Mena, Jaume Trepat, and Josep Hervas deserve special note. Mena, a militant from Lleida, was one of the first militia commissars. At the beginning of the repression, he was arrested and accused of having met conspiratorially with other officers. He was brought before a court martial in Lleida. The prosecutor demanded the death penalty. The officers who made up the court, some of them professionally ambitious and others obedient members of the P.S.U.C., condemned him to death. From the courtroom he was taken by truck to the cemetery. The firing squad was already waiting, since those who were responsible for Mena's trial knew what the verdict would be. The press reported the execution in only four lines, without mentioning Mena's P.O.U.M. affiliation nor the reason for the decision, noting only the accusation of indiscipline. What the communists sought—but did not obtain, because Mena did not "confess"—was to show that the P.O.U.M. militia had prepared to march from the front to Barcelona.

Among those P.O.U.M. members who were unable to get into C.N.T. divisions there were various murder victims. When the communists discovered P.O.U.M. members at the front, they would send them on missions in which death was certain, or they killed them and announced that they had deserted or were killed while trying to cross to the enemy lines. They robbed them, then, of life and honor. Jaume Trepat and Josep Hervas, two teachers who had been prominent in the post-July New Unified School

(ENU) movement, figure among these unfortunates. Because of special circumstances, their case became known. They were members of the communications department of the 141st Mixed Brigade, which was under the almost completely communist-controlled 32nd Division.

But the communications department had a C.N.T. commissar, José Meca Cazorla. On March 16, 1938, the commissar of the IX Army Corps received a note from the commissar of the 32nd Division informing him that Meca and Hervas had deserted. The commissar of the Army Corps, Juan Molina, was a C.N.T. member and knew the histories of the supposed deserters; he knew it could not be true. An investigation was ordered into their fate and that of Trepat, who had also disappeared. The investigation showed considerable evidence that all three had been killed by communists. A copy of the report was sent to the military section of the C.N.T. national committee, and thence to the defense minister, Prieto. Neither Prieto nor General Pozas, chief of the forces at the Aragon front, took any action in this matter, but at least in this case the honor of three victims was saved.[25]

The International Workers' Delegations

Many of those who were saved from communist *chekas* owed their freedom to the actions of an extensive secret intelligence network set up by the C.N.T., members of which hunted for the disappeared and tried to get them out of communist hands. The activities of the C.N.T. secret bodies have been partially described by the German historian Patrik von sur Muhlen, in his book *Spanien War Ihre Hoffnung,* published in 1983. If the majority of those who, in this way, were moved from the *chekas* to regular prison cells were not judged or executed, as the communists wished, this was due, above all, to international pressure.

The initiator of the international campaign, at a moment when the party membership was still trying to find out the fate of the first group of arrested P.O.U.M. leaders, was the secretary of the British I.L.P., John McNair. He had been in Barcelona before and during the May events, for the frustrated meeting of the London Bureau. He then returned to London, and once he found out about the arrest of the P.O.U.M. militants, went back to Spain on his own initiative. It was with his help that the P.O.U.M. organized its international solidarity network, coordinating and stimulating activities, seeking aid, and organizing legal and labor commissions, under the supervision of Molins i Fàbrega, whom the executive sent to Paris in this capacity. Victor Serge collaborated very actively in these tasks; it was his prestige that helped them collect the signatures of writers and to organize collective protests by intellectuals. The campaign was supported by the member parties of the London Bureau as well as certain organizations, such as the League for the Rights of Man, the Vigilance Committee of Antifascist Intellectuals, and the Association of Antifascist Lawyers, all in France. In Paris, a Committee to Defend the Spanish Revolution was set up by Molins, Serge, and another P.O.U.M. member, Bartolomeu Costa-Amic, with special support from Magdeleine Paz, Henry Poulaille, Victor Margueritte, and Marceau Pivert.

Three international commissions went to Spain. They visited Irujo, minister of justice, and Zugazagoitia, minister of the interior. Negrín refused to see them.

The first delegation was made up of British House of Commons I.L.P. member Fenner Brockway, with the French syndicalist Robert Louzon, the French socialist Charles Wolf and the Swedish socialist Robert Bilis. It was received by a blast from the communist press: "What has this court of miserable types who cover the name of the Soviet Union with mud abroad done for our struggle?", "Mundo Obrero" asked. "These gentlemen from the international delegation have nothing to do here and they should be driven rapidly to the border."

The delegation demanded juridical guarantees for those arrested and information on the fate of Nin. In a press release—published only by C.N.T. and Left socialist papers—the commission affirmed that it had "no intention of exercising pressure on the Spanish justice system, but, rather, wished to be certain that nobody would try to exercise such pressure"—an obvious reference to the Soviet Union. But the commission felt it had the right to be alarmed when "a man like Nin could be kept out of the hands of the legitimate authorities." It ended by declaring that it had asked for impartial justice for the members of the P.O.U.M., "whose revolutionary activity the delegation knows, although doubtless it is unknown by those who have recently joined a Marxist party."

A little later, a second delegation visited Valencia and Barcelona, without obtaining either further guarantees or further information. But the arrested members of the executive had by then been removed from the *chekas*—thanks to the pressure of the first delegation—and the presence of the second permitted Irujo to arrange their transfer to Valencia, where they ran fewer risks.

This second delegation was made up of the I.L.P. Commons member James Maxton; the French socialist A. Weil-Curiel; Yves Lévy, who had fought in the C.N.T. and P.O.U.M. militia, with, as its secretary, Pierre Foucaud of the Paris weekly "La Fleche." Although the communist press greeted it with its habitual sallies, the delegation on leaving the country issued a press release warning against "the attempt to introduce falsified documents into the judicial process against the P.O.U.M.," in which it saw "an intention to create an amalgam of proven antifascist elements and fascists."[26]

The third international commission, made up of I.L.P. Commons member John McGovern and professor Felicien Challaye of the Sorbonne, spent a week in Barcelona, during which they visited the city's Model Prison and found there 500 prisoners from the P.O.U.M. and other antifascist organizations, 500 fascists, and 500 common-law convicts. The visit took place in November 1937, at which time it was clear that the promises made to prior commissions had not been carried out. There was still nothing officially known of the whereabouts of Nin. The attorney who had taken over the defense of the P.O.U.M., Benito Pabón, a veteran lawyer for the C.N.T. and member of the Cortes for the anarchosyndicalist redoubt of Saragossa, found himself threatened with death. The apartment of Jeanne Maurín, in Paris, was burglarized by communists who destroyed many things while searching for imaginary compromising documents.

The report of the third commission was very detailed and outlined the antecedents that put the repression in a political context.[27]

This delegation enjoyed a certain success. A dozen of the less well-known prisoners were released, but when an attorney visited Zugazagoitia to demand the freedom of the others, he received this answer: "I have ordered five times that they should be let out. We'll see if even the janitors pay attention to me this sixth time."

But on the sixth time nobody obeyed, as well.

Some of the wives of the arrested and disappeared, who had declared a hunger strike and whom Irujo visited, were taken to the border in Irujo's own car, because otherwise there was no certainty they would not be arrested anew. The commission also visited these women before returning to France, but were unable to gain entrance to a *cheka,* where Russians and Germans blocked their passage, although they showed an authorization from Irujo to proceed. They telephoned the minister, and he said, "It is necessary that you not leave Barcelona with the impression that the government does not have this jail under its control. Trust us and we will assure your entry."

But the following day, the minister's secretary told them that it had not been possible to do anything. The report of the commission stated, "the mask was off . . . The ministers were willing but powerless. The *cheka* was unwilling and had the power."

This delegation heard from Zugazagoitia the following phrases: "What do you want? We have received aid from Russians and in exchange we have had to let them do certain things that do not please us."

But the truth about Russian aid was revealed by the historian and republican politician Claudio Sánchez Albornóz, who recalled the following in his memoirs, published in 1972:

> I have heard [the republican officer] Gordón Ordáz in Buenos Aires refer to the peripeties of his purchase of U.S. airplanes for the government of the republic during the first phase of the civil war and how he succeeded thanks to great zeal and against great difficulties in flying them to Europe via [the Soviet port of] Arkhangelsk. Gordón finished his account by declaring that the planes had never reached Spain; the Russians had kept them and sent an equal number of old machines.
>
> I have heard [José] Giral say that the Russian war materiel that, very slowly and very costly, came to the ports of Republican Spain, was not unloaded if the government did not accede to the provision of important military and political posts to the communists.
>
> And I have heard [Jiménez de] Asúa describe how, by way of some German socialists, he learned in Prague [where he was ambassador] about the negotiations between the governments of Stalin and Hitler, which were preparing the betrayal of the Spanish Republic. And he could not make the Negrín government believe him.[28]

The reports of the three commissions served as a basis for the counter-campaign that Molíns and Costa-Amic organized in Paris and London and that extended throughout Europe and the United States, although, lacking resources, it could not match the penetration and intensity of the communist attack. It was useful in at least saving the lives of some of the arrested, although not those of the murdered.

The roster of intellectual figures, particularly in France and the United States, that rallied to the P.O.U.M.'s defense includes many distinguished names: the French novelists André Gide, Georges Duhamel, Roger Martin du Gard, François Mauriac, and the ethnologist Paul Rivet addressed a protest telegram to Negrín. The surrealist poet André Breton made notable speeches defending the P.O.U.M. In the United States, V.F. Calverton, editor of the "Modern Monthly," a radical organ with a relatively wide circulation, defended the P.O.U.M. and the C.N.T against the Stalinists, publishing an important article by Anita Brenner that utilized the testimony of George Orwell. The New York group of writers around "Partisan Review" were active in solidarity with the party, as was the then-"rightist" communist Bertram D. Wolfe, a member of the grouping around Jay Lovestone.[29]

The communist slander campaign was orchestrated throughout the world. Ilya Ehrenburg, the Russian novelist, published an article in the Moscow newspaper "Izvestia" for November 3, 1937, datelined Bordeaux, in which he accused the French authors who signed the above-mentioned telegram of being "faint-hearted" and "allies of the Moroccans and the Blackshirts."[30]

Louis Aragon, the surrealist-turned-Stalinist, writing in the daily "Ce Soir" of which he was editor (a camouflaged communist newspaper set up with funds from the Ministry of Propaganda of the Spanish Republic), discussed the "crimes" of the P.O.U.M. and insinuated that Nin had fled to Germany. Even André Malraux, later so respectable as de Gaulle's cultural minister, approved of the persecution of the P.O.U.M. Victor Serge met him one day in a cafe, spoke to him of the P.O.U.M., and received the following reply: "I accept the crimes of Stalin wherever they take place."

Serge could not contain himself and threw his coffee in Malraux's face.

Apart from the aid and support of the C.N.T., the P.O.U.M. found a defense in the ranks of the Esquerra leadership from the first day, but in public only after Companys understood that the Negrín government was ready to leave the Generalitat with no important functions.

Companys sent Jaume Miravitlles, his propaganda commissar, to Valencia, as soon as he heard about Nin's arrest, with orders to say that for his part he was very surprised to learn that Nin was a spy and that, in any case, he demanded for his former *conseller* every judicial guarantee of impartiality and respect for the rights of the accused. Miravitlles spoke with the communist colonel Ortega, head of security, who told him that documents had been found signed with the initials "A.N." Miravitlles stated that this was the first case in the history of espionage where the spy signed his own initials to documents, and added that the initials could apply to any number of people besides Nin. Ortega broke off the meeting in a rage.[31]

The offices of President Companys and of chief *conseller* Josep Terradelles, who would become the first president of a legal Generalitat after the death of Franco forty years later, were always open to P.O.U.M. delegations, to which, unfortunately, they had little to say, since the rise of the P.S.U.C. and Negrín after May brought the steady diminution of the powers of the Generalitat.

On one occasion, against a backdrop of tension between Negrín and Companys, the latter announced over the radio in Barcelona that he had "received a delegation from the executive committee of the P.O.U.M." (made up of the Lleida leader Josep Rodés and the youth organizer Solano). This infuriated the communist press, which portrayed the P.O.U.M. as dissolved and annihilated. The Esquerra minister in the Negrin government, Jaume (*not* Artemi) Ayguadé, who quit in mid-1938 to protest the constant trimming of functions of the Generalitat, always voted in favor of freeing the antifascist prisoners, when Irujo presented the question in cabinet meetings.

The repression was individual, and the communists wanted it so, because they expected fear to induce many P.O.U.M. members to come over to their side; but in this they erred. But there was one case in which the repression was carried out collectively, en masse: This was the case of the 29th Division.

On July 19, 1937, Bilbao fell; beginning July 12 a major operation had been underway aimed at Huesca, in Aragon, using two International Brigades and the P.S.U.C. 27th Division. In its preparatory phase the Hungarian Communist I.B. commander, Mata Zalka, known as "General Lukács," died, some said by an enemy bullet, others by a "friendly" one, because he was suspected of contacts with other I.B. dissidents. The operation failed. When this became clear, the P.O.U.M. 29th Division was ordered to attack, although the militia fighters protested that they had insufficient weapons. The P.O.U.M. shock troops fought their way to the walls of the Huesca mental hospital, a prominent landmark, but their lack of ammunition did not permit them to maintain a position there, and they received orders to return to their original point of attack. General Pózas, through his commissar, Crescenciano Bilbao, a former follower of Largo Caballero, tried to put blame for the failure on the P.O.U.M. Division, but as soon as he began talking about "the treason of the P.O.U.M." Rovira cut him off by declaring that if treason had taken place it was carried out by the general staff when they sent badly armed men into combat, then leaving them without support.[32]

The P.S.U.C. 27th Division began putting patrols at the crossroads in the rear guard of the 29th Division, which beat up, insulted, and in some cases killed soldiers and officers of the P.O.U.M. unit. Rovira protested in vain in Barbastro and had to make a great effort to convince his men to continue showing patience and not respond to an obvious provocation aimed at presenting the P.O.U.M. forces as undisciplined and even as "Franco collaborators."

Rovira, on learning that the repression had begun in Barcelona, met with the heads of the C.N.T. divisions and proposed a coordinated action to prevent the repression from reaching the front, but he encountered the traditional anarchist response: "With us, they won't dare."

In reality, they did dare, for the government soon dissolved the C.N.T.-controlled governing council of Aragon and put its services in the hands of a pliable figure, Ignacio Mantecón. The communists dismantled the agrarian collectives, which were the most precious jewel to the C.N.T. militia at the front, and they attacked and even executed the C.N.T. members that resisted. (The American writer Lois Cusick later suggested that the German Trotskyist Moulin had been killed by the communists during a raid on an anarchist collective.) The C.N.T. national committee and the peninsular committee of the F.A.I. sent delegations to the front to calm the *cenetistes*.

With the "cleansing" of the anarchists, the 30th Division, mainly consisting of Esquerra volunteers with some P.S.U.C. officers, was ordered to replace the P.O.U.M. 29th Division in the front lines. The order specified that all withdrawn troops would surrender their arms, including their personal sidearms. But the militia members refused to give up their rifles. They knew what it had cost to obtain them and, further, feared that once they were disarmed, they would be annihilated.

Finally, Josep Miret, a P.S.U.C. officer in charge of the movement of troops, allowed them to keep their weapons. While negotiations went on, an outbreak of enemy fire took place in which Armand Cahué, commander of the 129th brigade, was killed; the same night, police in the Catalan factory town of Terrassa, Cahué's home, received orders to arrest him for membership in the P.O.U.M.

The 29th Division was ordered to regroup at Azlor, a town in the rear guard. Rovira received an order to present himself to the army Captaincy-General in Barcelona. He was received by a communist, colonel Antonio Cordón, who told him that he greatly regretted it, but he had been ordered to arrest him. Eventually, the C.N.T. commanders on the Aragon front found out about the arrest and informed Prieto, then defense minister, who ordered Rovira released. An office was set up in Barcelona to administer the demobilization of the 29th Division. Rovira arranged for most of the militia fighters to be transferred to non-Communist units. In this way, many lives were saved.

While the slow and bureaucratic work of demobilization went on, patrols from the P.S.U.C. 27th Division surrounded Azlor, arresting the soldiers who left the village and killing some of them.

These crimes were carried out without the knowledge of the public, because they were committed in concealment and far from the press. But one crime could not be hidden: the disappearance of Andreu Nin.

Where is Nin?

Many walls in Barcelona and other Catalan towns were painted in bold letters with a challenging question: "Negrín, Where is Nin?" (*"Negrín, On es en Nin?"*)

A clear answer has never emerged from this mystery. On July 30, 1937, the minister of justice announced that his ministry had received the statements of the police and had passed them on to the Special Espionage Tribunal, but that the sworn declarations elicited from Nin "were not accompanied by the arrested person." Irujo then ordered an investigation.[33]

On August 4, a government press release stated that, from the reports that had been gathered, it seemed that "Nin was arrested by policemen from the Seguridad General at the same time as the other P.O.U.M. arrests, that he had been moved to Madrid, to a specially equipped place, and from there he disappeared."

Arquer, when he visited Irujo, was given the following revelatory information: "Nin is in a private prison in Madrid. Don't try to find him, because no official safe-conduct pass can protect you."

It is interesting to follow the development of the affair from the point of view of those who should have prevented it from happening and who never would have dared to do it themselves.

Zugazagoitia, who, as interior minister had authority, at least theoretically, over all police forces, many years later related how he had acted:

The unfortunate Andreu Nin had to contend with a worse fate. Imprisoned as a P.O.U.M. militant, moved to Madrid according to police reports, isolated and held incommunicado on a property at Alcalá de Henares, his 'escape' became known, as well as his immediately previous whereabouts, after his 'flight,' about which I was informed, in a restaurant on the plaza in Valencia, where [General José] Miaja had invited a group of government officials to a party for the security director, Ortega.

'Don't worry,' Ortega said, 'we will find out where [Nin] is, dead or alive. Leave it up to me.'

'Take care,' I told him, 'I am not interested in Nin's corpse; his life is what I care about.'

Miaja, who was listening to the conversation, after hearing the probability that Nin might have hidden out in a 'P.O.U.M.' unit, interrupted with his customary verbal violence.

'If that is true,' Miaja declared, 'and if the soldiers arrest him, I will order that he be shot without any further discussion.'

'Pardon me, general,' I replied, 'The decision as to Nin belongs to the justice system, and you should order, in this sense, nothing.'

That evening, in my office, finding the news intolerable and fearing the worst, and with no other reason than my instinct as a journalist, I called Ortega and, on the pretext of asking him if there was more news of Nin, posed the question in depth.

'Is Andreu Nin alive or dead? Can you tell me?'

'I cannot say. I don't know anything more than what is contained in the teletype message I showed you this afternoon. I have given orders that he be searched for everywhere, according to your wishes. Who knows what can happen in this kind of business, where the Gestapo is involved. . .'

The unexpected mention of the Gestapo made my suspicions certain. I tried to find out what special information had led the security director to mix up in the story of Andreu Nin's 'escape' the fearful German police body, and he did not know how to explain it. It was a supposition he had . . . an intuition . . .

Our conversation ended with Ortega promising me that he would give new orders to Madrid that they not neglect to learn Nin's whereabouts and assuring me he would convey any news to me immediately. I asked for an interview with the head of the government, [Negrín] whom I felt obligated to inform of what had happened and of my suspicions. I provided him, at the same time, with notice of my irrevocable resignation if the life of Andreu Nin was not saved, as well as a warning of the international scandal that would be unleashed against the government over which he presided, if we did not succeed in rescuing him. Obtaining the interview, I told Negrín of the reports I had received and declared to him what I thought.

'If, as I fear, my suspicions are confirmed,' I declared, 'I emphatically ask that you find someone to succeed me. I cannot continue in the ministry. For me, human life has the highest value, and if I begin by admitting the existence of Gestapo [involvement], the story that began with the kidnapping of Nin will have an infinity of bloody chapters. If I have recourse to your superior authority, it is not only to gain information, but also to ask for your support in rescuing a disappeared person.'

'Don't exclude completely the possibility, which I consider highly likely, that a reprisal by the Gestapo is involved,' Negrín replied. 'I cannot affirm it, since I have no special information, you being the first to bring me any; but I know the Germans very well, and I know what they are capable of. You have no idea of their audacity! It surpasses every measure and whatever I would be able to tell you would be pale in comparison with reality. You should insist that the police provide you with exact information regarding what has happened and when you have it come to see me, since I want to know the truth. Certainly, if Nin is alive we will save him. As far as finding a successor for you, do not think about it. If there are people you do not have confidene in, we will replace them.'

'It was obvious that the president was suggesting that I fire the general security director [Ortega], whose nomination I had not supported, because, among other reasons, I did not know the person in question and the post was, in those circumstances, the only important one, and, further, the most delicate one in the ministry . . .

'Having finished the conversation with Negrín, I asked the head commissar in Madrid, who was a socialist, for a quick report of everything that had happened, with orders that it be brought to me personally, indicating that no notice of the report should be given to anybody else. The next day, in the morning, the general commissar from Madrid awaited me in my office with the report and a briefcase containing some documents, some German coins, and a German railroad ticket. the report was very precise and clear.

'What is your opinion? Do you think Nin is dead or do you believe he is still alive?' I asked.

'I have the impression he is still alive. I believe he is a prisoner in some unit at the front in Madrid . . .'

It was said that the kidnapping of Nin was the work of the Gestapo, interested in assuring that a collaborator of theirs of such value would not be interrogated by our police forces, which would, thanks to weakness or repentance, discover his services in republican Spain. The fakery could not have been cruder. Without personally knowing Andreu Nin, I rejected it. I said so to Negrín. He tried to convince me that anything was possible and that the unlikeliest underhanded marriages had been publicly and solemnly carried out; but not in the case of Nin. With the report of the general commissar from Madrid in hand, the attribution of responsibility to the Gestapo was still inadmissible. After two nearly violent meetings of the council of ministers, the Director General of Security resigned. The communist ministers defended their fellow believer with extraordinary passion. I affirmed that the Director General could continue in his post, but that in any case I would give up mine. Prieto, with firm words, reproached the communists for their way of leading the debate and declared that, in solidarity with my position, he would add his resignation to mine should Ortega not resign. My proposal was approved.

Ortega presented to me, on learning of the agreement, a sentimental and tearful scene, eluding the basis of the problem: the disappearance of Nin. The general commissar from Madrid made some personal efforts with the president of the appeals court, who believed Nin was still alive and that it was possible to recover him. He promised to do so, on the promise that no investigations be made or punishments be suggested. I gave my agreement for this proposal, declaring that I was only interested in finding him. The idea of saving Nin possessed, and disturbed me. Had he been saved, I doubt even his own comrades would have felt a joy as profound as mine would have been. I went to Madrid to follow the curious negotiations close up. After various attempts the president of the appeals court, who was using all his authority, declared his powerlessness in the affair. Was Nin still alive? We could not even find out the answer to that. The rumors were extremely varied. Some believed he had been taken by ship to Russia, as a prisoner; others believed he was executed by a battalion from the International Brigades. The police believed he was still a prisoner in a unit at the front. I finally convinced myself, without reason, that Nin had been killed within a few hours of his kidnapping.[34]

Manuel Azaña, president of the republic, in various entries in his diaries, mentions Nin, for whom it is obvious that he felt neither sympathy nor interest; only the possible international repercussions and the authority of the regime interested him.

On June 29, that is, thirteen days after the arrests, he wrote: "Prieto has turned up something very serious. The police arrested in Barcelona many members of the P.O.U.M., among them Andreu Nin. The motive was an espionage organization. I read in the papers that Nin had been taken to Valencia and that an indictment was being prepared. Prieto tells me that Nin was moved to the prison at Alcalá and that some individuals came there one night, I don't know whether from the police or with police authorization, or, simply, 'for the better,' and they took him away. Zugazagoitia has told Prieto that there is a trail. The kidnapers were communists. Prieto has written about this in a letter to Negrín, following a statement from Victor Basch [of the League for the Rights of Man in Paris], calling his attention to the importance of the incident. I will also speak to him tomorrow."

Azaña did not write down what Negrín had said to him in reply. He let almost a month go by, until July 22, 1937, before coming back to the matter of Nin. Negrín continued to hand out, pretending to believe it, the communist version of events, as if it was the truth. In passing, Negrín falsely informed Azaña that the arrested leaders had confessed:

President Negrín spoke to me of espionage. In Madrid, important discoveries have been made. A transmitter, installed in a cellar, gave news of everything to the rebels. A military map of Madrid has been found, made up by an architect named Golfin, who has been convicted and confessed, and which seems to have been used to transmit information on artillery positions. Negrín says that they have been able to decipher some lines written in invisible ink on the back of the map, some of it in open language, some in a code that was used by the general staff. From the information gained in the investigation, there resulted the arrest of Nin and of two hundred or more other individuals, almost all from the P.O.U.M., which does not deny its intelligence contacts with the enemy. Hearing this, I again asked about the case of Nin. The president said that one night some individuals in the uniform of the International Brigades came to the Alcalá prison, tied up the guards, and took away the prisoner. He does not believe what has been said about it being the work of the communists. Naturally, the communists are indignant and claim to be surprised. Negrín believes he was kidnapped in the interest of German espionage and the Gestapo, to prevent Nin from making revelations. It does not seem that they have killed him. The affair has been turned over to an examining judge, so that it can be cleared up.

'Doesn't it all seem a little like a novel?' (Azaña asked Negrín).

'No, señor. There was also the thing with the Russian General Staff in Madrid, which was apparently the work of the Gestapo.'

'What happened?'

'I thought you had been told. The Russian General staff, in Madrid, was staying in Gaylord's Hotel. One night, they almost all died from a poisoning. Two, among them the chief of staff, were between life and death. German espionage is formidable. The International Brigades have among them many Nazi spies. Some have been found out and shot.'

On August 6, Negrín visited Azaña and the latter wrote:

I asked him for news about the Nin affair. They now believe, after the careful examinations they have made, that Nin was not kidnapped and that it is a matter of escaping . . . Regarding this affair, I called the attention of Negrín to the ferocious campaign carried out by part of the press, demanding inexorable punishment, that an example be made, that all the P.O.U.M. defendants must be exterminated. I told him 'I don't know why you let this go on, having the censorship in your hands. Such a campaign would always be bad, but, applied to people who are already before the dock, is worse. Who are they trying to impress? The court, the government, or the public? Whatever the capacity for imitation of the communists, here we have no business adopting Muscovite methods, under which every three or four months a plot is discovered and they shoot a few political enemies. I suppose the trial will still be late, but you should know from now on, and the cabinet should know, that I am not ready to see the parties tear each other apart ferociously; tomorrow shooting the P.O.U.M., the next day the others.'

'I do not think things will go that far,' Negrín said. 'In any case, my government would never permit it.'

Azaña let himself be calmed by promises from this man who had already given his consent to everything the communists had done. A new entry into the Azaña diary mentions Nin, on October 18. Nin was the pretext, in this case, to speak of something that Azaña considered, as he himself said, more dangerous than the disappearance of the P.O.U.M. leader.

I have just received a visit from Manuel Moreno Laguía, an old personal friend, an examining magistrate, who was charged with investigating the disappearance of Nin. He brought two copies of everything he had done and prepared all his documents in consultation with the attorney general. From what emerged in the investigation, Moreno cannot be certain whether the disappeared person is being kept somewhere or has been killed, or if he is in hiding. What he is inclined to believe is that the police know everything, but aren't talking. There are still some types in the police that are hardly of the best quality, and they are not among the oldest personnel. It has emerged that Nin was not a prisoner in the prison cells at Alcalá, as [Negrín] believed when he spoke to me about the case, but in a little hotel in the outskirts [of Alcalá], on the Aragon road. It has not been possible for the judge to obtain keys to carry out a search of the building. The declarations of Nin's guards are contradictory. The judge, with the support of the attorney general, ordered the trial and imprisonment of various police functionaries, among them a certain Vázquez, who had been head commissar in Madrid. He was arrested in Valencia and held for trial at the Palace of Justice, when an emissary arrived from the Dirección de Seguridad, with a document ordering the prisoner be freed. The judge refused to hand him over, and added that if the Dirección General had reasons to take the prisoner, he would have to be told personally. In reply, a captain of the asaltos came to him with a platoon of guardias, looking for the arrested man, and with an order from the General Director to arrest the judge as well, if he resisted them. Moreno replied to the captain that he could not be arrested, and that he could do what he wanted to with him, but that he would not go with him. As to the arrested Vázquez, the judge spoke about him to the attorney general by telephone; but the latter, as the lesser of two evils and to avoid a scandal, asked him to allow the prisoner to be turned over. This was done. The man is now free. All this is even more disturbing than the disappearance of Nin.[35]

The members of the government seemed unhurried in their consideration of Nin, apart from Irujo who served as a lightning rod. Prieto declared a month and three days after Nin's disappearance, "The disturbing thing is that the arrest of the P.O.U.M. leaders was not a decision of the government and that the police carried out the arrests on their own account . . . The responsible parties are not the police chiefs, but those who surround them, among them infiltrated communists."[36]

Prieto would soon be discarded from the government by the communists. It was only then that he began criticizing Negrín, and in this interest he used the case of Nin to deliver blows to his rival for Socialist Party leaddership:

> "Hardly had the government found out about the disappearance of Nin, than the interior minister ordered an investigation of what had taken place. It was on the point of discovering the shameful truth, when Negrín ordered the inquiry suspended. I found out, not being minister at the time, from Zugazagoitia."[37]

Nin was mentioned on various occasions in the council of ministers. The only person who has offered a detailed account of these discussions is the ex-Communist Jesús Hernández, who was then minister of education:

> An urgent call from the president's office informed me that Negrín was waiting for me in his office. On my entering, the president sent away the stenographer, to whom he had been dictating, and without preamble asked me: 'What have you done with Nin?'
>
> 'With Nin . . . I don't know what has happened with Nin,' I told him, and it was the truth.
>
> 'Negrín, obviously upset, explained to me that he had been informed by the interior

minister that a whole series of criminal acts had been committed in Barcelona by the Soviet police, who were acting as if they were in their own country, without bothering to notify even for reasons of delicacy the Spanish authorities, while arresting Spanish citizens; that these arrested had been moved from one place to another without any judicial order or summons and that they were being kept in private prisons, totally outside the control of the legal authorities; that some of the arrested had been taken to Valencia, but that Andreu Nin had disappeared. The president of the Generalitat had called, alarmed and offended, considering the activities of Orlov and the G.P.U. on Catalan territory to be an attack on human rights. . .

Promising to find out what could be ascertained about the kidnapping of Nin and to inform him immediately, I left and went directly to the [Communist] Party office. In Diaz's office—he was away sick—I found Codovilla and Togliatti. Both put on looks of astonishment when I told them about my conversation with Negrín. I did not know if their reaction was real or if it was simply another act. Codovilla supposed the comrades from the special services would have held Nin to interrogate him or to carry out some kind of investigation before handing him over to the authorities. Togliatti, hermetic, by now over his astonishment, feigned or real, said nothing. In the face of my insistence that we must

know something concrete before four that afternoon, when the meeting of the council of ministers would begin, he parted his lips to tell me that we should not put such a tragic interpretation on the matter, since the comrades in the service knew what they were doing, that they were not new to their trade, and that above all else they were political people. He promised to go to the [Soviet] embassy to inform them of what had happened. And he left, going in that direction.

The Soviet embassy was only a few minutes away . . . I decided to wait . . .

From the balcony, I watched Togliatti's car return. A minute later, he told us that in the embassy nobody knew anything, neither the whereabouts of Nin nor of Orlov. All my concern and all my nervousness burst out brusquely. I told them I could not go to the meeting of the council of ministers, that I did not want to be a decoy for Orlov and Co. in an affair that from the first moment seemed to me baseless and dirty.

'Not to show up, to flee from the argument, would be the worst mistake,' I was told. 'Avoid the specific case of Nin and be firm as to the existence of proofs that will show that the P.O.U.M. leaders were in contact with the enemy. Don't fight on their terms; put the debate on the basis of the existence or nonexistence of an espionage organization. If it is demonstrated, as it is possible to demonstrate, that such exists, the scandal over the whereabouts of Nin will lose its vigor. And when Nin reappears, he will be a defendant on a treason charge . . .'

When the president opened the meeting that day, the interior minister, Zugazagoitia, demanded the floor to air a question previously on the agenda.

With incontrovertible reasoning, firm argumentation, and a respectful manner,

Zugazagoitia described how much he knew of the 'Nin case,' and of his comrades 'arrested, not by the authorities of the republic, but by a "foreign service," which acted, as was to be seen, omnimodally throughout our territory, knowing no other law than their wishes, nor any restraint than that of their caprices.'

'I would like to know,' he said in concluding, 'if my jurisdiction as interior minister is determined by the mission of my office or by the criteria of certain Soviet 'technicians.' Our gratitude to that friendly country should not oblige us to leave in tatters, at the political crossroads, our personal and national dignity' . . .

They all spoke. They demanded Nin and asked for the firing of colonel Ortega, the visible and direct, although unknowing, accomplice in the atrocities of Orlov.

We two communist ministers spoke. Our arguments were poor and colorless. Nobody believed we were sincere when we said we did not know the whereabouts of Nin. We defended the presence of the Soviet 'technicians' and 'advisers' as the expression of a 'disinterested' aid based on 'solidarity,' which was given to us by the Russians and which was accepted by prior governments. We expounded once again what the shipments of weapons from the U.S.S.R. and the aid on the international level given to us by the Soviet Union meant for our struggle.

Since, notwithstanding everything, the atmosphere remained hostile and the frowns were still visible, I agreed to the dismissal of colonel Ortega, as a scapegoat, for having exceeded his functions and not having informed the minister in due time; but I threatened to make public all the compromising documents on the P.O.U.M. and also the names of many within and outside the government who, 'on the basis of mere procedural problems,' were protecting the spies in this party.

This gambit was demagogic and dishonest, but I did not hesitate to use it.

Negrín, as a conciliator, proposed that the council leave the debate suspended until all the facts were known and all the proofs of which the communist ministers spoke were available, and in expectation that the interior minister would be able to provide concrete news of the whereabouts of Andreu Nin.

We had handled the first, the most dangerous test . . .

It took two or three more days for us to learn something concrete about Andreu Nin. Our Madrid organization told us that Nin was in Alcalá de Henares, in a private prison used by Orlov and his gang. When we brought this question up to the Soviet delegation we were told that they had, in effect, just had news—what a coincidence!—that Nin had passed through Valencia, without stopping, in the direction of Madrid; that Orlov intended to take him directly to the Cellular Prison in Madrid, but that he was afraid of an escape attempt by the accused and that he chose to put him in the brig at the General Barracks in Alcalá until the arrival of the other arrested, who had to be moved from the jail in Valencia to that in Madrid . . .

On one of those days, while visiting Negrín, I could see on the president's desk a mountain of telegrams from all parts of the world questioning the government on Nin and protesting against the arrest of the P.O.U.M. leaders. Negrín demanded that we come up with a solution that would put an end to this discredit of his government inside and outside the borders of the nation.

'There is no other remedy than to take into government hands the responsibility for the P.O.U.M. trial. When it is given an official status, the attacks against the G.P.U. as authors of the affair behind the backs of the Spanish authorities, which is the main point of all the protests, will cease,' I told Negrín.

'Why should I compromise the entire government in this hideous affair?' Negrín protested.

'Because at times, against our own wishes, we have to take the heat for others.'

I do not know what arguments served Negrín in convincing Irujo, the justice minister, a Basque Catholic, hardly fond of the communists and frankly opposed to helping the G.P.U. But the day after this conversation, an official communique from the ministry of justice appeared in the press, announcing the trial of the P.O.U.M. leaders, jointly with some Falangists headed by the engineer, Golfin, author of the millimeter-scale map of Madrid intended for Franco's use.[38]

Although the witnesses to and authors of the crime have not spoken about it, it is possible to reconstruct in broad details the murder of Nin. What is certain is the following: Nin was driven to Valencia and from there, immediately, to Alcalá de Henares, close to Madrid, where the communists had an isolated building ready to receive him and where he made declarations to the police on June 18, 19, 20, and 21. In these declarations, which were included in the indictment presented at the P.O.U.M. trial, there appears neither the place where they were taken down nor the name of the police agent who took them down, a departure from custom. On the night of June 22, an armed group of some ten men "assaulted" the prison, invaded the place where Nin was kept and took him away. Apparently, the group included Orlov, Vittorio Vidali, and a group of Germans from Orlov's personal guard.

The raiders spoke German and tied up the two guards, to make this "escape organized by Nazi agents" believable. Further, they left in Nin's cell a briefcase containing documents linking Nin and the P.O.U.M. to espionage.

Nin was driven to El Pardo. Nobody has ever said what happened next. Jesús Hernández states that Nin was tortured and killed; the ex-Communist general Valentín González ("El Campesino") says that they killed him and buried him in the palace gardens; an article in a national Spanish news magazine, "Cambio 16," in 1983, stated that Nin was killed by a guardia del asalto, Valentín de Pedro, the lover of the pro-Communist political figure Margarita Nelkén.[39]

They submitted him to torture lasting several days. Blows, long interrogations without sleep, and when they saw that he did not surrender, did not confess—having nothing to confess—they must have used more refined methods.

Gorkín has published the names of the Spanish collaborators who, under direct Russian supervision, inflicted tortures: Vicente Juarez, son-in-law of General Riquelme; a certain Armisen, delegate for the central zone on the tribunal for high treason; Santiago Garcés, Tomas Rebosam, Leopoldo Mejorada, Elías Díaz Franco, Juan Vidarte. The group was selected by the police chief Francisco Ordoñez.[40]

Nin resisted. He must have known that on him and him alone now depended not only his own place in the history of the international workers' movement, but also the lives of his comrades, the dignity of the P.O.U.M., even the integrity of the workers' movement in his country. Sick with a liver ailment, weakened by all-day interrogations, he still found enough strength to say no.

Lenin's old comrades had broken under torture and ended up confessing nonexistent crimes and imaginary complicities, linking them one after another in a monstrous web. But Nin, a less spectacular historical figure, resisted, remained unbroken, and did not confess.

Finally, he died at their hands. No confession was wrung out of him. The men from the Soviet *spetsnaz* must have been surprised; the methods that worked so well in the Lyubanka failed on the soil of Spain.

The P.O.U.M., in the face of the Moscow trials, saved the honor of the Spanish workers' movement, by refusing to join the chorus of assent organized by the adherents of the People's Front. Nin, facing the men of the *spetsnaz,* saved the honor of the P.O.U.M.

"Nin saved all our lives," Largo Caballero said much later.

On August 8, 1937, "The New York Times" reported the discovery of Nin's body. This was probably not premature in the sense that it announced his death; but no body was ever found. The corpses whose finding near Madrid made possible this report, which many people believed belonged to Nin and the other arrested members of the P.O.U.M. executive, were, as we have said, those of other, unidentifiable victims. The *Times* bulletin was datelined Paris. Two days later, the *Times* correspondent in Spain, the ineffable Herbert Matthews, cabled from Paris that "loyalist Spain has been threatened by a revolt," attributing to the anarchists and Largo Caballero the aim of repeating the May events in order to retake power.

Anybody who lived in Barcelona or Valencia at that time knows that public rumor credited the communists with coup intentions; the C.N.T. even published a manifesto putting the masses on alert. The *Times* correspondent not only served as a mouthpiece for communist disinformation on this issue, but also affirmed, in the same cable, that the arrest of Nin had been carried out when the authorities discovered "a fascist plot in which the P.O.U.M. was implicated."

Ernest Hemingway and Mikhail Koltsov were less credulous. In Hemingway's novel *For Whom the Bell Tolls,* a brief exchange takes place with a Soviet correspondent, Karkov, modeled on the latter:

'Where is [Nin] now?'

'In Paris. We say he is in Paris. He was a very pleasant fellow, but with bad political aberrations.'

'But they were in communication with the fascists, weren't they?'

'Who is not?'

'We are not.'

'Who knows? I hope we are not.'

Another U.S. citizen who, unlike *Times* man Matthews, was not tricked, the socialist Norman Thomas, on reading the news of Nin's death sent this telegram to Negrín:

The lynching of Andres Nin in Madrid is a blot on loyalist Spain. It is very probable that this new murder is part of a communist program to liquidate all critics, all those who, true or not, are called Trotskyites. For the honor of your government, which we support against Franco, we demand punishment for this lynching and an impartial trial for the others who have been arrested.[41]

Throughout the world, individuals and organizations that had supported the Spanish revolution mourned Nin. In San Francisco, the anarchosyndicalist leaning journal of a local trade union, the "West Coast Sailors," angrily declared:

> "When Andres Nin, who spent most of his life fighting for the Spanish workers ... sought to break the death-hold of the Communist Party over the government, he was arrested and never brought to trial. He was charged with being a fascist agent, just as any union man who criticizes the Communist Party is called a red-baiter. But because they did not dare to bring him to trial, where such a charge would not only be laughed down, but would expose the frame-up of the best fighters against fascism, he was murdered. This was another body that had to be stepped over . . ."[42]

Underground Action

The communists organized special teams to add a phrase to the graffiti painted by the P.O.U.M. on the walls, answering "Negrín, where is Nin?" the words "In Salamanca or in Berlin" (Salamanca was a Franco stronghold).

The P.O.U.M. members now acted on four fronts: aiding the arrested, whose number was growing; keeping alive the memory of Nin; serving at the front or at work, and at the same time watching their backs; and, finally, as militants, adopting political positions, propagating them, and defending them.

The first task was to reorganize the executive. With the members that had escaped arrest and some militants from outside Barcelona, an executive was formed composed of Arquer, who replaced Nin as political secretary, Coll, Rovira, Enric Adroher (Gironella), and Molins i Fabrega, from the "old" executive, with Rodés (as administrative secretary) and Farré from Lleida, Indigeta from Girona, Martí from Barcelona, and Solano from the Youth.

The P.O.U.M. and J.C.I. executives and the Barcelona local committee ended up fusing in order to simplify things. The committee's composition changed as the arrests of its members continued. Gironella was arrested soon, followed by Rovira's arrest and liberation, and in mid-1938 the police were hunting Arquer. The same thing happened to the local committees, in which arrests and military mobilization orders forced continuous changes.

It was necessary, above all, to help the arrested leaders. While some applied pressure on Companys and Terradelles, Arquer was in Valencia, and Molins and Costa-Amic in Paris did what they could to mobilize international opinion, mostly through a mimeographed press service in

French and English, "Independent News." Benito Pabón had been named as defense attorney. Money was collected through subscription, and the militants organized what activities they could in factories and offices, always under the threat that some P.S.U.C. member would denounce them. In general, they received a warm welcome, notwithstanding the risks, and in January 1938 Comorera went so far, in a P.S.U.C. plenum at Lleida, as to denounce "complicity or indifference regarding the clandestine leaflets circulating [in the factories], distributed by the counterrevolutionary Trotskyites."[43]

A large number of militants were in the armed forces, which made collection of dues difficult. But the London Bureau parties and other foreign subscription provided resources allowing the party not only to take care of the prisoners and their families, but also to maintain what was truly indispensable: the clandestine press.

For an illegal party, at a moment when, because of war, there could be neither strikes, nor demonstrations, nor conspiracies, nor mass actions, propaganda was essential as the only remaining weapon. The press, then, had to appear at any cost. "La Batalla" began appearing again in mid-July and "Juventud Obrera" (having dropped the word "Comunista" from its title) at the end of July. Thirty-five issues of each publication appeared.

Further, documents were published reporting on the repression and publishing the party's political theses. Notwithstanding the situation, the central committee, however its membership changed, continued to meet underground. During the whole of the Spanish Civil War, the P.O.U.M. spent only eleven months in legality (three in the Catalan government and eight in opposition), and nineteen months underground.

The history of these nineteen months will be necessarily briefer than that of the preceding eleven, not only because the action of the party was limited, but because from the moment Negrín and the communists took power, political life in Republican Spain declined, although, in a more subdued way, criticism and protests continued. The Negrín-communist-republican bloc that controlled the key posts in government and the armed forces smashed at their opponents: the C.N.T., the followers of Largo Caballero, non-Communists in the U.G.T., Companys and the Generalitat, and the Basque autonomous government all had to adapt or face the P.O.U.M.'s fate. The Russian arms blackmail was all-powerful.

One of the problems of the P.O.U.M.'s underground work was that serious activities could only be carried out by those who were either too old or too young to be eligible for the draft; but those in the first category had the handicap of being well-known, and many were arrested as leaders. Young people who had entered the Youth at an age no older than fifteen bore the brunt of the P.O.U.M.'s underground work, involved as much thanks to an adventurous spirit as to political convictions. An incredible but true experience was that new militants from this age group continued to join the movement even during the worst period of repression.

In examining the underground P.O.U.M. press, the most surprising thing is its independence. For their physical survival, the P.O.U.M. needed the C.N.T.'s help. Notwithstanding, they criticized the C.N.T. often and harshly. They reproached them, above all, for joining amorphous groupings such as the Antifascist Front (an extension of the People's Front) and the Antifascist Youth Front instead of organizing, as the P.O.U.M. counseled, a Revolutionary Workers' Front. They also criticized the followers of Largo Caballero for having confided in Léon Jouhaux, a French union leader, to arbitrate the conflict between communists and the supporters of Prieto and Negrín in the U.G.T., on one side, and those of Largo on the other; Jouhaux himself, who had admitted the communists into the French C.G.T. union federation, sought to avoid a conflict with them by siding against Largo Caballero. This made it possible for Negrín to send police into the U.G.T. unions, to dislodge Largo's partisans.

But the P.O.U.M. rapidly abandoned the illusions it had harbored as late as 1937. At the beginning of 1938, "La Batalla" noted that the party had entered a "period of recuperation and not of the revolutionary tide," and that it was impossible to pass over to the political offensive until the C.N.T., the Left Socialists, and the P.O.U.M. had recovered their strength. Anything else would be adventurism.

The Negrín regime was a "government of defeat and crime." The national parliament, when it began meeting again, was a "parliament of the bourgeois counterrevolution," and the year 1937 was "a mournful year for our revolution and our war."

In the face of constant military defeats, "Juventud Obrera" declared "We will resist and we will prevail," in contrast with the communist slogan "Resistance is victory."

"The defensive," "La Batalla" noted, "is defeat. We need a revolutionary military policy." But these were phrases that were not destined to become reality.

Reality was visible in other pages of the same underground publications: in the obituaries of dead militants, some at the front and others at communist hands, and the information on arrested militants (and only two items on the expulsion of members—no more than seven in all—for having gone over to the P.S.U.C.).

Reality was also to be seen in the Generalitat decrees removing all P.O.U.M. members from posts as municipal councillors, where they had been unable to continue functioning anyway, because had they shown up at the town halls they would have been denounced by the P.S.U.C., and lowering the number of C.N.T. councillors. It appeared as well in the news of a court-martial of three P.O.U.M. members, sentenced to twenty years' imprisonment for having stolen explosives during the May events. Or the sentence against the soldier Josep Cullares, for whom the prosecutor demanded a year in prison for indiscipline, but who was condemned to death once it was known he had served in the P.O.U.M. 29th Division (although he was not a P.O.U.M. member).

Reality was present in the report by Comorera at the first national conference of the P.S.U.C., in July 1937, during which, after calling for an end to all salary increases, he said "our enemies are the fascists, the Trotskyists, and the uncontrolled . . . as for Trotskyism and its expression in Catalunya, the P.O.U.M., we do not consider it a political party. It is not a political party; it is, as was clearly demonstrated in the counterrevolutionary rising [of May], the detractor of the U.S.S.R., the divisive factor in the Antifascist People's Front, the most dangerous, most hypocritical enemy of the proletariat and of the antifascist people."[44]

Reality is to be found, as well, in the speech by Santiago Carrillo on March 19, 1938, when the enemy had broken the Aragon front, blaming the P.O.U.M. for the reverses on the battlefield. "The Spanish youth," he affirmed, "point to the Trotskyites as those mainly responsible for the retreats and collapse of the Aragon front. Let us destroy them without regret, in order to secure our rear guard."

The underground P.O.U.M. press also published other statements that demonstrated a different sentiment. For example, in Abad de Santillán's book *La revolucion y la guerra de España,* published in January 1938, we find the following:

> Was it not possible for us to prevent [the suppression of the P.O.U.M.], if not out of solidarity with this party, than in recognition of the reactionary significance of its extirpation? We should have prevented by any means, including arms in hand, crimes such as those of which Andreu Nin was victim, and counterrevolutionary acts like the suppression of his party.

There are items in the underground P.O.U.M. press that show that party life continued, irregularly, in fits and starts, but in accordance with the organization's tradition of internal democracy. In Lleida, for example, a little before the city fell to the fascists, a local P.O.U.M.-J.C.I. conference met to demand that the Lleida be defended at all costs. In Barcelona the central committee met and decided to increase the dues for militants, to hold a party congress as soon as possible; it could not be held in January, May, or June 1937, or at that moment, since with the approach of the P.O.U.M. trial, the police had stepped up its persecutions.

The central committee protested against the new Moscow trials, criticized Trotsky for having forced his Belgian and Dutch followers out of the Fourth International over their support for the P.O.U.M., and thanked the London Bureau (from which the German S.A.P. had broken) for its solidarity, approving the slogan it had put forward: "Nothing for the Negrín government; everything for the Spanish workers." It finally demanded a return to legality, freedom for those arrested, and the truth about the disappearance of Andreu Nin.

In this tangle of news, there was a single note of joy. In September 1937, the underground press announced: "Maurín is alive. We must save Maurín."

Maurín Lives!

During the first weeks of the war, a press agency had reported that Maurín was executed in Galicia, which quickly fell to the rebels. Notwithstanding the efforts made by some Parisian friends of Maurín and the P.O.U.M., the report could not be confirmed.

In late Spring 1937, Jeanne Maurín, the P.O.U.M. leader's wife, received news indicating he was alive, arrested under a false name in the fascist zone. She told this to some intimate friends, asking them to keep it a secret while efforts to communicate with him were under way.

In September 1937, it was learned that he was not only alive, but had been identified and was to go on trial. The news came from a correspondent for an international news agency in the fascist capital of Burgos. On receiving the news, the president of the Cortes contacted the International Parliamentary Commission, hoping Maurín's status as an elected deputy would protect him. José María Arenillas, in France, proposed a plan to Nin: to kidnap the wife of general Franco during one of her frequent visits to Bayonne, and to exchange her for Maurín. A report on this proposal, transmitted to Nin via Costa-Amic, was found by the police when Nin was arrested; phases from the report, ripped out of context, were utilized by the communists in their attacks on the P.O.U.M.

The communists had included Maurín in their general campaign of defamation against the P.O.U.M. Already, in January 1937, the foreign communist press claimed that Maurín "was staying tranquilly in Burgos."

An inimitable communist hack, Manuel Benavides, claimed Maurín "established agreements with the Falange" in Galicia and later that he "served as an informer in Franco's prisons and made speeches in the prison patios for a conciliation between the P.O.U.M. and national-syndicalism [the ideology of the Falange]." Even when, at the end of the war, it became known that Maurín had survived and when he left prison in 1946 they continued circulating rumors against him; that in July 1936 he had been vacationing in Galicia and then that he had fled to Galicia.

Even in prison, Maurín disturbed the communists. British M.P. John McGovern, while participating in the third international commission of inquiry on the P.O.U.M., spoke with Irujo, asking him to exchange Maurín for some important fascist prisoner, pointing out that this had already been done with the sister and mother of José Díaz. Senor Irujo replied that the government had, shortly before, discussed the exchange of Maurín and that "only the communists opposed it."

Irujo authorized McGovern to ask the British Foreign Office to make efforts toward effecting the exchange.[45] Later, Maurín's name was added to a list of persons for which the republican government was willing to exchange rightist prisoners, through the international Red Cross.

This was decided, we now know, in a meeting of the council of ministers in which the communists, aside from some observations, made no objections.[46] But in a conversation with Víctor Alba in Mexico in June 1955, Jesús Hernández stated that the communists had agreed to the proposal but had privately told Negrín that they could accept Maurín's name figuring on a list of people to be exchanged, but that they would not tolerate such an action actually taking place.

The facts, naturally, were very different than those presented in communist propaganda. Surprised by the military coup in Galicia, Maurín presented himself to the civil governor of La Coruña, a loyal republican. Once the rightist officers had taken the city, he took a false name and checked into a modest hotel and after a few days went to see the French consul, intending to ask for help to get into France, given his wife's French citizenship. The French consul refused to help him. He succeeded in obtaining a false identity card in the name of Joaquín Julio Ferrer and with this was able to leave La Coruña on September 1, 1936, six weeks after the coup attempt. On the 2nd, he reached Saragossa, and on the 3rd, Jaca, on the border with France. While waiting to obtain a pass to cross the border, he was arrested as a suspicious personage by the guardia civil in Panticosa. He was put in prison at Jaca under the name J.J. Ferrer. Until spring 1937, he was unable to send any news to his wife, in Paris. At the beginning of September 1937, since there were no charges pending against J.J. Ferrer, he was freed. He had reached a border town, still trying to get to France, when a policeman stationed in the town, who had served in Barcelona, recognized him. The Burgos press published the news, and it was reprinted everywhere.

Jeanne Maurín then made contact with a cousin of Joaquím, a colonel of the chaplain corps in Franco's army, who later became Bishop of Seu d'Urgell. The cousin was able to prevent Maurín from being killed and even to delay his trial. He was moved, successively, to prisons in Saragossa and Salamanca, always in solitary confinement. In 1942, he was moved to prison in Barcelona, where his trial was to take place, but was soon returned to Burgos, as a dangerous prisoner. In 1943, he was brought again to Barcelona for a court martial, and received a thirty-year prison sentence. In 1946, he was released on parole under the obligation to reside only in Madrid, and in July 1947 succeeded in leaving Spain and joining his wife and his son in France, after eleven years in prison.

Maurín died in New York in 1973.

The P.O.U.M. Trial

While Maurín was held incommunicado in the fascist zone, in Barcelona the trial of his comrades was being prepared.

The trial was, as we have indicated, intended to serve a concrete function: that of proving that the Moscow trials were not a purely Soviet phenomenon, created by Stalin, but that such proceedings were possible wherever there were groups that Moscow called "Trotskyite."

On setting up his government, Negrín had announced. "We will not be able to speak of peace until we have secured the absolute calm of the rear guard."

There was neither peace nor any kind of calm, whether absolute or relative. The government itself took on the responsibility of continuing a losing policy on the war, while undermining the potential for calm by its measures against the revolutionary organizations: dissolution of the anarchist council of Aragon, prohibition on public speeches by Largo Caballero, who was put under house arrest, police-communist occupation of U.G.T. offices, some 250 executions in the International Brigades, militarization of the war industries, trimming of the authority of the Generalitat, leading to tension between the latter power and the central government, and, finally, the rise of the power of the communist-controlled Military Investigation Service (Servicio de Inteligencia Militar-S.I.M.).

The result of this "calm" was an atmosphere that a writer who sympathized with the communists, Arturo Barea, described as follows: "The government and war machinery worked as never before; now they had an efficient army and administration, two things necessary to wage a modern war, even on a limited scale. But the thirst for freedom, the desperate efforts to build a new and better social order, had been completely destroyed."

He added, "Today I went into a shop [in Barcelona] to buy a beret. The owner told me, very pleased, that business had begun to pick up; the wives of official functionaries had been told that they should go back to wearing hats, as propaganda to show that the turbulent period of the proletarian mob had ended forever."[47]

There was no better way to give an impression of enthusiasm than to hold military parades and writers' congresses. In July 1937, an "international congress of antifascist writers" was held in stages in Madrid, Barcelona, and Valencia. The participants, who included such luminaries of Anglo-Saxon literary fellow-travelling as Stephen Spender, spent most of their time condemning the recent book by André Gide, *Retour de l'U.R.S.S.* This task was taken up with special enthusiasm by the Catholic writer Jose Bergamín, who was also prominent in the attack on the P.O.U.M.[48]

However real the "calm" of the situation, dissident voices continued to be heard. Aside from the underground P.O.U.M. press, there appeared the semiclandestine journal of the anarchist Friends of Durruti, "El Amigo del Pueblo," as well as that of the official Trotskyists in the S.B.L., "La Voz Leninista," and the leaflets distributed in the Barcelona area by a secret group that called itself "The Controllers of the P.S.U.C."

With the coming of army "efficiency," militia equality disappeared. The soldiers now had to salute their officers if they saw them in the street, and while the soldier who did the saluting received 300 pesetas per month, the officer who was saluted received much more—General Pozas, for example, received 11,000 pesetas per month. Should it be any surprise, then, that in a letter to Prieto, in 1938, Companys revealed that production in the war industries had continued falling after June 1937, and that this decline had reached a level of 35% to 40% by the end of that year?[49]

And was it therefore strange to find that even in the official Communist Party there were concerns and doubts? Some members began to say the party had gotten too close to the bourgeoisie.

Such misgivings began to be reflected, even, in one of the central organs of the P.C.E., "Mundo Obrero," which, since it appeared in Madrid, was not subject to the immediate control of the Barcelona-based leadership of the party, whose official mouthpiece was the newspaper "Frente Rojo." On March 23, 1938, the editors of "Mundo Obrero" stated:

> It is impossible to say, as one paper does, that the only solution is for Spain to be neither fascist nor communist, because this is what France wants . . . The Spanish people will win despite opposition from capitalism.

The P.C.E. leadership reacted instantly. In a letter signed by José Díaz and published in "Frente Rojo" on March 30, the editors of "Mundo Obrero" were severely admonished:

> The statement that 'the only solution to our conflict is for Spain to be neither

fascist nor communist' is fully correct and corresponds precisely to the position of our party.

With regard to the thesis that "the Spanish people will win despite opposition from capitalism," José Díaz wrote that "it corresponds neither to the situation nor to the policy of our party and the Communist International."[50]

Did all this constitute calm? The calm of the communist leaders can be gauged by the statement of "La Pasionaria" in a speech at Valencia, during the period when the trial of the P.O.U.M. was approaching and the communist press was filled with imprecations against the party: "It is better to condemn a hundred innocents than to let a single guilty person go free."

The trial of the P.O.U.M. had to have some kind of judicial foundation, since it was insufficient for propagandistic ends to have a complacent judge willing to coordinate the farce. The Madrid police were charged with preparing the structure. The English historian Hugh Thomas, in one of the few instances where his version of events is largely accurate, agreed with Gorkín on the following:

> . . . in April, the communist-controlled police in Madrid unearthed a genuine conspiracy by the Falange. One of the conspirators, named Castilla, was induced by threats to become an *agent provocateur.* Castilla prevailed upon another Falangist in the capital, Golfin, to prepare a fraudulent plan for a military rising by the Fifth Column. Golfin did this, and he and his plan were apprehended. Next someone, probably Castilla, wrote a letter purporting to be from Nin to Franco on the back of Golfin's plan . . . At about the same time, another genuine Falangist agent, named José Roca, who kept a small bookshop, was discovered by the Catalan communists controlled by Erno Gerö. Roca's task was to pass on messages to a Falangist named Dalmau, a *hotelier* in the same town, the Venice of Catalonia. One day, some time after the dissolution of the P.O.U.M., a well-dressed individual came to the bookshop, left some money for Roca and a message for Dalmau, and asked if he could leave a suitcase in the shop for three days. Roca agreed to this request. Shortly after, the police arrived to carry out a search. Naturally, they came upon the suitcase, which when opened, was found to contain a pile of secret documents all sealed, oddly enough, with the stamp of the P.O.U.M. military committee. It was upon these documents, the letter from Nin to Franco, and the suitcase found in Gerona, that the communist case against the P.O.U.M. rested. Of course, all were forgeries.[51]

The "well-dressed man" who left the suitcase with the compromising "documents" was Victori Salá, a former representative in Barcelona for the left wing publishing house Editorial Cenit and a member of the Bloc who had gone over to the official party in 1932. The P.S.U.C. gave him a secondary post in the police. The compromising "documents" were prepared by one Arconada, later a translator in Moscow, with the aid of Wenceslao Roces, who was to become known as a translator of Marx and a university professor in Mexico. The man who found the suitcase with the "documents" was Hubert von Ranke, a German communist, an agent of the Soviet secret police who followed his work as an International Brigades political commissar with a period as head of interrogations at the portal de l'Angel *cheka*. Von Ranke claimed to have been with the Soviets after this experience and lived in hiding for many years.[52]

Along with the trial of the P.O.U.M. executive—utilizing an "amalgam" with Golfin and his friends—a second trial (which never took place) was ordered by judge Miguel de Mora, of the Special Tribunal for Espionage and High Treason, for the P.O.U.M. members arrested after June 1937. The technique of the "amalgam"—charging revolutionary dissidents along with counterrevolutionary agents—had been used extensively in Russia, but was neither exclusively Russian nor particularly novel; the same methods were used in the French Revolution to purge the extreme-left *Hebertistes* and *Babouvistes*. Golfin and 103 codefendants were sentenced prior to the P.O.U.M. executive; of them, thirteen were condemned to death, Golfin among them, twenty-five to light punishments, and the rest cleared. The condemned were told they would be exchanged for left-wing prisoners from the fascist side, but when the Red Cross had the transfer ready, they were executed. The communists did not want Golfin to be left free to speak and reveal that he had never had anything to do with Nin or the P.O.U.M. Roca, a timid and mean-spirited youth, was the only one who signed a statement implicating the P.O.U.M. Victori Salá, who had given him the suitcase with the "documents," took his declaration and told him that if he did not sign a statement that he was the contact between the P.O.U.M. and the Falange, his sister and father, who were under arrest, would be shot.[53]

The main judge in the trial of the P.O.U.M. executive was a Valencian named Taroncher, who had been expelled from the bar by his colleagues for unethical dealings, and whom Negrín restored to his professional status, for him to serve in the matter of the P.O.U.M. The prosecutor was a certain José Gomis, who was under the thumb of the communists; other, less submissive prosecutors had to be pushed aside, and Gomis placed at the top of the list, so that he could take over the P.O.U.M. case.

Finally, the moment for the trial approached. In September 1938, Negrín met in his office in Barcelona with the new minister of justice, Ramón González Peña, the president of the supreme court, Mariano Gómez, and the president of the Special Tribunal, Eduardo Iglesias Portal, to tell them that "the army demands the death penalty for the P.O.U.M. defendants," pointing to a mountain of telegrams. González Peña answered that the telegrams were all from communists. Negrín insisted, "The situation at the front is delicate and the morale of the troops has fallen somewhat. It is necessary to give the army satisfaction." Gómez told him that the administration of justice was independent of the army and that if the accused were guilty, they would be punished. Negrín became threatening, then: "I need the condemnation of these men. If necessary, I will side with the army against the courts."

Finally, seeing that Mariano Gómez was not in a mood to make promises, Negrín said, "High reasons of international policy oblige me to ask for this sacrifice. Condemn them, and I promise I will suspend [the sentences]."[54]

To pressure the government, groups of P.C.E. and P.S.U.C. members went from cafes to factories to barracks asking for signatures on petitions demanding the death penalty for the accused. They collected few names. People were too preoccupied with the bad war news and the rationing lines to be interested in a trial they knew little of and did not clearly comprehend. Only political activists were interested in the case.

The Spanish Republican embassy in Paris refused a visa to Henri Torres and Louis Nogueres—two French attorneys representing the Committee to Defend the Spanish Revolution who sought to attend the trial. No journalists not already in Spain were allowed visas to attend the trial.

The communists did not believe Negrín's promises. They had to prepare a pogrom atmosphere, so the judges would not dare to release the defendants. On November 13, 1937, Díaz declared before the central committee of the P.C.E. that "Since the treason of the P.O.U.M. is proven, the execution squad should function to finish off the traitors and terrorists." The entire communist press repeated this phrase for months.

To keep the campaign going, the Paris "L'Humanité," in February 1938, commenting on the trial and death sentence of Nikolai Bukharin, said, "The vigilance of the Soviet magistrates must be imitated. Our Spanish comrades will understand what we want to say."

They understood it well. A foreign "expert," using the false name of Max Rieger, prepared a book, *Espionaje en Espana,* dedicated entirely to the P.O.U.M. trial. Published in Barcelona in 1938, by Ediciones Unidas, a firm created for this purpose alone, the book was translated by Lucienne and Arturo Perucho—the latter was one of the prodigies of the team around the conservative Catalan politician Francesc Cambó, and had become editor of the P.S.U.C. daily "Treball." The book was published in editions around the world, supplemented by others with the same theme, such as that of the "L'Humanité" editor, Georges Soria (*L'Espionnage Trotskyste en Espagne*) and that of Carlos J. Contreras (Vidali, a leading servitor of the *troika*), *La quinta columna; como luchar contra la provocacion y el espionaje.*

Rieger's opus, which was given away free throughout the republican zone, carried a prologue by the Catholic Bergamín, whose style included barely veiled threats such as the following, directed to the P.O.U.M.'s defense counsel:

> "The defense of the delinquent is handled, in the court, by the defense attorney. But to defend the delinquent as such, a traitor or a spy, is not to defend a man, but to make a defense of his crime. And, in this wartime case, it is to identify totally with the enemy."

Bergamín claimed to be especially indignant over the protest by some French writers in defense of the P.O.U.M. (against which he had spoken out frequently at writers' gatherings and in the Paris press). About the French intellectuals he said, "Not long ago, some French intellectuals demanded by telegram, with anxious urgency, that the Spanish People's Government take measures guaranteeing the defense of certain defendants. They asked that juridical formalities be observed by a government that has, in practice, been excessively attentive to this, and that, in this concrete case, has demonstrated what one could call exaggerated concern. The anxious formalists perhaps forget that it would have been better for the Spaniards if this demand had been presented to the government of the protestors' own country, so as to attain their compliance with other international juridical formalities . . ."

The press did not report that when the defendants from the P.O.U.M. executive were taken to the state prison barbershop to prepare themselves for their appearance before the court, having been accused of contacts with the fascists, Doctor Negrín was meeting, in a small Swiss town, where he had gone for an international congress of biologists, with representatives of the German government, attempting to negotiate a withdrawal of German aid to Franco in exchange for special concessions by the republic. Such an agreement was obstructed by Russian pressure. Nor did the press mention that the newspaper writer Emérita Esparza, who lived in Berlin, often visited Barcelona, where she stayed in Negrín's home, because she was a friend of the actress who lived with him. Prieto, who revealed all this years later, asked if this newspaper writer was not carrying out the wishes of Negrín in maintaining contact between him and Berlin, exactly the charge leveled at the P.O.U.M.[55]

The trial lasted for eleven days, from October 11 to 22, 1938. The situation in the republican zone continued to be characterized by disintegration. Lleida was lost, and Catalunya was cut off from the rest of the republic when Vinyarós was taken by fascist troops. An Ebro river offensive, which had been imposed on the republican army staff by the Soviet advisers, who sought to end the war quickly and leave Stalin's hands free for a deal with Hitler, had debilitated the republican army. The people were exasperated by lines, bombings, and scarcities; the revolutionary spirit had dissipated, thanks to the policy of the communists; and for many defeat was an inevitability. The Generalitat and the Basque government, the latter having gone into exile under *lehendakari* Joseba Antxon Agirre, had broken with Negrín. Political life had virtually ceased to exist. Negrín dominated everything and the communists controlled everything.

On being brought to the buildings where the Special Tribunal for Espionage and High Treason was established, the arrested members of the executive crossed paths with a Catholic burial, with the crucifix raised high by a priest, something that would not have been seen in public in July 1936. In front of the building, numerous P.S.U.C. members formed a human barrier to prevent anybody sympathetic to the defendants from entering the spectators' section of the courtroom. In the hands of many of the P.S.U.C. were copies of a pamphlet published by the Communist Party which contained the prosecuting attorney's report, although this was supposed to be kept confidential until the presentation of pleas. Many foreign journalists along with some Spaniards and many police were in the courtroom.

The defense attorney was Vicente Rodríguez Revilla, an Asturian socialist who had taken over the defense a few weeks before; the original advocate, the Cortes deputy Benito Pabón, had fled the country after receiving numerous threats on his life. Pabón, all the way from Manila, in the Philippines, wrote to the defendants, "What guarantees do I have that in such an atmosphere my role as attorney will not change to that of one of the accused?" The communist press had naturally labeled him a "spy" for having defended "spies." Another attorney had expressed his willingness to defend the P.O.U.M. leaders, but only if a large sum of money was deposited in a Paris bank, in the name of his wife and children, in case he was killed.

The public was not allowed into the sessions and could not find out what had happened until October 23, 1938, when the censorship permitted reporting on the case.

The presiding judge was Eduardo Iglesias Portal, with four other members of the judicial panel. The prosecuting attorney was the previously mentioned José Gomis. The accused were Julián Gómez (Gorkin), Enric Adroher (Gironella), Juan Andrade, Pere Bonet, Jordi Arquer, Josep Escuder, and Daniel Rebull (David Rey).

In the indictment, the prosecutor argued that the P.O.U.M. executive committee was responsible for the party's activities, since, he said, it was the executive "that signed the subversive proclamations, the slogans against the governments of Catalunya and Spain, the People's Front, the Parliament, and the People's Army; that prepared and carried out the uprising of May 1937; that had dealings with fascist organizations; that used secret codes and radio broadcasts; that ordered and carried out the removal from Spain of a great quantity of gold and works of art, illegally acquired and even more illegally disposed of; that maintained relations with a constellation of foreign adventurers who under the mask of 'international soldiers' were brought into the ranks of the P.O.U.M. and whom the police have had to expel from the national territory because of vehement suspicions, at some times, and certainty, at others, that they were agents of the Gestapo and the O.V.R.A. [Italian secret police]; ... that ordered the 29th Division to abandon its positions at Huesca to join the May uprising ...

"All this," Gomis added in his opening argument, "constitutes a crime of high treason."

The tribunal called the defendants one at a time, from the cellars of the building where they were held. Escuder quickly answered some questions, and when it became obvious that he was nothing more than a technical employee at "La Batalla" and never a member of the executive, he was left aside by the prosecutor. Gorkín was the second to be examined, during five hours over two court sessions. Given the talents of Gorkín as a mass orator, there was tension between he and the prosecutor, when Gorkín would answer questions in a political manner.

The tone of the prosecutor was the same for all the defendants. The accusation was juridically based on the metric map of Madrid linked to Golfín, who in his own trial admitted it was his but denied that anything had been written on the back, in invisible ink or otherwise. Regarding the suitcase left in the Roca bookshop, the prosecutor hardly spoke of it. His questions tended to present the P.O.U.M. as subversive and corrupt. For example, he tried to demonstrate that the 29th Division abandoned the front during the May events and that the party had organized the same events. He insisted on connecting the P.O.U.M. with Trotsky (as if this was a crime in the eyes of anybody but a Stalinist). At times he would ask the accused if they had held meetings with falangists. He read excerpts from articles in "La Batalla" as if they were great secrets and showed surprise that the defendants would admit to writing and publishing them.

The third to be questioned was Andrade, who with his own questions presented the political character of the trial to the judges and the public.

The third day began with a blow for effect: The accused placed a large photo of Nin upright in a chair, with a wreath in front of it. Gironella made the judges laugh and exasperated the prosecutor when he answered one of the latter's questions, while maintaining a straight face, with the words,

"Yes, señor Vishinsky" (Andrei Vishinsky was the notorious prosecutor in the Moscow trials).

Bonet, the fifth to appear, answered questions about the financial aspects of the P.O.U.M.'s activities. The prosecutor was unable to get him to admit that the P.O.U.M. had gained access to a fortune in resources. And he was open-mouthed in astonishment to learn that, as Bonet pointed out, and as was the practice in all the workers' organizations, the members of the P.O.U.M. executive received 500 pesetas monthly salary, beginning in July 1936, and that if they received supplementary income for extra work, they turned it over to the party in its entirety.

Arquer, who had been away from Barcelona during the May events (he had gone to Valencia), mainly answered questions about the front, where he had been in July and August 1936.

The last to speak was David Rey. Had he visited Trotsky during a trip to Mexico? Yes, as he had visited that country's president, Lázaro Cárdenas, and, he said, "It was a great pleasure to meet the old Bolshevik."

The witnesses for the prosecution then came forward. Handwriting experts stated that, while the handwriting on the back of Golfin's map and in some other documents resembled that of some of the accused, it was, nevertheless, not the same. Roca, the bookseller from Girona, told how a suitcase had been left in his shop, how he had been obliged by threats to confess that he was the contact between the P.O.U.M. and the Falange, and how he had renounced such statements as untrue when he had left the hands of the police and appeared before a judge.

Then, the three "star" witnesses. The first, Virgilio Llanos, a former actor, a socialist before 1936 and later a communist and Commissar in the Army of the East, knew the accused. He did not say how he had met them, but it is worth noting: In the summer of 1934, to raise money for arms purchases, a socialist action group falsified some checks against the account of an aristocrat, and Llanos was charged with cashing them. After October 1934, fearful that the police would charge him with fraud, he asked Gorkín to help him hide and the Bloc got him over the border to France. In 1938, he acted as an accuser of those who four years before had saved him.

"Solidaridad Obrera," once the censors permitted it, published a summary of the prosecution witnesses' testimony. This is what they said about Llanos:

> He said that the P.O.U.M., through the 29th Division, carried away the F.A.I. forces and had absolute influence over the latter's division. That on May 28 the [anarchist] 28th Division rose and joined the 29th Division, in the absence of the commander of the 28th, and together they went to Binéfar . . . He stated that the 29th Division had left its sector of the front abandoned; the

fortifications looked good from outside but were weak, unable to resist the slightest onslaught by the enemy. He denounced a 'nonaggression pact' that existed between the P.O.U.M. and the fascists and said the latter fraternized with the 29th Division to the point of going back and forth between each other's trenches. That on a certain occasion he sent a commissar to the 29th Division who denounced the indicated anomalies and above all the fact that the 29th Division had received an order to 'open the front to the enemy.' The following day, the commissar alluded to was killed, doubtless because of an attack by elements of the 29th Division, since at that time there was no shooting from the enemy side. He said the entire activity of the 29th Division had been favorable to Franco and Mussolini.

He ended up stating that, on taking over the commissariat of the Army of the East, Largo Caballero (who did not know about his change of political affiliation) gave him "one recommendation: to keep a firm eye on the military elements of the P.O.U.M."

Ignacio Mantecón, a former republican put in charge of the liquidation of the Council of Aragon by Negrín, and then commissar of the communist-controlled XIth Army Corps, was another of the state's witnesses. He said, ". . . that he was not at the Aragon front during the May events. That he did not have any direct knowledge of the affair involving the 29th Division, but that he was told that there was a 'nonaggression pact' and that the rebel forces were in communication with them."

Finally, appearing in uniform, came colonel Antonio Cordón, undersecretary of war for the army and member of the Communist Party, who declared ". . . that he understood that the 29th Division belonged entirely to the P.O.U.M., and that, in that division, the underground and fascist press was continuously distributed, as evidenced by the content of the periodicals and other documents . . . He stated there was no relationship between the P.O.U.M. and the General Staff. He stated that the 29th Division abandoned the front during the May events in Barcelona and established its own control, which put in danger, because of its leaving, the front that it occupied."

The defense attorney gave special attention to this witness. What was the title of the "fascist newspaper, printed in Huesca," that the P.O.U.M. distributed at the front?

"La Batalla," Cordón answered.

Angel Galarza, interior minister under Largo Caballero, declared that, while he had suspended the P.O.U.M.'s newspaper on one occasion, it was for ignoring the censor, but not because he considered the paper favorable to Franco.

Finally, Largo Caballero, on whom a long silence had been imposed, and for whom the court testimony was something of a political testament, spoke.

"The May events," he declared, "were provoked by the conflict between the organizations." He was strongly pressured to dissolve the P.O.U.M., a course to which he was opposed and to which he would have remained opposed had he stayed at the head of the government. He knew some of the accused, whom he did not consider fascists, but rather intransigent.

The prosecutor read some criticisms of his government that had been published in "La Batalla," and Largo commented, "Other antifascist groups have attacked me more harshly." He finished by affirming the political character of the trial: "If Nin and other P.O.U.M. members are persecuted today for espionage, it is only for political reasons, only because the Communist Party wishes to destroy the P.O.U.M."

When the defense attorney asked him if he had ordered Llanos, as the latter claimed, to especially watch the military forces of the P.O.U.M., he answered, "That I would give such an order! Never. Why would I?"

The trial took on, with the appearance of the defense witnesses, Galarza, Largo Caballero, and Federica Montseuy, the tone of a political meeting. Without losing sight of the accusations against the defendants, the trial had become, in reality, an examination of the communist attempt, with the complicity of Negrín, to ideologically colonize Spain.[56]

Finally, the prosecutor and defense delivered their summations. Gomis shouted "There are the agents of Franco!", pointing at the defendants. As if the witnesses had not invalidated the accusations, he repeated them one by one, among them that of criticizing the People's Front, which, he said, "had led the Paris Commune [of 1871]".

The defendants burst out laughing; Gomis realized that he had put his foot in it and tried to clarify, whereupon the president interrupted him, saying, "We don't need explanations. We all know history."

Gomis ended with his definitive conclusions: Escuder should be freed, since he was never a member of the executive, while the others should each receive thirty years in prison. He did not dare to ask for the death penalty, or had received orders not to outdo himself, perhaps because Negrín did not feel certain of his power to grant a reprieve for a death sentence and feared this could pull public opinion out of its apathy.

The defense attorney insisted that the prosecutor was speaking under orders. He showed the falsification of the phrases written on the back of the map of Madrid and the provocation of the suitcase left in the Girona bookshop. He underscored the political motives of the trial. He recounted the history of the P.O.U.M. and the political biographies of the accused: David Rey, the only one aged over forty years, who had spent thirty years as a militant, including eleven in jail; Gorkín and Andrade, founders of the Communist Party in Spain; Bonet, an old trade unionist and founder of the Catalan-Balearic Communist Federation; Arquer, founder of the Partit

Comunista de Catalunya; Gironella, a trade union organizer among the teachers, implicated in the republican rising at Jaca in 1930. Could these be agents of fascism, or spies? He spent five hours analyzing the trial.

Only the verdict remained.

The Verdict

It took several days before the verdict was returned.

When it came, it was dated October 20, but another three days went by before the results were given to the public. Probably that period had seen gestures and pressures, but the judges remained firm. Their decision had not been an easy one. They were part of a political tribunal—one that could be nothing else, in a civil war—and, at the same time, a civil court. None of the accusations had been proven. But to free the accused was the same as allowing the communists to liquidate them and then say they had fled to Berlin, so the government would find itself, anew, in an embarrassing situation, as with the case of Nin. The best was to find them guilty, but supporting them on the issue that for them was basic: their integrity as revolutionaries.

The verdict, which was very long, affirmed among other things that the May events were provoked by the attempts by the Generalitat to take over the Telefónica, and that there was no proof that the accused had provided news of any kind to the fascists. On the contrary, the judicial panel found that their antifascism was well-known and intense and that their only motives in May or at any other time had been to set up a regime based on their social program. They were found guilty of one offense: "rebellion against the constituted government."

The P.O.U.M. and J.C.I. were both legally dissolved. Gorkin, Andrade, Bonet, and Gironella were sentenced to fifteen years imprisonment; Arquer received eleven years, since he had been away from Barcelona in May 1937; David Rey and Escuder were cleared.

As we can see, Barcelona was not Moscow. The Spanish judges had proven more vigilant than those in the Soviet Union of which "L'Humanité" spoke, because they had not submitted to the government. Politically, the trial had been worse for the Soviet secret police and its accomplices than for the P.O.U.M.; it showed that once such proceedings were submitted to the daylight of a court in a Western country, they could not hold up. The accused had gained what they most wanted: Not only were their lives saved, but the political personality of the P.O.U.M. as a Marxist, non-Trotskyist revolutionary party was intact. They had an opportunity denied to those Russian revolutionaries faced with the Stalinist terror—to undercut the trials staged by Stalin's agents, who corrupted and dishonored the international workers' movement. And they had not failed to take the opportunity.

The P.O.U.M. defendants refused to sign a petition asking for a reprieve, as had been suggested by their defense attorney on the prompting of the justice minister, the president of the supreme court, and the head of the Special Tribunal. As soon as this decision by the defendants became known, various individuals, on the initiative, apparently, of Companys, asked the government for a revision of the verdict. This petition was signed by the Generalitat president, the mayor of Barcelona, six former ministers and other political figures.

The petition for a rehearing went unanswered. The government did not dare to defy the communists, who persisted in their campaign. The readers of the C.N.T. and republican press learned of the verdict, but not those who read the Negrín-controlled socialist papers or the communist organs. "L'Humanité" reported that "when the prosecuting attorney asked the accused Gironella if he was a Franco spy, he paled and with trembling voice and eyes cast down confessed that it was true."

In these lines only one thing was true: the prosecutor had asked Gironella if he was a spy. His answer was to break out laughing and to offer this sarcastic confession: "Yes, in effect, I am a spy for Franco, Mussolini, Hitler, the pope, and the Moroccan leader Musa."[57]

The C.N.T. journals, to the extent they could under censorship, gave wide coverage to the case. Joan Peiró, after the trial, wrote a note about it whose publication was not permitted, because it could "poison relations" (a pretext that was not applied to the communist press). He said, among other things:

> The stigma of spies and traitors has not marred the reputations of the P.O.U.M. leaders or led to the Stalinists' being able to obtain the definitive death of their adversaries. The verdict conflicts with this aim and, further, makes clear the cowardice of the false accusers . . .

> If republican justice has moved, it is because the communist 'orthodox' have pushed it with scandal and tricks; and if they rejoice in the treatment of the P.O.U.M., they will not dare with the confederal and F.A.I. militants . . .

> Either way, an iniquity has been committed for which, on a day not far off, the people will demand an accounting.

> As they will demand an accounting regarding the death of Andreu Nin.[56]

It could be justly said that the demand for an accounting of which Peiró wrote has remained an active one since the time of the verdict. Certainly, such a demand is implicit in many of the best books written about the Spanish Civil War, beginning with Orwell's *Homage to Catalonia*, and as we have noted, the martyrdom of Nin continues to haunt the Spanish communists. An "official" call for clarification of the P.O.U.M. case and, in particular, the death of Nin, was issued in June 1987, on the fiftieth anniversary of his arrest, by a hundred former P.O.U.M. members, in a letter addressed to Soviet party leader Mikhail Gorbachev. A copy of this letter was taken to Moscow by Anna Balletbó, a socialist Cortes deputy for Barcelona, on the occasion of an international congress on women, held in the Soviet capital.

Perhaps the best commentary on this sinister chapter of history was provided by an old militant, in 1943, in the Model Prison in Barcelona, when he said to Víctor Alba that, according to Stalin, Hitler had agents much better placed than the P.O.U.M. for gaining information: General Berzin, the consul Antonov, ambassador Rosenberg, the journalist Koltsov and the economist Stashevsky were all executed in Moscow as Nazi agents. With these informants, why should Franco have needed the P.O.U.M.?

Toward the Future

The war agonized to an end. While the judges in the P.O.U.M. trial were writing their verdict, the volunteers from the International Brigades were being withdrawn from Spain, a second step, after the battle of the Ebro, in the Soviet plan to debilitate the republican army, ending the war and leading to a Moscow-Berlin rapprochement. On November 17, 1938, the republican forces retired from their positions west of the Ebro. A general mobilization was decreed. The P.O.U.M. prisoners wrote to the government and the antifascist organizations: "It is criminal that in these moments we should be kept immobile in a prison. We demand freedom to fight."

There was no answer, or, put better, the answer came when the communist police arrested all the P.O.U.M. members it could find, including those who had been freed by judicial orders and, even, the widow and two daughters of Nin. They were locked up in the *chekas*. As the communists saw the war was lost, they dedicated all their time and energy to their obsession: keeping the P.O.U.M. in Barcelona and leaving the Franco forces the task, which they had not been able to complete, of eliminating them.

The underground P.O.U.M. organization, in these last weeks, dedicated itself to two things: circulating the news of the verdict to the widest possible audience and trying to avoid letting the arrested P.O.U.M. members be caught in the trap when, as everyone knew it must, the moment to leave Spain finally came.

During these days of anguish, they had been cheered not only by the verdict, but also by the news from Paris. There the Committee to Defend the Spanish Revolution had gained the support of the anarchist International Antifascist Solidarity organization (S.I.A.), which covered the walls of the city with enormous posters: "Another Moscow Trial in Barcelona."

But everything became insignificant in the panicked atmosphere after Christmas 1938, when the Franco forces began their Catalan offensive and broke through the front.

One month later, they entered Barcelona. In the prisons they found no P.O.U.M. members, as the communists would have wished. On January 23, the fascist prisoners in the state prison had been allowed to leave and had hidden in the foreign embassies. On the 24th, the warden and assistant warden of the prison disappeared. The P.O.U.M. prisoners decided that the next day, if they were not moved elsewhere, they would try to escape.

The prison guards were found in a truck, preparing to save themselves, and the P.O.U.M. prisoners made them remove their luggage and take them along.

Everywhere P.O.U.M. members were imprisoned, groups of party members surrounded the jails and succeeded in gaining liberty for the antifascist prisoners. Thanks to them, the communist attempt to keep the P.O.U.M. members imprisoned failed.

On January 29, the group of imprisoned executive members, after wandering from city to city, got to Agullana, on the French border. The prison warden, who had reappeared, advised them to flee, but they did not allow him to leave, since he was their best security against the danger of communists finding and murdering them. They themselves began searching for a suitable building to use as a prison. Finally, the warden fled once more, leaving on the table a briefcase with the documents in his care. The prisoners took advantage of the situation to write out orders for their release. Early the next morning, they were in France.

Three days later, the P.O.U.M. executive committee held the first of many meetings in Paris.

Here this history ends.

Beginning February 4, 1939, the P.O.U.M. faced the same situation as the members of the other antifascist organizations: They were put in French concentration camps, they participated in the anti-Franco opposition in Spain and in the French resistance, they were sent to Nazi concentration camps, they died at the hands of the fascists, and, later, at the end of the Second World War those of the Communists. In the late 1940s, they divided into two groups, one of which kept the name of the P.O.U.M., and the other adopting the name of the Socialist Movement of Catalunya (Moviment Socialista de Catalunya). Eventually, the latter joined the Spanish Socialist Party. The history of the P.O.U.M. in the anti-Franco underground has been told in recent historical works.[59]

What we have narrated here is the history of a party that tried to be Marxist in an atmosphere reformist on the one hand and anarchist on the other, a party that gave all its members a reason to live (and many of them a reason to die), that often swam against the stream, that was always in a minority, and that never lost its self-respect, through correct and incorrect decisions.

The drama of the P.O.U.M. was a personal tragedy for many people in the Spanish and international workers' movement. But regardless of this, the authors of this work can sincerely say of it exactly what Orwell affirmed about his experience in Spain:

"When you have had a glimpse of such a disaster as this . . . the result is not necessarily disillusion and cynicism. Curiously enough, the whole experience has left me with not less but more belief in the decency of human beings."[60]

Notes

1. This text is to be found in Andreu Nin, *Los problemas de la revolucion Española,* pp. 217-ff.
2. See Victor Serge, *Birth of Our Power,* New York, 1967, and *Memoirs of a Revolutionary,* Oxford, 1963.
3. Gorkín, *Canibales politicos,* p. 89.
4. Guy Hermet, *Les Communistes en Espagne,* Paris, 1971, p. 46.
5. Valuable information on Soviet and East European veterans of the war in Spain is provided in Soviet War Veterans Committee, *International Solidarity With the Spanish Republic,* Moscow, 1975. On Gerö, see Jaume Miravitlles, "The Man Who Denounced Antonov-Ovsyeyenko," "The New Leader" (New York), August 6, 1956, as well as Branko Lazitch, *Biographical Dictionary of the Comintern,* p. 137-138.
6. An important document on Aleksandr Orlov is a letter from Bertram D. Wolfe to the "Slavic Review" (New York), June 1969. Also see Cyrille Henkine (Kirill Henkin) *L'Espionnage Sovietique: le cas Rudolf Abel,* Paris, 1981, for a strong argument against the credibility of Orlov's defection.
7. Walter Krivitsky, *In Stalin's Secret Service,* New York, 1939, pp. 101-102.
8. Raymond Carr, *España 1808-1939,* Barcelona, 1969, p. 634.
9. On the case of Joaquím Olaso, see "La Mort Troublante de Joaquím Olaso Piera et Dolores Garcia Echevarieta," in "B.E.I.P.I." (Paris), July 1-15, 1954.
10. For Carrillo's statement, see Santiago Carrillo, *Eurocommunism and the State,* Westport, 1978. Also see Rafael Vidiella, "La Generalitat Fué Maniatado," in "Historia," April 1977, and comments of Gregori López Raimundo in A. Gavilan, "El Maig Sagnant de 1937," in "Avui" (Barcelona), Sunday Supplement, May 3, 1987.
11. See "El Noticiero Universal" (Barcelona), April 23, 1974, and Teresa Pamies, *Quan Erem Capitans,* Barcelona, 1974, pp. 70-71.
12. See P.S., "No vivimos solo de verdades, dice Vargas Uosa," "El Pais" (Madrid) June 18, 1987, and Xavier Domingo, "El líder del P.S.U.C. reabilita a Nin," in "Cambio 16," August 3, 1987.

13. Jean Rous, *La Révolution Assassinée,* Paris, 1938, passim.
14. There is a considerable literature on the Zborowski case. See Isaac Deutscher, *The Prophet Outcast,* Oxford, 1957, *passim.* Also, *passim,* Elisabeth K. Poretsky, *Our Own People,* London, 1969 (by the widow of Ignace Reiss), Gerard Rosenthal, *Avocat de Trotsky,* Paris, 1975, and Georges Vereecken, *The G.P.U. in the Trotskyist Movement,* London, 1976, by a leader of the pro-P.O.U.M. Trotskyists in Belgium. Further, Stephen Schwartz, "Intellectuals and Assassins," "The New York Times Book Review," January 24, 1988.
15. Munis, op. cit., pp. 61-66.
16. Trotsky, op. cit., *passim.*
17. Gorkín, op. cit., p. 98-99.
18. See "Informe del Comite Regional de Levante del P.O.U.M. sobre la represión llevada a cabo contra dirigentes y secciones del Partido," undated typescript in Servicio Historico Militar, "Documentacion Roja," Madrid. Copy provided by Burnett Bolloten.
19. Herbert L. Matthews, *A World in Revolution,* New York, 1971, p. 44.
20. Manuel Tuñón de Lara, op.cit., p. 547, reproduces this phrase without giving a source.
21. Gorkín, op. cit., p. 130.
22. Information on Lev Narvich has been derived from the following sources: Narcís Molins i Fàbrega, conversations with Víctor Alba; Gorkín, op. cit.; "J.A." "L'Affaire Léon Narvich," in "Cahiers Léon Trotsky," July-September 1979, Jose Luis Alcofa Nassaes, *Los asesores sovieticos en la guerra civil Esñola,* Barcelona, 1971, p. 136; Munis, op. cit., p. 217, and conversations with Stephen Schwartz; Henkine, op. cit. p. 243. In addition, Stephen Schwartz wishes to thank Pierre Broué and Reiner Tosstorff for special help in investigating the Narvich case, as well as Professor Simon Karlinsky of the University of California, on Kirill Henkin.
23. On the repressions in the International Brigades, see, in particular, Cecil Eby, *Between the Bullet and the Lie,* New York, 1969, *passim*; William Herrick, interview, in Paul Berman, "Spanish Betrayals," "The Village Voice" (New York), July 22, 1986, and Schwartz, *Brotherhood of the Sea,* pp. 123-24. On the persecution of the P.O.U.M., see Katia Landau, *Les Staliniens en Espagne,* Paris, 1938; Rolf Reventlow, *Spanien In Diesem Jahrhundert,* Frankfurt, 1970, and Marcel Ollivier, *La G.P.U. a Barcelone,* Paris, 1937.
24. For more information on Kulcsar, see Landau, ibid., p. 40, as well as Hans Schafranek, "Kurt Landau," in "Cahiers Léon Trotsky," January-March 1980. The treatment of the arrested women is also discussed in the narrative of Lois Cusick, for which see chapter 7 of the present work.
25. The report on the investigation is discussed in detail in José Peirats, *Anarchists in the Spanish Revolution,* Toronto, n.d., pp. 313-14.
26. Pamphlet editions of the two reports of the delegations appeared in Paris and London; in addition, the documents plus extracts from the communist press may be found in Lazarillo de Tormes, *España, cuña de la libertad,* Valencia, 1937, pp. 182 and ff.
27. The report of the third delegation was also published as a pamphlet in Paris and London, and was utilized by McGovern in writing his short book on the P.O.U.M., *Terror in Spain,* London, 1938. The full text of the report appears in Rudolf Rocker, *Extranjeros en España,* Buenos Aires, 1938, pp. 145 and ff.
28. Claudio Sánchez Albornoz, *De mi anecdotario político.* Buenos Aires, 1972, p. 150.

29. For further information on the impact of the P.O.U.M. case in the United States, see Allen Guttmann, *The Wound in the Heart,* New York, 1962, pp. 156 and ff.

30. An excerpt from this article and the commentaries it provoked from Gide, as well as Gide's correspondence with Jean Guéhenno on the same subject are to be found in André Gide, *Littérature Engagée,* Paris, 1950, pp. 194 and ff. Gide wanted to publish these remarks in the antifascist weekly "Vendredi" of which Guéhenno was the editor, but the latter refused and the documents were printed instead in "La Fleche."

31. Jaume Miravitlles, *Episodis de la Guerra Civil Espanyola,* Barcelona, 1972, pp. 188-189.

32. Verle B. Johnston, *Legions of Babel,* University Park, Pa., 1967, p. 187.

33. One of the statements by Nin to the police, a kind of autobiography, appears in Nin, *Los problemas de la revolución Española,* pp. 36 and ff. The statements were included in the evidence presented at the P.O.U.M. trial, and, during the twenty-four hours that defense counsel had access to them, they were copied by party militants, who later reproduced them.

34. Julián Zugazagoitia, *Guerra y vicisitudes de los españoles,* Paris, 1968, vol. I, pp. 219-ff. This book is the second edition of the one published in Buenos Aires a little after the end of the civil war under the title *Historia de la guerra de España.*

35. Azaña, *Memorias politicas y de guerra,* pp. 638, 692, 699, 700, 711, 746, 768, 828, and 831.

36. "La Fleche" (Paris), August 18, 1937.

37. Indalecio Prieto, *Como y por que sali del Ministerio de Defensa Nacional,* Mexico, 1940, p. 54.

38. Hernández, op. cit., pp. 263-ff.

39. Rafael Cid, "Que Pasó en Paracuellos?," in "Cambio 16" (Madrid), February 21, 1983.

40. Gorkín, op. cit., p. 248. It is worth noting that an activist in Russian secret police work in both Spain and France was the sinister Leonid Eitingon ("General Kotov" in Spain), who organized the assassination of Trotsky in Mexico in 1940. See Schwartz, "Intellectuals and Assassins," op cit.

41. Quoted in Jacinto Toryho, *La Independencia de Espana,* Barcelona, 1938, pp. 226-227.

42. See unsigned, "Stalinism (Red Fascism) Grows Fat on Dead Bodies of Sailors," in "West Coast Sailors" (San Francisco), December 23, 1938, published by the Sailors' Union of the Pacific; see Schwartz, *Brotherhood of the Sea,* passim. There is a strong probability this article was written by Ralph Chaplin, the American anarchist poet and author of the words to the labor hymn "Solidarity Forever."

43. Munis, op. cit., p. 385.

44. "Treball" (Barcelona), July 24, 1937.

45. Rudolf Rocker, op. cit., pp. 155-56.

46. Julian Zugazagoitia, op. cit., vol. I, p. 108.

47. Arturo Barea, *La forja de un rebelde,* Buenos Aires, 1951, p. 769.

48. For discussion of the 1937 writers' congress, see Jef Last, "Noble Pages in History's Book," in Valentine Cunningham, *Spanish Front,* Oxford, 1986, as well as Ronald Radosh, "'But Today the Struggle': Spain and the Intellectuals," "The New Criterion" (New York), October 1986, and Ricard Blasco, "El Segon

Congrés Internacional d'Escriptors," "Revista de Catalunya" (Barcelona), May 1987.
49. See *Documentos sobre la industria de guerra en cataluña,* Buenos Aires, 1939.
50. Claudín, op. cit., p. 234-235.
51. Hugh Thomas, *The Spanish Civil War,* London, 1961, p. 452.
52. Clara and Pavel Thalmann, *Revolution Fur Die Freiheit,* Hamburg, 1977, pp. 254-256.
53. Gorkín, op. cit., p. 260.
54. Gorkín, ibid, pp. 265-266. Luis Araquistain confirmed this attitude of Negrín verbally and in an article (see "Carta de Luis Araquistáin a Norman Thomas," in "La Batalla" (Paris), October 20, 1945.)
55. See Indalecio Prieto, article in "El Socialista" (Toulouse), February 1957.
56. Jaume Miravitlles recounts (*Episodis de la Guerra Civil Espanyola,* p. 183), a fact that shows how far the Negrín regime was willing to go to gain a guilty verdict against the accused. Miravitlles was in Paris when the trial began. Companys telephoned him and asked him to return to make a declaration for the defense. He could not do it, so he went to the Republican embassy in Paris and dictated the text of his declaration, so that it would be sent to the court through the Ministry of Foreign Relations, but the document was never received by the judges.
57. Ibid, p. 184.
58. Joan Peiró, *Problemas y cintarazos,* Rennes (France), p. 191-ff.
59. See Víctor Alba, *Historia de la resistencia antifranquista* (1939-1955), Barcelona, 1978 and Carme Molinero and Pere Ysas, *L'Oposició Antifeixista a Catalunya (1939-1950),* Barcelona, 1981.
60. Orwell, op. cit., p. 220.

7

Orwell and Others: Foreigners and the P.O.U.M.

Stephen Schwartz

The name of the English writer George Orwell is inextricably linked with the history of the P.O.U.M. His service in the party militia was a central experience of his life, if not, indeed, the single most important for his development as a writer and social theorist. His *Homage to Catalonia* is considered by some to be the most significant political work in English in this century. It is no exaggeration, to say, further, that were it not for Orwell's account of the fate of the party and of the events of May 1937, the events themselves, most probably, and the P.O.U.M., certainly, would be largely forgotten outside Spain today.

Of course, Orwell was not the only foreign writer to involve himself in the activities of the Bloc and the P.O.U.M. The first was probably the previously-mentioned French surrealist, René Crevel, who participated in Bloc cultural events. Pride of place as the first English-speaking writer to publish on the P.O.U.M. belongs not to Orwell but to another English intellectual, and, later, eminent scholar of Buddhism, Edward Conze. Years before distinguishing himself as a translator of such classic Buddhist texts as the *Heart Sutra* and many other Pali, Sanskrit, and other writings, Conze maintained a friendship with Maurín that culminated in a short book of observations, useful for gauging the atmosphere in Spain directly before the civil war, titled *Spain Today* and published in London within weeks of the war's beginning in 1936. However, Conze's Spanish work seems to have enjoyed little success, and is largely unknown to scholars of the civil war. Conze taught for many years at Oxford, London, and other universities. He died in 1979.

The same obscurity that closed over Conze's book claimed Mary Low and Juan Breá's *Red Spanish Notebook,* which we will discuss further along. Indeed, in hindsight it seems nothing short of miraculous that other works sympathetic to the P.O.U.M., such as those of Gerald Brenan and Franz Borkenau, did not suffer a similar fate; although undoubtedly these latter writers' continuing interest in the subject and their prominence in later life played a role in rescuing their Spanish war books. In the case of Orwell, it is a commonplace of his biographers to note that *Homage to Catalonia* was originally read by few and bought by fewer.

This early "failure" of the book was undoubtedly inherent in its character as a great document of moral protest as well as the unpopularity of its basic subject, the P.O.U.M., in Anglo-Saxon "liberal" circles. For *Homage to Catalonia* is a good deal more than a lucidly and elegantly written account of a sensitive intellectual's encounter with war and revolution; it is also a unique warning against the rise of totalitarian thinking in the West.

Orwell's dedicated effort to reconstruct and dispassionately examine the "May events" has a remarkable similarity to the case of Émile Zola in his intervention into the frameup of Captain Dreyfus; chiefly, in the obvious flimsiness of the evidence against both the Jewish officer, and, forty years later, a despised revolutionary minority. But among the differences there is one very depressing one: Zola's act relatively quickly mobilized a much more considerable sector of the political public than Orwell's. By the 1930s, the Left was already too totalitarianized, under the influence of the People's Front, to rally to the P.O.U.M. The ambivalent reaction of the international Left and its intelligentsia to Stalinism is no better expressed than by the hesitation, when not hostility, of the P.O.U.M.'s treatment by historians outside Catalunya in the decades immediately after the civil war. It was not so long ago that Hugh Thomas delivered himself of the opinion that *Homage* is "more accurate about war itself than about the Spanish war," a statement breathtaking in its disingenuousness.

Because it is a protest against, above all, Stalinism, *Homage* is often considered as a book about breaking with the Left; but, in reality, it expresses a point of view that was and is as distasteful to the Right as to the Left in showing the fundamental humanity of revolutionary movement, particularly the most extreme elements, P.O.U.M. members and anarchists.

It has been largely forgotten today that at the time of the book's publication this opinion was as scandalous to conservative society as Orwell's anti-Stalinism was to the Left. Jejune critics from today's hyper-Stalinist British Left (about which more below) have attacked the book's title, saying that the text "is not about Catalonia." They have apparently never heard that at the time of the book's writing Catalonia was on the front pages of daily papers around the world, not because of its ancient culture and its artistic and literary achievements, but as a kind of hell on earth ruled by criminal demons, in which the public roasting of nuns, etc., was supposed to be commonplace, and in which the wearing of neckties was undertaken at the risk of one's life. (With regard to the latter cliché, although Orwell is correct in noting that the great mass of men in revolutionary Barcelona did not wear ties, there are many photographs of prominent anarchist, P.O.U.M., and other leaders, some of them quite irreconcilable, wearing the offending item.)

That Orwell's moral protest in the name of a difficult truth remains a source of dismay for the Left—the Right has largely forgotten the Spanish Civil War—is shown by a recent volume of anti-Orwell musings edited by Christopher Norris, a literary ideologue of the "post-modernist" kind whose works are probably in every university library in the United States. Significantly, this book titled *Inside the Myth,* is published by Lawrence and Wishart, the official publishing house of the British Communist Party. In it, some rather elaborate academic huffing and puffing produces little more than the charge that the book contains errors. That it does, as Orwell himself warned his readers; however, the errors in Orwell are considerably fewer than in the great bulk of other contemporary accounts, including Borkenau and Brenan. Sadly, such critics never seem to do any spadework outside their own gardens: thus it must seem strange and outlandish to them that *Homage to Catalonia* has, in the period since the 1950s, been unreservedly accepted by Catalana and other Iberian historians, not an easy group with which to pass muster, as the best account of the "May events" and the fate of the P.O.U.M.; it has, as well, been acclaimed as a basic work on the overall civil war. Also, there are today various other eyewitness accounts, including those from P.S.U.C. members, such as Rafael Vidiella, that Orwell's critics would do well to correlate with their adversary's version—except that this would force them to abandon their prejudices.

Valentine Cunningham, in introducing a recent anthology of writings on the civil war, *Spanish Front,* notes that a major attack on Orwell has come from another direction, out of the mouth of the Nobel laureate novelist, Claude Simon, a pioneer of the French "new novel."

Simon, who fought in Spain in the ranks of the Stalinists, has made his memories of the civil war a subject in several of his novels (such as *Le Palace*), and in his most recent work, considered his most important, *Les Géorgiques*, he has incorporated Orwell and his trajectory in Aragon and Barcelona into his own narrative, subsuming the action of *Homage to Catalonia* into his fiction.

It is not enough, however, for M. Simon to appropriate the work of another for his own literary needs; he has also defamed him, M. Simon's most gentlemanly pronouncement on *Homage* is that it is "faked," whatever that means. M. Simon complains that in Orwell's account the street fighting in Barcelona is incomprehensible. It is certainly true that Orwell's account of revolutionary Barcelona lacks the sectarian self-consciousness present in most leftist works of the time—indeed, Orwell's main concerns in the book palpably included that of reconstructing his own state of mind and his slow coming to full awareness about the nature of Stalinism and its role in the Spanish struggle. *Homage* is not an easy book to immediately grasp in its fullness. But everything we know of its author's life before his arrival in Spain shows that his self-description as, at that time, little more than a naive antifascist, is a truthful one. He was no Borkenau, and not by any means a Mary Low. But in the end this very nonpoliticism was, clearly, a virtue, for it allowed him to tell an objective and truthful tale, largely uncomplicated by matters of doctrinal theory of the kind that led other observers to confuse the communist attack on the revolution with "capitulation to the bourgeoisie." Orwell saw unequivocally that the communists aimed at power alone, and he further perceived a truth that has escaped many if not most commentators even today: that the old morality of the labor and socialist movements had given way to a new and sinister one.

However, it is one of the gratifications of Orwell as a historical subject that his case needs little argument. In the past three decades, *Homage to Catalonia* has risen to the status of a genuine classic. In that, Orwell has done better than Zola; while the latter called more people to his side in the short term, his declarations in defense of Captain Dreyfus today go unread. By contrast, Orwell's *Homage* has attained a permanence that will probably be granted no other political work of this century. And for every Claude Simon, seizing upon Orwell in an effort to destroy him, there are writers like the Spanish novelist Juan Marsé, whose *Si te dicen que caí* (*The Fallen*) is widely considered the best fictional work on the effects of the civil war on Spain; in it also Orwell appears.

Finally, a word should be said about Orwell's narrative in the context of the attention given by today's historians to daily life during the Spanish Civil War.

In trying to understand daily life in Barcelona during the Spanish Civil War, we have many resources. Each of the Left parties published newspapers, magazines, bulletins, and other printed sources. In addition, many participants and observers, both Iberian and foreign, have contributed narratives. Although most of the foreigners suffered from ignorance of the Spanish background of the 1936-39 war (including Orwell), with their fresh perspectives, their broad insights, and their special political education they often set down details of their own and others' experience that might otherwise have passed unrecorded.

Orwell, in his *Hòmage*, begins his account with an evocation of revolutionary Barcelona in the period just after his arrival. Although months had passed since the convulsion of July 1936, Orwell noted that the aspect of the city was clearly that of one where "the working class was in the saddle." Revolutionary posters, slogans, ballads, and other immediate indicators contributed to an impression that was fortified by the dress of the urban masses and their very habits of speech. Hats and neckties were rare, while words like *Don* had disappeared, the familiar form *tú* was on everyone's lips, and words with a religious connotation such as *adios* (*adéu* in Catalan) were replaced by neutral greetings such as *salud*.

Further, at the point in his book where Orwell begins to outline his unease with the decline of the revolutionary impulse, he presents evidence derived from daily life: the reappearance of fashionable women's clothing and the availability of gourmet meals to those with money—a situation where, to paraphrase Orwell, fat men feasted on quails while children begged in the streets for bread. Indeed, throughout Orwell's book, a fundamental concern is his awareness that propaganda, particularly that of the press, and political guidelines, as put forward by the competing leftist parties, are much less faithful sources of truth than one's own eyes and ears, given common sense and the ability, therefore, to understand one's daily life experience. (In a way, Orwell reaffirms the wisdom of the Greek pre-Socratic philosopher Herakleitos, whose fragments include the statement that "eyes and ears are untrustworthy witnesses for men, if they are unprepared to understand.")

An appeal to the verities of common sense in daily life is an implicit element in much writing about the Spanish conflict by unorthodox supporters of the republic's struggle, Marxists or otherwise, who found themselves obligated to combat the increasing influence of Soviet-molded propaganda on world opinion. The same insistence on the value of direct witness is to be found in Borkenau, in Gerald Brenan's *The Spanish Labyrinth,* and, above all, the great masterpiece of Spanish Civil War history, Burnett Bolloten's *The Spanish Revolution*.

One can link this moral conception of historical truth with the "critical-revolutionary" tendency that, in combination with a healthy dose of sentimentalism, makes the Spanish anarchist historians so vivid and concerned with detail: but also, with methodological principles derived from historians like Jules Michelet, and with an overall ethical vision of the writer's role, as expressed in Orwell's fine essay "Politics and the English Language." But, perhaps as a matter of course, daily life in revolutionary Spain receives much more comparative attention from Orwell, a volunteer soldier, in regard to specifics and details, then from Borkenau, Brenan, or Bolloten, all in Spain as writers or journalists.

Mika Etchebehere: Woman Commander at Madrid

Although one should not belabor the point, the Spanish Civil War, more than any other in this century, could be called a "women's war." Images of women with rifles in the streets of Spain inspired independent-minded women around the world, through the medium of the newsreel. Women played a prominent role as symbols of the leftist parties—the Stalinist icon Dolores Ibárruri ("La Pasionaria") has as her positive counterpart the anarchist leader Federica Montseny. In addition, the anarchist Grouping of Free Women played an outstanding role as a force for social reform during the war.

Mika Etchebehere is a special example of the revolutionary woman as she existed in the ranks of the P.O.U.M. militia. Born in Argentina, while still little more than a teenager she had come to Europe in the company of an Argentine man of French citizenship, Hipólito Etchebehere. They considered themselves Trotskyists; Mika sold the leftist paper "Qué Faire?" in the toughest streets of Paris. Their closest friends were Alfred and Marguerite Rosmer and Kurt and Katia Landau, all of whom, with Nin, had been driven away from the official Trotskyist movement by the sectarian suspicions of Trotsky himself.

Mika and Hipólito arrived in Madrid only a few days before the coup attempt in July 1936. With the beginning of fighting, they immediately enlisted in the P.O.U.M. militia and went to the nearby front. There, Hipólito Etchebehere became column commander and was killed; Mika took his place in the front lines, rising to the rank of commander. This woman who, only months before, had come to Spain very young, became a heroine of the Madrid front. In the terrible fighting at Siguenza, when the town was retaken by the fascists after nearly a week of desperate combat, including German bombardment, Mika Etchebehere led the defense from the town's barricaded church; finally, after great losses on the antifascist side, there was no choice but to retreat from the town. Mika and the other survivors made their way to safety over a further twenty-four hours of mad, confused flight, harried by fascist bullets and thick fog.

Because Mika Etchebehere, as a militia commander, was always in the front lines, exposed to the greatest danger, it is not surprising that she was reported for dead in *Red Spanish Notebook*, by Mary Low and Juan Breá. But Mika was not killed. She remained hidden in Spain for several months after the fall of the republic, making her way to France, where she has lived since then. In 1976, a Parisian publisher brought out her magnificent memoir, *Ma Guerre D'Espagne a Moi,* an inspiring document that is an important testament to the spirit of the P.O.U.M., and an extremely valuable account of P.O.U.M. participation in the defense of Madrid.

It was Mika Etchebehere who arranged for Kurt and Katia Landau to come to Spain, where a tragic fate awaited them. It is also Mika Etchebehere whose memoirs note that the communist unit at Madrid, named after "La Pasionaria," refused to allow women to take arms, keeping them behind the lines for cooking and laundry duties![1]

Katia (Julia) Landau

Katia Landau is mainly known because she carried out the political work her disappeared companion Kurt was prevented from completing. Having led a hunger strike in the *chekas,* once she had left Spain for France she dedicated herself to the difficult work of finding press and other outlets in which to defend the P.O.U.M. against the Stalinist frame-up. The most important contribution from her hand was, undoubtedly, the pamphlet *Les Staliniens en Espagne*, published in Paris in 1938.

One of the most interesting aspects of the P.O.U.M.'s history is the phenomenon of the "revolutionary couple" as exemplified by many foreign militants, such as Hipólito and Mika Etchebehere, Kurt and Katia Landau, Mary Low and Juan Breá, Lois Cusick and Charles Orr, and Pavel Thalmann and Clara Ensner. Within such relationships there was a real commitment to strict equality of man and woman. From them emerged a creative or constructive work that cannot be said to represent an effort of either partner alone, but which was truly a product of both. In the cases of Mika Etchebehere and Katia Landau, the female members of the couple, left alone by the death or disappearance of the other, took on the full burden of the other's mission—Mika's in the military field and Katia's in politics—with a strength and courage that fulfilled the faith on which their relationship with the other was based. The same may be said of Jeanne Maurín and Olga Nin.

Mary Low [2]

Mary Low's book, written in collaboration with a Cuban Trotskyist, Juan Breá, and titled *Red Spanish Notebook,* was first published in London in 1937, by Martin Secker and Warburg, who also issued Orwell's *Homage.* The book features an undeniably feminist organizational principle that even today is somewhat novel: each of the chapters is designated as to whether it was written by her or by Breá, her companion. This allows the authors to escape the stigma of a subordination of the female that might one day be called "sexism," but also provides a useful means for the later analyst to trace the thoughts of each participant in the collaboration.

In the *Red Spanish Notebook,* Mary Low's chapters show many aspects that distinguish her discourse from that of Breá, although one would be wary of assigning a feminist content to these textual components. Perhaps it is because she was an Anglo-Saxon, unlike the Spanish-speaking Breá, that she concerns herself as a writer with the immediate impressions of a new environment in a way that would be considered typical of the travelers' genre were the book not put under the sign of revolution. The first chapter, titled "Journey There," bears the caption "(Narrative by Mary Low)," and the remaining ten chapters signed by her, out of a total of eighteen, all record daily life, with titles like "Round the Town," "Communal Life," A Meeting at the Grand Price Theatre," "Women . . . ," and "The Changing Aspect."

The eight chapters signed by Juan Breá (none are co-signed) focus, by contrast, on military and political topics. It is an irony that, while this division of responsibilities might logically be considered a product of what we today call "sexism"—in which the role of a woman is that of sub-mergence in daily life and superficial impressions, with the man assigned the "serious" topics—the effective consequence of "discrimination" in this instance is to preserve, for today's historians, a much more valuable record from the woman's pen than from the man's. For, ultimately, the truths to be mined from a veridical account of daily life are always fresh and useful, while the facts of war and the arguments of politics are accessible to all, to the point of satiety.

Mary Low's narrative occasionally falls into a sentimental mode that might be labeled, unfairly, "feminine," but in the main her contributions to the book provide important details, concrete and surprisingly objective, that are present nowhere else. During her stay in revolutionary Barcelona Low worked on *Spanish Revolution,* the English-language P.O.U.M. bul-letin, as well as in the Propaganda Commissariat of the Generalitat under Jaume Miravitlles, with an office in the Generalitat Palace on the plaça San Jaume. For this reason alone, given the relative paucity of documentation of the internal life of the extremist movements during the war, the work of Mary Low has great value apart from its intrinsic characteristics, be they artistic, psychological, or feminist.

One of the most interesting chapters by Mary Low is that titled "A Meeting at the Grand Price Theatre." The meeting in question was a rally of the P.O.U.M., with a speech by Andreu Nin, the leader of the party in the absence of its imprisoned cofounder and more important founding leader, Joaquím Maurín. Hers is one of the few primary source accounts we shall ever have of Nin and his ability to influence (or not influence, in some cases) the Barcelona masses, as a political speechmaker.

"The balconies were crammed full of people," Low notes. A portrait of Lenin was present, without Trotsky, but also without Stalin. "Over all, the red light poured down like continuous rain."

The spectators included militiamen, militiawomen, children, peasants. "It was a very responsive audience. The moment any of the speakers touched on some constructive measure to which the party was feeling its way, the listeners replied with cheers and loud, excited cries. There was hand-clapping and fists were raised. Anything really revolutionary which was said earned violent applause."

Low described Nin as "speak[ing] like a plain man . . . [without] embroidered phrases . . . He goes through one thing after another point by point, and hammers each of them into you, and the effect comes from the simplicity and the sureness . . . The people react strongly . . . The vast majority . . . responded to him as a single man. [Nin spoke] with his face turned passionately toward us while the light beat down in torrents upon him; his gaze was so intent that he scarcely blinked."

More important, perhaps, than her accounts of Nin and other figures in the P.O.U.M., are the chapters in her book on "Women . . ." and "The Changing Aspect." The chapter on women includes a description of some German volunteer nurses, one of them "under the thumb of a thick German man, with a squashed nose and hairy hands, who had done great deeds at the front . . . He wouldn't let her go back to the militia." Then, watching the column of P.O.U.M. volunteers, with "trumpets blowing . . . dust rising and the red flag fluttering," she could not resist. She was soon dead, on the Aragon front.

In the same chapter, Low further describes her discussions with the architects of revolutionary Catalunya's marriage and divorce law, then the most enlightened in the world (and largely drafted by Andreu Nin during his brief tenure as *conseller de justicia de la Generalitat*). The reader encounters the test of hypocrisy undergone by many of the Spanish revolutionaries of that time, for both among the *poumistes* and the anarchists there were many men who kept their wives at home, as before, or objected to the anarchist Free Women's campaign against prostitution, or obstructed women's military involvement in the struggle, while professing support for "the revolution that had restored [women] to their natural place in society and [which] would admit of no sex domination."

In her examination of Spain's "changing aspect," with the decline of the revolutionary impetus, the rise of the Muscovite Communists, and the politically defensive posture of the P.O.U.M. and anarchists, Low, like Orwell, found symptoms of decay in daily habits and mores.

"Nearly all the men were wearing ties again. The workman's overalls had largely disappeared off the streets. More and more, elegantly dressed women could be seen daily everywhere." Some wore furs, an affectation unimaginable in the period of the revolution's apogee. As in Orwell, we find that the militia costume has been replaced by a regular army uniform. But unlike Orwell, Low notices the reapparition of the *senyera*, the Catalan national flag, after months of Barcelona's domination by red and black banners. Also, fewer women join the men on the way to the front. And the first clues of the coming Stalinist repression are to be seen as well, although unlike Orwell (and Lois Cusick, as we shall see), Low left Spain before the purge began in earnest, and therefore, also unlike Orwell (and Cusick) was spared the experience of the *chekas* and prisons.

But even in the crucible of the counterrevolution, Low observed those elements of working class culture that gave the anarchists much of their great prestige with the Spanish masses and with others around the world. She describes how, following an alarming report of a fascist attack on the coast, "A small crowd was stationed in the center of the Ramblas. Ten minutes after the first alarm the lorries were roaring down on each side of the central avenue, the men standing up in them, packed tightly one against the other in their blanket coats, and the guns standing with their pointed profiles above their backs. They cheered as they went by, waving wildly, and the dark mass rocked and swayed.

"'F.A.I.! F.A.I.! C.N.T.!'

"We roared back at them."

Luckily, the 1937 edition of *Red Spanish Notebook,* which fell into obscurity although cited by other writers, including Orwell (who had high praise for it) and Borkenau (who was less enthusiastic), was not the last. In 1979, the book was reissued by City Lights Books, in San Francisco, with a new introduction from the pen of Eugenio Fernández Granell, a Galician musical prodigy and painter who was first a founder of Andreu Nin's Communist Opposition, one of the first Spanish Trotskyists to serve time in prison, and who in exile became a close confidante of Joaquim Maurín.

As Granell declares in this essay, which is itself an important restatement of such issues in the Spanish revolution as the conflict between the P.O.U.M. and Trotsky, "The present edition of *Red Spanish Notebook* . . . fills an enormous lacuna in the formidable biography of the civil war in Spain . . . Not only in being among those which began the historic recording of events, but because its eighteen chronicles offer an incomparably faithful vision of days which were believed would change the face of the world." To emphasize, this vision was not simply in advance of its time thanks to its rooting in daily life; but also, thanks to its pioneering feminism. While others who had encountered the book must have assumed, along with City Lights' editorial staff, that Mary Low was dead, she remains alive today, a vigorous and clear-minded woman who now spends her time between Miami (where she maintains a kind of "base" among Cuban anarchist exiles), and France, where she lectures on classic Roman and Gallic art.

Lois Cusick

There are many differences between Mary Low's account of revolution and war in Spain and that of Lois Cusick. To begin with, Low's was an immediate eyewitness testimony, while Cusick's manuscript, titled "The Anarchist Millenium, Memories of the Spanish Revolution, 1936-37," was composed some forty years later, finished in 1979, although based on an archive dating from the war, and including extensive original notes, accumulated between 1937 and 1942, and impregnated with a striking ring of truth.

Sadly, Lois Cusick died in the early 1980s, without her work seeing print. Even more unfortunately, after her death her important archive, including her manuscript, was disposed of casually and unwisely. Her memoirs came into the hands of the Hoover Institution virtually by accident, in the form of a xerocopy. At the present moment, very little in the way of biographical information about Lois Cusick may be confirmed. We know she was the companion of an American Trotskyist named Charles Orr and was known as Lois Orr during the 1930s. (The Charles Orr-Lois Orr archive was also utilized by Felix Morrow in the preparation of *Revolution and Counter-Revolution in Spain,* a book mainly remarkable for its Trotskyist biases.) And we know that she arrived in Spain on September 14, 1936 (Low had come in the final days of July; Orwell did not arrive until December.)

Cusick indicates a greater sympathy for the anarchists than for either the P.O.U.M., or the official Trotskyists. This contrasts strongly with Low, who, at the time, worked in the P.O.U.M. while also participating in the official Trotskyist group.

There are other points of contrast between the Low and Cusick narratives. Cusick's manuscript is extremely rich in details of daily life, to an even greater extent than Low; but Cusick concerns herself less with the women's movement in the revolutionary matrix. Perhaps most importantly, rather than a simple description and defense of the revolution in its early stages, Cusick produced an extended account of the destruction of the revolution through the influence of the Soviet Union, leading to the end of the "anarchist millenium." Cusick thus produced an important, extended historical polemic, vigorous and transparent.

Cusick's memoir begins with an evocation of the Cathar heretics' pilgrimages through the Pyrenees, comparing them to the revolutionary pilgrims that streamed across the Franco-Spanish border in the weeks after July 19, 1936. She provides extensive anecdotal material, describing in sharp relief her encounter with anarchist border militia who required proof of revolutionary reliability from every incoming visitor.

In one of the most interesting of her chapters, titled "Feeding the Revolution" Cusick begins, "Food was one of the first problems to which the revolution addressed itself. In the first chaotic and Glorious Days, the C.N.T.'s big three supply unions, Food, Transport, and Distribution, set up a supply committee in Barcelona. It opened canteens at the union and antifascist party headquarters to feed 120,000 people daily during the fighting . . . When we enrolled in the P.O.U.M. militia in September, 1936, the Supply Committee fed us. We lived gratis at the P.O.U.M.-confiscated Hotel Falcón . . . Every day trucks brought huge rounds of bread to the manager's office, to be stacked next to 100-kilo bags of potatoes and big wicker-covered bottles of Catalan red wine. The P.O.U.M. gave free meals to the wives and children of its militiamen at the front, to militia on leave in Barcelona, and those who worked in the rear as we did. The food was plain but good, soup, a stew or meat dish, salad, bread, and wine." She then provides an extensive discussion of the feeding of the republic through the three years of the war, and the relationship of the revolutionary forces with the peasants.

Nearly all the data Cusick present involves a melding of documentary citations with her own insights and observations, which are clear-sighted and vivid. The result is a fascinating panorama of how the revolution and the war came to affect the life of the mass of people. This is, I believe, a signal contribution to the emerging tradition of a historiography based on "working class culture."

In addition, because she, like Low, worked in the Generalitat propaganda office, Lois Cusick was able to observe from within the sequence of events that made up the transition from the apogee to the decline of the revolutionary impetus. She outlines intimately the process of strengthening of the guardia del asalto and other police bodies, the increasing influence of Soviet political operatives, and the attempts of the C.N.T. and other noncommunist forces to maneuver in response to these manipulations. Significantly, she centers her narrative, after a certain point, on the *tertulias* (café groups of friends), which she visited on a daily basis.

Describing the arrival of the first Russian supply ship in Barcelona, the *Ziryanin,* on October 15, 1936, Cusick writes:

> Suddenly the excitement and enthusiasm of July 19, raced through the *tertulias* with the news, 'We are not alone! Help has come!'

> Collectivized factory whistles all over town shrilled a half-holiday. Thousands of anarchists flooded the Ramblas and the port in disorderly masses, carrying their factories' somber black or *rojinegra* banners. The F.A.I.'s Free Women (Mujeres Libres) went down the Ramblas eight abreast, breaking all anarchist tradition by singing and shouting in their excitement. Usually anarchist parades achieved their effect by massing silent thousands of black-clad workers in an austere, serious or threatening manner. They dislike the gay color and

sound demonstrations of the 'carnival revolutionists' (as they called the communists).

The Stalinist Partit Socialista Unificat de Catalunya (P.S.U.C.) sent just such a colorful delegation to greet the *Ziryanin*. The revolutionary Patrols of Control cordoned off the pier and did not let the P.S.U.C. on the ship. Instead, the F.A.I. cadres searched it for arms. They found a cargo of beans and chocolate. The disgusted anarchists hauled down the hammer and sickle and ran up the libertarian *rojinegra*. Food was not what the antifascists needed in October, 1936.

A great deal of Cusick's narrative is concerned with the study of the "anarchist economy" set up in Catalunya on the bases of the collectivized factories and peasant collectives. However, unlike later commentators, Cusick does not primarily defend the collectivizations as an expression of revolutionary will, or as a fulfillment of the anarchist ideal. Rather, she examines the "anarchist economy" in the context of the war needs of the republic and of conflicts involving fear of Catalan domination (felt in Madrid) as well as bourgeois fear of the revolutionary impetus.

One of the most significant components of the Cusick memoir is her description of the May days of 1937, and her subsequent imprisonment in the communist *cheka* at portal de l'Angel, 24. As Orwell and so many others have noted, May Day 1937 went without official celebration in Barcelona, the effective "capital of the world revolution." Nevertheless, Cusick describes a situation on May 1 in which "thousands of workers milled through the streets . . . daring the police to disarm them. That was heat lightning," she declares. On May 3, with fighting at the Telefónica, the open conflict began. She points out the somewhat enthusiastic response of Barcelona's anarchist masses to the provocation of Erno Gerö: "At last there was something to DO, something to release the unbearable tension . . . Again time slowed down and sped up simultaneously."

The next day, the city was in the grip of a complete work stoppage.

The Patrols of Control took Montjuic fortress and trained its cannon on the Palau de la Generalitat . . . The block-long Popular Army poster on the communist Karl Marx House came down to reveal machine guns controlling the Passeig de Gracia, which the defense committees took over . . . Tuesday morning, the C.N.T. printers allowed only two papers to appear, *Solidaridad Obrera* and the P.O.U.M.'s *La Batalla* . . . The Friends of Durruti and the genuine Trotskyites (Munis and Moulin) separately printed handbills calling for a revolutionary Junta to take over the government buildings. Josep Rebull's P.O.U.M. left wing tried to win over the syndicalists at the barricades in another part of town for a march on the government buildings. Nothing came of these isolated initiatives . . . But the reputation of the P.O.U.M. shot up in the anarchist ranks. C.N.T.-F.A.I.-P.O.U.M. was the password at the barricades . . .

Wednesday morning the general strike continued. The workers stayed at the barricades and ignored Casa C.N.T.'s orders [to abandon the strike and leave the barricades]. The city's life was suspended in a will conflict between the anarchist masses and their leadership. . . . The communists tried to take advantage of their truce with Casa C.N.T. to put the city's bus system back to work. They used U.G.T. members the anarchists had always said were scabs from a big strike years ago. The sight of their red and black pointed trams run by communist scabs started the fighting all over. Barricades went up across the tracks, and the trams stopped running. . . .

With the eventual collapse of the May defensive action by the anarchists and P.O.U.M., and the transfer of central authority in Valencia from Largo Caballero to Negrín, Cusick and her associates in Barcelona entered a kind of limbo. C.N.T.-F.A.I. price control was abolished, and black market food items appeared at high prices, including such delicacies as asparagus and peaches, with "confections of chocolate and mocha for sale at outrageous prices."

In the wake of the May tragedy, "the P.S.U.C. and the Generalitat mounted one . . . event after another . . . We had a week devoted to the Battle of the Egg (*La lluita de l'ou*). This was a four-year plan to make Barcelona self-sufficient in eggs by having a chicken on every balcony. Then, the first week of June, we had Book Week. The carnival revolutionists filled the Ramblas with colorful bookstalls selling old parchment manuscripts from the burnt-out churches and new bright paperbacks of communist-approved authors. No more Kropotkin or Bakunin. This was the week we learned the Russians had arrested Bob Smillie of the P.O.U.M.'s [English] I.L.P. column while he was in Valencia." Soon Cusick was dismissed from her job at the Generalitat, on the instance of the P.S.U.C.

On June 16, 1937, Nin and the P.O.U.M. executive committee were arrested. On June 17, the same fate struck the P.O.U.M. foreigners at the Hotel Falcon. The next morning, the expropriated apartment at Avinguda Republica d'Argentina *2 bis* that had been given to Cusick and her companion, Charles Orr, by the anarchists, was raided by four *guardias de asalto*, a Russian, and three plainclothes men. That night, after having first been transferred to a police station on the Via Durruti, they and the other P.O.U.M. foreigners were marched "through the blacked out streets to the Portal de l'Angel, 24. There were no Patrols of Control on the streets . . .

"Portal de l'Angel, 24 was a Russian *cheka*, an old house, elegant upstairs. They put eight women in a windowless basement room about fifteen feet square . . . The walls of our cell were dirty grey plaster, covered with graffiti by the prisoners before us, in all the languages of the International Brigade." Among the women with whom Cusick was imprisoned was Katia Landau.

However, few political colloquies seem to have taken place in the *cheka*. Silence was dictated as much by fear of provocateurs as by reaction to the grim situation. Eventually, the lives of Cusick and Orr were saved, apparently by the action of George Tioli, a journalist who warned friends of the imprisoned about their whereabouts. Russell Blackwell (Rosalio Negrete) and America Escuder, the wife of the "La Batalla" managing editor Josep Escuder, prevailed on a U.S. consul named Perkins to visit the *cheka*, but he was turned away without an answer. Returning a few days later, he again was denied contact with the U.S. citizens, although he left them two peaches, which they divided into eight pieces. At that moment, Cusick believed that this "outside contact" originated with Eileen Orwell.

On a third visit, the consul was allowed to speak face-to-face with Cusick. On July 1, at the end of almost two weeks, Cusick and Charles Orr were finally released. Others were not so fortunate. Tioli was placed in a prison ship in Barcelona harbor, along with Col. Georges Kopp, the close friend of Orwell. Moulin, the Trotskyist whose real name was Hans Freund, "was killed when his C.N.T. collective was raided," Cusick writes.

When the U.S. consul finally put Cusick and Charles Orr on a vessel bound for Marseilles, on July 3, 1937, "it felt like a wake," Cusick noted.[3]

Russell N. Blackwell (Rosalioi Negrete)

Negrete, as he preferred to be called in Spain, was born in New York on March 24, 1904. During the 1920s, he had functioned as a Comintern operative in Mexico, where he acquired excellent Spanish and the name "Rosalio Negrete," a rough translation of his born name, Russell Blackwell. His responsibilities included the leadership of the Mexican communist children's group, the "Pioneros Rojos."

He had broken with Moscow and become a Trotskyist. He came to Spain in picturesque fashion, presenting himself to the Spanish Consulate in New York in the company of two authentic Spaniards who testified that he had been born in Spain and brought to the United States as an infant by his now-dead parents. As a Spanish subject, he sought repatriation. The story was believed, and a Spanish passport was issued; he then stowed away on the passenger liner "Normandie." Caught by officers and locked in the brig, he would have been returned to the United States when the liner docked in France had he not convinced the French authorities to deport him to Republican Spain.

When he arrived in Barcelona, in November 1936, he immediately went to the P.O.U.M. headquarters and presented himself as a representative of the Revolutionary Workers League of the United States, a small, extreme, and unorthodox Trotskyist splinter group led by one Hugo Oehler. The

R.W.L. had very little weight in American political life but it had an advantage with the P.O.U.M. that no other American leftist group could claim: Josep Escuder, a well-known member of the Bloc and P.O.U.M., had become involved with the R.W.L. while living in New York and working for daily newspapers. Negrete immediately pressed Oehler to arrange for Escuder's passage to Spain, which was accomplished in December. Escuder disappointed Negrete by adopting a supportive attitude toward the P.O.U.M. quite out of line with the acidulous commentaries of even dissident Trotskyists such as Negrete and Oehler; as we have noted, he became managing editor of "La Batalla," and was a defendant in the P.O.U.M. trial. But Escuder was not the only associate of Negrete to come to Barcelona; America Escuder, born in Tampa, and married to Josep, came, and soon Oehler himself arrived as well. Oehler did not remain long and, although according to Charles Orr his conduct while imprisoned during the repression was that of "a good revolutionary," his main "achievement" with regard to the Spanish revolution was to pen a pamphlet excoriating the P.O.U.M. in classic Trotskyist style.

Negrete shared Trotskyist criticisms of the P.O.U.M., but did not fully support the sectarian spirit of attack employed in these "debates." In his letters to Oehler, which are presently housed at Brandeis University, he insists on a conciliatory attitude toward the P.O.U.M. in writing and speaking publicly about the party, and strongly criticizes the record of the S.B.L. of Munis and Carlini. He met and discussed with Andrade, Molins i Fàbrega, Low and Breá, Carlini, Fosco, Enrico Russo and others, assiduously noting and classifying their degrees of political agreement or conflict. He met frequently with the Greek Archiomarxist leader Vitte, about whom we know little, and an Albanian, Jovan, about whom we know even less.

But Negrete was capable of rising above this political miasma, and acted in solidarity and courage during the May days as well as the period of repression. In May, he fought with the P.O.U.M. and C.N.T. on the barricades, and was wounded in the thigh, suffering a noticeable limp for several months thereafter. In the company of America Escuder he braved the custodians of the portal de l'Angel *cheka* to visit the group including Katia Landau, Lois Cusick, and Charles Orr, and then sought the help of the American consul in Barcelona, who arranged the freeing of Cusick and Orr.

Negrete did not escape the communist dragnet, although he was able to function underground in Spain until his arrest on March 17, 1938, in the town of Cuenca, between Madrid and Valencia. He was jailed in Valencia, where he remained for two months until released, again through U.S. consular efforts. He was placed on a British freighter but arrested once again, by the S.I.M. once the American consul, Woodruff Wallner, left. He was accused of plotting to assassinate Prieto, among the usual charges. He was interrogated and beaten. On May 9, he was able to send a postcard to his wife Edna in the United States. Thanks to pressure from then-secretary of state Cordell Hull, with a campaign to publicize his case through a committee on which Norman Thomas and a brace of prominent writers and other intellectuals served, he was freed on December 30, 1938.

It is worth noting that Negrete and Oehler were the only Trotskyists, Spanish or foreign, to make serious contacts with dissidents inside the P.O.U.M., in the form of the grouping around Josep Rebull, younger brother of Daniel Rebull (David Rey), in cell 72 of the party.

For the rest of his life, Blackwell/Negrete ardently defended the revolutionary movement to which he finally felt closest in Spain: the C.N.T. He eventually founded a small anarchist grouping, the Libertarian League, which published a newsletter, "Views and Comments." He died in New York in 1969.[4]

Pavel Thalmann and Clara Ensner

The case of Pavel Thalmann, the former Comintern functionary from Switzerland, and of his companion Clara Ensner, is a difficult one for historians of the P.O.U.M. Both were active in pro-P.O.U.M. journalistic work from very early in the civil war, Clara having arrived in Barcelona just before the outbreak of the conflict. During the 1970s, they published a widely read and admired book of memoirs, first in German (*Revolution Für die Freiheit,* Hamburg, 1977), and then in French (*Combats Pour La Liberté* (Paris, 1983). These volumes have been taken up and cited by a number of historians of the Spanish Civil War.

The Thalmanns' memoirs are vivid and detailed, although they betray a curious disinterest in the political activities of the P.O.U.M., if not, at some points, downright hostility, reflecting their status as foreign observers less interested in the constructive work of the Spanish working class movement than in the desiderata of the sectarian battle with the various groups of Trotskyists.

Further, there are important elements of the Thalmanns' narrative that, while absorbing and compelling, do not correspond with the accounts of others. Perhaps the most serious such instance involves the relationship between Moulin, the young member of the Trotskyist group around Munis, and the anarchist grouping of the Friends of Durruti. The Thalmanns' highly colored account of the relations between Moulin and Jaume Balius, the main figure in the Friends of Durruti, would have the reader believe that the Friends were virtually under the guidance of Moulin; ironically, exactly the charge made by the Stalinists. In this, the Thalmanns seem motivated by a "Trotskyist" disbelief in the ability of the anarchists to do anything "really revolutionary" or even commonsensical without the intervention of Marxists. Such considerations have led other commentators, including some eminent historians, to ascribe to Balius a clearly nonexistent former membership in the B.O.C.

There are other mistakes in the Thalmanns' account, which it would be tedious to enumerate here, but which are obvious enough. While the Thalmanns were gallant in their fidelity to their own revolutionary dreams during the 1930s, it is our judgment that their work must be used, as an authority, with great care. (Pavel Thalmann died in 1980, and Clara in 1987 as this book was being finished.)

Benjamin Péret

Benjamin Péret, the great French surrealist poet, is another example, like that of the Thalmanns, of an individual whose generous impulses led him to the Spanish struggle but whose attachment to sectariana prevented him from exercising a really positive influence in the P.O.U.M. However, he never let his disagreements with the P.O.U.M. lead him to the kind of heedless attack favored by others who, like him, were under the very strong influence of Trotsky.

Péret arrived in Barcelona the third day after July 18, according to Juan Andrade. In letters to André Breton, beginning in mid-August, Péret indicated a clear awareness of the reactionary role assumed by the official Communists. He fought in the battle of Somosierra, in the outskirts of Madrid. In September, following the visit of the official Trotskyist Jean Rous to Barcelona, Péret served as Rous's stand-in, representing the Trotskyist international secretariat although he was not, himself, an actual Trotskyist militant.

It is worth noting that, although already well-known as an author—the Trinidadian leftist C.L.R. James, in his introduction to the first (1937) edition of Low and Breá's *Red Spanish Notebook* refers to him as "the famous French poet"—Péret showed no taste for the safe, glamorous work of the "revolutionary writer" on a propaganda tour of the Spanish battlefront. Low and Brea's book illustrates Péret's modesty and, even, diffidence, with a recounting of their amusement when he went to visit Jaume Miravitlles, who had expressed great admiration for Péret's work but who, confronted with a middle-aged, unprepossessing looking individual in militia overalls and *espardenyes* (Catalan sandals), took him for "just another worker" and directed him to an electrical fixture in need of repair! However, it is possible Péret would not have found such a task onerous; he seems to have sought nothing more than to make a simple contribution, without fanfare.

A major concern, expressed in a letter to Breton, was to have the American-born avant-garde photographer and painter Man Ray collect x-ray negatives for the Spanish hospitals. After working for the P.O.U.M. radio, where he broadcast in Portuguese (which he learned during a sojourn in Brazil), he returned to the front at Huesca. His combative personality seems to have provoked some resentment in Barcelona, for his friend G. Munis admits that Péret was forced to take refuge in an anarchist unit, following threats to his life. His last letter from Spain to Breton, dated March 7, 1937, is headed "First Company, Nestor Makhno Battalion, Durruti Division, Piña de Ebro, Aragon Front."

Perhaps because of his deep streak of rebelliousness, visible in his poetry, Péret found himself attracted to the irreconcilable Munis. Following his return to France, while in exile in Mexico, during the Second World War, Péret collaborated, under the name "Peralta," in a series of Trotskyist journals edited by Munis. This collaboration continued until the 1950s, when Péret organized, along with the Mexican poet Octavio Paz, the rescue of Munis from a Spanish prison. The "Munis-Péret" group, supported by Trotsky's widow, Natalya Sedova, eventually broke with Trotskyism, forming a small political tendency that, amazingly enough, continues today in France and Spain. However, although Munis remained unrepentant in his bilious condemnation of the P.O.U.M., Péret, as noted by Andrade, was never so small-minded, and, at his passing in 1959 (he was born in 1899) he was mourned by the *poumistes* as a comrade.[5]

Nancy Macdonald and William Herrick

Mention should also be made of two Americans who, although not directly active in the P.O.U.M., have nonetheless helped aid its survival, physically and in history.

Nancy Macdonald, the companion of the radical cultural critic Dwight Macdonald, became actively involved in efforts after the Second World War to organize relief for P.O.U.M. and other Spanish refugees living in France and elsewhere. Under the umbrella of an organization titled Spanish Refugee Aid, Macdonald organized support campaigns by prominent anti-Stalinist intellectuals around the world, and managed over some four decades to provide a great quantity of financial and other resources to the P.O.U.M. refugees. This irreplaceable solidarity work is described in Nancy Macdonald's memoir, *Homage to the Spanish Exiles* (New York, 1987), a work that is useful, although uneven as a historical source.

William Herrick's solidarity with the P.O.U.M., although less practical than that of Nancy Macdonald, cannot be ignored. A young communist from New York, Herrick fought in the ranks of the Abraham Lincoln Battalion and was badly wounded in the battle for Madrid. But unlike so many other Lincoln veterans, whose ability to discern the truth about Spain has been clouded by sentimentality as well as a tenacious Stalinism, Herrick clearly perceived the terrible character of the P.O.U.M.'s persecution. In 1969, Herrick published a novel, *Hermanos!,* that is a strong defense of the P.O.U.M., aside from being, however fictionalized, the only fully truthful memoir of the Lincoln Battalion. In a virile "war prose" that has nothing in common with the excesses of Malraux and Hemingway, Herrick describes his own horror at the use of American volunteers in anti-P.O.U.M. execution squads.

Naturally, Herrick's work has incurred the anger of those communist veterans of the war who cannot accept the ambivalence and, even, the evil that was present in "the good fight." But his book remains in print and deserves to be read by everybody interested in the experience of the Spanish Civil War.

Herrick has followed *Hermanos!* with a series of novels on the subject of revolt and violence and lives today in upstate New York, with a Franco bullet still inside his body.

Notes

1. Mika Etchebehere, op. cit., p. 58.
2. Material in this chapter on Mary Low and Lois Cusick was presented by Stephen Schwartz under the title "Dues Anglo-Saxones a la Barcelona Revolucionaria," at the second international colloquium on the Spanish civil war, "War and Revolution in Catalunya," sponsored by the Universitat de Barcelona and held at the Institut d'Estudis Catalans, Barcelona, 1986. The paper is available in Catalan from the latter Institut.
3. I have also consulted, on Cusick and Orr, a typewritten document by Charles A. Orr, "Some Facts on the Persecution of Foreign Revolutionaries in 'Republican' Spain," n.d., copy provided to me by Burnett Bolloten.
4. Russell Blackwell's correspondence with Hugo Oehler, before the latter's arrival in Spain, is on deposit in the Hugo Oehler Papers, Brandeis University, Waltham, Mass. Biographical information presented here is drawn from John Nicholas Beffel, "Russell N. Blackwell," in "España Libre," November-December 1969, and unsigned, "Rosalio Negrete," in "Cahiers Léon Trotsky," July-September 1979.
5. Sources on Péret are: Low and Brea, op.cit., including the preface by C.L.R. James to the first edition; Claude Courtot, *Introduction a la Lecture de Benjamin Péret,* Paris, 1965, which includes his letters to Breton from Spain; interviews with Munis, Jaime Fernández Rodríguez (Costa), and Octavio Paz; and the following pamphlets: *De la Part de Péret,* published by the surrealist group, Paris, 1964; Stephen Schwartz (S. Solsona), *Incidents From the Life of Benjamin Péret,* San Francisco, 1981, and *A Propos de Péret*, Paris, 1987, published by the Association des Amis de Benjamin Péret.

Bibliography

Alcofa Nassaes, José Luis, *Los asesores soviéticos en la guerra civil española*, Barcelona, 1971.

Alvarez del Vayo, Julio, *Freedom's Battle*, New York, 1940.

Amicale des Anciens Volontaires des Brigades Internationales, *Deroulements de la Guerre*, Paris, 1956.

Amigos de Durruti, *Hacia una nueva revolución*, Barcelona, 1938.

Andrade, Juan, *La burocracia reformista en el movimiento obrero*, Madrid, 1935.

Angulo, Enrique de, *Diez horas de Estado Catalán*, Barcelona, 1935.

Archives Secretes de la Wilhelmstrasse, (Les) Paris, 1952.

Arlandis, Hilario, *Los anarquistas en Rusia*, Barcelona, 1924.

Arquer, Jordi, *El Comunisme i la qüestió nacional i colonial*, Barcelona, 1930.

_____, *Salvador Segui*, Barcelona, 1932.

Azaña, Manuel, *Memorias politicas y de guerra, in Obras Completas*, vol. IV, Mexico, 1968.

Balcells, Alberto, *Crisis económia y agitación social en Cataluña*, Barcelona, 1973.

_____, *El arraigo del anarquismo en Cataluña*, Barcelona, 1973.

Barea, Arturo, *La forja de un rebelde*, Buenos Aires, 1951.

Bates, Ralph, *"Introduccion"-Unidad proletaria U.G.T.-C.N.T.*, Mexico, 1938.

Benavides, Manuel D., *Guerra y revolución en Cataluña*, Mexico, 1944.

Benson, Frederick R., *Writers in Arms*, New York, 1967.

Berneri, Camilo, *Scritti Scelti: Petrogrado 1917, Barcelona 1937*, Milan, 1964.

Bolloten, Burnett, *The Grand Camouflage*, London, 1961.

_____, *The Spanish Revolution*, Chapel Hill, 1979.

Bonamusa, Francesc, *Andreu Nin y el movimiento comunista en España, 1930-37*, Barcelona, 1977.

_____, *El Bloc obrer i camperol 1930-32*, Barcelona, 1974.

Borkenau, Franz, *The Spanish Cockpit*, Ann Arbor, 1963.

Bowers, Claude G., *My Mission to Spain*, New York, 1954.

Brandt, Willi, *El exilio y la lucha*, Barcelona, 1973.

Brenan, Gerald, *The Spanish Labyrinth*, Cambridge, 1943.

Breton, André, *What is Surrealism*? New York, 1978 (translations by Stephen Schwartz).

300

Brockway, Fenner, *The Truth about Barcelona*, London, 1937.
Broué, Pierre, and Temime, Emile, *Guerre et Revolution en Espagne*, Paris, 1961.
Buenacasa, Manuel, *El movimiento obrero español*, Barcelona, 1928.
Bullejos, José, *Europa entre dos guerras, 1918-1938*, Mexico, 1945.
Cambó, Francesc, *Les Dictadures*, Barcelona, 1929.
Carr, Raymond, *Spain 1808-1939*, London, 1966.
_____, *The Republic and The Civil War in Spain*, New York, 1971.
Carrillo, Santiago *Conferencia de Santiago Carrillo, secretario de la J.S.U. en el teatro Apolo de Valencia, el 16 de diciembre de 1936*, Valencia, 1936.
_____, *Eurocommunism and the State*, Westport, 1978.
_____, *Polemica Maurín-Carrillo*, Barcelona, 1937.
"Casanova, M.," *La guerra de España*, Barcelona, 1978.
Castro Delgado, Enrique, *Mi fé se perdió, en Moscú*, Mexico, 1948.
_____, *Hombres Made in Moscu*, Mexico, 1960.
Cattell, D.T., *Communism and the Spanish Civil War*, Berkeley, 1956.
_____, *Soviet Diplomacy and the Spanish Civil War*, Berkeley, 1957.
Churchill, Winston, *Journal Politique*, Paris, 1948.
Claudín, Fernando, *La crisis del movimiento comunista mundial, de la Komintern a la Kominform*, Paris, 1970.
Colodny, Robert G., *El Asedio de Madrid*, Paris, 1972.
Comin Colomer, E., *Historia del Partido Comunista de España*, Madrid, 1962.
_____, *Conferencia de la Industria Textil del P.O.U.M.*, Barcelona, 1937.
Contreras, Carlos J., *La quinta columna, Cómo luchar contra provocación y el espionaje*, Barcelona, 1938.
Conze, Edward M., *Spain Today*, London, 1936.
Costa I Deu, Josep, La Veritat del 6 d'Octobre, Barcelona, 1935.
Courtot, Claude, *Introduction a la Lecture de Benjamin Péret*, Paris, 1965.
Crozier, Brian, *Franco*. Boston, 1968.
Cruells, Manuel, *El Fets de Maig de 1937*, Barcelona, 1970.
_____, *El 6 Octubre a Catalunya*, Barcelona, 1970.
_____, *L'Expedició a Mallorca, Any 1936*, Barcelona, 1972.
Cuadrado, Miguel M., *Elecciones y partidos politicos en España, 1868-1931*, Madrid, 1969.
Cunningham, Valentine, *The Penguin Book of Spanish Civil War Verse*, Harmondsworth, 1980.
_____, *Spanish Front*, Oxford, 1986.
Cusick, Lois, *The Anarchist Millenium*, Unpublished Manuscript.
De Julio a Julio, Barcelona, 1937.
Degras, Jeanne, *The Communist International*, London, 1961.
Diaz, José, *Por la unidad hacia la victoria*, Valencia, 1937.
Documentos sobre la industria de guerra en Cataluña, Buenos Aires, 1939.
Eby, Cecil, *Between the Bullet and the Lie*, New York, 1969.

Estivill, Angel, El 6 d'Octobre, l'Ensulciada dels Jacobins, Barcelona, 1935.
Etchebehere, Mika, Ma Guerre d'Espagne a Moi, Paris, 1976.
Foix, Pere (Delaville), Los archivos del terrorismo blanco, Barcelona, 1932.
Fontenis, Georges, Le Message Revolutionnaire des Amis de Durruti (Espagne 1937), Cangey, France, 1983.
Foreign Relations of the United States, Diplomatic Papers, Vol. 1, 1937, Washington D.C., 1954.
Fraser, Ronald, Blood of Spain, New York, 1979.
Friends of Durruti Group, Towards a Fresh Revolution, Sanday (Orkneys), 1978.
Gabriel, José, La vida y la muerte en Aragon, Barcelona, 1938.
Garosci, Aldo, Gil Intellectuali e la Guerra di Spagna, Turin, 1955.
Gide, André, Retour de L'USSR, Paris, 1935.
_____, Litterature Engagée, Paris, 1950.
Gorkin, Julian Canibales politicos, Mexico, 1941.
_____, España, Primer ensayo de democracia popular, Buenos Aires, 1961.
Grossi, Manuel, La Insurrección de Asturias, Barcelona, 1935.
Guerra i la Revolución a Catalunya en el Terreny Economica, La, Barcelona, 1937.
Guerra y revolución en España, Moscow, 1966.
Guttmann Allen, The Wound in the Heart, New York, 1962.
Hemingway, Ernest, For Whom the Bell Tolls, New York, 1962.
Henkine, Cyrille, L'Espionnage Sovietique, Paris, 1981.
Hermet, Guy, Les Communistes en Espagne, Paris, 1971.
Hernandez, Jesus, Negro y rojo, Mexico, 1946.
_____, Yo fui un ministro de Stalin, Mexico, 1952.
Herrick, William, Hermanos!, New York, 1969.
Hidalgo, Diego, Un notario español in Rusia, Madrid, 1931.
Historia del Partido Comunista de España, Paris, 1965.
Huit Cent Quatre Vingt Jours, Paris, 1963.
Humbert-Droz, Jules, Dix Annees au Service de l'Internationale Communiste, Neüchatel, 1971.
Ibárruri, Dolores, Memoires de la Pasionaria, Paris, 1963.
Iglesias, Ignacio, El proletariado y las clases medias, Barcelona, 1967.
_____, Trotsky et la Révolution Espagnole, Lausanne, 1974.
L'Insurrecció d'Octubre a Catalunya, Barcelona, 1935 (no author).
Jackson, Gabriel, The Spanish Republic and the Civil War, 1931-39, Princeton, 1965.
Johnson, Verle B., Legions of Babel, University Park, Pa., 1967.
Koltzov, Mikhail, Diario de la guerra en España, Paris, 1963.
Kom, Prof. I., La revolución española, Barcelona, 1932.
Krivitsky, Walter, I Was Stalin's Agent, London, 1939.
Landau, Katia, Les Staliniens en Espagne, Paris, 1938.
Largo Caballero, Francisco, Mis Recuerdos, Mexico, 1954.
Lazarillo de Torres (Benigno Bejarano) España, cuna del la libertad, Valencia, 1937.

Lazitch, Branko, *Biiographical Dictionary of the Comintern*, Stanford, 1987.

A Lead to World Socialism, London, 1937.

Lichtheim, George, *Europe in the 20th Century*, New York, 1972.

London, G., *Espagne*, Paris, 1966.

Longo, Luigi, *Las Brigadas Internacionales en España*, Mexico, 1966.

Losovsky, A., *Programa de acción de la Internacional Sindical Roja*, Barcelona, 1923.

_____, *Tres anos de lucha de la I.S.R.*, Barcelona, 1924.

Low, Mary and Brea, Juan, *Red Spanish Notebook*, San Francisco, 1979.

Macdonald, Nancy, *Homage to the Spanish Exiles*, New York, 1987.

Macia i la seva actuacio a l'estranger, Mexico, 1963.(no author)

Madariaga, Salvador de, *España*, Buenos Aires, 1945.

Madrid, Francisco, *Film de la republica libertaria comunista*, Barcelona, 1932.

Manzanera, E., *Documento historico (La Columna de Hierro)* Barcelona, 1981.

Marba, Palmiro, *El movimiento sindicalista obrero espanol*, Barcelona, 1921.

Marse, Juan, *The Fallen*, New York, 1979.

Martin, J. G., *Political and Social Changes in Catalonia During the Revolution, July 19-Dec. 31, 1936*, Barcelona, 1937.

Marx, Karl, *La revolucion espanola*, Madrid, 1929.

Matthews, Herbert L., *A World in Revolution*, New York, 1973.

Maurín, Joaquím, *El sindicalismo a la luz, de la revolucion rusa*, Barcelona, 1922.

_____, *La Crísis de la Confederacion Nacional del Trabajo*, Barcelona, 1924.

_____, *Los hombres de la dictadura*, Madrid, 1930.

_____, *La revolucion española: de la monarquía absoluta a la revolución socialista*, Madrid, 1932.

_____, *El Bloque Obrera y Campesino*, Barcelona, 1932.

_____, *Alianza Obrera*, Barcelona, 1935.

_____, *Hacia la segunda revolución*, Barcelona, 1935.

_____, *Revolucion y contrarrevolucion en España*, Paris, 1966.

_____, *Polemica Maurin-Carrillo*, Barcelona, 1937.

_____, *Intervenciones Parlamentarias*, Barcelona, 1937.

_____, *En las prisiones de Franco*, Mexico, 1974.

McGovern, John, *Terror in Spain*, London, 1938.

Merkes, Manfred, *Die Politikenuber des Spanische Burgerkrieg*, Bonn, 1961.

Milany, Joan de, *Un aviador de la republica*, Barcelona, 1970.

Minor, Robert, *Mi adhesion al Comunismo*, Barcelona, 1932.

Mintz, Frank and Pecina, Manuel, *Los Amigos de Durruti, Los Trotsquistas, y los sucesos de Mayo*, Madrid, 1978.

Miravitlles, Jaume, *De Jaca a Sallent*, Barcelona, 1932.
_____, *Perqué Soc Comunista*, Barcelona, 1932.
_____, *Contra la Cultura Burgesa*, Barcelona, 1932.
_____, *El Discurso de Stalin*, Barcelona, 1932.
_____, *Ha Trait Macia*, Barcelona, 1932.
_____, *Los obreros y la politica* Barcelona, 1933.
_____, *Episodis de la Guerra Civil Espanyola*, Barcelona, 1972.
Molas, Isidre, *Lliga Catalana*, Barcelona, 1972.
Molinero, Carme, and Ysas, Pere, *L'Oposició Antifeixista a Catalunya (1939-50)* Barcelona, 1981.
Molins I Fàbrega, Narcïs, *U.H.P.*, Barcelona, 1935.
Montseny, Federica, *Mis primeros cuarenta años*, Barcelona, 1987.
Mora, Constancia de la, *Fiere Espagne*, Paris, 1946.
Morrow, Felix, *Revolution and Counter-Revolution in Spain*, New York, 1939.
Munis, G., *Jalones de Derrota, Promesa de Victoria*, Mexico, 1948.
Nin, Andreu, *El sindicalism revolucionario y la Internacional*, Barcelona, 1923.
_____, *Fachism i Profsoyuzi*, Moscu, 1923.
_____, *Struggle of the Trade Unions Against Fascism*, Chicago, 1923.
_____, *Le Anarchistes et le Mouvement Syndical*, Paris, 1924.
_____, *Opasnost Voini Mejdunarodnoye*, Moscow, 1925.
_____, *Professionalno Dvizhenie y Ispanii*, Moscow, 1926.
_____, *Les Dictadures dels Nostres dies*, Barcelona, 1930.
_____, *Reacción y revolución en España*, Barcelona, 1934.
_____, *El proletariado español ante la revolución*, Madrid, 1931.
_____, *Lo que són los soviets*, Madrid, 1931.
_____, *Manchuria y el imperialismo*, Valencia, 1932.
_____, *La huelga general de enero y sus ensenanzas*, Madrid, 1932.
_____, *Los anarquistas y el movimiento sindical*, Barcelona, 1933.
_____, *Las organizaciones obreras internacionales*, Madrid, 1933.
_____, *Els moviments d'Emancipació Nacional*, Barcelona, 1935.
_____, *Los problemas de la revolucion espanola*, Paris, 1971.
Norris, Christopher, *Inside the Myth*, London, 1984.
Ollivier, Marcel, *La Guépéou en Espagne, Les Journees Sanglantes de Barcelona*, Paris, 1937.
Oltra, Pico J., *el P.O.U.M. i la Col.lectivizacio d'Industries i Comercis*, Barcelona, 1937.
Orlov, Alexander, *The Secret History of Stalin's Crimes*, New York, 1953.
Orwell, George, *Homage to Catalonia*, London, 1938.
Ossorio y Gallardo, Angel, *Vida y sacrificio de Companys*, Buenos Aires, 1943.
Pagès, Pelai, *Andreu Nin, su evolución política (1911-1937)*, Barcelona, 1975.
_____, *El movimiento Trotskista en España* (1930-1935), Barcelona, 1977.

_____, and Virós, Xavier, *El P.O.U.M. ante la revolución española*, Barcelona, 1971.

Palacin, Santiago, *La revolución y el campo*, Barcelona, 1937.

Pámies, Teresa, *Testament a Praga*, Barcelona, 1971.

_____, *Quan Erem Capitans*, Barcelona, 1974.

Payne, Stanley G., *The Spanish Revolútion*, New York, 1970.

Peirats, José, *Lá C.N.T. en la revolución española*—Buenos Aires, 1955.

Peiro, Juan, *Problemas y cintarazos*—Rennes, 1946.

Perez Baro, Albert, *Trenta Mesos de Collectivitzacions a Catalunya*, Barcelona, 1969.

Perez Baró, Albert, *Els "Felicos" Anys Vint*, Palma de Mallorca, 1974.

Pérez Salas, Jesús, *Guerra en España*, Mexico, 1947.

Pestana, Angel, *Setenta dias en Rusia*, Barcelona, 1921.

Pla, Josep, *Andreu Nin*, in *Homonots*, Barcelona, 1957.

Pleno Ampliado del CC del Partido Comunista de España, Valencia, 1937.

P.O.U.M. en el banquillo, El, Barcelona, 1938.

Preston, Paul, *The Coming of the Spanish Civil War*, London, 1985.

Prieto, Indalecio, *Cómo y porqué salí del Ministério de Defensa Nacional*, Mexico, 1940.

Puig I Vila, Nonit, *Qué es la Unio de Rabassaires*, Barcelona, 1935.

Qué es y Qué Quiera el Partido Obrero de Unificación Marxista, Barcelona, 1935.

Ramos Oliviera, Antonio, *Politics, Economics and Men of Modern Spain*, London, 1946.

Rappoport, C. *Qué es al Comunismo*, Barcelona, 1924.

_____, *Resoluciones Aprobadas en el Pleno Ampliado del CC del P.O.U.M., 12 al 16 de Diciembre de 1936*, Barcelona, 1937.

_____, *Resoluciones de la Juventud Comunista Ibérica, Comite Central Ampliado*, Barcelona, 1937.

Reventlow, R., *Spanien in Diesem Jahrhundert*, Frankfurt, 1970.

'Revolution Espagnole, La', Etudes Marxistes, Nos. 7-8, Paris, 1969.

"Rieger, Max," *Espionaje en Espana*, Barcelona, 1938.

Rios, Fernando de los, *Un Viaje a la Rusia Sovietica*, Madrid, 1972.

Rocker, Rudolf, *Extranjeros en España*, Buenos Aires, 1938.

Rosa, Carmel, *Quan Catalunya era Revolucionario*, Salt, 1986.

Rosal, Amaro del, *Los Congresos Obresos Internacionales en el Siglo XX*, Mexico, 1963.

Rosenthal, Gerard, *Avocat de Trotsky*, Paris, 1975.

Rosmer, Alfred, *Moscou sous Lenine*, Paris, 1958.

Rous, Jean, *la Revolutión Assassinée*, Paris, 1938.

Sanchez Albornoz, Claudio, *De mi anecd. tario político*, Buenos Aires, 1972.

de Santillan, Diego Abad, *Los anarquistas y la insurrección de Octubre*, Barcelona, 1935.

_____, *La Revolución y la Guerra de España*, Barcelona, 1938.

_____, *Porqué perdimos la Guerra*, Buenos Aires, 1940.

Sardá, Rafael, *Las colectividades agricolas*, Barcelona, 1937.

Schwartz, Stephen, *Brotherhood of the Sea*, New Brunswick, 1986.

_____. *Incidents From the Life of Benjamin Péret*, San Francisco, 1981.

_____. *The Transition*, San Francisco, 1987.

Semprun, Jorge, *The Autobiography of Federico Sanchez*, New York, 1977.

Serge, Victor, *El nacimiento de nuestra fuerza*, Madrid, 1932.

_____, *Mémoires d'un Révolutionnaire*, Paris, 1953.

Sharkey, Paul, *The Friends of Durruti, A Chronology*, Tokyo, 1984.

Solano, Wilebaldo, *Andreu Nin*, Barcelona, 1977.

Soria, Georges, *L'Espionnage Trotskyste en Espagne*, Paris, 1938.

Souchy, Augustin, Bolloten, Burnett, Peirats, José, and Goldman, Emma, *The May Days Barcelona 1937*, London, 1987.

Souvarine, Boris, *Stalin*, New York, 1939.

Soviet War Veterans Committee, *International Solidarity with the Spanish Republic*, Moscow, 1975.

Stansky, Peter and Abrahams, William, *Orwell the Transformation*, New York, 1979.

"Suárez, Andrés" *El proceso contra al P.O.U.M.*, Paris, 1974.

Thalmann, Pavel and Clara, *Combats pour la Liberté*, Paris, 1938.

_____, *Revolution für die Freitheit*, Hamburg, 1977.

Thomas, Hugh, *The Spanish Civil War*, New York, 1959.

Toryho, Jacinto, *la Independéncia de España*, Barcelona, 1938.

Tosstorff, Rainer, *Die P.O.U.M. Im Spanischen Burgerkrieg*, Frankfurt, 1987.

Trotsky, Leon, *Leçon d'Espagne*, Paris, 1936.

_____, *Manual del Ejercito Rojo*, Barcelona, 1937.

_____, *Ecrits, Vol. III*, Paris, 1963.

_____, *Escritos Sobre Espana*, Paris, 1971.

_____, *la Révolution Espagnole (1930-1940)*, Paris, 1975.

_____, *The Spanish Revolution (1931-39)*, New York, 1973.

Tuñon de Lara, Manuel, *La Espana del siglo XX*, Paris, 1968.

Urgell, Ferran, *La Lluita de Classes al Camp*, Barcelona, 1933.

V. zur Muhlen, Patrik, *Spanien War Ihre Hoffnung*, Bonn, 1983.

Velarde Fuentes, Juan, *España ante la Socialización Económica*, Madrid, 1970.

Vereecken, Georges, *The GPU in the Trotskyist Movement*, London, 1976.

Vidarte, Juan Simeon, Todos fuimós culpables, Mexico, 1973.

Vidiella, Rafael, *De Paris a la carcel de Madrid*, Barcelona, 1932.

Viros, Xavier, and Pages, Pelai, *El P.O.U.M. ante la revolucion espanola*, Barcelona, 1971.

Watkins, K.W., *Britain Divided*, London, 1963.

Wolfe, Bertram D., *Civil War in Spain*, New York, 1938.

Zugazagoitia, Julian, *Guerra y vicisitudes de los españoles*, Paris, 1968.

Correspondence and Interviews by Victor Alba and Stephen Schwartz

Alberti, Santiago—Barcelona
Altman, Georges—Paris
Antic, Marcel.lí—San José, Costa Rica
Arquer, Jordi—Paris
Benedet, Vicente—San Francisco, Ca.
Bolloten, Burnett—Sunnyvale, Ca.
Bonet, Pere—Paris
Brandon, Herbert—San Francisco and New York
Coll, Josep—Paris
Costa-Amic, Bartolomeu—Mexico, D.F.
Cowl, Carl—San Francisco and New York
Fernández Grandizo, Manuel (G.Munis)—Paris
Fernández Granell, Eugenio—New York
Fernández Rodríguez, Jaime—Paris
Ferrer, Miquel—Barcelona
Gorkín, Julián Gómez—Mexico and Paris
Grossi, Manuel—Brignoles, France
Hernández, Jesús-Mexico
Herrick, William—Old Chatham, New York
Iglesias, Ignacio—Paris
Kupinsky, Wolf (Harry Milton)—Mill Valley, Ca.
Largo Caballero, Francisco—Paris
Lovestone, Jay—Washington, D.C.
Machado, Mary Low—Miami, Fla.
Marsal, Salvador—Barcelona
Maurín, Jeanne—New York and Lancaster, Pa.
Maurín, Joaquim—New York
Miravitlles, Jaume—Barcelona
Molins I Fàbrega, Narcís—Mexico, D.F.
Nin, Olga—Mexico
Panades, Enric—Barcelona
Pané, Josep—Lleida
Paz, Octavio—Mexico and Miami
Petel, Phyllis—Paris, Washington, San Francisco
Pi I Sunyer, Carles—London
Portela, Lluis—Barcelona
Rebull, Daniel (David Rey)—Barcelona
Rocabert, Joan—Barcelona
Rosa, Carmel—Barcelona
Rovira, Josep—Barcelona
Sánchez, Manuel—Barcelona
Sans, Martí—Barcelona

Santillán, Diego Abad de—Buenos Aires
Serge, Victor—Mexico
Sharron, Mark—San Francisco
Solano, Wilebaldo—Paris and Barcelona
Sole-Martí, Antoni—Lima
Tussó, Tomàs—Mexico
Van Heijenoort, Jean—Palo Alto, Ca.
Wolfe, Bertram D.—New York and Stanford U., Palo Alto, Ca.
Wolfe, Ella—Palo Alto, Ca.
Xammar, Eugeni—L'Ametlla del Vallès

Periodicals

Adelante." Alacant.
"Adelante." Barcelona.
"Adunata dei Refrattari." New York.
"Ahora." Madrid-Valencia.
"The Alarm." San Francisco.
"Alarma." Paris and Barcelona.
"Alerta." Siétamo.
"American Historical Review." Washington.
"El Amigo Del Pueblo." Barcelona.
"La Antorcha." Madrid.
"Avance." Oviedo.
"Avant." Barcelona.
"Avant." Figueres.
"Avant." Lleida.
"Avant." Balaguer.
"Avui." Barcelona.
"El Baix Penedès." El Vendrell.
"La Batalla." Barcelona and Paris.
"Beipi." Paris.
"El Be Negre." Barcelona.
"Butlleti de l'Aliança Obrera." Barcelona.
"Butlleti Interior del P.O.U.M." Barcelona.
"Cahiers Léon Trotsky." Grenoble.
"Castilla Libre." Madrid.
"Catalunya." Barcelona.
"Catalunya Roja." Barcelona.
"Ce-Soir." París.
"Claridad." Madrid.
"Clave." Mèxico, D. F.
"C.N.T." Madrid.
"Combat." Lleida.
"El Combatiente Rojo." Madrid.

"Comunismo." Madrid.
"Los Controladores del P.S.U.C." Barcelona.
"La Correspondencia." Valencia.
"Correspondencia Internacional." Moscow.
"Cruz y Raya." Madrid.
"Cuenta y Razón." Madrid.
"The Daily Worker." London.
"El Debate." Madrid.
"El Dia Gráfico." Barcelona.
"Dissent." New York.
"España Libre." New York.
"L'Espurna." Girona.
"L'Esquella de la Torratxa." Barcelona.
"Est et Ouest." París.
"L'Estrella Roja." Barcelona.
"La Flèche." París.
"Frente Rojo." Valencia.
"Front." Barcelona.
"Front." Barcelona (Gràcia).
"Front." Sitges.
"Front." Terrassa.
"Il Grido del Popolo." Paris.
"Guerra di Classe." París.
"Historia." Madrid.
"L'Hora." Barcelona.
"La Humanitat." Barcelona.
"L'Humanité." París.
"El Ideal." Lleida.
"Inprecorr." Moscow.
"La Internacional." Madrid.
"La Internacional Comunista." Moscow.
"La Internacional Sindical Roja." Moscow.
"International Press Correspondence." Berlin and London.
"Izvestia." Moscow.
"La Jornada." Lleida.
"Juillet." Barcelona.
"Justicia Social." Barcelona.
"Juventud Comunista." Barcelona.
"Juventud Obrera." Barcelona.
"El Leninista." Barcelona.
"Leviatán." Madrid.
"Lluita." Paris.
"Lucha Obrera." Barcelona.
"Lucha Social." Lleida.
"Manchester Guardian." London-Manchester.

"Mirador." Barcelona.
"Le Monde." Paris.
"El Mono Azul." Madrid.
"Mundo Obrero." Madrid.
"The New Criterion." New York.
"The New Leader." New York.
"The New York Times." New York.
"News Chronicle." London.
"La Noche." Barcelona.
"Nosotros." Madrid.
"Nosotros." Valencia.
"Las Noticias." Barcelona.
"El Noticiero Universal." Barcelona.
"La Novela Ideal." Barcelona.
"Nuestra Bandera." Alacant.
"Nuestra Bandera." Paris.
"La Nueva Era." Barcelona.
"Nueva Senda." Madrid.
"Nuevo Mundo." Madrid.
"L'Opinió." Barcelona.
"Paris-Midi." París.
"Partisan Review." New York.
"El Pla de Bages." Manresa.
"El Poble Català." Barcelona.
"Politica." Madrid.
"Por Una Paz Duradera." Bucharest.
"Pravda." Moscow.
"La Publicidad." Barcelona.
"La Publicitat." Barcelona.
"La Rambla." Barcelona.
"Renovación." Madrid.
"La Revista Blanca." Barcelona.
"Revista de Catalunya." Barcelona.
"La Révolution Espagnole." Barcelona.
"La Révolution Prolétarienne." París.
"Rote Fahne." Zurich.
"Ruta." Barcelona.
"Serra d'Or." Montserrat.
"Sindicalismo." Barcelona.
"Slavic Review." New York.
"El Socialista." Madrid.
"El Sol." Madrid.
"Solidaridad Obrera." Barcelona.
"El Soviet." Barcelona.
"TeleXpres." Barcelona.

"La Tierra." Madrid.
"Treball." Barcelona.
"Tribuna Socialista." Paris.
"Triunfo." Madrid.
"UHP." Lleida.
"Ultima Hora." Barcelona.
"Unitat." Terrassa.
"Vanguardia." Madrid.
"La Vanguardia." Barcelona.
"La Vanguardia Española." Barcelona.
"Vendredi." Paris.
"Verdad." Valencia.
"La Veu de Catalunya." Barcelona.
"La Vie Ouvrière." Paris.
"The Village Voice." New York.
"La Voz Leninista." Barcelona.
"Xaloc." Mexico.

Index